JUTLAND

THE NAVAL STAFF APPRECIATION

JUTLAND

THE NAVAL STAFF APPRECIATION

Edited, annotated and introduced by

William Schleihauf

Additional text by

Stephen McLaughlin

Diagrams redrawn by

John Jordan

Seaforth

PUBLISHING

This book is dedicated to those men in both navies,
who fought for their Sovereign and Country
on that misty Wednesday in May, 1916
'and at the going down of the sun, we shall remember them'

and to the memory of my Father
William Franklin Schleihauf
Royal Canadian Tank Regiment
who volunteered to serve his King and Country, 1944–1945

Edited text copyright © The Estate of William Schleihauf 2016
Additional text copyright © Stephen McLaughlin 2016
Drawings © John Jordan 2016

First published in Great Britain in 2016 by
Seaforth Publishing,
Pen & Sword Books Ltd,
47 Church Street,
Barnsley S70 2AS

www.seaforthpublishing.com

British Library Cataloguing in Publication Data
A catalogue record for this book is available from the British Library

ISBN 978 1 84832 317 9

Typeset in 11/14 Ehrhardt by M.A.T.S, Leigh-on-Sea, Essex
Printed and bound in Great Britain by CPI Group (UK) Ltd, Croydon, CR0 4YY

Contents

List of Diagrams   vii
Abbreviations   ix
William Roger Schleihauf, 22 September 1958 – 27 January 2009:
  An Appreciation   xi
A Note on the Text   xiv
A Note on the Diagrams   xvi
Editor's Introduction – The Mists of Jutland   xvii
A Cautionary Note   xxx
A Few Basics   xxxii

Naval Staff Appreciation of Jutland   1
Introduction   2
I   The Situation in 1916   10
II   The Grand Fleet Battle Orders of May, 1916   17
III   Preliminary Movements, May 28–30   38
IV   The Battle Cruiser Action from 3.40 pm to 4.40 pm   59
V   German Battle Fleet in Sight. The Action from 4.40 pm
            to 5.40 pm   70
VI   Commander-in-Chief's View of the Situation, 2 pm to 5 pm   82
VII   Commander-in-Chief in touch with Battle Cruiser Force,
            5.35 pm to 6.15 pm   89
VIII   Remarks on the Deployment at 6.15 pm   107
IX   The First Half Hour, 6.15 pm to 6.40 pm   117
X   The Second Engagement and Scheer's Turn Away. The Turn
            to South-East and South   136
XI   Proceedings during the Night   167
XII   Destroyer Actions during the Night   194

Appendices

A   Preliminary Distribution of British Ships, with names
              of Commanding Officers   209
B   Organisations of the British Fleet   215
C   British and German Casualties   219
D   Damage sustained by British and German Ships   221
E   List of Ships Sunk   228
F   Summary of Reports of Enemy received in *Iron Duke*   229
G   German Signals   233

Editor's Afterword   243
Annexe I: *Jellicoe's Letter to the Admiralty, 30 October 1914*   268
Annexe II: *Excerpts of the Grand Fleet Battle Orders in Force at Jutland* 271
Annexe III: *Cover Letter for Admiral Jellicoe's Despatch*   276
Annexe IV: *Enemy Sighting Reports, 8 pm Through Midnight, 31 May*   279
Annexe V: *Pre-war Tactical Instructions, 1913–1914*   283
Annexe VI: *Surviving Copies of the* Naval Staff Appreciation of Jutland:
              A Bibliographical Note   294
Bibliography   298
Index   307

List of Diagrams

Number		Page
1.	Disposition of Battle Cruiser Force (*Lion*) at noon, 31 May, and redisposition ordered at 1.30 pm	48
2.	Battle Cruiser Force. Position at 2.20 pm 'Enemy in sight'	49
3.	Disposition of 1st and 2nd Scouting Groups, 2.00 pm	52
4.	Position of Forces, 2.30 pm	52
5.	*Galatea* and 1st Light Cruiser Squadron closing enemy, 2.30 pm	53
6.	Closing enemy, 3.00 pm	54
7.	Battle Cruiser Squadron engaging 1st Scouting Group, position 3.50 pm	60
8.	Battle Cruiser Action. Position 4.02 pm	62
9.	Battle Cruiser Action. Position 4.30 pm	64
10.	Enemy Battle Fleet in Sight, 4.40 pm	71
11.	Approximate positions of Main Squadrons at 5.00 pm	77
12.	The Run to the North. Approximate positions at 5.15 pm	80
13.	Hood proceeding to support Beatty. Position at 4.06 pm	85
14.	Position of Enemy Battle Fleet at 5.00 pm. Reconstruction of reports	87
15.	Cruiser formation L.S.1	90
16.	Discrepancy between reckonings of *Iron Duke* and *Lion*	91
17.	Approximate relative positions at 5.42 pm	93
18.	*Falmouth* in touch with *Black Prince*. Position at 5.30 pm	101
19.	Reports of enemy, 5.40 pm to 6.12 pm	103
20.	Last reports, 6.14 pm	105
21.	Showing effect of new estimate of enemy's position on bearing of guides	109
22.	Probable effect of deployment on right wing	111
23.	Probable effect of deployment on *Iron Duke*	113

24. The deployment. Approximate position at 6.19 pm   119
25. 1st and 2nd Battle Cruiser Squadrons at 6.15 pm   120
26. 3rd Battle Cruiser Squadron and 1st Scouting Group
        at 6.20 pm   121
27. 5th Battle Squadron. *Warspite* and *Warrior* at 6.18 pm   123
28. Deployment Diagram   125
29. Light Cruiser Squadrons at 6.15 pm   125
30. Destroyer Flotillas at 6.15 pm   127
31. Approximate position at 6.29 pm   131
32. Scheer's first turn away. Position at 6.35 pm   133
33. British Fleet turned by Divisions to South-East at 6.44 pm
        Approximate positions at 6.45 pm   137
34. Approximate positions at 6.56 pm   139
35. Approximate positions at 7.12 pm and tracks to 7.20 pm   143
36. Approximate positions at 7.22 pm   147
37. Approximate positions at 7.25 pm   148
38. Approximate positions at 7.35 pm   152
39. Approximate positions at 7.42 pm   153
40. Approximate positions at 8.00 pm   154
41. Approximate positions at 8.10 pm   157
42. Approximate positions at 8.15 pm   158
43. Approximate positions at 8.17 pm and tracks to 8.36 pm   160
44. Redisposition of German Forces, 8.40 to 9.00 pm   163
45. Approximate positions at 9.00 pm   168
46. Errors in plotting due to the difference in reckoning
        of the *Iron Duke* and *Lion*   169
47. British and German minefields up to 1 June, 1916, and
        the German swept channels in the Heligoland Bight   174
48. Position of the fleets at 9.00 pm and their approximate tracks
        until 2.30 am (daylight)   176
49. Approximate positions at 10.41 pm and interpretation
        of the Admiralty signal   181
50. Approximate positions at 2.45 am, 1 June   186
51 Approximate movements of the 4th Flotilla from 10 pm
        to 12.30 am   195
52. Approximate movements of the 9th and 10th, and the
        13th Flotillas between 11.00 pm and 3.30 am   203
53. Approximate movements of the 12th Flotilla from 11.00 pm
        to 3.30 am   205

Abbreviations

Note: For ease of reference, this listing combines abbreviations used in the original *Naval Staff Appreciation of Jutland* and those introduced by the editor.

APC: 'Armour Piercing, Capped', that is, a type of shell designed to penetrate heavy armour.

BCF: Battle Cruiser Fleet (or Battle Cruiser Force).

BCS: Battle Cruiser Squadron, e.g. the 2nd BCS.

BS: Battle Squadron, e.g., the 5th BS.

CAC: Churchill Archives Centre, Churchill College, Cambridge.

CPC: 'Common, Pointed, Capped', i.e., a type of shell with a heavier bursting charge than APC, but without APC's ability to penetrate heavy armour.

CS: Cruiser Squadron, consisting of the older type of armoured cruiser.

DID: Director of the Intelligence Division of the War Staff.

DOD: Director of the Operations Division of the War Staff.

German I, II, etc.: These refer to the numbered charts of German movements from Scheer's report issued with the *Official Despatches* (see below).

G.F.B.O.: Grand Fleet Battle Orders.

Harper I, II, etc.: These refer to the numbered charts accompanying Captain Harper's original record of the Battle of Jutland. These were not included in the *Reproduction of the Record of the Battle of Jutland* as published in 1927, and the charts have since been lost. The closest approximation to them are the diagrams included in vol. III of Corbett's *Naval Operations*, which were based more or less directly on Harper's charts.

HE: High Explosive shell, filled with Lyddite, a form of picric acid.

LCS: Light Cruiser Squadron.

Marder, *FDSF*: Arthur J. Marder, *From the Dreadnought to Scapa Flow*.

(r): Reports from individual ships or admirals reproduced in the *Official Despatches* (see below).

NARA: National Archives and Records Administration, Washington, D.C.

NMM: The National Maritime Museum, Greenwich.

Official Despatches: Cmd. 1068, *Battle of Jutland, May 30 to June 1. Official Despatches with Appendices*. A collection of reports and other documents related to the battle, published by HMSO in 1920.

RMA: Royal Marine Artillery. At this point in time, Britain's Royal Marines were split into the RMA (the 'Blue Marines'), and the Royal Marine Light Infantry (the 'Red Marines').

(s): Signal log.

(s^1): *Iron Duke*'s compiled signal log (see the original Introduction, Section 3 for an explanation of this term).

(s^2): *Iron Duke*'s contemporary signal log (see the original Introduction, Section 3 for an explanation of this term).

SO: Senior Officer; thus, 'SO BCF' is the Senior Officer, Battle Cruiser Fleet, i.e., Admiral Beatty.

TNA: The National Archives (formerly the Public Record Office), Kew.

TS: Transmitting Station: A below-decks compartment which housed the Dreyer Fire Control Table, and which was the centre of gunnery communications.

Von Hase: The *Naval Staff Appreciation* was printed before the commercial version of Georg von Hase's book *Kiel and Jutland* was published; instead, the authors used a translation prepared by the Intelligence Division (usually – but not always – cited as 'I.D. 1220' in the footnotes), as well as the original German edition. No attempt has been made to update these citations, as there are at least two versions of von Hase's book in English, with different pagination.

(w): wireless log (see the original Introduction, Section 3 for an explanation of this term).

(w/e): wireless entry log (see the original Introduction, Section 3 for an explanation of this term).

W/T: Wireless Telegraphy, i.e., (Morse) radio

William Roger Schleihauf,
22 September 1958 – 27 January 2009:
An Appreciation

This project was the brainchild of Bill Schleihauf, yet tragically he did not live to see its fulfilment. So it is fitting that before plunging into the text we take a moment to say a few words about him.

Bill was interested in all things nautical, a fact reflected in the many organisations to which he belonged and contributed – he was president of the Montreal Branch of the Naval Officers' Association of Canada (although he never served in the RCN), long-time secretary to the Canadian Nautical Research Society and editor of *Argonauta*, its bulletin, a trustee of the Canadian Naval Memorial Trust, member of the Friends of HMCS *Haida*, and an experienced scuba diver. He was also an ardent supporter of the Monarchy. The depth of Bill's interest in Canadian and British naval history may be gauged from the select bibliography below. He was especially interested in fire control, and his three-part article on the Dumaresq and the Dreyer Tables will likely remain a standard work on these devices for many years to come.

It was because of our mutual interest in fire control that Bill and I first began our correspondence, sometime back in the mid-1990s. Bill's personality came through clearly in every email message – his commitment to the British Commonwealth, his love of good beer, his disdain for Microsoft® software, and his wry sense of humour. But what I remember most was his intellectual honesty. This aspect of his personality was demonstrated when I chanced to meet a famous naval historian. I asked his opinion of one of Bill's articles; the historian criticised the article rather severely – criticisms that in my view were totally unwarranted. When I reluctantly mentioned this incident to Bill, he immediately asked me exactly what the criticisms were, so that he could consider them and decide if they were valid. He wasn't defensive or offended – he just wanted to learn as much as he could from a historian whose views he respected.

After corresponding through email for a decade, I finally met Bill in April

2004 when we visited the battleship USS *Massachusetts* as members of a group of fire-control enthusiasts. We were shown through many areas of the ship usually off-limits to visitors, including the fire-control room, where we were allowed to play (respectfully) with the equipment. It was a memorable gathering, but unfortunately it was destined to be the only time I met Bill face-to-face. We made plans to get together when I visited Washington, D.C. in the spring of 2008; Bill was going to drive down from Quebec so that we could both do research at the U.S. National Archives. But it was not to be; I got an email from Bill after I arrived at the hotel – his (unspecified) illness had laid him up. Less than a year later that illness – non-Hodgkin lymphoma – took his life.

Bill had largely completed the manuscript of this book when he died; it is yet another indication of his intellectual honesty that, while he recognised the flaws of the *Naval Staff Appreciation of Jutland*, he also knew that it offered many valid criticisms, and that it is an important historical document. It has been used by many of the historians who have written about Jutland, a sort of grey eminence that stands behind many accounts of the battle. He therefore believed that it was worthy of publication, so that a larger audience could have access to it. And with the publication of the *Appreciation* the interested reader now has access to all the major sources involved in the Jutland Controversy – the *Official Despatches*, Corbett's *Naval Operations*, the Admiralty *Narrative*, the 'Harper Record', the Harper Papers, and the relevant correspondence available in the published Beatty and Jellicoe papers. This annotated edition of the *Naval Staff Appreciation of Jutland* is therefore a fitting capstone to Bill's career as a naval historian.

Steve McLaughlin

Select Bibliography

Works by Bill Schleihauf:

Note: In addition to the articles listed below, Bill also wrote numerous book reviews, many of which appeared in *The Northern Mariner/Le Marin du Nord* in the period 1994 to 2006.

'Admiral Sir Frederic Dreyer's visit to Canada, January 1940', *Argonauta: The Newsletter of the Canadian Nautical Research Society*, vol XXIII, no 4 (October 2006), pp 15–22.

'The Ancestral Asdic', *Warship International*, vol XXXVII, no 3 (2000), pp 272–83.

'The Baden Trials', in John Jordan (ed.), *Warship 2007* (London: Conway Maritime Press, 2007), pp 81–90.

'Battle Cruisers', *The Naval Review*, vol 90, no 1 (January 2002), pp 72–3.

'A Concentrated Effort: Royal Navy Gunnery Exercises at the End of the Great War', *Warship International*, vol XXXV, no 2 (1998), pp 117–39.

'Disaster in Harbour: The Loss of HMS *Vanguard*', *The Northern Mariner/Le Marin du Nord*, vol X, no 3 (July 2000), pp 57–89.

'The Dumaresq and the Dreyer', *Warship International*, vol. XXXVIII (2001), part 1: no 1, pp 6–29 (with colour illustrations on the inside front and back covers); part 2: no 2, pp 164–201; part 3: no 3, pp 221–33.

'The Final Blossom: HMCS *Sackville*', *Naval History*, vol 13, no 6 (December 1999), p 72.

'*Hood*'s Fire Control System: An Overview', The official website of the H.M.S. *Hood* Association (http:www.hmshood.com/ship/fire_control.htm).

'The Last of Her Tribe: HMCS *Haida*', *Warship International*, vol XXXIII, no 4, (1996), pp 344–77.

'A Naval Bandersnatch' (Warship Note), in John Jordan (ed.), *Warship 2005* (London: Conway Maritime Press, 2005), pp 173–4.

'"Necessary Stepping Stones": The Transfer of *Aurora*, *Patriot* and *Patrician* to the Royal Canadian Navy after the First World War', *Canadian Military History*, vol 9, no 3 (Summer 2000), pp 37–48.

'The Restoration of HMS *M33*', *Warship International*, vol XXXVII, no 2 (2000), pp 170–6.

'Some Tidbits Relating to HMS *Canada*', *Argonauta: The Newsletter of the Canadian Nautical Research Society*, vol XXIV, no 2 (April 2007), pp 13–18.

'State of the Art – Topics in Royal Navy Gunnery ca. 1919', *Warship International*; forthcoming.

'What Happened to the *Campania?*' *Mariner's Mirror*, vol 90, no 4 (November 2004), pp 464–6.

Works about Bill Schleihauf:

Adamthwaite, Paul, 'William Roger Schleihauf, 1958-2009', *Argonauta: The Newsletter of the Canadian Nautical Research Society*, vol XXVI, no 1 (January 2009), p 2. See also in this issue: Maurice D Smith, editorial, p 1; and Paul Adamthwaite, 'President's Corner', p 3, for additional tributes.

Jurens, Bill, 'Bill Schleihauf, September 1958-January 2009', *Warship International*, vol XLV, no 4 (2008), pp 259–60. (Note: This obituary does not indicate prescience on the part of the journal; at this time, *Warship International* was generally published several months after the nominal date of the issue.)

McLaughlin, Stephen, 'William Schleihauf: In Memoriam', in John Jordan (ed.), *Warship 2010* (London: Conway Maritime Press, 2010), p 8.

A Note on the Text

In addition to transcribing the *Naval Staff Appreciation of Jutland* and annotating the text, Bill wrote most of the Editor's Introduction, selected the supplementary materials and had made a start on the Afterword; however, aside from its first section ('Jellicoe Bad/Beatty Good'), Bill left only a few scattered notes. This presented me with something of a quandary when I was asked to complete the book; Bill had been in and out of hospital for some time before his death, and I knew from our email discussions that he was rethinking some of the views he had expressed in these notes. Should I simply try to complete the Afterword as it stood, or should I make changes in light of Bill's emails? I opted for the latter course. Therefore the Afterword combines Bill's notes, some of the thoughts he expressed in emails, and my own thinking. I hope the result will do justice to Bill's intentions. But for better or worse, the overall responsibility for the bulk of the Afterword rests with me. I have also added a bibliographical note on the surviving copies of the *Appreciation*.

This book is not a facsimile of the original *Naval Staff Appreciation of Jutland* (which for the sake of simplicity and variety will often be referred to as 'the *NSA*' or 'the *Appreciation*' in the pages that follow). Although the complete text has been reproduced, a few changes have been made for clarity's sake. The *Appreciation* was printed as proof copies, and was never subjected to the final editing that a finished work would have received. As a result, there are inconsistencies in how times are given, in the manner in which works are cited in the footnotes, and in the punctuation. There are also a few spelling errors. As far as possible, these have been corrected, and some of the cryptic footnote abbreviations of the original have been changed to a more complete form of citation. But the wording and substance of the work has not been altered in any way.

One important change is that the pagination is different, and therefore the numbering of the footnotes has been altered; instead of being numbered starting from note 1 on each page, their enumeration is now continuous throughout each chapter. Interfiled with the original notes are explanatory footnotes, most written by Bill Schleihauf, with some added by me; these always begin with the words '*Editor's note*'. In many cases, these are appended to an original note, rather than being separately numbered. A few long editorial notes, which expand upon some points in the *NSA*, appear at the end of the relevant chapter. The term 'High *Sea* Fleet' has been retained in the original text, but the more familiar 'High *Seas* Fleet' has been used in the new material; hopefully this will not prove too jarring. Various documents relevant to the *Naval Staff Appreciation*, called 'Annexes' to avoid confusion with the appendices of the original text, can be found at the end of the book.

A few words of thanks are in order. I owe a special debt of gratitude to the various archives that have tolerated – with unfailing patience and grace – my ceaseless demands for documents. Jenny Wraight of the Admiralty Library and Heather Johnson of the National Museum of the Royal Navy's library (both in Portsmouth) have been very kind in providing access to their remarkable collections under difficult circumstances. The amazingly efficient staff of the Churchill Archives Centre, Cambridge, produced file after file in a twinkling; and The National Archives (still the PRO in my mind) in Kew cannot be bettered as far as national archives go. The staff of the Caird Library of the National Maritime Museum have been very both tolerant and welcoming. I am especially grateful to Nicholas Roskill, son of Captain Stephen Roskill, for last-minute permission to reproduce the note on page 296, and to Ceri Humphries of the Churchill Archives Centre for handling my unreasonable request so speedily. The quotations from Add. MS. 49042 on page 297 are © The British Library Board and I am grateful for permission to use them. I am also grateful to all the members of a certain listserv (which must remain nameless – but they know who they are) for their help in tracking down details and skewering my wilder ideas as I worked to complete this project. Rob Gardiner of Seaforth Publishing cleared the way with diplomacy and tact. John Jordan not only redrew the diagrams but also provided help with some editorial and formatting decisions. Bill's widow, Cathy Bonneville, showed great patience with my delays in getting started on this project. Vince O'Hara did some emergency proof-reading work. And as usual, my wife, Jan Torbet, served as an excellent editor.

Steve McLaughlin

A Note on the Diagrams

The original edition of the *Naval Staff Appreciation* was illustrated with fifty-three diagrams. All have been specially redrawn for this publication. The originals were drawn by hand and reproduced in the two-tone printing format common to the period: ships and formations, lines of course/bearing and annotations were in black for ships of the Grand Fleet, red for the German High Seas Fleet. When the diagrams were subsequently photocopied or scanned in greyscale, much of the red disappeared altogether, which proved problematic for the illustrator until the British Library posted a copy online which was scanned in colour. However, even the British Library copy is not perfect: some details at the edges of the diagrams are missing, so some cross-referencing was necessary.

The guiding principle we agreed for this new edition of the *NSA* was that the diagrams should be as faithful as possible to the originals, even where these have subsequently proved to be in error. The style of the originals has been reproduced as far as possible, with the individual ships represented by arrowheads and grey substituted for the red. Times are annotated in one of two ways: the 12-hour clock (e.g. 6.15) is used for positions and events, the naval 24-hour clock (e.g. 1815) for the timing of signals. This matches the recording of times in the narrative and the appendices (see in particular Appendix F).

There were small inconsistencies in the originals – not uncommon with hand-drawn diagrams – and these have been ironed out in the re-drawing process. There were occasions, particularly with the complex 'theoretical' diagrams showing actual versus projected ranges and bearings between the different components of the fleets, when the original illustrator had become confused and used black in place of red (and vice versa) or had confused the annotation for 'movement' times with 'signal' times; there were also diagrams which formed part of a series where a detail present on all the other diagrams in the series (such as the flag marking out the flagship) had been omitted. These have been corrected to ensure consistency and clarity, but any substantive changes to the information on the diagram have been noted for the reader.

John Jordan

Editor's Introduction –
The Mists of Jutland

The horizon ahead of us grew clear of smoke, and we could now make out some English light cruisers which had also turned about. Suddenly my periscope revealed some big ships. Black monsters; six tall, broad-beamed giants steaming in two columns. They were still a long way off, but they showed up clearly on the horizon, and even at this great distance they looked powerful, massive.[1]

'Jutland' – the merest whisper of the word conjures up images of majestic dreadnoughts, steaming implacably through the North Sea mists. Wednesday, 31 May 1916, was the only time two complete fleets of dreadnought battleships met in combat. This is enough, perhaps, to fire the imagination. Mixed with the less than decisive result, the fact that both sides can plausibly claim victory, and that for the British it was hugely disappointing, there are plenty of reasons for historians, not to mention naval officers, to take an interest. One 1992 bibliography lists 528 books and articles on the subject, and many more have been published since.[2] Perhaps more ink has been spilt over Jutland than any naval action ever fought.

If this weren't enough, on the British side there arose a rift between the supporters of Admiral Sir John Jellicoe, the Commander-in-Chief of the Grand Fleet, and those of Admiral Sir David Beatty, Commander of the Battle Cruiser Fleet and Jellicoe's subordinate. This 'Jutland Controversy' generated rather more smoke than light, but nevertheless kept public interest alive during the 1920s and 1930s. The document in your hands falls out of that very debate. It has long been hidden away, rumoured to be much too explosive to ever be made

---

[1] The words of Commander Georg von Hase, Gunnery Officer of *Derfflinger*, describing his first sight of the British battle cruisers. Hase, *Kiel and Jutland*, 142 (full details for all works cited in the notes can be found in the bibliography).

[2] Rasor, *The Battle of Jutland: A Bibliography*.

public. The editor was fortunate enough to receive a copy of the microfilmed version at the University of California at Irvine, part of the legacy of Professor Arthur J Marder. Only four copies are known to have survived the destruction orders given by the First Sea Lord, Admiral Sir Charles Madden, in 1930.[3] (See Annexe VI, 'Surviving Copies of the *Naval Staff Appreciation of Jutland*: A Bibliographical Note' for details.) This book is a transcript from the microfilm, verified against one of the original copies, in the Beatty Papers at the National Maritime Museum, Greenwich.

There are two reasons why this is being published. First and foremost is its importance to those who steep themselves in Jutland Lore – in any recounting of the Jutland Controversy, there will be mention of the *Naval Staff Appreciation*. The aura of mystery that surrounds it has given it an almost legendary status, while very few alive today have had the opportunity to actually read it. It is, therefore, an important historical document in its own right.

Second, although a bowdlerised version – the *Narrative of the Battle of Jutland*, often referred to as the 'Admiralty Narrative' – was published in 1924, purged from it, along with some very barbed commentary, was valid analysis that merits publication.

The Jutland Controversy

A survey is in order, if only to put the *Naval Staff Appreciation* into perspective. It is fair to say that the seeds of the controversy were planted immediately after the battle, while some ships of the Grand Fleet were still at sea. The German commander-in-chief, Vice-Admiral Reinhard Scheer, returned to the Jade during the morning of 1 June, and the next day, the *Admiralstab* (German Admiralty Staff) issued a press communiqué, listing British losses as *Warspite*, two battle cruisers, two armoured cruisers, a light cruiser, a submarine, plus destroyers, while acknowledging only the sinking of the predreadnought *Pommern* and the light cruiser *Wiesbaden*, with the light cruiser *Frauenlob* and a few destroyers not yet returned.[4] It was this news which first hit every newsstand in the world. Not until the evening of the 2nd did the British Admiralty make a statement, which would appear in the next day's newspapers:

> On the afternoon of Wednesday, May 31st, a naval engagement took place off the coast of Jutland.
>
> The British ships on which the brunt of the fighting fell were the Battle

---

[3] Marder, *FDSF*, 5:360; Roskill, *Admiral of the Fleet Earl Beatty*, 334; and *Beatty Papers*, 2:425.

[4] Marder, *FDSF*, 3:234.

Cruiser Fleet and some cruisers and light cruisers supported by four fast battleships. Among those the losses were heavy.

The German Battle Fleet, aided by low visibility, avoided prolonged action with our main forces, and soon after these appeared on the scene the enemy returned to port, though not before receiving severe damage from our battleships.

The battle cruisers *Queen Mary*, *Indefatigable*, *Invincible*, and the cruisers *Defence* and *Black Prince* were sunk. The *Warrior* was disabled, and after being towed for some time had to be abandoned by her crew.

It is also known that the destroyers *Tipperary*, *Turbulent*, *Fortune*, *Sparrow-hawk*, and *Ardent* were lost, and six others are not yet accounted for.

No British battleships or light cruisers were sunk.

The enemy's losses were serious.

At least one battle cruiser was destroyed, and one severely damaged; one battleship reported sunk by our destroyers during a night attack; two light cruisers were disabled and probably sunk.

The exact number of enemy destroyers disposed of during the action cannot be ascertained with any certainty, but it must have been large.[5]

Honestly intended, this statement confirmed the seriousness of the Royal Navy's losses. To a British public brought up on tales of Nelsonic heroics and the overwhelming victory of Trafalgar, this sounded very much like a defeat. Certainly the Germans won the opening round of the public relations campaign. British attitudes would swing round within the next few weeks, as further information was released by the Admiralty (Jellicoe's despatch was published on 6 July). Nevertheless, people wanted to know what really happened during the battle, and the great unanswered question remained: why wasn't Jutland a second Glorious First of June?[6]

Within the Navy itself, a slight fault line was beginning to open up. The men of the Battle Cruiser Fleet (BCF)[7] had long considered themselves an elite

[5] Quoted in Fawcett and Hooper, *Fighting at Jutland*, 1.

[6] The victory of Admiral Howe against the French in 1794, which was fought so far out in the Atlantic that it was named for the date and not the nearest point of land. It saw six French ships captured and one sunk, but it is often forgotten that the French grain convoy – crucial to the survival of a starving country – escaped unscathed. For a complete and engaging examination of this battle, see Willis, *Glorious First of June*.

[7] Initially Beatty's command was designated the Battle Cruiser Squadron; in February 1915 it was renamed the Battle Cruiser Fleet (*Beatty Papers*, 1:204). It was renamed the Battle Cruiser Force on 28 November 1916, the day before Beatty hoisted his flag in *Iron Duke* as Commander-in-Chief (Marder, *FDSF*, 4:25–7). The *NSA* uses both 'Battle Cruiser Force' and 'Battle Cruiser Fleet' indiscriminately.

force, the seagoing equivalent of dashing Napoleonic light cavalry. They were under the command of the colourful Sir David Beatty – with a rich American wife and a knack for getting his name in the newspapers – and they served in the glamour ships of the Fleet: the very latest 'New Testament' ships, in the words of Admiral Sir John Fisher. The BCF had already been tested in action, and both Heligoland Bight (28 August 1914) and Dogger Bank (24 January 1915) were considered battle cruiser victories. Of course, the fact that the BCF was based in the Firth of Forth, close to the bright lights of civilisation and within easy reach of the Press, did their reputations no harm.

The Battle Fleet was based in the remote fastness of Scapa Flow, virtually inaccessible to reporters. Its officers and men had been busy, with much sea time, and although their activities were vital, they were for the most part routine, and consequently unheralded. Before Jutland they had not actually met the enemy in battle. At long last, they finally fired their guns in anger on 31 May 1916.

The rivalry between the BCF and the Battle Fleet, and particularly their geographical separation and lack of personal contact, led to a certain amount of ill-feeling after the battle.[8] The battle cruiser men felt that they had borne the brunt of the fighting, only to be let down by the Battle Fleet. Within the battleships, there was a belief that the battle cruisers had been over-confident, and that neither their gunnery nor reconnaissance had been up to scratch. With time, and the closer integration of the two forces later in the war, these feelings would subside; nevertheless, there would remain a distinct clustering of officers into those who had served with Beatty in the Battle Cruiser Fleet, and those who were with Jellicoe in the Battle Fleet. But it was only after the Armistice that the Controversy began to flare up in earnest.

In early 1919, the First Sea Lord, Admiral Sir Rosslyn Wemyss, ordered Captain J E T Harper[9] to 'prepare a Record, with plans, showing in chrono-logical order what actually occurred at the battle. No comment or criticism was to be included and no oral evidence was to be accepted. All statements made in the Record were to be in accordance with evidence obtainable from Admiralty records.'[10] Harper was finished by the beginning of October 1919, having used

---

[8] Recounted by Admiral of the Fleet Lord Mountbatten, who joined *Lion* as a midshipman a few weeks after the battle: 'An Appreciation Given at the Annual Jutland Dinner in HMS *Warrior* on 25 May 1978'. Sub-lieutenant Charles Daniel (1894–1981), who served in *Orion*, recorded his own displeasure at the 'wretched piece of ingratitude' towards Admiral Jellicoe; CAC: DANL/2.

[9] John Ernest Troyte Harper (1874–1949). He was a 'dagger N' – i.e., a specialist in navigation.

[10] 'Facts Dealing with the Compilation of the Official Record of the Battle of Jutland and the Reason it was Not Published, by Captain J. E. T. Harper' (hereafter 'Harper's Narrative'), 1928, reproduced in *Jellicoe Papers*, 2:462.

the wreck of *Invincible* (located 3 July) as a datum point. The results came within inches of receiving Admiralty approval and being published. At the end of the month, the Deputy Chief of the Naval Staff, Vice-Admiral Sir Osmond de B Brock, was about to sign the document on behalf of Wemyss, who was then on leave, when he decided that it really ought to wait for the incoming First Sea Lord. On 1 November, Earl Beatty took up his appointment as the professional head of the Royal Navy. Almost immediately, Beatty was asking Harper to make changes to the *Record* – some of a trivial nature, others more serious. Perhaps the most egregious example was the attempt to suppress the 360° turn made by the battle cruisers at 7.05 pm. The circle itself was of little consequence tactically, and all indications are that it came about through simple inattention on *Lion*'s bridge. Despite incontrovertible evidence that the turn did take place, Beatty insisted that his ships had followed a kind of 'S-shaped' track, 16 points (180°) to starboard, followed by a 16-point turn to port. Worse still, it is clear that Beatty made a flimsy attempt to forge proof for his claim, but the way in which his own signature changed over the years gave him away.[11] Harper demanded written orders before he would alter his findings, which he would receive, but ultimately (no doubt after the First Lord, Walter Long, had a 'chat' with Beatty) these were rescinded on 11 March 1920.[12] Nevertheless, further alterations were called for, some of which were contrary to the findings supported by the data from the battle cruiser and gunnery records.

Meanwhile, Jellicoe had not as yet seen the *Record* (but through inside contacts may have had some indication as to its contents[13]), and indeed was strongly of the opinion that it should not be read by himself or Beatty until after publication. However, when he learned of the various changes, and of the proposed Admiralty preface (one version of which went so far as to assert that there had been no engagement between the British and German battle fleets[14]), he became concerned and eventually, at the request of the First Lord, examined a draft along with the proposed alterations. He was not pleased, and was prepared to delay his departure for New Zealand, where he had been appointed Governor-General, unless matters were resolved to his satisfaction. Long promised that no changes to Harper's original would be made without Jellicoe's approval, but that created an impasse as Beatty wanted modifications. This dilemma was inadvertently solved by the publishers of the Committee of Imperial Defence's Official History, *Naval Operations*, when they pointed out

---

[11] See Roskill's account in *Admiral of the Fleet Earl Beatty*, 326–7.

[12] Harper's Narrative, 468.

[13] Roskill, *Admiral of the Fleet Earl Beatty*, 328.

[14] *Beatty Papers*, 2:440.

that Harper's *Record* would be competing directly with their own volume on Jutland, and moreover, that publication of the *Record* would be a contractual violation.[15] So the *Record* was shelved for the time being; but it remained a recurring topic of interest in the House of Commons,[16] and ultimately it would be published in 1927, by which time the now-retired Rear-Admiral Harper had published his controversial anti-Beatty book *The Truth About Jutland*. The *Record* appeared *sans* diagrams[17] as Cmd. 2870 – 'prepared by Captain J E T Harper . . . and other officers by direction of the Admiralty in 1919-1920' (as is stated on the title page). It was, of course, a version of the *Record* that included some of Beatty's alterations.

The Writing of the Naval Staff Appreciation

Meanwhile, in November of 1920 the Naval Staff College, through the Director of Training and Staff Duties (DTSD), Captain Walter M Ellerton, directed Captains Alfred C Dewar and his brother Kenneth G B Dewar to prepare an appreciation of the battle:

> 1. You are desired to write a full appreciation of the battle of Jutland, to serve as a groundwork for a further Staff appreciation. Your appreciation should include any operation orders issued prior to the battle and a full analysis of the movements of the British Fleet, including the Harwich Force, from the time of leaving harbour on 30th May until its return on 2nd June.
>
> 2. The appreciation is to be regarded as secret; you are to avoid any reference to the fact that it is being compiled.
>
> 3. The Secretary will be requested to give you access to all papers you may require, including all the papers of Captain Harper's committee.
>
> 4. You will be attached to the Training & Staff Duties Division while carrying out this duty.[18]

Despite the intended secrecy, the *Evening News* of 29 November reported that a naval officer had been brought in to write a 'Staff Appreciation' in place of the Harper report.[19]

---

[15] *Jellicoe Papers*, 2:400–1.

[16] Questions were asked in the House of Commons twenty-two times between 1919 and 1927! Roskill, *Admiral of the Fleet Earl Beatty*, 324.

[17] Supposedly because of the expense! Beatty's 'Minute on the Publication of the Harper Record', 10 May 1927, quoted in *Beatty Papers*, 2:477–8.

[18] Letter from Admiral Osmond de B. Brock, Deputy Chief of the Naval Staff, 15 November 1920, to the brothers Dewar; NMM: BTY/9/5.

[19] Clipping in NMM: BTY/9/5.

Alfred Charles Dewar (1875–1969), then retired, had been instrumental in setting up the Admiralty Historical Section – under the Training and Staff Duties Division – and had begun work in March 1919 on a series of monographs and historical papers on the War.[20] His brother, Kenneth Gilbert Balmain Dewar (1879–1964), was part of the Navy's intelligentsia and one of the founders of *The Naval Review*. His wartime service had ended in the Admiralty, in the Plans Division under then-Captain Dudley Pound. Kenneth Dewar was an acolyte of Captain Herbert Richmond and one of the 'Young Turks' bent on reforming the Royal Navy. He would eventually gain notoriety in the '*Royal Oak* Court-martial' in 1928, and retired in 1929 as a rear-admiral (promoted to vice-admiral on the retired list in 1934).

More than just a simple narrative, the Dewars' *Appreciation* was to include analysis and commentary. In composing it, they had the assistance of Lieutenant John Pollen,[21] who had worked with Captain Harper on the diagrams. An early draft was submitted in September 1921, but both Beatty and the Assistant Chief of the Naval Staff, Rear-Admiral Alfred Chatfield (who had been Beatty's flag-captain throughout the war), called for revisions to tone down the severe criticism of Jellicoe.[22] The *Appreciation* was finished in December 1921, and 100 proof copies were printed in February 1922.[23] The intent at that time was to produce three versions: the full *Appreciation* (as reproduced here), including secret information and 'criticism approved by the Board'; a 'Fleet Edition', fundamentally the same, but with certain 'critical remarks' expunged; and a sanitised version for public release.[24]

Sir Julian Corbett was given access to both the *Staff Appreciation* and Harper's *Record* in the preparation of the *Naval Operations* volume of Jutland (issued, be it noted, under the auspices of the Committee of Imperial Defence, *not* the Admiralty). Corbett's impression of the Appreciation was not favourable:

---

[20] Marder, *From the Dardanelles to Oran*, 60–1. In the 1920s, the Historical Section would consist of just A C Dewar and Lieutenant-Commander Lloyd-Owen RN (retired), paid at a rate of about £450 per large monograph of 120,000 words: about £270 a year for Dewar and £180 to Lloyd-Owen (note entitled 'Historical Section of the Naval Staff'; NMM: DEW/4).

[21] Nephew of Arthur Hungerford Pollen, the inventor of what might have become the RN's fire-control computer during the First World War.

[22] Roskill, *Admiral of the Fleet Earl Beatty*, 333.

[23] Roger Keyes, who took over as Deputy Chief of the Naval Staff in October 1921, wrote to the First Sea Lord on 20 December that final proofs and plans of the Staff Appreciation would be brought to the Admiralty on the 22nd. In October, the book had been allocated Confidential Book Number 0938, to be printed in size Royal 8vo, and at some point thereafter 100 copies were to be printed; NMM: BTY/9/5.

[24] Memorandum to the DCNS dated 15 February 1922; NMM: BTY/9/5.

. . . my reading of the whole affair differs materially from the 'Staff Appreciation'. After I had read it – for they were good enough to let me have a copy – it appears to me that merely as a piece of history it ought not to go out with the Admiralty imprimatur. The presentation of the facts seemed to me so faulty that I felt it my duty to intimate that my narrative would have to be entirely different. [25]

Indeed, although its authors denied being influenced by Earl Beatty,[26] the *Appreciation* was very much a Battle Cruiser Fleet account of the battle and was highly critical of Jellicoe – so much so that the new head of the Training and Staff Duties Division, Captain Vernon S H Haggard (who replaced Ellerton on 1 January 1922), did not think it could be issued as-was:

The mental attitude of the writer was rather that of a counsel for the prosecution than of an impartial appraiser of facts, and obvious bias animates his statements throughout the book, leading to satirical observations and a certain amount of misrepresentation.[27]

Even Chatfield and Roger Keyes, both staunch Beatty supporters, advised:

It is not considered . . . that any sufficient cause exists at the moment to justify the issue to the Fleet of a book that would rend the Service to its foundations.[28]

They recommended not only that the *Staff Appreciation* should not be issued, but that all but a handful of existing copies should be destroyed and that the printers ensure that even the type used in printing the proofs be broken up.[29] The DTSD asked Corbett to return his copy on 23 February 1922, because the Board of Admiralty had decided against issuing it.[30] In 1930 all copies of the *Staff Appreciation* then on personal loan were recalled,[31] and subsequently, Beatty's successor as First Sea Lord, Admiral Sir Charles Madden (Jellicoe's brother-in-law and erstwhile chief of staff), issued an order to destroy all copies. And thus it was that the same North Sea mists that obscured the scene for

---

[25] Corbett to Jellicoe, 10 March 1922, quoted in *Jellicoe Papers*, 2:413.

[26] Kenneth Dewar, *Navy From Within*, 267.

[27] Memorandum by V S H Haggard to the First Sea Lord (Beatty) and the Deputy Chief of the Naval Staff (Keyes), 26 July 1922, quoted in *Beatty Papers*, 2:454–5.

[28] Memorandum by the Deputy Chief of the Naval Staff (Keyes) and the Assistant Chief of the Naval Staff (Chatfield), 14 August 1922, quoted in *Beatty Papers*, 2:455–6.

[29] Ibid.

[30] Letter in NMM: BTY/9/5.

[31] Letter from the Training and Staff Duties Division to K G B Dewar, 14 April, 1930; NMM: DEW/3. Beatty was most unhappy about being ordered to return his copy of the *Naval Staff Appreciation* – and as it remains in the Beatty Papers in the National Maritime Museum, clearly he didn't comply! In a letter to Roger Keyes, 10 April 1932, he described Madden's destruction

Admirals Jellicoe, Beatty, Scheer and Hipper seemed to swallow up the *Naval Staff Appreciation of Jutland*.

The Influence of the *Naval Staff Appreciation*

Nevertheless, the *NSA* was out there, and like a fleet-in-being, has had considerable influence on the writing of the British side of the Jutland story. Much of the Dewars' work made its public debut in the guise of the *Admiralty Narrative*, published in 1924, which is fundamentally the *Naval Staff Appreciation*, although much interesting material had to be expunged from it. The original intention was to produce a volume suitable 'for issue to the Fleet on the ground [*sic*] that many valuable lessons from the action ought to be placed at the disposal of those who it is necessary should profit by them'.[32] In October 1921, K G B Dewar recommended that Lieutenant-Commander Pollen prepare the abridged version of the *NSA*, under his supervision – Pollen, in Dewar's opinion, having 'no qualification for original work and is in fact peculiarly bad at expressing himself'.[33] This was agreed to, but there was some confusion over how much original writing Pollen was to do (to the dismay of the Dewar brothers), and on 28 November, Pollen received clear instructions to

> edit the appreciation already prepared by Captain Kenneth G B Dewar, CBE so as to produce a narrative of the battle of Jutland free from criticism and comment. The wording of the narrative contained in the appreciation is to be adhered to and as few alterations made as possible. You are to consult Captain Dewar from time to time as the work progresses and to be guided by him in all matters and in suggested alteration in the text of the narrative.[34]

With the suppression of the Harper Record and the mounting public pressure for some form of official description of the battle from the Admiralty, the abridged version acquired a new purpose: by July 1922 it was 'in preparation for public issue'.[35] Chapters I, II and VIII were deleted, as were all references

---

order as a 'crime against Contemporary History' and that he would 'be court-martialled before he would give his up'. Keyes was of like mind, and his copy also survives in his papers in the British Library (Add. MS. 82490). Both letters may be found in *Keyes Papers*, 2:298, 299.

[32] Haggard to DCNS and 1st Sea Lord, 26 July 1922, quoted in *Beatty Papers*, 2:454.

[33] Letter from K G B Dewar to Admiral Ellerton, 17 November 1921; NMM: BTY/9/5. Pollen's abilities were appreciated by Sir Julian Corbett, who found it difficult to work on his account of Jutland without him, and asked Sir Roger Keyes for the return of his services (letter to Keyes, 25 January 1922; NMM: BTY/9/5).

[34] Letter from DTSD to Lieutenant-Commander Pollen, 28 November 1921; NMM: BTY/9/5.

[35] Haggard to DCNS and 1st Sea Lord, 26 July 1922, quoted in *Beatty Papers*, 2:454.

to the deciphering of German signals, and many changes were made to individual passages throughout the text to remove the more severe criticisms. Nevertheless, much controversial material remained. In March 1922 a copy of an early typescript draft of the *Narrative* was sent to Admiral Jellicoe for his remarks. There followed much to-and-fro between the Admiralty and Jellicoe over the tenor of the work and the details of the battle. The *Narrative* eventually appeared in 1924; although a few changes had been made in the text as a result of Jellicoe's comments, the bulk of these were consigned to appendix – introduced by the Admiralty's curt statement that

> Where ... the Appendix differs from the Admiralty Narrative, Their Lordships are satisfied that the Narrative is more in accordance with the evidence available.[36]

For every one of the points raised by Jellicoe there was a rebuttal in the form of a footnote – some of them longer than the original statement. But if the *Narrative* was an attempt to satisfy or at least deflect the calls for the publication of Harper's Record, it was a failure, as demands for the latter continued.

The year 1924 also saw the *Naval Staff Appreciation* put in a cameo appearance in the *Naval Review*, the service's professional journal. In May Alfred Dewar published what amounted to a condensed version of the *NSA* in the guise of a review of Sir Julian Corbett's account of the battle in the third volume of *Naval Operations*.[37] In criticising Corbett's pro-Jellicoe interpretation of the battle Alfred Dewar raised many of the same points and even used some of the phrasing of the *NSA*. The review generated a back-and-forth debate that continued into the following year.

The *Naval Review* was a confidential publication, and so its contents could have little impact on the public discussion of Jutland; the same could not be said of Winston Churchill's description of the battle in his multi-volume combined memoir and history of the Great War, *The World Crisis*.[38] Although he had served as First Lord of the Admiralty in 1911–15, Churchill admitted that he had 'only the vaguest idea of what had taken place' at Jutland,[39] and so he asked Beatty for assistance in writing this section of his work, and Beatty

---

[36] *Narrative of the Battle of Jutland*, 106.
[37] A C Dewar, 'Naval Operations of War, Vol. III, the Battle of Jutland'.
[38] Churchill, *The World Crisis*, vol. 3, part I, 108–70.
[39] Churchill to Keyes, 25 August 1924, reproduced in *Keyes Papers*, 2:104.

recommended none other than Kenneth Dewar.[40] Moreover, sometime in 1924 Churchill was given or loaned a copy of the *Naval Staff Appreciation*, which he found 'admirable'.[41] Not surprisingly, Churchill's account strongly reflected the views put forward in the *NSA*, and several of the diagrams were in fact prepared by Dewar himself.[42] Also not surprisingly, Churchill's account was severely criticised by Jellicoe's chief public champion, Admiral Sir Reginald Bacon.[43]

The *Naval Staff Appreciation* also had some influence on another popular account of the battle – although not in the manner intended by its authors. According to Captain J E T Harper, despite the secret classification of the *Naval Staff Appreciation*, Beatty showed a copy to the American journalist Langhorne Gibson.[44] Gibson was delighted, and asked Harper to buy a copy on his behalf – obviously under the impression that it was available to the public! According to Gibson's son, Langhorne Gibson was much impressed by Jellicoe, but not so with Beatty,[45] so perhaps it is unsurprising that he would later partner with Harper to write the pro-Jellicoe book *The Riddle of Jutland*, published in 1934.[46]

But by the time *The Riddle of Jutland* had appeared, interest in the battle was waning as the peoples of Europe worried more about the possibility of a future war than the controversies of a past one. Interest in the battle began to revive only in the late 1950s and 1960s when new accounts began to appear, most by retired naval officers – Donald Macintyre (*Jutland*, 1958), Geoffrey Bennett (*The Battle of Jutland*, 1964) and John Irving (*The Smoke Screen of Jutland*, 1966). Some of these writers had access to the *Appreciation*, but the old controversy appears in all these accounts in a muted form, and there is little of the passionate partisanship of the pre-war debate.

There can be no doubt that the *Naval Staff Appreciation* influenced Arthur Marder, the leading naval historian of the era – he admits to its value in his seminal *From the Dreadnought to Scapa Flow*[47] – and that influence can be seen in the similarity of these passages:

---

[40] Prior, *Churchill's 'World Crisis' as History*, 198, 207, 308 n.47, 309 n.79. Bill Schleihauf had the unexpected pleasure of stumbling across a note from Churchill to Dewar, covering a draft of his Jutland chapters, and inviting him 'to luncheon & stay the night' at Chartwell in August 1926; NMM: DEW/3.

[41] Churchill to Keyes, 25 August 1924; *Keyes Papers*, 2:104.

[42] Prior, *Churchill's 'World Crisis' as History*, 308 n.58.

[43] Bacon, 'Mr. Churchill and Jutland'.

[44] *Jellicoe Papers*, 2:482n.

[45] Email, Gibson to Schleihauf, 7 February 2002.

[46] Gibson and Harper. *The Riddle of Jutland: An Authentic History*.

[47] Marder, *FDSF*, 3:viii–ix.

From the *NSA*, Chapter II, Section 11:

Three main conceptions dominate the [Grand Fleet Battle] orders:
(a) The single line and the parallel course.
(b) Long range.
(c) Defensive action against the torpedo.

And this, from Marder:

Three main conceptions dominate the GFBOs: A subordination of the offensive spirit to defensive precautions, especially against the torpedo; the single line, parallel course, and long range of the plan of battle; and centralized command.[48]

NSA, Chapter III, Section 30: '"No division on the eve of battle" is an axiom as true at sea as on land.'

Marder: '. . . the decision to hold Tyrwhitt back disregarded the axiom that forces, whether on land or sea, should be concentrated on the eve of battle.'[49]

But do such superficial similarities indicate that Marder relied too heavily on K G B. Dewar and the *NSA*? Certainly in the first volume of *From the Dreadnought to Scapa Flow*, published in 1961, Marder was dismissive of the Royal Navy's pre-war tactical thinking, and he quoted extensively from Kenneth Dewar's published writings.[50] This led another great naval historian, Stephen Roskill, to believe that Marder had depended too heavily on K G B Dewar and the *NSA*.[51] But in fact Marder's views moderated over time, and he was much less harsh in his Jutland volume, which appeared in 1966. Here we may see the influence of Marder's long-time correspondent, Captain John Creswell. A former lecturer at the Tactical School, Creswell was much more favourably inclined toward the line of battle, the tactical formation employed by Jellicoe and severely criticised by the Dewar brothers.[52] As for Roskill, his account of Jutland in his biography of Beatty is well balanced; although he considers Jellicoe's command style too centralised and the line of battle too rigid, he is equally critical of Beatty.[53]

If the general view of Jutland had moderated over the years, that of Kenneth Dewar never did. In 1959–60 he published a three-part series on Jutland in

---

[48] Marder, *FDSF*, 3:5.

[49] Ibid, 3:51.

[50] Ibid, 1:395–404.

[51] Letter from Roskill to Drax, 26 July 1963; CAC: DRAX 6/18.

[52] Creswell, *British Admirals in the Eighteenth Century*, *passim*; for his influence on Marder, see the letters in the Marder Papers, Box 1, University of California, Irvine. Note that Marder dedicated his book *From the Dardanelles to Oran* to Creswell, calling him a 'gentleman, scholar and dear friend'.

[53] Roskill, *Admiral of the Fleet Earl Beatty*, 149–88.

The Naval Review that was in almost every detail a rehash of the *Naval Staff Appreciation*.[54] The tone of the articles still reads as though he were 'counsel for the prosecution', indicting the Royal Navy's leadership in the years prior to the First World War, Jellicoe's command style during the war and his tactics during the Battle itself. It was a sign of changed times, however, that the correspondence generated by the articles, while often praising individual points, condemned the bitterness that continued to mar Dewar's writing forty years after the original suppression of the *Naval Staff Appreciation of Jutland*.[55]

---

[54] Kenneth Dewar, 'Battle of Jutland'.

[55] See the letters published in the July 1960 (vol. XLVIII, no. 3) issue of *The Naval Review*, 377–89.

A Cautionary Note

A general assessment of the issues raised by the *Appreciation* is given in the Afterword. There is much of value in what the Dewar brothers wrote, but there are errors, and, to put it charitably, misinterpretations as well. The *Appreciation* must not be treated as an authoritative source, and its conclusions need to be judged against modern scholarship. It certainly isn't suitable as a first introduction to the battle! For those readers not already familiar with Jutland, there are several excellent English-language accounts, at least one of which ought to be read beforehand. Amongst the foundational accounts is that of Sir Julian Corbett in *Naval Operations*, volume III. Originally published in 1923, a revised version was published in 1940, which included material from German sources that was unavailable to Corbett, as well as information about Room 40's deciphering of German wireless messages, which was still secret when Corbett wrote. It remains a very good, albeit dated, rendering of the battle from the British point-of-view.[56] A collection of valuable first-person recollections may be found in H W Fawcett and G W W Hooper, *The Fighting at Jutland*, first issued in 1921 and recently reprinted. This compendium is not only entertaining and illustrative of what Jutland felt like to those who took part, but buried within the stories are some useful nuggets unavailable elsewhere.

A modern, complete account is that of Arthur J Marder, in his five-volume set *From the Dreadnought to Scapa Flow*. Volume III, *Jutland and After*, first appeared in 1966, and was revised and enlarged in a second edition in 1978. Eminently readable, it is mandatory reading for any student of Jutland, although some of Marder's conclusions have been challenged by later scholars.

---

[56] Sadly, most of the printed copies of the 1940 revision were destroyed during the Blitz before they could be sold (see Bennett, 'The Harper Papers', 23–4). In the 1990s, the complete set of *Naval Operations* (including the revised version of vol. III, but unfortunately without the separate case of illustrations) was re-issued by the Imperial War Museum and The Battery Press.

Three books are musts for the 'advanced' reader. In 1996, Dr Andrew Gordon published *The Rules of the Game*, which looks in much detail at the ethos within the Royal Navy's officer corps and suggests reasons why Jutland went as badly as it did for the British. For those interested in a technical analysis of the ships that took part the ultimate source is John Campbell's *Jutland: An Analysis of the Fighting*, which provides a hit-by-hit examination of the battle. Finally, John Brooks' *Dreadnought Gunnery and the Battle of Jutland: The Question of Fire Control* goes into a wealth of detail on the underlying fire-control equipment, requirements and calculations of both sides, and gives new insight into the controversy regarding the relative merits of the Dreyer and Pollen fire-control systems. Brooks' analysis of the battle itself, from a gunnery and tactical standpoint, is definitely worth reading. Marder, Campbell, Gordon and Brooks have been considered the authoritative accounts against which the *Naval Staff Appreciation* has been checked. Additionally, the serious scholar will want to track down a copy of Cmd. 1068, *Battle of Jutland 30th May to 1st June 1916: Official Despatches*; this thick volume contains a wealth of primary source material and the reports of proceedings of the commanders immediately after the battle. It was reprinted by the Naval & Military Press Ltd. in 2006.

A Few Basics

It is assumed that the reader has a basic understanding of Great War naval technology and the more important players on each side. However, it should be borne in mind that the *Naval Staff Appreciation of Jutland* was written almost a century ago for the use of naval officers; it assumes that its audience would be aware of many things that may be unfamiliar to a modern reader. Therefore it may be helpful to explain a few of the details that were part of everyday life in the Royal Navy of 1916.

    1. *Time:* All times given in the *NSA* are Greenwich Mean Time (GMT). These are always to some degree approximate; it may be surprising to the modern reader, living in a world where to-the-second precision in time is commonplace, that the Royal Navy in the early twentieth century was generally unconcerned about discrepancies of several minutes or more. Keep in mind the fact that precise timekeeping was generally only of interest to the navigator, and that the technology of the day (manually-wound timepieces) simply did not allow for greater accuracy.[57]

    2. *Navigation:* The vagaries of reported positions played a major role in the battle. Before GPS, there were three basic methods of navigation: 1) Coastal, which relied on taking the bearings of two or more landmarks on shore to determine a ship's position; 2) Celestial, which involved 'shooting the sun' with a sextant to fix one's position; and 3) Dead Reckoning (DR), which was an estimated position, based on courses steered and speeds maintained since the last known position, adjusted for winds, currents and tides. Throughout the Battle of Jutland, ships had to rely on dead reckoning; radical manoeuvres while

---

[57] More disturbing was the occasional confusion over the actual time zone. There is an interesting anecdote from *Prince George* in the Dardanelles, which mistook the time to begin moving up for bombardment by two hours because of 'the orders given did not say whether it was local time or G.M.T.' (Lieutenant-Commander A R Hammick, 'Dardanelles Notes', 200).

under fire made it almost impossible to keep accurate track of courses and speeds. As a result there were inevitably errors, and differences of several miles were quite common. Although Jellicoe broadcast 'reference' positions to the Battle Fleet, allowing ships in company to adjust their reckoning to that of the flagship, this could not help in establishing the relative positions of Jellicoe's and Beatty's forces, which were not in sight of one another until about 6.00 pm; as a consequence their rendezvous in the midst of the battle took place on an unexpected bearing.

3. *Courses, Bearings, Distances:* Courses and bearings are magnetic except when they are reckoned from 0 to 360 degrees. Although gyrocompasses were coming into widespread use by the time of Jutland, all courses and bearings reported by British ships throughout the battle were based on magnetic compasses. Because the North Pole and the North Magnetic Pole do not coincide, these will differ from 'true' courses based on the North Pole; this variation was about 13° West in the vicinity of the battle. The difference can be plainly seen in the *Reproduction of the Record of the Battle of Jutland* (the 'Harper Record'), where both true and magnetic courses are usually given side by side; for example, on page 19 we find that at about 3.07 pm 'the course of the Battle Cruisers . . . was changed to 77° (East)'. A true course east would of course be 90°. Another form of notation that crops up from time to time follows this format: 'S 16° E'; in this example, the direction being indicated is 16° East of South, and in all cases these are also magnetic. Note also that courses and bearings were usually expressed in terms of 'points', with 32 points making up a circle of 360° – that is, a point is equal to 11¼°. Thus, a 4–point turn is one of 45°, 8 points 90°, 16 points 180°.

Bearings are occasionally given in the form 'green 115°' or 'red 60°' – these are measured from the ship's bow, green being starboard and red port (the mnemonic is 'port wine is red').

All distances are given in nautical miles of 2,026.667 yards each. The usual 'back of the envelope' approximation is 2,000 yards to the mile.

4. *Signalling:*[58] Signals could be conveyed by visual means (flags, signal lamps, searchlights or masthead semaphores) or by wireless (W/T, 'wireless transmission' or 'wireless telegraphy'). Visual signals could generally not be seen by an enemy, so could be made in plain language (although there may have been a major indiscretion here regarding night recognition signals). Wireless messages could be picked up by any suitably-tuned receiver, and so had to be

---

[58] In his forthcoming book on Jutland, John Brooks provides a lucid and detailed description of RN signalling practices; I am very grateful for an advance copy of this material, which was of great assistance in writing this section.

encrypted. The encryption and decryption process took time, and so there were often considerable delays in the delivery of messages. For this reason, both navies manoeuvred their ships with visual signals – flags and signal lamps – supplemented by W/T. In the case of flag signals, they were hoisted by the ship giving the order. There was no separate flag hoist to order their execution. Instead, the 'execute' was given by their being hauled down.

There were several 'mutilated' W/T signals during the battle, that is, signals that were in some sense garbled. One example came at 4.45 pm, when *Lion* sent a sighting report to Jellicoe (via *Princess Royal*, as *Lion*'s wireless transmitter had been damaged in action):

Have sighted enemy's Battle Fleet bearing SE.

This was received in *Iron Duke* as:

26 to 30 battleships probably hostile, bearing SSE steering SE.

The discrepancy between these two versions of the signal is probably explained by the fact that signals, whether visual or wireless, were not spelled out word-by-word or letter-by-letter; instead, all the words and phrases likely to be needed were accorded two-letter codes in the signal book, and in the case of wireless they were transmitted in Morse code. Thus if a single two-letter code group was incorrectly encoded or decoded, or if the sender made a mistake in keying a group, or the recipient misheard the dots and dashes of the messages (due to noise or interference), the entire purport of a message could be altered beyond all recognition.

5. *Helm Orders*: Up until 1933,[59] ordering 'Hard a starboard' would turn a Royal Navy ship to port (i.e., to the left)! This was because the order was given in terms of the helm – the tiller, actually – and not the rudder. Sailors of small boats will recognise that putting the tiller over to starboard is how they turn their boat to port, and vice versa.

6. *Tactical Units:* The Grand Fleet was divided into a variety of sub-units for tactical purposes.

a) Squadrons: Battle squadrons, composed of battleships, consisted of eight ships; cruiser squadrons, including battle cruiser squadrons, consisted of four ships. The unique 5th Battle Squadron of fast *Queen Elizabeth* class battleships had four ships at Jutland (a fifth ship, the *Queen Elizabeth* herself, was in dockyard hands at the time of the battle).

b) Divisions: Battleship divisions consisted of four ships, hence a battle squadron was composed of two divisions; the entire squadron would be

---

[59] Harland, *Seamanship in the Age of Sail*, 175–6.

commanded by a vice-admiral, with a rear-admiral commanding the second division.

c) Flotillas were the basic unit for destroyers; their composition varied during the war. At a conference on 18 March 1916 it was decided that the nominal strength of a flotilla would be eighteen destroyers; allowing for boats undergoing refits and repairs, this would provide an effective strength of sixteen destroyers.[60] Each flotilla would have one light cruiser and one flotilla leader (an enlarged destroyer; these vessels offered better communications facilities than normal destroyers). Flotillas were led by a Captain (D); individual destroyers were usually commanded by lieutenant-commanders or lieutenants. The post of Commodore (F) had been introduced shortly before the battle; the commodore was to be in command of all the Battle Fleet's flotillas. However, this officer (Captain J R P Hawksley) had little time to train his force, and the reorganisation agreed in March was still far from complete. The actual strength of the flotillas during the battle can best be gleaned from studying Appendix A.

In addition to Commodore (F), there were also the 'Commodore (S)', in charge of submarines, and Commodore Reginald Tyrwhitt of the Harwich Force, who went by the title of 'Commodore (T)' and commanded the 'torpedo craft' (light cruisers and destroyers) that operated in the southern part of the North Sea.

Note that in contemporary RN usage the term 'ship' did not include destroyers, but referred to battleships and cruisers; hence the frequent appearance in documents of the phrase 'ships and destroyers'. The origins of this distinction probably lie in the origins of destroyers themselves, which evolved from torpedo *boats*.

Another terminological peculiarity was that the unadorned word 'cruiser' referred to armoured cruisers, an obsolescent type; 'light cruisers' referred to the smaller, faster, more modern vessels. Thus at Jutland there was a 2nd Cruiser Squadron *and* a 2nd Light Cruiser Squadron; the two should not be confused.

Finally, note that the term 'Special Intelligence' refers to the British interception and decryption of the German signals traffic by 'Room 40'.

---

[60] See Corbett, *Naval Operations*, 3:318–19 for more details.

C. B. 0938

NAVAL STAFF
APPRECIATION OF JUTLAND

WITH APPENDICES AND DIAGRAMS

———————

NAVAL STAFF.
Training and Staff Duties Division.
January, 1922.

INTRODUCTION

1. The Battle of Jutland must appear to many as a grey mass of ships manœuvring in and out of the battle smoke with no possibility of ascertaining their movements with clear and definite precision. To attempt to do so is certainly no light task. The official reports of individual captains represent only an effort, often necessarily hasty, to reduce the observations of a number of observers into one story; and similarly the despatches of the Admirals can be regarded only as a provisional attempt to reduce the reports of individual captains to a single focus.

From a historical point of view both must be regarded merely as rapid preliminary surveys. By their very nature they could be no more, for a complete survey requires the careful and critical examination of every source of information – every log, every signal log, every individual report.

But in a battle where 154 British flags and pendants were flying this in itself is a heavy and laborious task, and when in addition it is remembered that in the case of most ships the signal volumes alone number at least three or four[1] and the total number of volumes runs into hundreds, the mere physical labour of arrangement and custody is a considerable item of work.

2. The Ships' Logs and Signal Logs in conjunction with the official reports may be regarded as the principal sources available. But in a large number of ships the logs unfortunately are of little assistance. Many navigators merely say 'Courses as requisite'. Very few, as in the case of the *Marlborough*, insert a complete and detailed account of every alteration of course and speed. The details are presumably to be found in the navigator's notebook, but these are not

---

[1] Signal and Wireless, Odd Day and Even Day, Auxiliary Wireless and Wireless Entry. In the case of the *Iron Duke* there were some seven or eight volumes kept, of which a number were wireless entry registers.

available,[2] though an unimpeachable source from an historical point of view.

The deficiencies of the logs are, however, in this case largely supplemented by information appended to the captains' reports.

But even where there is sufficiency of information, visual discrepancies in time and place arise. Times differ in different ships and in the same ship the times of different observers may differ, and different observers see the same incident from different points of view. One sees the destruction of the *Indefatigable* in the explosion of the bursting salvos, another in the disappearance of her hull beneath the waves.

On the whole, however, the discrepancies in time are not very serious. The wireless logs rarely differ by more than two or three minutes and in many cases are synchronous.

The discrepancies in reckoning are more serious and practically render latitude and longitude reports valueless for establishing relative positions when the ships are close to one another. The *Southampton*'s reports between 5 pm and 6 pm and the *Falmouth*'s between 8.15 pm and 8.45 pm are instances of this deficiency. In all probability its cause is partly to be found in the cumbersome latitude and longitude code in force at the time.

In addition to the difficulty of establishing relative positions, these discrepancies introduce an element of complexity, for three positions have to be considered. For instance, in the case of the bearing of the *Iron Duke* and *Lion* when they were approaching one another at 5.30, there are the *Iron Duke*'s reckoning position, the *Iron Duke*'s actual position, and the *Iron Duke*'s bearing according to the *Lion*'s reckoning all to be considered in arriving at an estimate of the situation.

3. The Signal and Wireless Logs constitute another valuable source. All the signals made have been collated by the Signal Division in a record of messages.[3] This has been carefully done, but one or two signals of minor importance are not to be found in it, and in some cases the time of receipt has become merged in the time of origin. Amongst the signal logs is the signal log of the *Iron Duke* handed in to M. Branch. This is written in ink, and from a historical point of view bears all the signs of having been compiled subsequently[4] to the battle

---

[2] The navigator is bound to produce it at a court-martial touching the safe navigation of his ship, but on his safe return to harbour he can drop it overboard with the anchor.

[3] Record of Messages, Battle of Jutland, S.P.02085. Signal Division 21.12.18 (printed folio). This is the source of the signals in Harper, Appendix VIII, and in Jutland *Official Despatches* (1920), Appendix II.

[4] Includes May 31 to June 1 only; the handwriting is the same throughout.

from other signal logs. Only two contemporary signal logs proper[5] of the *Iron Duke* have been seen, both written in pencil, one rather more carefully than the other, both omitting a number of important signals probably because the pressure of work of a fleet flagship led to the systematic use of files and the logs were not carefully written up.

It is difficult otherwise to account for the fact that the contemporary signal log of the *Iron Duke* is one of the most incomplete logs in the fleet for the actual battle.[6] In the case of the *Lion*, a fire apparently destroyed a number of the original forms.[7] A word of thanks is due to the *New Zealand*'s wireless log which was evidently kept by an officer who noted all the 'check and repeats' and repetitions, which are very helpful. All these signal logs are kept at Deptford Yard.[8] A careful compilation[9] of material from the ship's logs, signal logs and reports of all ships which embodies all the relevant information they contain was made by Captain J. E. T. Harper's Committee, and a complete compilation of all the material in ships' logs has also been made by Lieutenant-Commander J. F. H. Pollen (Historical Section, C.I.D.).

It might be thought that Wireless Entry Logs which merely register the time of receipt or despatch and the sender were of little use, but this is far from being the case. They are useful in checking times and actual receipt. Mention has already been made of one or two signals omitted from the Record of Messages and consequently from the Command Papers. One is a signal made by the Admiralty to Commander-in-Chief, May 31, 1235, stating that the enemy's flagship was in the Jade at 11.10 am.[10] The original is to be found in the War Registry files. As it is one of the Special Intelligence telegrams its text would not be in the wireless log, but in the *Iron Duke*'s 'In' telegrams.[10] It is not

---

[5] There are several volumes of various logs, including auxiliary logs, wireless entry logs, cypher registry logs, etc.

[6] *Editor's note*: There will be other instances where the authors of the *Naval Staff Appreciation* hint at conspiracy and cover-up in Jellicoe's flagship!

[7] *Editor's note*: Here is the pertinent extract from *Lion*'s signal log:

4.55 pm. Most of the records of the outgoing visual signals were lost and destroyed in the action. The records had been sent down to the Port Signal Station to be logged, but, on account of bursting shells and smoke and fire, they got lost or destroyed. This log was preserved with difficulty, not before a hose had been turned on it (Cmd 2870, 'Harper Record', 24).

[8] *Editor's note*: Sadly, these were eventually destroyed: see Marder, *FDSF*, 3:46 n.13. However, there is a small collection of signal chits from *Iron Duke* in the National Maritime Museum; see Mead, 'Jutland Signals'.

[9] Extracts from reports, logs and signal logs of the ships present at the Battle of Jutland (typescript folio).

[10] These are in Historical Section C.I.D., classified as in *Iron Duke*, under six headings,

there and has evidently gone astray. Here the wireless entry logs come in useful. The *Iron Duke*'s wireless entry has an entry, 'Cleethorpes, received 12.48, Cypher 1235, Admiralty to Commander-in-Chief', and *Lion*'s wireless entry has a similar entry, clearly proving that it was received. The signal had no direct incidence on the battle but is of interest as introducing another very important collection of records, namely, those of Room 40,[11] where German messages were decyphered.

On May 30, at 5.41 pm, the German Flagship made a signal to the *Ostfriesland* to say that the direction of wireless would be carried out by Wilhelmshaven third entrance, which would have the wireless call of the Commander-in-Chief, High Sea Fleet. This was in a new key and was not decyphered till the 31st at 6 pm. Meanwhile, in the forenoon of the 31st, directionals placed the Commander-in-Chief's wireless call in the Jade and the above signal went out to this effect. This and infinitely more is to be found in this unique collection which stands as a monumental product of British genius in a field practically untouched before the war.

The I.D. History,[12] compiled by Lieutenants F. Birch and W. F. Clarke, R.N.V.R., from these materials must be regarded as a most valuable and indispensable contribution to the study of the war and has been very helpful in presenting the German view of the battle.[13]

4. The next large collection consists of the Admirals' despatches and the reports of individual ships.[14]

Admiralty to all ships, ditto W and X cyphers, Private and Personal, B and other Secret (this includes Special Intelligence), Intercepted and General.

[11] These were arranged by Lieutenant-Commander Frank Birch, R.N.V.R., and Lieutenant W. F. Clarke, R.N.V.R., in 1919-20, in the Historical Section I.D. The records comprise over 2,300 volumes and include the valuable collection of the German Section of the Intelligence Division (Room 14, Commander Brandon) which contains the material taken from captured and sunken ships.

[12] Contribution to the Study of German Movements, Volumes I and II, four volumes, typescript folio, by Lieutenants Birch and Clarke, Intelligence Division, 1919-20.

[13] *Editor's note*: This is probably a reference to 'A Contribution to the History of German Naval Warfare 1914-1918' by Birch and Clarke, kept in the Naval Historical Branch library; a copy may be found in TNA: HW 7/1 through HW 7/4; volume one signed by Frank Birch 2 July 1920. There is a handful of undated marginal notations in The National Archives copy by Captain Alfred Dewar. This work has recently been published in two volumes as *Room 40: German Naval Warfare 1914-1918*, edited by Hans Joachim Koerver.

[14] M. Branch dossier, four volumes, folio, cardboard bound – Commander-in-Chief's Despatch, Battle Fleet, Battle Cruisers and Light Cruisers, Destroyers.

These were photostated for Captain Harper's use in 1920 but have become more readily accessible in the Jutland Papers.[15]

It should be noted that the Commander-in-Chief's first despatch and plan is dated June 18, 1916 (M.05697/16); on June 24 a second version of his despatch was forwarded (M.06495/16). This omitted the introductory remarks and the details of our ships being sunk and gave a short list of enemy vessels put out of action, in place of the long list of Certains and Probables in the first version. The despatch in the printed Command Papers is the fuller and earlier despatch of June 18, 1916. Three tracings were also sent at different times by the Commander-in-Chief, the first dated June 18, 1916, with the report of June 18, 1916; a second, dated June 19, 1916, sent on July 8, 1916; and a third, sent on August 29, 1916. These tracks differ in the adjustment of the track of the battle cruisers to that of the Battle Fleet. The Jutland Papers give the Plan of June 18, 1916 (Plan 1A) and of August 29, 1916 (Plan 4A).[16]

5. In addition to these sources, Captain J. E. T. Harper's record and diagrams of the battle[17] have been of very great assistance and really represent the first stage of this work. But as there is no such thing as finality in historical work, so there are certain points where the record is considered open to revision, more particularly in its representation of the movements and courses of the German Fleet which differ widely from those of Scheer. Until the

---

[15] (Command Papers, 1920) *Battle of Jutland, May 30 to June 1, 1916, Official Despatches, with Appendices* (603 pp., 8vo). This is based on the M. Branch dossier, but omits lists of recommendations. The Appendices are very valuable. Appendix I: Information from Gunnery Records; Appendix II: Record of Messages (from Signal Division compilation); Appendix III: Admiral Scheer's Report of July 4, 1916 (but not his supplementary Report of July 16, 1916); Appendix IV: Letter, Commander-in-Chief (Admiral Sir John Jellicoe) to Admiralty, of October 30, 1914, which throws valuable light on the tactical views held by the Commander-in-Chief. There are 31 diagrams in the book and in a separate case 12 British and 7 German, the latter being reproductions of the diagrams attached to Scheer's report. The work unfortunately lacks an index.

Editor's note: Hereafter this compilation will be referred to as '*Official Despatches*'. Some interesting gunnery material, now of interest to technical historians, was removed before publication. The original despatches may be found in the TNA: ADM 137/302.

[16] Lord Jellicoe expressed the opinion that the later plan of August 29, 1916, is the more correct, and has pointed out that the note on page 51 of the *Official Despatches* is not correct.

[17] Official Record of the Battle of Jutland, with Appendices and Plans (proof print 8 vo, 349 pp.), with 18 diagrams. The 'German' diagrams have been reproduced in the Command paper.

Editor's note: Published in 1927 as Cmd. 2870, *Reproduction of the Record of the Battle of Jutland Prepared by Captain J.E.T. Harper*. It was unfortunately issued without the original diagrams referred to so frequently in the *Naval Staff Appreciation*.

German Staff account of the battle is issued a certain element of uncertainty must surround the German movements, but Scheer's report and diagrams provide a large amount of reliable material, and pending further information must be accepted as the nearest approach to accuracy.

It is certain, for instance, that at 7.15 pm when the German Fleet turned away the second time, the First Squadron was practically in line with the Third Squadron, otherwise the turn of the *Friedrich der Grosse* to port, specifically stated and clearly explained in Scheer's book,[18] would be meaningless. These courses have been carefully revised with the assistance of Lieutenant-Commander J. F. H. Pollen, and the diagrams attached to the appreciation are based on this revision.

6. It has not been considered necessary to attach a complete plan showing the continuous track of each ship; nor is it altogether desirable. A plan of this sort is necessary in the historical reconstruction of the battle as a norm or standard to test the reliability of particular statements, but it must not be regarded as more than the adjustment of a number of varying observations to a general mean. In some cases the course of a ship or squadron is certain, in others less certain, in others again it is largely supposititious. A continuous track of a battle tends by its very nature to convey an impression of absolute accuracy which may be very misleading unless accompanied by a critical commentary assessing the relative degree of credence to be given to particular portions of it, and it is considered that a commentary of this sort would overload the appreciation. Also a complete and continuous track of the movements of all vessels in a battle, however desirable, may not always be possible. If the incident is on a small scale, and the facts were accurately recorded, it is easy to construct such a track. But when the incident is on a very large scale or the facts are not recorded[19] or are insufficiently or inaccurately recorded, then it is better to confine oneself to the main outlines of the battle. For instance, in the case of destroyer actions at night, the information is generally so scanty that only an approximate plan of their movements can be reproduced.[20]

Where the discrepancies occur in time, courses, ranges and bearings, these all have to be adjusted so as to harmonise with one another and with criterions of possibility and probability. The final adjustment which gives a generally

---

[18] Scheer, *Germany's High Seas Fleet*, 158.

[19] To carry the argument to its extreme limit, it is useless to attempt to draw an accurate track of each ship in the Battle of Salamis. The information is not there.

[20] The movements of some of the 12th Flotilla during the attack on the German 2nd Squadron must remain uncertain, and the individual reports of the boats of the 11th Flotilla were not sent in by the Captain (D).

correct view of the battle is not based on any one record, but is more of the nature of a complicated mosaic or puzzle picture whose composition requires a great deal of knowledge, skill and patience – how much can only be known to those who have tried it. When the general variations in time have been ascertained by a study of the logs and records there remain three elements of place to be adjusted – the geographical position in latitude and longitude, the relative position of the enemy, and the relative position of one's own squadron and ships. In Captain Harper's diagrams of the latitude and longitude of the *Invincible*, subsequently ascertained by careful survey, have been used as a datum point, and the position of the *Iron Duke* adjusted to it. For the relative position of the enemy there are numerous bearing and ranges, but the bearings were usually in terms of red or green, and the ranges were rapid rangefinder observations on a misty day and not carefully surveyed distances.

In the case of the relative positions of our own ships and squadrons, the number of recorded observations is small.[21]

For these reasons it has been thought better to confine the appreciation to diagrams of the more important phases of the battle, which are also simpler and clearer than a continuous track.

The chapter on the Grand Fleet Battle Orders is based on the collection made by the Training and Staff Duties Division.[22]

Lord Jellicoe's *Grand Fleet* has been used to supplement the despatches, and mention should be made of *The Fighting at Jutland*, a valuable collection of personal narratives largely based on notes made during the action, compiled by Lieutenants H. W. Fawcett and G. W. W. Hooper.

7. Finally there are some sources which have not been used because they do not exist, but whose non-existence it is just as well to emphasise; for instance, 'instructions of the Cabinet' to the Commander-in-Chief.[23] The War Council did a number of things which may be open to criticism, but it never got the length of issuing instructions to the Commander-in-Chief of the Grand Fleet

---

[21] For the relative position of the Battle Fleet and Battle Cruiser Fleet between 7 pm and 8 pm, there are only four recorded observations, viz., *Minotaur* at 7.10 pm (*Official Despatches*, 272) and at 8 pm (*Minotaur's* track, Plate 24), *Shannon* at 6.58 (*Official Despatches*, 280) and *Calliope* at 7.28 (*Official Despatches*, 385). Again there was considerable bunching in the Battle Fleet during deployment, but the observations are too few to enable one to plot it.

[22] Grand Fleet Battle Orders (photostated), 3 volumes, folio, Training and Staff Duties Division, 1919. Volume 3 gives the orders in force at Jutland.

Editor's note: These volumes are now available in TNA: ADM 116/1341, GFBOs before Jutland; ADM 116/1342, GFBOs after Jutland; and ADM 116/1343, GFBOs in force at Jutland.

[23] It would be hardly necessary to mention this point had it not been seriously discussed in certain quarters.

as to the tactics he was to adopt on meeting the enemy. Nor does the appreciation venture to deal with any personal factors. It may be said, of course, that no one can criticise the battle, for no one can place himself in the position of a Naval Commander-in-Chief surrounded by mist, battle-smoke and uncertainties with the safety of a huge fleet on his shoulders and measureless and untold responsibilities looming before and behind him. Such an argument merely leaves the battle where it was and fails to distinguish between the subjective personality of the Commander-in-Chief (which is not in question here) and the objective events of the battle. Its acceptance would mean the negation of history whose task it is to dispel the mist and uncertainties arising both in the battle and out of it and to tell us whether, and how far, they were inevitable. The appreciations is written more particularly for the use and instruction of staff officers and is an endeavour in the light of fuller knowledge and careful analysis to deduce lessons for their future guidance and investigation. Let no one think that there are no lessons to be gleaned from it or that a battle can be 'ancient history' before its history has been written. To those who study it carefully and intensively there still remains a rich, ungarnered harvest. Out of the sea where so many of our sailors lie sleeping there arise two subjects of absorbing and perennial naval interest which were certainly not solved at the Battle of Jutland and may not have been completely solved since – an adequate system of naval tactics and an adequate system of staff work and command.

CHAPTER I

THE SITUATION IN 1916

Function of the Battle in Naval Strategy

1. The Battle of Jutland will rank as one of the great battles of naval history, but it cannot be understood without a clear grasp of the influence of a decisive naval battle on the general situation at the time.

With the exception of occasional sorties, the German Fleet had been confined to its harbours from the beginning of the war, and it is maintained by some that this form of blockade dispensed with the necessity of a battle, and that the defeat of the enemy fleet in battle would not have influenced the course of events.

This argument demands careful scrutiny. Was the Battle of Jutland merely an incident of the blockade? Was its object merely to maintain the blockade? Was it won when the Germans were driven back to harbour? Such a theory, which would make the battle merely an aspect of the blockade, is inadmissible. Naval warfare has only four principal aspects, viz:

Invasion, and counter invasion;

Attack of trade, and defence of trade.

These ends, which loom behind every naval operation, can only be completely achieved by the destruction of the enemy's forces. The struggle may be spread over long years of suffering and uncertainty, or it may be greatly abbreviated by battle.

There has been a tendency in recent years to depreciate the function of the battle in naval strategy, but it must always play an essential part in the economy of war, for it embodies two great principles of war – concentration, and the economy of the decisive blow.

The High Sea Fleet and the Baltic

2. Besides, the German High Sea Fleet stood for two things outside the blockade – the control of the Baltic, and the control of the Heligoland Bight.

10

Germany's practically undisputed control in the Baltic was a grave obstacle to the blockade, and acted as a powerful impetus to neutral trade.[1] In addition to supplies from the West, it covered the important Swedish iron ore traffic[2] which, in the opinion of the French General Staff, was as vital to Germany as the supplies from the Lorraine and Luxembourg districts. But it had a still more important aspect. It closed direct sea communication with Russia. The stream of munitions, food, and raw material that flowed by sea to Great Britain, France and Italy from all over the world was the life blood of the Allies' armies, and it was the failure of this stream which led to the collapse of Russia and Roumania.

The situation would have been greatly influenced in our favour by the presence of British naval forces in the Baltic co-operating with the Russians,[3] but so long as the High Sea Fleet was 'in being', they could not be spared from the more important area of the North Sea.[4] The High Sea Fleet held the gate of the Baltic in its hand: if it had been decisively defeated, a British squadron could have entered the Baltic. Operating from Russian bases such a squadron would have tightened the commercial blockade, and opened a road of moral and material support to the Russian armies.

The High Sea Fleet and the Heligoland Bight

3. But it was in the Heligoland Bight that the control exercised by the High Sea Fleet exerted its vital influence on the war. Shut off from the high seas and not daring to risk a battle, the Germans had recourse to the *guerre-de-course* with the submarine as its principal weapon, and by June, 1916, the destruction

---

[1] The traffic was gradually reduced by direct interception and economic pressure in various forms, but these measures did not become fully effective until the U.S.A. entered the war in 1917.

[2] Amounting in 1916 to 4.35 million tons. Swedish iron ore contains roughly double the quantity of iron in German and Belgian ore. It was of the greatest importance to Germany, and an officer on Ludendorff's staff is reported to have said that without it Germany could not have continued the war after January, 1918.

[3] In the first two years of the war, the Russian Baltic Fleet showed itself an effective force in several conflicts with the enemy, and with the help of a few British submarines it succeeded in temporarily interrupting the German-Swedish trade on more than one occasion.

[4] At a conference held on September 17, 1914, in the *Iron Duke*, attended by the First Lord, Chief of War Staff, DID, and several flag officers, including Commodores (T) and (S), when the question of operations in the Baltic was discussed, it was decided that forces could not be spared for the purpose. M.0078/1914.

wrought by it was already reaching alarming proportions.[5] Even at that stage, the menace to our mercantile marine dominated every other naval consideration, and the possibility that lack of shipping might end the war before the Allied armies won it, was already assuming a very insistent and definite form.

The most favourable areas for intercepting the submarine was, of course, the vicinity of the German rivers and the narrow channels of the Kattegat. Was it not possible to close these passages completely by mines and other measures? This was the first question[6] considered by the Planning Section of the Navy Staff on its constitution in July, 1917, and after exhaustive investigation it was decided that the High Sea Fleet rendered the performance of this task impracticable.

Less ambitious schemes for intercepting the submarines were, however, tried, and not without a considerable measure of success. Early in 1917 a large area in the Bight was notified as a mined area, and measures set on foot which resulted in the laying of nearly 37,000 mines in the Bight in 1917 and 1918.[7]

The High Sea Fleet the Power behind the Submarine Campaign

4. This attempt to block in the enemy submarines developed into a protracted struggle between British minelayers and German minesweepers, in which the former had the immeasurable advantage of knowing the position of the German swept channels. The enemy was thus forced to accompany the submarines on both their inward and outward journeys by minesweepers, barrier breakers, and torpedo boats. These escorts had to be supported, and from 1917 onwards the main task of the High Sea Fleet was the support of the sweeping forces working far afield on the submarine routes.[8]

---

[5] Gross tonnage of British, Allied and Neutral ships sunk up to June, 1916:-

	By surface craft	By submarine	By mines	Total	Percentage by submarines
1914 ..	222,432	2,950	78,152	303,534	.9
1915 ..	59,076	1,048,293	170,380	1,277,749	82
1916 ..	52,160	576,725	191,629	821,484	70
	(six month)				

(Statistical Review of the War against Merchant Shipping, Admiralty, November 23, 1918)

[6] The plan included a complete blocking of the Elbe, Kattegat and Jade.

[7] Mines laid in the Bight were: 1914, nil; 1915, 4,538 in 9 minefields; 1916, 1,782 in 17 minefields; 1917, 15,686 in 76 minefields; 1918, 21,105 in 129 minefields.

[8] History of German Movements (typescript), I.D., Section 25, by Birch and Clarke, 81, 84, 85; Scheer, *Germany's High Seas Fleet*, 291. By the end of the war some of the swept channels extended more than 150 miles from the Jade, and from November, 1917, there was generally a whole Battle Squadron a considerable distance out in support of the sweepers.

This is clearly described in the History of German Movements.[9] 'Gradually, as British mining activities increased, the operations of the minesweeping units had been extended, and the provision of an adequate force to protect the vessels engaged, from raids, had become imperative. This force had steadily been reinforced. At first merely a half flotilla of destroyers, strengthened by a light cruiser or two; by June, 1917, it was thought necessary to have battleships in support'. All German Commanders-in-Chief recognised 'that if the Battle Squadrons were destroyed it would be impossible to use the Bight. It was only the support of the battleships which enabled the German minesweepers to carry out their tasks undisturbed. If that support perished, or was seriously weakened in a fleet action, then one of two things were bound to happen. Either British mining would render all approach to the bases impassable, or the defensive minefields, left without adequate support, would be forced and the Bight overrun by British craft. Not one of them, not even Scheer, dared to risk a fleet action which might have had such disastrous results'.

As time went on the difficulties of egress and ingress increased. The 'ways' in the Bight were frequently closed, and from April, 1917, homeward bound submarines began to be deflected through the Kattegat, whilst by the end of the year that channel was also frequently used by outgoing submarines. Early in 1918 about 1,400 deep mines were laid in the northern part of the Kattegat,[10] but as the minefield was not patrolled by surface craft, it did not exercise any real influenced on the German submarines. The intensive mining of the Bight just failed to achieve complete success because of the difficulties of attacking the German sweeping craft and the inability to provide destroyers, etc., for the control of the Kattegat. These difficulties would have been greatly reduced if the High Sea Fleet had been decisively defeated, but so long as it remained intact it was the bulwark behind which the submarines were able to continue their campaign.

Other Influences of the High Sea Fleet

This latent power of the High Sea Fleet to hold our forces immobilised from other spheres of work adversely affected anti-submarine measures of every sort. In October, 1917, a combined operation with mines, mine nets, and Grand Fleet torpedo craft and submarines, resulted in the destruction of three submarines.[11] The operation was a decided success, but was never repeated

---

[9] Ibid.

[10] The question of laying mines in the Kattegat was of course complicated by neutral interests.

[11] U.50, U.66 and U.106. H. S. Operations, October 11, 1917. The submarines were sunk in the mine nets and minefields. The destroyers drove the submarines down but saw nothing themselves and were inclined to depreciate the value of the operation.

owing to the demands for convoy reducing the Grand Fleet destroyer force to the lowest possible limits of battle requirements.

5. Dover Straits can be cited as a contrast to the Heligoland Bight. There the surface control was in British hands. As soon as the mines were properly laid and the minefields were patrolled, the route became exceedingly dangerous and the enemy could only hope to reopen it by direct attack on the patrols. Similarly, the gigantic task of mining the Norway-Shetland area,[12] was forced upon us by the High Sea Fleet, in order to bring the minefield under the direct control of the Grand Fleet and beyond the reach of the enemy's sweepers.

Measures to prevent the submarines coming out went hand in hand with measures to protect the trade by means of convoy. But convoys suffered in the same way. It was not possible to supply enough destroyers for convoy and at the same time keep the Grand Fleet ready for battle, and it was only the delivery of British and the arrival of American destroyers in the end of 1917 and in 1918 which relieved the situation.[13]

In dealing with the possibility of raids and invasion, the same malignant influence was at work. So long as the High Sea Fleet was 'in being', intact, and undefeated and able to come out in force, defensive measures had to be adopted against a raid. Thus at the commencement of hostilities only four out of six divisions of the expeditionary army were despatched to France, and throughout the war a large force was retained in the Kingdom for home defence.

Effect of a Decisive Naval Victory

6. The influence of the High Sea Fleet can be traced in every phase and aspect of the war. If it had been decisively defeated, the complete blocking of the Kattegat and Heligoland Bight would have become practicable. This measure would have meant the end of the submarine campaign and a consequent shortening of the war. Its defeat would also probably have opened up communication with the Baltic and have had the two-fold effect of increasing the economic pressure of the blockade and encouraging the Russians. In every other aspect of the war, a naval victory would have simplified

---

[12] This minefield was designed to close an area 220 miles broad and 50 to 160 fathoms deep. It was not in existence long enough to judge of its success, but it probably destroyed six submarines.

Editor's note: Robert Grant, *U-Boat Intelligence 1914-1918*, 109, confirms that six or possibly seven submarines were sunk in the Northern Barrage.

[13] See Naval Staff Memorandum on 'British Naval Policy' circulated to War Cabinet on July 4, 1917, which stated, 'the Grand Fleet, Harwich, and Dover flotillas must be kept up to strength, and the task of finding additional numbers for convoy work is the only obstacle to its general adoption'.

operations and reduced the strain on the British Navy. Shipbuilding could have been stopped, and men, munitions, and machinery diverted to the services of the war on land.

7. But vitally important as a fleet action may be, it may not be possible to bring it about. The weaker fleet may avoid battle. Meantime the trade must be protected, and one of the great problems of naval strategy is to combine the demands of commerce defence with the requirements of a prospective battle. In the intervening period, the attacks on trade may be so serious, or the necessities of troop transport so urgent, that the Main Fleet may have to be called upon to assist them, which may entail limitations on its instant readiness for battle.[14]

Under ordinary circumstances, and in default of special intelligence, the only way to bring about a fleet action would have been for the Grand Fleet to oppose the German submarines so effectively as to force the High Sea Fleet to come out and support them.

The ascending degree of offensive action which might have followed such a policy is illustrated in the case of the Scandinavian trade. The Germans attacked with submarines; we answered with destroyers and escorts; the enemy replied with light cruisers,[15] which were in turn countered by a battleship or battle cruiser force from the Grand Fleet covering the convoys whenever they were at sea. Finally, the whole High Sea Fleet sallied out on April 23, 1918, with the intention of attacking the convoy off the Norwegian coast. The German attack miscarried owing to faulty information and an accident to the *Moltke*; but had it been accomplished the Grand Fleet would have had a good chance of intercepting the High Sea Fleet. These are the normal methods by which a battle is brought about.

8. In practice, little or no attempt was made during the first two years or so of the war to amalgamate the policy of trade protection with that of battle. The Grand Fleet and all its attendant light craft stood aside as if it had no concern with the submarine campaign. The brunt of the enemy's main line of attack was therefore borne by the mercantile marine, whilst the bulk of the anti-submarine work was left to slow trawlers and drifters manned by untrained ratings lacking proper equipment and without skilled direction or control. The

---

[14] For example, if Grand Fleet destroyers were carrying out anti-submarine operations in the northern area, the Grand Fleet could probably be ready for battle at short notice in that particular area, but these destroyers would have to be recalled and fuelled before accompanying the Grand Fleet to, say, the southern area.

[15] *Brummer* and *Bremse*.

trade had in fact to look after itself whilst the fleet was waiting for a decisive battle.

Here a new element had entered naval war. Special intelligence[16] greatly increased the chance of battle, for the movements of the enemy could be closely followed. This gave rise to what may be called a policy of immediacy. The Grand Fleet was kept ready to move at any hour of the night or day on information of enemy movements, and under these circumstances any systematic co-operation of Grand Fleet destroyers in anti-submarine operations became impracticable. The normal methods of bringing about an action had been superseded.

But as this policy of immediacy, based on the hope of a fleet action, meant the sacrifice of very important interests, it was essential that every effort should be made to make the action decisive. The fleet stood apart from the protection of trade only in order that it might deal one crushing and final blow at the High Sea Feet. The whole policy of immediacy was indissolubly linked with the idea of a decisive battle and a vigorous tactical offensive. Divorced from these conceptions, British strategy in the North Sea becomes futile and meaningless.

---

[16] *Editor's note*: That is, the interception and decyphering of the German signals traffic.

THE GRAND FLEET BATTLE ORDERS OF MAY, 1916

Tactics before the War

9. The key to a battle is to be found in the Battle Orders which may be presumed to embody the tactical conceptions prevailing in the mind of the commander. These conceptions will partly depend on the general level of tactical thought at the time, and a few remarks on this point will not be out of place.

When war broke out there was no comprehensive or authoritative tactical doctrine, and conflicting views were held on fundamental questions of principle.

In the long period of peace after 1815, the real art of tactics seems to have died with Nelson. Formal movements took their place, and a system of manœuvring was built up which bore no relationship to the realities of war. Biddlecomb's Book of Tactics, published in 1850, marks a step towards the quadrille-like movements which characterised the latter part of the nineteenth and the beginning of the twentieth century. Not only did these so-called tactics neglect the aspects of gun and torpedo fire, but quite apart from the movements involved, they tended to produce a faulty system of command which, even in peace time, was responsible for at least one serious disaster.[1] Centralised and mechanical command became the vogue, and officers were moulded to a system which had been responsible for most of the errors and failures of the eighteenth century. Exactitude of station-keeping and rigidity of formation were practised to the detriment of self-confidence and initiative. The stress laid on accurate station-keeping as an end in itself, the sextants, speed cones, and signalling which accompanied the most simple movements, were all representative of a system out of touch with the well-proved principles of command.

There had been a renaissance in tactical thought during the decade prior to

---

[1] Loss of the *Victoria*, June 22, 1893.

the war, and the parade movements which passed for tactics at the end of the nineteenth century had been left behind; but there was still no systematic study of the subject either afloat or ashore, and there was no staff competent to deal with tactical questions. A great deal of work was done at sea, but there was no continuous plan[2] running through it. Piles of P.Z. diagrams were accumulated, but, starting without any clear principles or line of investigation, they frequently ended where they started. At the War College[3] the geometrical and mechanical side of the subject received more attention than the vital principles of command, and historical research – a necessary branch of tactical study – was neglected.

10. At the outbreak of war, the only orders bearing on the battle tactics of the Home Fleet are to be found in a short memorandum[4] which defined the functions of the various types of vessels, and laid great stress on the necessity for initiative on the part of officers in command of squadrons and flotillas.[5] They avoided the pitfall of laying down any hard and fast plan, and thus left the Commander-in-Chief free to conduct the battle according to circumstances, but they lacked the clear definition of principle required to ensure convergence of effort.

---

[2] The tactical exercises carried out in the Home Fleet during Sir William May's period of command (1909-1911), showed a marked advance on contemporary thought and methods, and his investigation into divisional tactics was peculiarly applicable to a large fleet. Under the prevailing system, however, there was no continuity, and they came to an abrupt end when he hauled down his flag.

[3] The principal instrument of instruction was the competitive tactical game; but the Tactical Board has very definite limitations, and what the games really amounted to was a comparison between the gunnery and torpedo *matériel* of the opposing fleets. Scoring rules took no cognisance of such factors as initiative, decentralisation of command, co-operation of different arms, etc., and these were neglected, if not actually discouraged by the system.

[4] Remarks on the conduct of a fleet in action, based on the experience gained in the manœuvres and exercises of the Home Fleets during the year 1913. Sir George Callaghan, M. 02124/13.

[5] *Ibid*, paras. 1 and 6. 'Officers commanding squadrons and flotillas in the first place, and all officers in command in the second place, must at all times be ready to act if circumstances require it on their own initiative and judgment in assisting the Admiral to defeat the enemy . . . vessels outside the line of battle must not rely on receiving orders; none should remain inactive if they are able to make effective use of their force . . . It must be borne in mind the preconceived ideas in action may be upset by unlooked-for tactics by the enemy: it is for this reason as much as for any other that Officers must be trained to act on their own initiative when it is clear that by doing so they can . . . materially assist in the enemy's defeat'.

Editor's note: The complete text of Admiral Callaghan's October 1913 Memorandum has been reproduced in Annexe V.

This memorandum does not appear in the Grand Fleet Orders,[6] which were compiled after the outbreak of war when a vast amount of business had to be transacted with great urgency. There was probably little time to go into side issues of investigation or to study the evolution of tactical thought discernible during Sir William May's and Sir George Callaghan's command of the Home Fleet. The lack of a staff must, however, be held responsible for any deficiencies in this respect, for tactical research is a function of the Staff and not of the Executive Command. If tactical principles, standing orders for manœuvring, etc., were embodied in a suitable manual, and continually revised in the light of current experience, an Admiral on taking command should only have to prepare a short memorandum explaining his particular methods of attack.

Grand Fleet Battle Orders

11. The orders actually in force at Jutland consist of some 75 sheets containing detailed instructions on battle tactics and various other subjects.[7] They should be read in conjunction with an important letter[8] from the Commander-in-Chief to the Admiralty, written in October, 1914 (30/10/1914, in M. 03177/1914),[9] which throws light on much which they contain.

Three main conceptions dominate the orders:

(a) The single line and the parallel course.

(b) Long range.

(c) Defensive action against the torpedo.

The principles of tactics tend to be lost sight of in long detailed instructions, and the orders never seem to get much beyond the idea of a battle in a long single line against an enemy steering a parallel course. But if the enemy refused

---

[6] Lord Jellicoe says his battle orders were based on a Battle Memorandum prepared by him when in command of the Atlantic Fleet (Jellicoe, *Grand Fleet*, 49).

Editor's note: There was, however, this statement in the section of the GFBOs pertaining to destroyers: 'Act quickly, and do not hesitate to use initiative; no orders can be expected from the Admiral after the battlefleets commence action' (Grand Fleet Battle Orders, 'Destroyer Addendum', 1 October 1915, 3).

[7] These will be found in Training and Staff Duties Division collection, Vol, III. They are divided into 30 sections, together with a Destroyer Addendum and Diagrams. They are grouped under six headings: Battle Orders (for Battle Fleet), Sections I to XXII; Gunnery Instructions (XIV to XIX); Cruiser Instructions (XX to XXV); Submarine Instructions (XXVI); Destroyer Instructions (XXVII to XXX); Destroyer Addendum with Deployment Diagram and Memorandum H. F. 0034/39 of May 1, 1916, on Destroyer Attack, with six plans. It appears that the plans accompanying this Memorandum, although dated 1st May, were not issued to the Fleet until 12th June, 1916.

[8] *Official Despatches*, Appendix IV.

[9] *Editor's note*: Jellicoe's letter to the Admiralty is reproduced in Annexe I.

to engage and turned away, the superior fleet would then have to adopt what may be termed tactics of pursuit. Here one is faced with the fact that the letter of October, 1914, practically rules out the possibility of immediate pursuit, and nothing definite on the subject is to be found in the Battle Orders.

Two sections deal more particularly with the tactics of the Battle Fleet.[10] One deals exclusively with the tactics of the Main Battle Fleet, and confines itself to the idea of an action on parallel courses in one long line which may be regarded as the Commander-in-Chief's ruling tactical conception.[11] Attacks by divisions or squadrons are forbidden,[12] and a definite intention to fight at long range and avoid close action is expressed.[13] The 5th Battle Squadron is certainly detached from the Main Fleet, but the general idea is to use it for a prolongation of the battle line to the van or rear, according to the direction of deployment.[14]

The 3rd Battle Squadron (pre-Dreadnoughts of the *King Edward* class) is given the right of independent manœuvre evidently on account of its inferior speed and separate command.

Menace of Torpedoes and Submarines

12. Running right through the Orders is a cautionary note as to the use which the Germans may make of submarines and mines in a fleet action. Great stress is also laid on the menace of torpedo attack by the opposing battleships and torpedo craft, and the intention is expressed of keeping outside torpedo range until the enemy is beaten by gun-fire.[15] An attack by the enemy's torpedo craft will be met by turning the fleet away two or more points.[16]

The warning that the enemy will endeavour to draw the fleet over an area previously prepared with mines or occupied by submarines frequently appears

---

[10] Sections VII, VIII.

[11] Battle Tactics, Section VII, para. 3, says: 'In all cases the ruling principle is that the Dreadnought Fleet as a whole keeps together . . . and so long as the fleets are engaged on approximately similar courses, the squadrons should form one line of battle'. Again, in para. 13: 'Action on approximately similar courses will be one of the underlying objects of my tactics - (1) Because it is the form of action likely to give the most decisive results; (2) Because it is probable that the Germans will make use of mines if they can do so'.

[12] *Editor's note*: See Chapter II Endnote 1 for the relevant text of the GFBOs.

[13] In paras. 5 and 7: 'I shall probably deploy or move to a flank with A arcs bearing at a range of about 18,000 to 20,000 yards' . . . 'In weather of good visibility the range should be between 15,000 and 10,000 yards, the latter being reached as the enemy's fire is overcome; in the early stages of action I do not desire to close the range much inside 14,000 yards'.

[14] *Vide* Section V.

[15] Section VII.

[16] Section IX.

in the Orders, which state that the Commander-in-Chief will not follow if the enemy turns away shortly after deployment, as the movement would probably be intended to draw the fleet over submarines.[17]

The Flag Officer leading the line is consequently warned to exercise great judgment in leading in to close the range,[18] and in the event of the fleet deploying on opposite courses, the Vice-Admiral leading the van is definitely forbidden to circle the rear in case the enemy may have dropped mines. These precautions, arising from the threat of the minelayer and submarine, tended to limit the action of divisional leaders and possibly contributed to a state of mind which saw submarines where they did not exist.[19]

A careful study of the Battle Orders leaves the distinct impression of a centralised system of command. It is true that decentralisation is mentioned. For instance, the difficulty of the Commander-in-Chief exercising control over the battle line after the action commences is pointed out,[20] and Vice-Admirals are given discretionary power to manœuvre their squadrons independently whilst conforming generally to the movements of the Commander-in-Chief.[21] But this delegation is practically overridden in the next paragraph, where it is laid down that the Dreadnought Fleet as a whole is to keep together, and that attacks by divisions or squadrons are to be avoided. Finally, various conditions are enumerated which might call for separate action on the part of divisional or squadron commanders,[22] and from these it can be seen that the discretion given to them refers merely to protective measures against destroyers, submarines, and mine-layers, or to alterations of course to avoid an attack on the van or rear. There is no mention of delegating authority to attack or close the enemy. Independent action was confined to defensive measures.

Some of the instructions dealing with the 'Conduct of a Fleet in Action'[23] seem to clash with those mentioned above. For example, the instructions for the

---

[17] Compare letter of October 30, 1914.

[18] Section VII, para. 9.

[19] There were numerous reports of submarines during the battle, though Scheer states definitely that there were none in the vicinity, which is confirmed by Admiralty special intelligence.

[20] Section VII, para. 1.

[21] *Ibid*, para. 2. Jellicoe, *Grand Fleet*, 49 also says that the necessity for wide decentralisation of command after the deployment of the fleet for action was emphasised. A careful study of the G.F.B.O. shows that it amounted to little, and, in the actual battle, practically to nothing so far as the Battle Fleet was concerned.

[22] *Ibid*, para. 12.

[23] Section VIII. It is stated at the head of Section VIII that it is supplementary to the instructions issued by the Admiralty in M. 0426 13/A of October, 1913, and perhaps this accounts for the difference between it and Section VII.

guidance of leading ships of columns imply the possibility of the van, centre and rear divisions acting independently, and actually state the exact bearing on which the leading ship should alter course if it is decided to circle the enemy's rear, though circling of the rear was forbidden in the previous section.[24] The necessity of closing the range to obtain decisive results is also laid down as an abstract principle, but is at variance with some of the previous instructions.

Deployment

13. The deployment of the fleet receives considerable attention in the Orders. The conventional methods of deployment from cruising formation are dealt with,[25] and an important diagram is included giving the position which each squadron and flotilla is expected to occupy after deployment. The Battle Fleet is shown in one long line 18,000 yards from the enemy line with the 5th Battle Squadron and Battle Cruiser Force two points on the engaged bow of their own Battle Fleet, one and five miles distant respectively. All the cruisers, light cruisers and destroyers, except one squadron of each and one flotilla, are disposed ahead of the battle line and Battle Cruiser Force. The remainder are stationed at the rear of the line on the engaged quarter. In the event of the enemy deploying away from Heligoland, the 5th Battle Squadron is allotted a position at the rear of the line instead of the van. These Orders are representative of the level of tactical though existing at the time. They are carefully thought out, but are confined to the idea of a battle in a long straight line. They never reached tactics of pursuit, and when the fleet turned into divisions at 6.55 pm, they broke down.

Cruisers and Destroyers

[14.[26]] A general explanation of the duties of cruisers is to be found in the instructions to cruisers employed on screening and looking out for the Battle Fleet.[27] Stress is laid on the urgent necessity of the Commander-in-Chief getting reliable bearings and distances of the enemy relatively to himself or one of the Battle Fleet,[28] and it is pointed out that when the visibility is less than 12 miles references to the enemy's latitudes and longitudes are quite useless, and that visual touch must then be maintained between the reporting ship and the Commander-in-Chief by means of linking cruisers.

---

[24] Section VIII, para. 2.

[25] Section XXIII.

[26] *Editor's note*: This was presumably to have been numbered paragraph '14', but that number was omitted in the original.

[27] Section XXII.

[28] Section XXII, paras. 6, 19 and 20.

The duties of battle cruisers, cruisers and light cruisers in a fleet action are explained at great length.[29] The gist of these instructions is that the primary duty of all classes of cruisers is to attack vessels of a similar class so as to prevent any interference with the Battle Fleet, which must be left free to engage the enemy Battle Fleet.

Stress is also laid on the necessity of keeping a look-out for submarines and driving off all ships which might be employed in concealing their position. Armoured cruiser squadrons are detailed to prevent mines being laid in the path of the Battle Fleet, and are ordered to act widely from the Battle Fleet for this purpose and without regard to any other consideration. Particular stress is laid on the necessity of the light cruisers attacking the enemy torpedo flotillas and supporting their own flotillas in the performance of this duty. They are only to attack the enemy battle line with torpedoes if they can do so without prejudice to this duty.

Instructions for destroyers are contained in an Addendum to the Grand Fleet Orders. They are in great detail, but their primary duty is stated to be that of stopping enemy destroyers by engaging them at close range before they can fire their torpedoes.[30] Attack on the enemy's Battle Fleet is definitely relegated to a secondary position.

The detailed plans for destroyer attacks given in the Memo. of May 1 form a striking commentary on the actual events of the night of May 31.

15. The letter of October 14, 1914,[31] deals mainly with the question of submarines co-operating with the German Battle Fleet, and also with that of attack from German torpedo craft. It conforms with the principles embodied in the Battle Orders of 1916. Their Lordships are informed that if 'the enemy's Battle Fleet should turn away from an advancing fleet, I should assume that the intention was to lead us over mines and submarines, and *should decline to be so drawn*'. It is then stated that 'the safeguard against submarines will consist in moving the Battle Fleet at very high speed to a flank before deployment takes place or the gun action commences'. It is recognised that the enemy may refuse to follow, and that this action might be deemed a refusal of battle, and might possibly result in failure to bring the enemy to action as soon as was expected and hoped: but the Commander-in-Chief states that so long as he had the confidence of Their Lordships he intended to pursue this policy, which in his considered opinion was the proper course to defeat and annihilate the enemy's Battle Fleet.

---

[29] Section XXIV.

[30] *Editor's note*: See Chapter II Endnote 2 for the text of this section of the GFBOs.

[31] M. 03177/1914, *Official Despatches*, Appendix IV, 601.

This letter, which received the general approval of Their Lordships, also emphasises the desirability of despatching the Harwich Force to join the fleet should an action be probable, and requested that this might be done.

Tactical Conceptions of the Battle Orders

16. One of the main points arising out of a study of these Orders is whether the tactical conception of an action in one long line on parallel courses was sufficient to meet the situation. Was it capable of forcing an action on a reluctant fleet?

In the sailing ship period, the rigid formula of the long line always failed to bring about decisive results, and it was finally discredited after numerous failures[32] and endless courts-martial. Although steam ships can be manœuvred with greater freedom, the same faults tend to develop unless definite precautions are taken to avoid them. Divisional leaders must either be encouraged to attack on their own initiative in order to prevent the escape of a retreating fleet, or a strong detached force must be used for that purpose.[33]

17. The decision of the Commander-in-Chief to keep outside of the effective range of the torpedo, combined with the lack of any definite idea of concentration,[34] meant that under the most favourable circumstances the battle must develop into a ship to ship artillery duel at long range. But the whole art of tactics consists in massing superior forces against part of the opposing fleet, and battles are not won by applying equal pressure all along the line. In every case there is one part of the line the defeat of which will bring about the collapse of the whole.

---

[32] Battles of Lowestoft, Toulon, Minorca, Rodney and De Guichen (April 17, 1780), Chesapeake Bay (September 5, 1781), etc.

[33] *Editor's note*: Beatty, in his copy, has placed a question mark against this sentence, and has underlined the word 'retreating', adding the note 'but not beaten'.

[34] The word concentration is used here in its tactical and not in its gunnery sense. At the time of Jutland the technique of modern gun concentration was comparatively undeveloped, but tactical concentration is as old as fighting at sea. De Ruyter and Nelson brought it to a fine art despite the difficulties of movement inherent in the sailing ship.

Editor's note: At the time of Jutland, the method of concentrating the gunfire of several ships onto one target was based 'time sectors'; under this scheme each ship in a group was to fire during a specific period of time, keeping track of her salvoes by using time-of-flight stopwatches (Home Fleets General Orders No. 15, 'Distribution of Gunfire', 8 Dec. 1913; TNA, ADM 137/260). However, wartime experience demonstrated that this method was woefully ineffective, and an entirely new, and very effective, system was developed by 1918. See Schleihauf, 'A Concentrated Effort' for details.

Envelopment, or an overpowering attack on part of the German Fleet, was the only certain method of forcing a decision, and whether this attack were carried out against the van, centre or rear, the one essential factor was that it should be inspired with a determination to break up and intimidate the enemy, upset his plans, and cut off his line of retreat.

The Orders to the Battle Fleet do not express any such intention, but the 5th Battle Squadron and Battle Cruiser Force were detached from it, and at first sight this might seem to imply an intention for this fast and powerful force to co-operate with the Battle Fleet in an overwhelming attack on part of the High Sea Fleet. But this was apparently not the intention of the Orders, for these vessels were merely directed to engage the opposing battle cruisers and prolong the line of deployment,[35] whilst the primary function of the light cruisers and torpedo craft was definitely stated to be the protection of their own Battle Fleet from the German torpedo craft.[36] The use of these forces was therefore governed by the conception of like attacking like, which was at variance with the idea of uniting all available forces in an overwhelming attack on part of the opposing fleet.

Functions of Auxiliary Craft based on the idea of Defence

18. In dealing with the functions of various craft the Battle Orders state: 'The aim of our Battle Fleet is the destruction of the enemy's battleships, and to enable this to be done with the greatest certainty, and in the shortest time, it is of primary importance that the whole attention of ships in the line should be given to this object, and should not be diverted by the proceedings of other classes of enemy vessels such as battle cruisers, cruisers, light cruisers, torpedo craft or minelayers, all of which possess the power to inflict great damage if the opportunity is given to them. The duty of preventing interference with our Battle Fleet belongs to vessels of generally similar type to those of the enemy ... and is not purely defensive but should be achieved by attack'.[37]

But if the various craft mentioned 'possessed the power (when used by the enemy) to inflict great damage', could they not be used by us to inflict reciprocal damage on the enemy's Battle Fleet, for when it was defeated, the battle would be won and other craft would not matter? The mere fact of attacking would force similar craft on the German side to protect their Battle Fleet, and thus

---

[35] Deployment diagram and Section XXIV.
[36] Section XXIV (d) and destroyer addendum.
[37] Section XXIV.

prevent them interfering with the British Battle Fleet.[38] This policy of cruiser fighting cruiser and destroyer destroyer is based on the doctrine that the battle is to be won by artillery fire[39] alone and not by tactics.

The Orders practically renounced the use of the torpedo, although the greatest results can only be obtained by the co-operation and full use of all arms, and the gun by itself cannot achieve the effect of a skilfully combined attack.

It would be difficult to maintain that this policy was not a purely defensive one. What else could it be? It meant that the British light cruisers and destroyers had to wait for the enemy's moment of attack, for the latter, sheltering behind the guns of their Battle Fleet, were not likely to expose themselves until that moment arrived. The policy of awaiting attack must be regarded as a defensive one, for it surrenders the initiative and power of surprise to the enemy, and the result was seen in the attack delivered by the enemy at 7.25 pm.

19.   Destroyers first took a regular part in fleet tactical exercises during Sir W. May's command of the Home Fleet, and the instructions[40] which he suggested for their guidance make it clear that they were primarily intended to attack the enemy's battleships with torpedoes. Sir George Callaghan's memorandum favoured the same view.[41] It laid down the functions of attack and defence, but stated that the chances of performing the second are more uncertain owing to the difficulty of preventing the opposing torpedo craft from reaching a favourable position for torpedo attack.

The following extracts show that great stress was laid on the defensive rôle of destroyers in the Grand Fleet Battle Orders:[42]

> *Unless conditions are clearly very favourable for our light cruisers to be able to deal effectually with the German destroyers, it is impressed on all destroyer officers that their primary duty is to stop the German destroyers by engaging them in close action before they can fire their torpedoes. If, therefore, their duty is to act against the*

---

[38] As in the attack of the 13th Flotilla at 4.15 pm and of the 4th Light Cruiser Squadron and 11th Flotilla at 7.35 and 8.15.

[39] Grand Fleet Battle Orders. Destroyer addendum, para. 5: 'It is undoubtedly to our advantage to endeavour to obtain the final decision in a fleet action by means of superior gun power. Our tactics must consequently be based on this plan'.

[40] Notes on Tactical Exercises, Home Fleet, 1909–1911, 424.

Editor's note: The reference here is to Admiral Sir William May, 'Notes on Tactical Exercises. Home Fleet. 1909–1911'; a copy exists in the Admiralty Library, Portsmouth.

[41] Remarks on the Conduct of a Fleet in Action, M. 02124/1913.

[42] Underlined in the original.

German flotillas, torpedo attack on the German Battle Fleet is secondary to gun attack on their destroyers. . . .[43]

The question (i.e., of attack) depends to a certain extent on relative strength in torpedo craft. Were the numbers in our favour or nearly equal, we could afford to give our destroyers greater freedom in taking the offensive. . . . *At the same time, it must be understood that our flotillas are not to miss a favourable opportunity for successful torpedo attack on the enemy's Battle Fleet.*[44]

The general summary runs as follows: 'Take up the best position you can for offensive action for operating against both the German Battle Fleet and its destroyers, having always in view the relative number of destroyers present on the two sides. . . . If we have an approximately equal number of destroyers (which is improbable), or if our light cruisers have the destroyer menace well in hand, one of the two van flotillas should attack the enemy Battle Fleet immediately the opportunity occurs after the fleets are engaged, assuming the range to be not greater than 13,000 yards. If you have to decide between his Battle Fleet and destroyers, the latter are to be given primary attention, so as to stop them before they can fire their torpedoes at our Fleet'.[45]

It would appear from the foregoing that the action of destroyer officers was partly to depend on the strength of the enemy flotillas, and that they would have to ascertain this before deciding on their course of action. But even on days of clear visibility it was more than probable that some of the enemy's torpedo craft would be out of sight from our flotillas,[46] and it is difficult to see how they were expected to obtain this information. Flotilla Commanders were instructed not to miss a favourable opportunity of attacking, but each succeeding set of instructions laid stress on the necessity of defending the Battle Fleet, and impressed on officers that this was their primary function.

With these Orders in front of them, and with only a very limited view of the

---

[43] *Editor's note*: Not included in the NSA is the following paragraph:

5. The reason for this decision is that, as we shall probably be largely outnumbered in torpedo craft and the enemy will strive to weaken us by their attack, it is of the utmost importance that we should be prepared to meet it with superior force composed of vessels of high speed and good gun power, both of which are possessed by our destroyers. (GBFOs, 'Destroyer Addendum', 1 October 1915.)

[44] Destroyer addendum, paras. 4, 5 and 6.

[45] Destroyer addendum, para. 24.

Editor's note: The part not quoted reads: 'It may be assumed that the Germans will have at least eight flotillas, viz., eighty-eight boats'. In fact, at Jutland, there were only 55 German destroyers in seven flotillas (plus two light cruisers in 'leader' roles) against 77 British destroyers (78 including *Oak*, which was tender to *Iron Duke*), also in seven flotillas (three light cruiser leaders).

[46] The German plan of stationing their flotillas on the disengaged side and attacking through their line was well-known before the war.

battle, officers who wished to attack would be faced with the heavy responsibility of jeopardising their primary duty in sending vessels to attack the enemy's Battle Fleet, and in fact they made little attempt to do so.[47]

Further, the idea of attacking with one flotilla and holding back the other when a favourable opportunity of attack offered, had distinct disadvantages, for success in such an attack depends largely upon the force with which it is delivered, and to produce the fullest effect, the fullest use must be made of all available craft.

Conception of Defensive Tactics

20. The spirit in which an action is commenced is, however, more important than the particular dispositions adopted. The self-confidence of a leader is the determining factor for or against victory, and so long as the command is inspired by the determination to destroy the opposing fleet, the initial handicap of a faulty tactical plan may sometimes be overcome.[48]

The theory of the defensive is, however, so consistently implied in the Grand Fleet Orders, that a determination to run no risks must be regarded as part of its Commander-in-Chief's considered policy.

This conception displays itself in two very startling decisions, viz.: the refusal to follow the High Sea Fleet should it turn away during the opening phase, and the pre-determined movement to a flank before engaging. If these proposals were carried out, delay must inevitably occur in commencing the action, and, what is more serious, the German Fleet would be given a very good opportunity of escaping altogether.[49] It was as certain as anything is certain in war, that the German Fleet would not follow the Grand Fleet, and that the only hope of a decisive action lay in making the most of any opportune contact and denying the High Sea Fleet any opportunity of escape. When the Commander-in-Chief's letter was written, the system of special intelligence had not been

---

[47] Only two flotilla attacks were made during the day – by the 13th Flotilla at 4.15 on Hipper's squadron (by order of the S.O.B.C.F.) and by the *Shark* and its small division at 5.55 pm. The attacks by the *Moresby* and *Onslow* were individual attacks.

[48] Previous to the battle of Camperdown, Duncan intended to maintain the long line and repeat the inconclusive tactics of the battle of June 1. A tendency to retreat on the part of the enemy induced him to hurry on the action, and, signalling to Onslow [Admiral Onslow, not the destroyer named for him!] to attack the rear, he steered for the centre of the Dutch line. The approach therefore developed into two more or less perpendicular attacks led by the flagships. With the exception of Nelson's victories, this was the most decisive and hard fought battle of the century, and it was fought in direct opposition to his own original and faulty plan.

[49] This was recognised by the Commander-in-Chief, for he says that the enemy may refuse to follow, and that his action (the Commander-in-Chief's) may be deemed a refusal of battle. Commander-in-Chief to Admiralty, October 30, 1914. M. 03177/1914.

developed, and the chances of a fleet action were very remote.[50] So far as could be foreseen at that time, the opportunity, if it arose, was not likely to recur, and in these circumstances the letter of October 30, 1914, must be regarded as embodying a conception of tactics which could not be reconciled with a decisive action.

The menace from mines and submarines will be considered in greater detail later, but if it were so serious as to justify these decisions, it was hardly sufficient to say: 'Exercises at sea and exercises on the tactical board show that one of the most difficult movements to counter on the part of the enemy is a turn away of his line of battle'.[51] When such a vital issue was at stake, a solution had to be found, and this was not far to seek, for the difficulties referred to could have been sensibly diminished by a more flexible tactical system. If the enemy line turned away in succession, an attack on the rear by a strong detached force would be one method of checking the retreat without drawing the attacking force over the supposed submarine area; or, again, the Grand Fleet was sufficiently strong to detach the battle cruisers, and a strong squadron of fast battleships to operate on the German van or rear; but such methods entailed a considerable degree of dispersion[52] and decentralisation of command, and they were not possible under the system outlined in the Orders.

Similarly, the danger of torpedo attack was a necessary corollary of the long single line, and it was frequently pointed out before the war that it could be greatly reduced by divisional tactics. There were, no doubt, strong objections to adopting a new system of tactics after hostilities commenced, but the system was not entirely new, for Admiral Sir William May had pointed out its advantages, and if the accepted and orthodox tactics of the single line were so vulnerable to torpedo attack, the difficulties of adoption should have been faced and overcome.

Also, if the risk from submarines and mines was so great as to prevent the British Fleet moving to attack across a certain area, was it not equally possible

---

[50] 'There seems to be very little chance of bringing on a general engagement . . . the dream of most naval officers seems to be a great sea fight in which by some means or other we are to be enabled to collect all our forces together and crush the Germans at one blow. This, however, is only a dream. What we have to do is to dispose our forces so as to prevent the Germans from doing us more injury than we can possibly help and never to miss a good opportunity of injuring them'. Sir A. K. Wilson's minute on M. 03177/1914.

[51] *Vide* Section VII, para. 8.

Editor's note: See Annexe II for the full text of this section of the GFBOs.

[52] 'Dividing the fleet at once gives freedom to subordinates, and in so doing, strikes at the root of the purely defensive formation of the single line, and leads to an offensive method of engaging'. Notes on Tactical Exercises, Home Fleet, 1909-1911. Admiral Sir William May.

for British submarines and minelayers to prevent the German Fleet escaping over a similar area? If we could not use them, why should the Commander-in-Chief infer that the Germans could?

21. The true significance of the Commander-in-Chief's letter of October 30 does not appear to have been appreciated, and the sweeping nature of the tactical considerations involved seems to have been overlooked, for Their Lordships made no remarks or criticisms on the fundamental questions raised therein. The only minute of any importance is by Admiral of the Fleet Sir A. K. Wilson,[53] who points out that there are great practical difficulties in bringing submarines to the scene of action, and that even if they do accompany the fleet on the surface, they will almost certainly be left behind when the action commences.[54] The fact that such a very important letter could pass through the Admiralty without thorough examination must be attributed to the lack of an adequate staff organisation. Read in the light of later events, it can be seen that the conception of battle tactics it contained, practically ruled out the idea of a decision by gun-fire and spelt the negation of the battleship. But the Battle Orders were based on obtaining a decision by gun-fire, and so the whole tactical system became infected with an element of inconsequence. It is also important to note that at the time of the Battle of Jutland the then First Sea Lord was unaware of the existence of this letter,[55] although it governed the tactics of the Grand Fleet, and should, if approved, have led to a very great modification in our North Sea strategy.[56]

Centralisation of Command

22. Before discussing the Battle Orders from the point of view of tactical command, it is desirable to recall the two conflicting conceptions which characterised it in the past. On the one hand was a stereotyped centralised system directed from the flagship which left as little as possible to chance. Opposed to this was a flexible system in which the admiral conveyed a general tactical idea of attack, set it going, and left it to subordinate leaders to execute as the particular circumstances of the moment might require. Risks were freely

---

[53] Sir A. K. Wilson acted in an advisory capacity to the Board.

[54] Remarks on Commander-in-Chief's letter of October 30, 1914, M. 03177/1914.

[55] 'This letter appears to have been stowed away, as I have never seen it till yesterday'. Minute of Sir Henry Jackson, September 18, 1916.

[56] It was pointed out in Chapter 1, para. 8, that British strategy in the North Sea was based on the idea that the one and only function of the Grand Fleet was to seek out and destroy the High Sea Fleet, and that the protection of trade and anti-submarine operations were subordinated to this idea.

accepted and offensive action encouraged. The fighting instructions of the eighteenth century typify the former system, and Nelson's method of command the latter.[57]

The Grand Fleet Orders indicate a reversion to the formal system, for they were based on the conception of a ship to ship artillery duel developing on orderly and methodical lines in accordance with a stereotyped plan to which both sides would mutually adjust their movements. The battle plan of the Grand Fleet in fact depended neither on the will nor intention of its leader, nor on the information gained by his cruisers, but on the readiness of the enemy to conform to its movements. This was a very uncertain basis to build on, for the leader of a weaker fleet was hardly likely to conform to the idea[58] of a parallel course unless he were forced to do so. The very first thing Scheer did immediately he appreciated that he was confronted by the whole British Fleet was to turn and run away.

Besides the conception of a formal battle on stereotyped lines, the Orders indicated a tendency to prescribe the actual methods of fighting, and to lay down in detail how subordinates are to act, though general experience of war has shown that it is better to leave officers to use their own judgment according to the particular circumstances of each case.

For example – in endeavouring to legislate for a divisional destroyer attack by the Germans after the British deployment, the Orders, instead of giving general directions, endeavour to provide for three possible situations, and lay down the procedure to be followed in each, even to the number of vessels to be detached to meet the German attack.[59]

But the consensus of experience in war, both on land and sea, tends to show that when attempts are made to provide for such cases by detailed instructions, some wholly unforeseen contingency arises, and subordinates are then inclined to await further instructions which are probably not forthcoming at the critical moment.

A battle in which the reciprocal action of the enemy must be a matter of conjecture cannot be embodied in a single formula. Mist and low visibility were

---

[57] Somewhere between the two was the signal book system introduced by Howe and Kempenfelt, which led to the abolition of the Fighting Instructions and left an admiral free to adopt any tactical plan he desired. Signals alone have, however, always failed to obtain a high degree of co-operation, and it was left to Nelson to introduce the perfect system, based on offensive action, decentralisation of command, a common doctrine and co-operation as opposed to mechanical obedience.

[58] Section VII, para. 13: 'Action on approximately similar courses will be one of the underlying objects of my tactics'.

[59] Section VII, para. 14.

probable conditions in the North Sea. Was the fleet, under these conditions, still to keep outside torpedo range, a course tantamount to refusing action? Similarly, was the principle of the single line to be adhered to and divisional attack forbidden, if half the fleet were engaged and the other half were out of sight of the enemy? Or, if the battle cruisers and 5th Battle Squadron found themselves in favourable positions for attacking in conjunction with the Battle Fleet whilst falling back after reconnaissance, were they to abandon them in order to take up the positions laid down in the Deployment Diagram? Or, if the conditions of meeting were such as to render the presence of submarines unlikely, was the leader of the van still to exercise great caution in 'leading in'? – and so on through all the doubts and perplexities which must accompany this system of command, and which generally result in subordinate leaders, hampered by innumerable instructions, doing nothing or doing the wrong thing when some unforeseen contingency arises.

23. The direction of the battle should be centred in the Commander-in-Chief, but instead of trusting to signals to meet emergencies as they arise, or to cut-and-dried plans for meeting emergencies which may not arise, he should rely on the trained judgment and spontaneous action of subordinates to carry out his ideas. This relationship may be the product of a general body of doctrine, as in the case of the French or German armies, or of individual teaching as in the case of Nelson, who instinctively grasped all the essential principles of successful command. It appears that at Jutland the system of command was limited to the signal book, and a cut-and-dried plan suitable only to one particular set of circumstances.[60]

Only the initiative of subordinate leaders can produce results in modern battle, but initiative can only produce convergent results when it is guided by some general tactical idea. Instructions for cruising dispositions, station keeping, deployment, etc., may be important, but they are subsidiary details. The main thing – very often the only thing – for the higher command is to define clearly, briefly and broadly the idea of manœuvre or attack, so that everyone may act with the maximum degree of confidence and determination in destroying the opposing fleet.

This was lacking, and although in theory the orders seemed to recognise the necessity for initiative, in nine cases out of ten the adoption of a strictly

---

[60] *See* Deployment Diagram of April 7, 1916. It is very possible that the Commander-in-Chief endeavoured conscientiously to adopt a system of decentralisation, but it must have been difficult for him to do so. Centralisation had become an inherent part of naval command; it had crept into the bones of almost every naval officer of the eighties and nineties, and had become ingrained in the subsequent generation of fleet commanders.

defensive policy entails surrendering the initiative to the enemy. How, for example, could flotilla leaders exercise initiative if their primary function were defined as the protection of their own battleships? Under these circumstances, the initiative lay with the enemy torpedo craft which could generally fire their torpedoes long before the opposing destroyers could attack them. Instructions for maintaining definite formations, detailed procedure for avoiding torpedo attack, orders as to the number of ships to be detached in certain eventualities, etc., give no opportunity for the initiative of subordinates. They are the orders for the sentry not to leave his post, and belong to a highly centralised system out of touch with the well-proved principles of command.

Submarines, Mines and Torpedoes

24. The menace of the submarine, mine and torpedo, will now be examined in greater detail. Firstly, with regard to submarine traps. At the time of Jutland, neither this country nor Germany possessed submarines capable of accompanying the Battle Fleet without greatly hampering its movements, and this reduced the chances of German submarines playing as important rôle in a fleet action. Considering the great British superiority in cruisers, it would have been extraordinarily difficult for the Germans to foretell the exact meeting place of the two fleets, much less to manœuvre submarines into a favourable position for attack. They could only hope to do so by reducing the speed of the Battle Fleet, and working their submarines on the surface after the two fleets had sighted each other: but this would preclude the idea of surprise and concealment.[61]

The inherent qualities of the submarine were also unfavourable to its employment in a fleet action, for its vulnerability and comparative blindness place it at a disadvantage when working with surface craft, whilst its power of evasion makes it more or less independent of their support. Being the only type of vessel which suffers from close co-operation with other craft, the German submarines were likely to co-operate more effectually by taking up strategical positions in the vicinity of British harbours (as they actually did) than by entering an area in which hundreds of vessels including destroyers are moving about at high speed.[62]

The possibility of enticing the Grand Fleet over a minefield during the opening phase of an action in the open sea, was also more remote than might

---

[61] Special cases can be imagined when the danger of a submarine trap would be considerable, such as one fleet pursuing another through a deep water channel such as the Straits of Gibraltar, but these were not the conditions of the North Sea.

[62] The Germans had never practised the co-operation of submarines and battleships; Scheer, *Germany's High Seas Fleet*, 104. On the only known occasion before Jutland when a German submarine (U.19) got in amongst the Grand Fleet, it missed its mark and was rammed by the *Dreadnought*.

appear at first sight. At the best of times a tactical minefield closes an area to friend and foe alike, and tends to limit mobility just when mobility may be all important. It was fair to assume that the movements of the British Fleet, with its immense superiority in cruisers, would be hidden from its opponent, and that the latter would not be in a position to foretell the exact direction and nature of the British attack until it actually developed. Part of the British Fleet, for instance, might cross the German line of retreat and drive them back over their own minefield if it were laid too early. The Germans might certainly endeavour to cover their retirement by dropping mines, but they probably would not dare to do so until the two fleets were close to each other, when the operation would probably be observed by the pursuing fleet. Action of this kind might effectually delay the attack, but the element of concealment would be lacking. Hipper, in the early part of the afternoon during his action with Beatty, ran through the very area traversed later by the German Battle Fleet. How is one to know where to lay one's mines in the open sea? To lay them as the *Abdiel* did on a definite return route is another matter.

25. Again, there was the danger of the torpedo fired from surface ships. It was stated in the Orders that the enemy might possibly have torpedoes with a range of 15,000 yards or more, and the diagram of deployment was apparently based on this assumption.[63] But in January, 1916, the latest Admiralty information[64] gave the maximum range of the German 19.7 in. and 17.7 in. torpedoes as 10,000 and 6,500 yards respectively, and the extra 5,000 yards seems to have been of the nature of a margin of safety.[65]

The torpedo itself is an inferior weapon. Its aim is very uncertain, and although it may strike a very heavy blow,[66] it has no effect on the personnel except on the very rare occasions when it actually sinks a ship. The gun, on the other hand, by the frequency of its hitting, demoralises the personnel, destroys the gun and torpedo control, and interferes with the power of hitting back.

---

[63] Section VII, para. 7.

[64] German Torpedoes, Mines, etc., Addenda to Foreign Naval Ordnance, Torpedo, Mines, etc., 1916, p. 4.

[65] *Editor's note*: However, it must be noted that each British battleship and cruiser had one 'ER' (Extreme Range) torpedo that could reach out to 17,000 yards at the admittedly slow speed of 18 knots (see Brown, 'Torpedoes at Jutland').

[66] Prior to the Russo–Japanese War, so little attention was given to under-water protection that the ordinary merchant ship was probably less vulnerable to torpedoes than the pre-Dreadnought battleship. There can, however, be no comparison between that class of battleship and the Dreadnought battleship with its continuous transverse bulkheads.

The chances of a torpedo hitting a line of ships being proportionate to the space between the ships, the British Fleet might, from a purely geometrical point of view, counter a torpedo attack by:

(a) Keeping outside torpedo range or running outside when the attack takes place.

(b) Presenting a narrower target by turning towards the attacking vessels.

(c) Presenting a narrower target by turning away.

(d) Dividing the long line into separated divisions or sub-divisions.

With regard to (b) and (c), a turn towards the enemy produces a narrower target than a turn away, as torpedoes are generally fired from well before the beam of the target.

Comparison in Torpedo Power

26. In any case, there was little justification for the theory that the British Fleet was inferior to the Germans in power or torpedo attack. Ship for ship the German capital ship and torpedo boat mounted more tubes than the British, but this was balanced by numbers, and the fact that the British carried a larger proportion of long-range torpedoes. In a fleet action, the German 17.7 in. and British 18 in. were of relatively little use.

The torpedo strength of the fleets present at Jutland is shown in the following table:

TORPEDO TUBES AT BATTLE OF JUTLAND[67]

Type of Vessel	British 21 in.	18 in.	German 19.7 in.	17.7 in.
Battleships and Battle Cruisers	86	40	80	64
Cruisers	–	29	–	–
Light Cruisers	60	6	16	10
Destroyers	236	–	266	33
	382	75	362	107

In the event of a fleet action there was, however, good reason to expect reinforcements by the Harwich Force, and if the Admiralty had carried out what really amounted to a pledge, the Grand Fleet would have had 14 more 21 in. tubes in light cruisers, and 72 in destroyers.

This would have increased the British margin of superiority in long-range torpedo tubes from 20 to 106, and the British torpedo flotillas would also have had a greater number of tubes than the German. In preparing the Battle Orders

---

[67] From information supplied by Torpedo Division, Naval Staff, in 1921.

there was, therefore, no reason to assume that the Grand Fleet would be relatively weak in power of torpedo attack. With regard to range, the maximum range of the British 21 in. was 10,750 yards at 29 knots. The Germans had three marks of 19.7 in. torpedo in their fleet at Jutland, and, failing information as to the proportion in which they were carried, their mean maximum range may be taken, which was 10,090 yards at 28 ½ knots.[68] The British 18 in. torpedo had also a greater maximum range than the German 17.7 in. The superiority of the Germans in torpedo attack was therefore based largely on assumption, and even if inferiority in torpedo power were admitted, it constituted only one arm of the fleet. The object of battle is the destruction of the enemy fleet, and to attain that end, the attack must be made with every available weapon. Gun-fire can cover and support torpedo attack by light craft, and the torpedo can drive home and complete the work of the gun. Weakness in one arm can be balanced by strength in another, and if the British Fleet were weak in torpedoes, it constituted all the more reason for vigorous attack with the gun. This was precluded by a turn away, which must increase the difficulty in hitting, if it did not actually run the fleet out of gun-range. If the doctrine of systematically turning away to keep out of a weapon's range (and not of a particular torpedo track) were applied to the gun, fleets would keep out of gun-range and naval warfare would come to an abrupt end.

Chapter II Endnotes

1. It is worth reproducing the full text of the paragraph quoted in note 11 (the part excised by the Dewars is shown in italics); strictly speaking, divisional tactics are not prohibited:

3. In all cases the ruling principal is that the 'Dreadnought' fleet as a whole keeps together, *attempted attacks by a division or squadron on a portion of the enemy line being avoided as liable to lead to the isolation of the ships which attempt the movement*, and, so long as the fleets are engaged on approximately similar courses, the squadrons should form one line of battle.

See Annexe II where the Deployment and Battle Tactics sections are copied in their entirety.

2. In January 1916, Section XXX, 'General Instructions by which Our Destroyers are to be Guided' read (the underlining is in the original):

Unless the conditions are clearly very favourable and enable our light-cruisers to deal effectively with the German destroyers, it is impressed on all destroyer officers that their primary duty is to stop the German destroyers engaging them in close action before they can fire their torpedoes, and that torpedo attack on the German battlefleet is secondary to gun attack on their destroyers. The two exceptions to this rule are stated in paragraphs 6(b) and 7.

The two exceptions noted were: (6b) in bad weather, when the Grand Fleet's light cruisers

---

[68] From information supplied by Torpedo Division, Naval Staff.

were to break up the enemy flotillas if they attacked, the destroyers then having torpedo attack on the German battle line their primary role; and (7) when the fleets were on parallel courses, when a commanding presence of British cruisers and battle cruisers in the van would preclude a German destroyer attack – then the leading British destroyers and light cruisers were to move across and attack the head of the enemy line.

CHAPTER III

PRELIMINARY MOVEMENTS – MAY 28-30

27. The appointment of Admiral Reinhard[1] Scheer to command the High Sea Fleet in place of Von Pohl was the first sign of a more offensive policy. As Admiral Commanding the Second Squadron he had chafed at the inactivity of the Fleet and had advocated a bolder strategy. His star was now in the ascendant. He received his formal appointment as Commander-in-Chief of the High Sea Fleet on January 18, 1916, and in February proceeded to Berlin to a conference with the Chief of the Naval Staff, Admiral Von Holtzendorff, where it was decided to adopt bolder measures.[2] Victory on land had not been achieved; the pressure of the blockade was being keenly felt; and it was hoped that the fleet by resolute and skilful sorties might do something to break the enemy's stranglehold by sea. The Emperor in person visited Scheer's flagship and publicly expressed approval of his policy.

Scheer was a strong advocate of ruthless submarine warfare, and he had hardly been in command a month when the attack on the *Sussex*[3] led to an outburst of neutral feeling and to a decisive Note from President Wilson threatening to break off relations with Germany. The German Government temporarily abandoned the idea of ruthless warfare, and issued orders on April 24 that the submarine campaign was to be conducted in accordance with Prize regulations involving visit, search and capture in due form. Tirpitz resigned. Scheer, then at sea on his way to bombard Lowestoft, recalled all submarines and announced that the campaign had ceased. This placed a number of submarines at his disposal, and plans were now drawn up for co-operation with them based primarily on the stratagem of enticing out the Grand Fleet and attacking it with submarines in the vicinity of the East Coast.

---

[1] *Editor's note*: Spelt 'Reinold' in the original.
[2] Scheer, *Germany's High Seas Fleet*, 105.
[3] March 25, 1916.

It was intended at first to despatch a Battle Cruiser Squadron to bombard Sunderland in order to draw out the British Fleet, which was then to be attacked by submarines stationed on the East Coast and, if a favourable opportunity presented itself, by the High Sea Fleet itself.[4] Sixteen U boats and a half-dozen boats of the Flanders Flotilla were to be stationed in suitable positions with orders to remain at their posts from May 23 to June 1, reporting any movements of British ships, and seizing any favourable opportunity for attack. Clear weather was, however, an essential condition for an operation of this sort, for air reconnaissance would be necessary to give the High Sea Fleet ample warning of the approach and composition of any British force. Unfortunately, a spell of bad weather had set in: day after day the airship commander reported air reconnaissance impossible, and the Commander-in-Chief finally decided to try the less risky operation of enticing the British Fleet out by a sortie in the direction of the Skagerak and the coast of Norway.[5]

The submarines had been ordered to take up their position by May 23, and as they were only to remain out till June 1, this became the last day for any operation in conjunction with them. On May 30,[6] therefore, the High Sea Fleet was ordered to be in the outer roads of Wilhelmshaven by 7 pm. Thirteen submarines were by this time lying off the British coast,[7] and U.75, after laying on May 29 off the West coast of Orkney the mines which were to sink the *Hampshire* and lead to Lord Kitchener's untimely end, was on her way home.[8]

28. These precursory movements had not been made without attracting attention. The British Admiralty was already on the alert. On May 16 and 17 signals had been taken in reporting the departure of nine submarines,[9] an incident sufficiently unusual in itself to arouse attention, and as several days elapsed without any sinkings being reported, it became clear that some special

---

[4] Scheer, *Germany's High Seas Fleet*, 134.

[5] Scheer, *Germany's High Seas Fleet*, 135.

[6] At 0944, Birch and Clarke, 377.

[7] Off Scapa, U.43, 44; off Kinnaird Head, U.47; off the Forth, U.66, U.63, U.51, U.32, U.70, U.24, U.52; on the way to the Tyne, U.24; off the Humber, UB.22, U.21; south of Dogger Bank, U.67. Harper Diagram, German II.

[8] *Editor's note*: On 5 June 1916 *Hampshire* was on her way to Archangel, Russia with Field Marshal Earl Kitchener, the secretary of state for war, aboard. While steaming along the western coast of the Orkney Islands in a very severe gale she struck a mine laid by U.75; the ship sank within sight of the shore, but because the weather was so rough, only twelve men survived. Kitchener and his entire staff were lost.

[9] Special Intelligence Records.

movement was afoot. But its precise nature still remained obscure,[10] and there was nothing tangible to indicate that it was part of a larger operation to be carried out in direct conjunction with the High Sea Fleet.

On May 28, however, it became apparent that a more extensive operation was on foot, for a signal[11] from the Commander-in-Chief directed all forces in harbour to be ready in accordance with his orders for March 30. This was supposed in Room 40, at the time, to refer to the despatch of forces to Terschelling and Horns Riff to meet airships returning from a raid.[12] But on May 30 it was followed by a signal[13] ordering the High Sea Fleet to be assembled in the outer roads of Wilhelmshaven by 7 pm, which was confirmed an hour or so later by a signal from Bruges to the submarines of the Flanders Flotilla, telling them to reckon on German forces being at sea on May 31 and June 1. It was clear that some considerable movement was on foot, and at noon on May 30 a message was sent to the Commander-in-Chief, Grand Fleet, that there were indications of the German Fleet proceeding out.[14] The position still remained obscure, but steps were taken to meet the contingency. Harwich destroyers and minesweeping sloops on the East Coast were recalled, and Commodore (S) was ordered to have all submarines ready for sea. At 1536 a signal was made by the German Commander-in-Chief, of which only a brief portion was received, namely, 'May 31, most secret', but to the workers in Room 40 this was enough to indicate that on May 31 most secret orders of some previous date were to be executed, and at 5.16 pm a message went off to the Commander-in-Chief and Senior Officer, Battle Cruiser Fleet, to raise steam, followed by a further wire at 5.40 pm as follows: 'Germans intend some operations commencing to-morrow and leaving viâ eastern route and Horns Reef. Operation appears to extend over May 31 and June 1. You should concentrate to eastward of Long Forties[15] ready for eventualities'. The operations had begun.

---

[10] A clear distinction must be drawn between the inferences drawn in Room 40 and the final appraisement given to them by the DOD and the Chief of the War Staff and First Sea Lord.

[11] Reported to Operations Division, 9.40 am, May 28.

[12] Birch and Clarke, 377.

[13] 0944 reported to Operations Division, 11.30 am. See Appendix G.

[14] 'There are indications that the German Fleet are to be in outer roads by 7 pm to-night, and may go to sea early to-morrow. Object may be to have them ready to support returning Zeppelins. Sixteen German submarines are now at sea, most of which are believed to be in North Sea; two are off Terschelling'. Sent by land wire to the Commander-in-Chief, noon, May 30.

[15] Long Forties lies about 60 miles east of Scottish Coast. Sent to Commander-in-Chief and Senior Officer, Battle Cruiser Fleet, at 5.40 pm, May 30.

Disposition of the Fleet[16]

29. The Grand Fleet on this date was distributed between Scapa Flow, Invergordon and Rosyth.

The major portion was with the Commander-in-Chief at Scapa Flow, including the 1st and 4th Battle Squadrons and 3rd Battle Cruiser Squadron, with the 2nd Cruiser Squadron (only organised that day from the 2nd and 7th Cruiser Squadrons), and the 4th Light Cruiser Squadron. With them were the 4th Flotilla, part of the 11th Flotilla (*Castor* and 4 boats) and 12th Flotilla.

At Invergordon were the 2nd Battle Squadron, the 1st Cruiser Squadron, and part of the 11th Flotilla (*Kempenfelt* and 9 boats).

Vice-Admiral Sir David Beatty was at Rosyth with the *Lion* and 1st and 2nd Battle Cruiser Squadrons. The 5th Battle Squadron was there, too, with the 1st, 2nd and 3rd Light Cruiser Squadrons and the 1st Flotilla (*Fearless* and 9 boats); the 13th Flotilla (*Champion* and 10 boats); part of the 9th Flotilla (4 boats); and part of the 10th Flotilla (4 boats); also the seaplane carrier *Engadine*.

The usual bustle of preparations for leaving harbour ensued, and at the various ports the fleet began to raise steam.[17]

Before sailing, a message from the Admiralty stated that the eight submarines which had sailed between May 16 and 20 were believed to be still in the North Sea.[18]

The Commander-in-Chief had now to arrange for the concentration of his forces. He decided to proceed to a rendezvous in Lat. 57° 45' N, Long. 4° 15' E, 240 miles from Scapa, and sent a telegram at 7.37 pm to Admiral Beatty informing him of this position and directing him to proceed with the 5th Battle Squadron to a position in Lat. 56° 40' N, Long. 5° E (260 miles from the Forth). If he had no news of the enemy by 2 pm he was to stand towards the Commander-in-Chief, who would steer for Horns Riff. Beatty was also informed that the 3rd Battle Cruiser Squadron, *Chester* and *Canterbury*, would leave with the Commander-in-Chief, but might be sent on to the battle cruiser rendezvous.[19] These two rendezvous were 64 miles[20] apart, a distance which in the light of later events must be regarded as excessive, and which meant in fact that the two portions of the Fleet were never actually in visual touch before the action.

---

[16] For details, see Appendix A.

[17] At Rosyth, signal 5.45 pm, steam for 22 knots; at Invergordon, signal 6.05 pm, for 18 knots; at Scapa, signal 7.05 pm, Battle Fleet raise steam for 19 knots; at 6.25 pm, 3rd Battle Cruiser Squadron for 22 knots; at 7 pm, cruisers and destroyers for 20 knots.

[18] Admiralty to Commander-in-Chief and Senior Officer, Battle Cruiser Fleet, 1812.

[19] Commander-in-Chief to Senior Officer, Battle Cruiser Fleet, 1937, received 8.15 pm.

[20] Admiral Beatty's rendezvous was 64 miles 157° from that of the Battle Fleet.

It may be assumed that the Commander-in-Chief in selecting the battle cruisers' position, expected to get into touch with the enemy there, in which case no real advantage could accrue from the main body being over 60 miles away. The nearer the Grand Fleet was to the enemy, the more time would be available to bring the enemy to action, quite apart from the difficulties that might arise and did arise in reporting the enemy, due to the squadrons never having been in visual touch. The Commander-in-Chief states[21] that he felt no anxiety in regard to the advanced position of Sir David Beatty's force, and it is true that, supported by the 5th Battle Squadron, it could hold its own against the 1st Scouting Group, the only force able to compete with it in speed, but there still remained the likelihood of delay in bringing the enemy to action, and of possible errors in reporting his position.

There can be little doubt that the Commander-in-Chief should have been as close as possible to the Battle Cruiser Force, subject only to the condition of keeping out of sight of the enemy. These conditions would have been met by a rendezvous in 57° N, 4° 15' E, 255 miles from Scapa,[22] and 28 miles 300° from the Battle Cruiser Force. Such a rendezvous would have ensured visual touch, and would probably have led to direct contact between the Main Fleet and the enemy nearly an hour sooner, about 18 miles to the southward of where it actually took place.[23]

The necessity of concentration was evidently felt by the Commander-in-Chief after the battle, for one of the questions which he noted for discussion at the Admiralty on June 22 was the importance of moving the Battle Fleet to Rosyth.

---

[21] Despatch, June 18, 1916 (*Official Despatches*, 1).

[22] The Commander-in-Chief's rendezvous was 240 miles from Scapa, requiring an average speed of 15¼ knots for the [*sic*] 15¾ hours. The above rendezvous would have been 255 miles, requiring a speed of 16.2 knots. The separation of the Battle Cruiser Force had given rise to a dangerous situation at 7 am, December 16, 1914, when the 2nd Battle Squadron and the Battle Cruiser Force were in the proximity of the High Sea Fleet. Little was known of this at the time, however, and the separation had become customary. During 1915 the Fleet had been ordered to sea on Special Intelligence reports on about seven occasions; the rendezvous ordered were on January 24, 1915 (Dogger Bank), 110 miles apart; March 29 (by Admiralty), 60 miles apart; April 17 (by Admiralty), 80 miles apart; April 21, 60 miles apart; May 18, 40 miles apart. During 1916 up to May 31 the Fleet had been ready for sea or ordered to sea on six occasions. The rendezvous were on March 6, 1916, 35 miles apart; on April 22, 44 miles apart. See Summary of Operations of the Grand Fleet, Naval Staff Monograph 13.

[23] Assuming that the Commander-in-Chief followed the Battle Cruiser Fleet the former would have been about 13 miles 282° from the enemy's battle squadron at 5.15 pm.

The Harwich Force

30. Just before 6 pm the Commander-in-Chief was informed by the Admiralty that the Harwich Forces and 3rd Battle Squadron lying in the Swin would not be sent out till more was known.[24] This episode forms a little story in itself. Early in the war the Commander-in-Chief had written to the Admiralty an important letter[25] emphasising the desirability of all available ships and torpedo craft being ordered to the position of a fleet action as soon as it was known to be imminent.

Though the letter had received the general approval of the Admiralty,[26] Admiral of the Fleet Sir Arthur Wilson had not concurred in the proposal to despatch the Harwich flotillas, 'First, because there would be no possible chance of their arriving on the scene till many hours after the action was over, and, secondly, because the enemy's intention would probably be to enable a landing to be effected on the coast'. The letter then seems to have been laid aside, for Sir Henry Jackson, who succeeded Lord Fisher as First Sea Lord, never saw it till some months after the Battle of Jutland.[27]

Sir Arthur Wilson's minute gives a clear summary of the strategical principles involved, entirely applicable to the time, and points out that there was little chance of bringing about a general engagement. But conditions had changed since he wrote it, and in 1916 the work of Room 40 made it possible to determine the position of the enemy and to foretell an impending action with some degree of probability. One point seems fairly certain, that the question was settled in 1916 without any reference to the letter of November 7, 1914, which remained snugly reposing in its safe till unearthed for the First Sea Lord's perusal three months after the action. The precise reasons for retaining the Harwich force remain obscure and were perhaps so at the time. Three possible contingencies were probably in the minds of those who made the decision. First: the German High Sea Fleet might come south. But if it did, how could Commodore Tyrwhitt with five light cruisers and 20 destroyers oppose it? The situation would merely have been a repetition of Heligoland Bight, with the positions reversed. Again, the Admiralty may have expected a repetition of the Lowestoft raid of April 25, 1916. But what could Commodore

---

[24] Admiralty to Commander-in-Chief, 5.55 pm, May 30.

[25] Commander-in-Chief to Admiralty, October 30, 1914, M. 03177/1914, printed in *Official Despatches*, 601, para. 17. See para. 11, *supra*.

Editor's note: Reproduced in Annexe I.

[26] November 7, 1914, *Official Despatches*, 603; also Sir Arthur Wilson's Minute of November 22, 1914.

[27] See *supra*, para. 21.

Tyrwhitt do in that case? No more than he did on April 25 – namely, retire. If the Harwich forces were kept back to prevent a raid by the High Sea Fleet, it was being used wrongly for a task it could not perform. Was it retained for the purposes of reconnaissance near the coast? Surely not, for this could be better done by seaplanes. The only other possible contingency was an invasionary raid: this had been Admiral Wilson's objection to moving the Harwich force north, but the possibility of this did not come into the picture in 1916; and if it did, decisions should for preference be based on intelligence which embodies something clear and precise.[28] In this case Room 40 supplied sufficient information to ensure the probability of an impending battle. Why, then, sit waiting for information about something else? Manœuvre based on conjecture fails against manœuvre based on a clear and definite plan. But it was not merely bad policy to wait for further information. It was bad strategy to retain the Harwich force even in the event of an invasionary raid. What could such a raid have achieved, tied down to a definite landing spot, with the whole British Fleet at sea between it and its base? It seems probable that the matter never received the consideration it deserved. One of the previously recognised duties of the Harwich flotilla was to support and assist the Commander-in-Chief in a fleet action, and this important function was to a large extent forgotten or overlooked. All that was done was to order Commodore (T) to have his light cruisers and destroyers ready to sail at daylight if required: he reported his probable strength[29] as five light cruisers, two flotilla leaders and 21 destroyers, including eight detached for screening the 3rd Battle Squadron then lying in the Swin. For a time there seems to have been some intention of sending both the Harwich force and the 3rd Battle Squadron to sea, for at 10.35 pm Commodore (T) was ordered to hold his squadron at one hour's notice after daylight and to send eight destroyers to join the 3rd Battle Squadron in the Swin. At 4.50 am he began to fear that he might not reach even the fringe of the impending action, and sent an urgent telegram to the Admiralty pointing out that no orders had been received. The reply that came back savours of routine. 'Orders are to remain at one hour's notice'. At daylight he was still at Harwich. His retention there must be regarded as a grave mistake. 'No division on the eve

---

[28] *Editor's note*: According to Admiral Sir Henry Oliver, chief of the Admiralty War Staff at the time, the Staff was actually concerned about the possibility of a German 'attempt to block the Channel ports and destroy our line of communications with the Army in France, such as rushing the Dover Straits with pre-dreadnought type of ship and using them as blockships' (Marder, *FDSF*, 3:50). He therefore held back the Harwich Force, so that they could act as escorts for the pre-dreadnoughts of the 3rd Battle Squadron, based in the Thames estuary, in case the old battleships were needed to counter such an attack.

[29] Admiralty to Commodore (T), 6.20 pm, May 30. Reply 7.40 pm.

of battle' is an axiom as true at sea as on land. From Harwich to Admiral Beatty's rendezvous was some 330 miles: at an economical speed of 18 knots[30] it would have taken the Harwich flotilla 18 hours to reach this rendezvous. To join Beatty, they would have had to leave at 8 pm. They remained at Harwich straining at their leash.

31. Meanwhile the various portions of the fleet had left harbour, and by 10.30 pm on May 30 the whole force was at sea. The Main Fleet under Sir John Jellicoe had cleared Hoxa by 10.15 pm, leaving the harbour almost empty. Only the *Royal Sovereign*, recently commissioned, and a couple of destroyers were left behind.[31]

The *Iron Duke* shaped course S 73 E at 17 knots. At 1.47 am[32] the cruisers formed disposition No. 1[33] with some modifications arising from the recent formation of the 2nd Cruiser Squadron. The 1st and 2nd Cruiser Squadrons were spread 10 miles ahead of the Battle Fleet and the 3rd Battle Cruiser Squadron 10 miles ahead of the cruisers.

One or two reports of submarines came in during the night. The *Trident* had been attacked by one off the Forth at 7.45 pm, and another had been seen on May 30 at 11.15 am, 45 miles east of Aberdeen,[34] both belonging to the German force sent out in conjunction with the coming sortie, but the Battle Fleet saw nothing and the night passed without any incident.

At dawn, the Battle Fleet formed divisions in line ahead disposed abeam to starboard, columns eight cables apart, the 3rd Division on the port hand, the 4th, 5th and 6th Divisions on its beam. At 9 am speed was reduced from 17 to

---

[30] At 18 knots they would burn on average 2.5 tons per hour – a total of 45 tons.

[31] There were left behind only the *Royal Sovereign* of the 1st Battle Squadron, which had arrived at Scapa on May 25 newly commissioned, the destroyer *Victor* of the 4th Flotilla, the *Phoenix* of the 1st Flotilla and the *Nepean* of the 13th.

Editor's note: The seaplane carrier *Campania* did sortie, but because she had missed the signal – not, as described in the original *Naval Staff Appreciation* Appendix A because of mechanical difficulties – and left harbour two hours late. She was ordered to return and thus missed the battle. In addition to the 10 seaplanes embarked, she also carried a kite balloon which might have been of some use, despite the visibility prevailing during the battle. See Layman, *Naval Aviation in the First World War*, 178–9; Schleihauf, 'What Happened to the *Campania?*', and TNA: ADM 1/8682/124.

[32] Senior Officer Cruisers to Cruisers, 1.47 am.

[33] Grand Fleet Battle Orders, 28, December 1915, Cruisers' Instructions. This disposition gives the 4th Light Cruiser Squadron spread four miles ahead of the Battle Fleet, the 5th Battle Squadron and *Blonde* six miles ahead of 4th Light Cruiser Squadron, the 1st, 2nd, 3rd and 7th Cruiser Squadrons 10 miles ahead of the 5th Battle Squadron, spread 10 miles apart over a front of 50 miles.

[34] U.63 or U.66.

16 knots,[35] and shortly afterwards contact was effected with the cruisers of the 2nd Battle Squadron from Invergordon. At 11.15 am this squadron joined[36] and took station on the port beam of the Fleet. At noon the *Iron Duke* was in Lat. 58° 09' N, Long. 2° 59' E[37] (position obs.) and reduced to 15 knots with a speed of advance of 14. The fleet had been steering S 50 E since 5 am, and by 2 pm the *Iron Duke* had reached a position according to her reckoning in Lat. 57° 57' N, Long. 3° 46' E.[38] The rendezvous for 2 pm was in Lat. 57° 45' N, Long. 4° 15' E and she was still 19½ miles[39] from it, or over an hour late. The fleet had been zigzagging since 2.35 am and the examination of neutral trawlers had given rise to further delay.[40]

The Battle Cruiser Force

32. Meanwhile the Battle Cruiser Force,[41] zigzagging on a course S 81 E was approaching the two o'clock rendezvous (56° 40' N 5° E). It had cleared the Forth by 11 pm and had gone at 18 knots through the night, increasing to 19½ knots at 2.45 am, and reducing to 19 at 4 am. The cruisers had taken up disposition No. 6 on passing May Island, and were disposed at noon on a line of direction 31° with the centre of the screen 87° from the *Lion*,[42] and the *Galatea* and *Phaeton* at the north-east end of the line (Diagram 1).

Several reports of submarines in the North Sea had been received. The *Trident* had reported two submarines off the Forth[43] in the evening and had been attacked by one to the north of it during the afternoon.[44]

---

[35] Courses and speeds. Courses S79 E to 1.30 am, S 73 E to 5 am, S 50 E to 3 pm. Speeds 17 knots to 9 am, 16 knots (speed of advance 15 knots) to noon; 17 knots 2.43 pm, 18 knots 2.52 pm.

[36] In Lat. 58° 12' N, Long. 2° 42' E, 58 miles from the Battle Fleet's rendezvous.

[37] *Official Despatches*, Plate 6A. *Official Despatches* makes *Iron Duke*'s longitude at noon 3° 0' E, but signal 12.40 pm and 1.05 pm give 2° 59' E. Her position deduced from mean of all ships' noon positions was 58° 7' N, 3° 1' 30" [E], i.e. 2¼ miles SSE (mag.) from her reckoning.

[38] *Official Despatches*, Plate 6A, *Iron Duke*'s track. (Harper places her at 2 pm in Lat. 57° 54½' N, Long. 3° 52' E, four miles S 42 E from her reckoning.)

Editor's note: Underlined in Beatty's copy of the *NSA* – clearly something he thought important.

[39] According to Harper, 15 miles.

[40] 'The Fleet had been slightly delayed to enable the usual and necessary practice of examining trawlers and other vessels met with en route to be carried out'; Jellicoe, *Grand Fleet*, 319.

[41] Comprising 1st Battle Cruiser Squadron, 2nd Battle Cruiser Squadron, 1st Light Cruiser Squadron, 2nd Light Cruiser Squadron, 3rd Light Cruiser Squadron, 1st Flotilla, 13th Flotilla, 9th Flotilla (part), 10th Flotilla (part), 5th Battle Squadron and *Engadine*.

[42] At 10.02 am the line of direction had been altered to 31°, centre to bear 87° from *Lion*. The 5th Battle Squadron at the same time took station five miles 301° (NW) and 2nd Battle Cruiser Squadron three miles 31° (NE) from *Lion*.

[43] U. 32 or U.24.

[44] U.63.

There were actually no less than seven submarines lying off the Forth, but none of them appear to have attacked the Battle Cruiser Force on its way out.

The *Galatea* in the early morning reported a torpedo fired at her at 3.55 am[45] and the *Yarmouth* and *Turbulent* made similar reports during the forenoon,[46] the former involving the fleet in an eight-point turn to port for 20 minutes, but nothing in the shape of a submarine was seen by the larger ships. At noon the *Lion*'s estimated position was 56° 44' N, 3° 45' E,[47] though she was actually some 5½ miles to the north-westward of it. At 1.30 pm the line of direction of the cruiser line was swung through 23° to 54° (ENE) with its centre bearing 144° (SSE) from the *Lion*. At the same time the bearing of the 5th Battle Squadron was altered to 324° (NNW) five miles and that of the 2nd Battle Cruiser Squadron to 54° (ENE) three miles (Diagram 1). The *Lion*, like the *Iron Duke*, was behind time, and at 2 pm according to her reckoning, was still some 10 miles to westward of her rendezvous.[48]

The Enemy in Sight

The Vice-Admiral had orders if nothing was in sight to close the Battle Fleet, and at 1.58 pm the signal had already been made to alter to N by E at 2.15 pm. Ten minutes later the *Galatea* at 2.10 pm sighted a steamer bearing 95° some eight miles away, blowing off steam and apparently stopped, and closed to examine her. The light cruisers were taking up their new line of direction and the Vice-Admiral at 2.15 pm had already turned to N by E to get in touch with the Commander-in-Chief, and had told the 5th Battle Squadron to look out for the latter's cruisers. Five minutes later the *Galatea* at 2.20 pm made the signal 'Enemy in sight', at the same time sending the following signal by wireless: 'Urgent. Two cruisers probably hostile in sight bearing ESE course unknown. My position Lat. 56° 48' N, Long. 5° 21' E'[49] (Diagram 2).

---

[45] Possibly by U.32, which at 0650 GMT reported two battleships and two cruisers in 56° 15' N, 0° 42' W. U.32 had been out since May 18 and her position may have been considerably out.

[46] *Yarmouth* in about 56° 50' N, 2° 55' E; *Turbulent* at 9.08 am in about 56° 52' N, 3° 5' E. There is no trace of any German submarines in these vicinities in any enemy record hitherto available.

[47] The signalled and other positions have been carefully reduced to positions observed and D.R., and a mean of positions observed places *Lion* at noon in Lat. 56° 46' N, Long. 3° 36½' E.

[48] Her position according to Harper was 56° 48½' N, Long. 4° 41' E, or 13 miles N 37 W of the rendezvous in Lat. 56° 40' N, Long. 5° 00' E.

[49] *Galatea*'s log says 2.07 pm sighted enemy T.B.D.s [torpedo boat destroyers]. *Engadine* remarks: '2.20 sighted two enemy cruisers bearing East'. Harper puts *Galatea* at 2.20 in 56° 52½' N, 5° 27' E, i.e., 5½ miles N 50 E of her signalled position.

Diagram 1

DISPOSITION OF BATTLE CRUISER FORCE (*Lion*)
AT NOON, MAY 31st

By signal 10.05 am:
2nd BCS NE (31°) 3 miles, 5th BS NW (301°) 5 miles from *Lion*. *Lion*'s course S 81°E (85°);
centre of screen E by S (87°) from *Lion*, 8 miles; line direction of screen NE (31°) and SW
(211°), 5 miles apart.

Re-disposition ordered by signal 1.30 pm:
2nd BCS ENE (54°) 3 miles, 5th BS NNW (324°) 5 miles, centre of screen SSE, 8 miles from
Lion; line direction of screen ENE (54°) and WSW (234°).

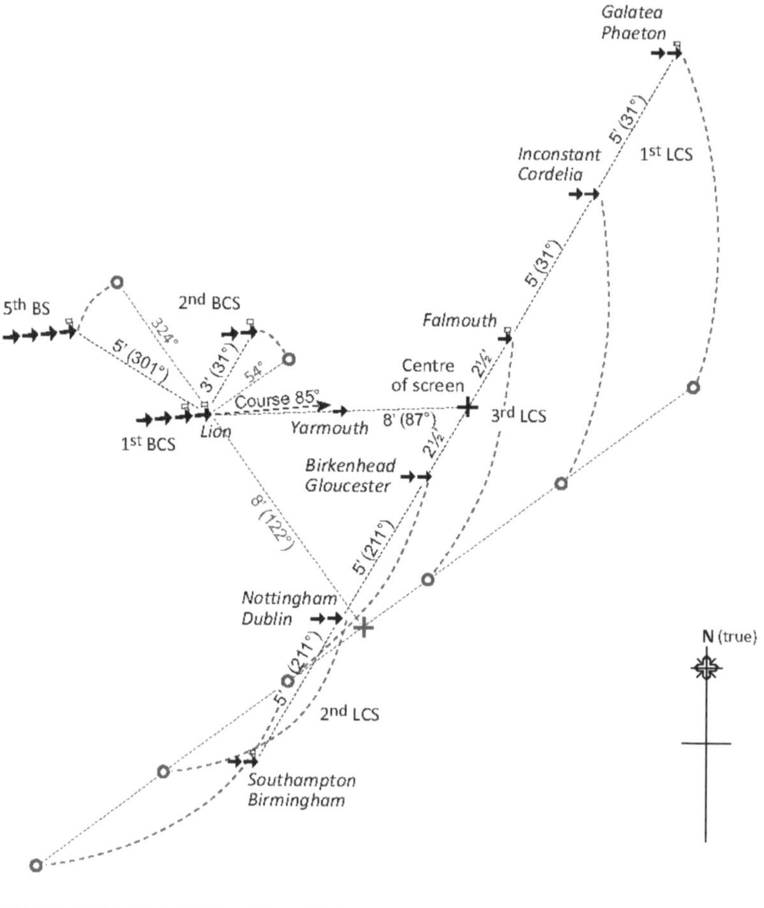

Notes

1. *Yarmouth*, as signal relay ship, was stationed half-way between the flagship and the centre
of the screen (ie at a distance of 4 miles).

2. Unusually, the change of alignment of the scouting line is depicted from the perspective of
Lion, which in effect remains stationary (together with the 1st BCS) relative to the movement
of the other ships and squadrons.

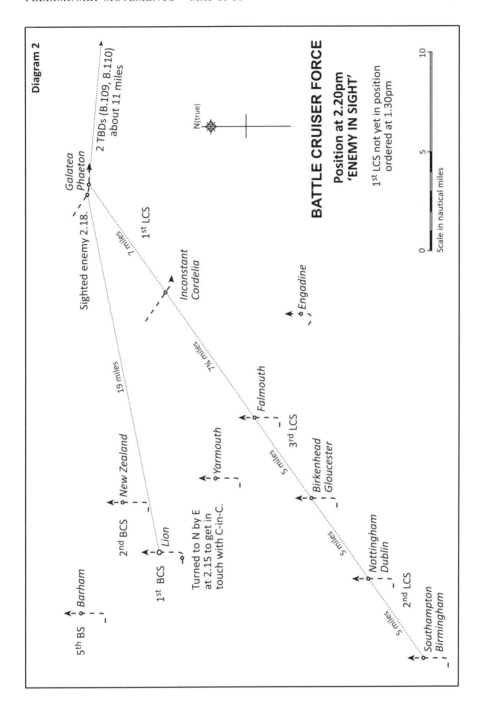

Diagram 2

BATTLE CRUISER FORCE

**Position at 2.20pm
'ENEMY IN SIGHT'**

1st LCS not yet in position
ordered at 1.30pm

0   5   10
Scale in nautical miles

2 TBDs (B.109, B.110)
about 11 miles

Galatea
Phaeton

N(true)

Sighted enemy 2.18.

1st LCS

7 miles

Inconstant
Cordelia

Engadine

7¼ miles

19 miles

Falmouth

3rd LCS

Birkenhead
Gloucester

New Zealand

2nd BCS

Yarmouth

5 miles

Lion

1st BCS

Turned to N by E
at 2.15 to get in
touch with C-in-C.

5 miles

Nottingham
Dublin

Barham

5th BS

2nd LCS

5 miles

Southampton
Birmingham

This report may have been received at first with some degree of doubt, for only an hour or two before a signal had been intercepted from the Admiralty to the Commander-in-Chief, which stated that the German flagship was still in the Jade at 11.10 am.[50]

But the *Galatea* was closing the suspicious craft and at 2.28 pm her guns opened fire. The whole situation was now assuming a new aspect. The Vice-Admiral turned at 2.32 pm and increased speed to 22 knots with the intention of cutting the enemy off from Horns Riff. His cruisers without further orders began to close the *Galatea*.

Movements of the German Fleet

33. The vessels seen were the German destroyers B.109 and B.110, which were in company with the 2nd Scouting Group, and had stopped to examine a merchant ship. The German cruiser force[51] had left the Jade at 2 am, followed at 2.30 am by the Main Fleet. The latter included the 2nd Battle Squadron with its six[52] ships of the *Preussen* class (four 11 in.). They were slow and ill-armed, and Admiral Scheer had not intended to take them with him, but when the time came sentiment prevailed over reason, and he gave way to the Admiral and officers of his old squadron when they begged him not to leave them behind. The battle cruisers were to proceed to the Naze and show themselves there on the evening of May 31, in the hope that the Grand Fleet would put to sea to intercept them and give the submarines lying in wait an opportunity to attack. The main body of the High Sea Fleet was to pick them up on the morning of June 1. The battle cruisers drew rapidly away on their separate quest and between 11.30 noon and 1 pm no fewer than five airships were

---

[50] Admiralty to Commander-in-Chief, 12.35 pm: 'No definite news of enemy. They made all preparations for sailing early this morning. It was thought fleet had sailed, but directional signal places flagship Jade at 11.10 GMT. Apparently they have been unable to carry out air reconnaissance which has delayed them, 1235'. This signal is in War Registry Out Telegrams and was received in *Iron Duke* 12.48 and in *Lion* 12.53 (*Lion*'s wireless time was then four minutes fast on *Iron Duke*), but there is no copy of it in *Iron Duke*'s In Telegrams, and it is not included in Harper's Appendix, nor in the Jutland Papers. There are grounds for the belief that it was sent without Room 40's cognisance or confirmation. Wilhelmshaven had taken over the Commander-in-Chief's wireless call and a signal (in a new cypher) made on May 30, 5.41 pm, to this effect could not be decyphered till 6.40 pm, May 31. Room 40, however, was not taken in by the ruse and remained positive that the High Sea Fleet was at sea.

Editor's note: See Chapter III Endnote 1 for more details of this incident.

[51] For constitution see Appendix B. The 2nd Scouting Group consisted of *Frankfurt* (Rear-Admiral Boedicker), *Wiesbaden*, *Pillau*, *Elbing*. The *Regensburg*, Commodore Heinrich, Second Senior Officer (T), was with them.

[52] The *Preussen* was in the Baltic, *Lothringen* unfit for sea.

despatched for reconnaissance, but owing to poor visibility they saw nothing of the British Fleet, nor did they hear or see anything of the engagement.[53] The German Commander-in-Chief was not left, however, without intelligence of the British movements. At 5.29 am U.32 reported two battleships, two cruisers and destroyers in a position 56° 15' N, 0° 43' W, approximately 60 [miles] East of May Island.[54] At 6 am Neumünster[55] reported that there were indications in an English message that two battleships or battle squadrons had just left Scapa Flow and at 6.47 am U.66 sighted eight battleships[56] in 57° 45' N, 0° 7' W about 60 miles East of Kinnaird Head. In Scheer's opinion the information was too vague to affect his plan. The forces seemed too far apart and their courses too divergent to be associated with an advance into the Bight or to have any connection with his enterprise. He continued his course, and at 2.30 pm the main body of the High Sea Fleet was well past Horns Riff with the scouting groups some 50 miles ahead. Spread ahead of the 1st Scouting Group in a fan formation were the four light cruisers of the 2nd Scouting Group, accompanied by the *Regensburg*, Second Senior Officer (T), and the 11th and 12th Half Flotillas. The *Elbing* was to westward on the port hand (Diagram 3). About 2.15 pm the latter sighted a neutral steamer and detached a couple of destroyers, B.109 and B.110, to examine it. At 2.28,[57] while busy with this task, they observed smoke to the westward, and shortly afterwards sighted enemy vessels steering East. The *Elbing* immediately closed to investigate, followed by the *Frankfurt*, *Pillau* and *Wiesbaden*. The squadrons were in touch, and their general position at 2.30 pm is shown in Diagram 4.

The *Galatea* in Touch. 2.30 - 3.30 pm

34. At 2.28 the *Galatea* making to the eastward opened fire on the two destroyers which made off to the northward, and a few minutes later sighted the *Elbing* coming down on a SSE course.[58] The German cruiser opened fire at 15,000 yards (Diagram 5). The *Galatea* and *Phaeton* altered course to the NE, and then at 2.37 pm turned sharp round to the NW, the 2nd Scouting Group following them in pursuit 7 miles astern.

---

[53] Scheer's Despatch, *Official Despatches*, 589.

[54] This was the Battle Cruiser Force.

[55] The German intercept station.

[56] The 2nd Battle Squadron.

[57] Scheer, *Germany's High Seas Fleet*, 141.

[58] Signal 2.34; time of origin 1430. Note *Galatea*'s 1430 position is 9 miles 254° (approximately West) from Harper's position.

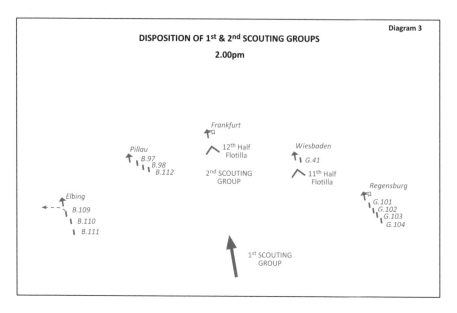

Diagram 3

DISPOSITION OF 1st & 2nd SCOUTING GROUPS

2.00pm

Note

The original diagram does not show a flag on the cruiser *Frankfurt*, flagship of Rear-Admiral Bödicker and leader of the 2nd Scouting Group.

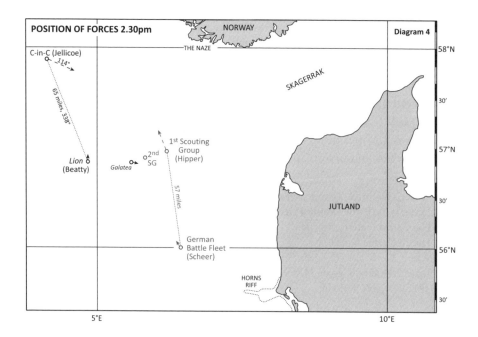

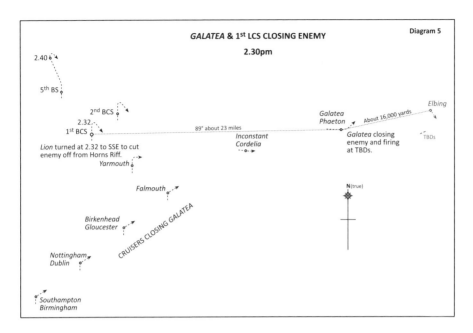

GALATEA & 1st LCS CLOSING ENEMY

2.30pm

Diagram 5

Two more cruisers of the 2nd Scouting Group were now in sight, and a large amount of smoke was visible to the ENE.[59] This was evidently a force some 15 miles to the eastward, and Beatty now felt confident that the enemy were to the north-eastward, and could be brought to action before reaching Horns Riff.

The *Inconstant* and *Cordelia*, the cruisers next to the *Galatea*, were hurrying up, and the whole light cruiser line without orders was closing to the north-eastward in support. The *Galatea* continued to run to North-West, keeping just out of range, with the intention of drawing the enemy on, while the Battle Cruiser Force altered course to SSE at 2.32 pm in order to cut him off from Horns Riff. But by this time the 1st Scouting Group had heard the call of their light cruisers, and was making westward to support them. The two forces were thus rapidly closing the distance[60] between them, and an action was now imminent.

The *Barham*, however, instead of turning with the *Lion* at 2.32 pm, when the two were only 4½ miles apart, held on till 2.40,[61] and opened her distance to over ten miles, a very considerable increase which delayed her getting into

[59] *Galatea* to Senior Officer, Battle Cruiser Force, 1435. The smoke seen by the *Galatea* may have been that of destroyers ahead of the German battle cruisers.

[60] At 2.32 about 40 miles when the *Lion* turned SSE.

[61] *Valiant* (r) 2.40 pm, *Malaya* (r) 2.40 pm, *Warspite* (r), track chart (*Official Despatches*, Pl. 17) 2.40 pm, *Barham* (r) says 2.38 pm.

Editor's note: See Chapter III Endnote 2 for a discussion of the controversy surrounding the reasons for *Barham's* late turn.

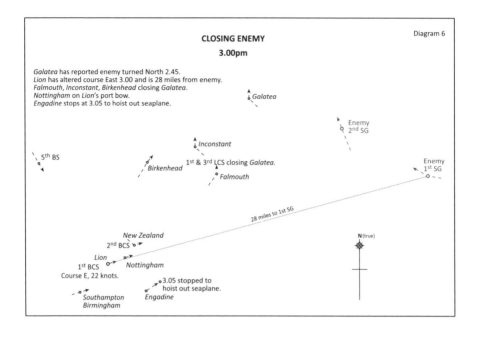

CLOSING ENEMY

3.00pm

Diagram 6

Galatea has reported enemy turned North 2.45.
Lion has altered course East 3.00 and is 28 miles from enemy.
Falmouth, Inconstant, Birkenhead closing Galatea.
Nottingham on Lion's port bow.
Engadine stops at 3.05 to hoist out seaplane.

Galatea

Enemy
2nd SG

Inconstant

5th BS

Birkenhead   1st & 3rd LCS closing Galatea.   Enemy
                                                            1st SG
                         Falmouth

28 miles to 1st SG

New Zealand   N (true)
2nd BCS
Lion
1st BCS   Nottingham
Course E, 22 knots.

                     3.05 stopped to
                     hoist out seaplane.
    Southampton   Engadine
    Birmingham

action later on. At 3.05 pm the *Galatea* reported the enemy had turned North, and the *Lion* altered course to SE, and at 3.0 to East. (Diagram 6).

The enemy was still some thirty miles away, though his light cruisers had come in sight of the *Falmouth* at 2.45 pm,[62] and between 3 pm and 3.30 pm the *Galatea* and *Phaeton* with the other light cruisers closing on them were drawing them to the North-West at a range which gradually increased from 17,000 to 20,000 yards.

At 3.07 the *Galatea* reported the enemy cruisers had altered course North-East, and at 3.13 pm the *Lion* altered course to North-East, going on to 23 knots. A few minutes later the *New Zealand*, three miles ENE, sighted five enemy ships on her starboard bow.[63]

The *Engadine* and her aircraft now joined in the reconnaissance. She had been told at 2.47 pm to send up her seaplane, and it got off the water by 3.08 pm and flew off northward. Though the visibility was poor (only some four miles at 1,000 feet), the observer sighted three enemy cruisers[64] and several destroyers, and between that time and 3.45 sent three signals reporting their

[62] *Falmouth* (r). But her log says 3.00 and her signal is timed 1500. *Falmouth*'s signal position at 3 pm is eight miles 47° from Harper's position.

[63] *New Zealand* (s). Probably the battle cruisers 19 miles East by North of her on Harper's Diagram III. The light cruisers were 18½ N 54' E, or almost ahead.

[64] Evidently the 2nd Scouting Group.

course and their alteration to the South at 3.35.[65] Her signals, however, never got past the *Engadine*:[66] engine trouble forced her to descend, and the *Engadine* picked her up while the battle cruisers passed swiftly on to the eastward.

At 3.29[67] the *Lion* altered course to East, increasing to 25 knots, and at about 3.31 sighted the enemy, which was made out to be 2, 3, 4 and finally 5 battle cruisers. The *Galatea* was then some 16 miles to the northward with the six cruisers of the 1st and 3rd Light Cruiser Squadrons. The 2nd Light Cruiser Squadron was close at hand, the *Nottingham* and *Dublin* four miles on her starboard bow, the *Southampton* and *Birmingham* 3½ miles astern. The *New Zealand* and 2nd Battle Cruiser Squadron were three miles on the starboard bow bearing ENE: rather more than five miles off on the port beam, the 5th Battle Squadron could be seen bearing N 54 W.

The enemy was some fourteen miles off:[68] the visibility was good, the wind South-East with the sun behind, and everything seemed favourable for the approaching action. The 2nd Battle Cruiser Squadron was now ordered to form astern in line of battle,[69] and the two flotillas were ordered to take station – the 13th, two points before the starboard beam, and the 9th, right ahead.[70] The 1st Scouting Group, on receiving the report of the British cruisers, had turned to the westward, and were some ten miles behind their light cruisers which were chasing the *Galatea* to the north-westward. Hipper had received no word of the proximity of British battle cruisers, when at 3.20 he suddenly sighted Beatty's force to the westward[71] approaching at full speed. Its appearance must have been disconcerting in the extreme. The whole original plan of operations now fell to the ground. Hipper recalled the 2nd Scouting Group at once, and after continuing a little way to the northward, turned at 3.33 to a Southerly course, with the evident intention of closing his Battle Fleet.[72] The *Lützow* was leading,

---

[65] *Engadine* observer's time 3.33.

[66] *Editor's note*: See the Chapter III Endnote 3 for more information on *Engadine*'s reports.

[67] *Nottingham*, four miles ahead of *Lion*, had reported smoke ENE at 1522; *Nottingham*'s signalled position is 56° 46' N, Long. 5° 14' E, which is 7¾ miles, 208° (S 41 W) from Harper's position.

[68] This is from Harper (Plate III). Chatfield (r) says 23,000 yards at 3.30 (*Official Despatches*, 143); Harper's text says a range of 23,000 yard was obtained from *Lion* at 3.30 pm, but Plate III gives 29,000 yards at this time.

[69] Signal 3.34.

[70] Signal 3.42.

[71] Harper makes them 19 miles apart at 3.20 pm.

[72] Scheer's report says the enemy deployed to South, and Hipper followed the movement, but it seems clear that the Germans turned first. Von Hase, 87; also Austrian Naval Attaché's report of June 17, 1916 (translated I.D.).

carrying the Admiral's Flag, and behind her in single line, steering a SSE[73] course, and on a line of bearing NW, came the *Derfflinger*, *Seydlitz*, *Moltke*, and *Von der Tann*, with the *Regensburg* (Commodore Heinrich, second senior officer of torpedo craft) and the 9th Flotilla on their port bow. The 2nd Battle Cruiser Squadron had turned, and was taking up its position astern of the 1st, when Admiral Beatty gave orders to form on a line of bearing NW[74] to clear the smoke, and the signal went up almost simultaneously with a signal to alter course together to ESE.

The enemy was now plainly visible on the port bow, and the two forces were closing rapidly. At 3.49,[75] the *Lützow* fired the first gun, and shortly afterwards the *Lion* opened fire in reply. The action had begun.

Chapter III: Endnotes

1 The origin of the Admiralty's signal that the High Seas Fleet was still in the Jade is a frequently told tale (e.g., Marder, *FDFS*, 3:45–7; Beesly, *Room 40*, 155). The usual telling goes something like this: The Director of Operations, Captain Thomas Jackson (who should not be confused with Admiral Sir Henry Jackson, then serving as First Sea Lord), asked the watchkeeper in Room 40 where directional bearings placed the call sign 'DK'. He was told that 'DK' was in Wilhelmshaven. Upon learning this, Jackson immediately left and reported to Rear-Admiral Henry Oliver, the Chief of the War Staff, that the High Seas Fleet's flagship, *Friedrich der Grosse*, was still in harbour – 'DK' being that ship's call sign. Oliver thereupon sent the infamous signal to Jellicoe (it was also picked up by Beatty) at 12.30, indicating that the High Seas Fleet was still in harbour.

The staff of Room 40 apparently knew that the standard German procedure was to transfer the DK call sign to the W/T station in Wilhelmshaven Dockyard when the fleet went to sea. In other words, DK was *always* located in Wilhelmshaven. Jackson, through his ignorance of German W/T procedures, had asked the wrong question, and the officer on duty in Room 40 had not volunteered any further information because of Jackson's well known disdain for the mostly civilian staff of Room 40.

That is the generally accepted version, but Jason Hines casts some doubt it. He argues that Room 40 actually did *not* know that the High Seas Fleet was at sea because the signal transferring the DK call sign to Wilhelmshaven dockyard was in a new cipher that Room 40 did not break until well after Jackson asked his question. He also quotes a note by Captain Herbert Hope, whose job was to analyse decoded signals: 'As far as Room 40 was concerned, there was nothing to actually show that the [High Seas] Fleet was at sea until 2.40 pm', when directional stations located the German light cruiser *Elbing* at sea (Hines, 'Sins of Omission and Commission', 1129). Hines notes that the source of the story of Jackson's apparently obtuse question is a manuscript by William F. Clarke (TNA: HW 3/2: 'An Admiralty Telegram', 10 August 1924), one of the staff of Room 40, and writes:

---

[73] Harper, Plate V.

[74] Signal 3.45 pm.

[75] Chatfield gives 3.47 for enemy, 3.47½ for *Lion*; *Lion* (s) 3.47; *Tiger* 3.49 (enemy), 3.50 *Lion*; Brock 3.50 (enemy), 3.51 (British); Hase 3.48 (*Lützow*); Scheer 3.49.

It is not clear whether the inaccuracies in Clarke's story were simply a case of faulty recollection, a move to place the blame squarely on the shoulders of someone Clarke clearly disliked, or rather an attempt to minimize any role Clarke may have himself had in the Admiralty signal to Jellicoe – Clarke's story doesn't reveal whether Clarke himself was the watchstander who answered Jackson (Hines, 'Sins of Omission and Commission', 1130 n.75).

Thus the precise origin of the signal, which during the battle led Jellicoe to doubt other, more accurate intelligence sent by the Admiralty, is another of Jutland's many mysteries.

Worth noting is that this signal was deliberately not included in the *Official Despatches* – Oswyn Murray noted this in a memorandum to the First Sea Lord, Admiral Beatty, in November 1926, with reference to the signal being included in a draft of Winston Churchill's book: additional evidence of Kenneth Dewar's assistance to Churchill (TNA: ADM 1/8697/64). The second, 1940, edition of *Naval Operations* does include this signal.

2. The reason for *Barham*'s delay in turning to support Beatty is one of the more controversial aspects of Jutland. Gordon (*Rules of the Game*, Chapter 6) examines the issue in exhaustive detail, and only the main points need be touched upon here.

At 1.30 Beatty changed the station of the 5th BS from five miles NW of *Lion* to five miles NNW of *Lion*; although this signal was made by flags, it was apparently repeated by searchlight to *Barham* by *Tiger*, the rear ship of the 1st BCS and therefore the closest ship to *Barham* (at 9.09 am *Lion* asked *Tiger* if she had repeated a submarine warning to *Barham* and received an affirmative answer). Most other signals to the detached formations (e.g., the 2.15 signal to the 5th BS telling it to look out for Grand Fleet's cruisers and several signals to the cruiser screen, the destroyers and the seaplane carrier *Engadine*) were sent by searchlight.

When the BCF and the 5th BS turned N by E at 2.15, *Tiger*, now the farthest ship from the 5th BS, probably assumed *Lion* had taken over the responsibility of sending signals by searchlight, since she was now the closest ship to Evan-Thomas' squadron. But when Beatty altered course to SSE at 2.32 the signal was sent only by flags, which were unreadable aboard the *Barham*, five miles away. As a result, while the BCF was turning to the southward, the 5th BS continued northward, and the gap between the two forces increased from five miles to nine or ten miles. Although his flag captain, Arthur Craig, had been urging him to turn to follow the BCF for several minutes, it was only at 2.40 that Evan-Thomas did so. Subsequent turns by the BCF in response to the developing situation (SE at 2.52, east at 3.01, NE at 3.13) provided an opportunity for Beatty to concentrate his forces, but this was not done, and when the BCF first turned east (3.30) and then began a series of turns toward the south (3.45), the 5th BS was again left behind. As a result, the fast battleships were not able to open fire on the German battle cruisers until a little after 4.00.

Despite the fact that the issue has often been treated as a zero-sum, either-or matter (either Beatty was at fault or Evan-Thomas was), both admirals clearly bear some responsibility for the gap between their forces. Evan-Thomas was certainly slow to react to the situation, perhaps out of sheer procidural fussiness (along the lines of 'I'm not going to turn until I get a proper signal'). Beatty – and/or his signals organisation – was at the very least sloppy and unobservant, and more than one opportunity to concentrate the British forces was overlooked.

But if that's Beatty's minimum degree of fault, there is also what might be termed a 'maximum fault' possibility, although a purely speculative one. Stephen Roskill, in his biography of Beatty, reluctantly suggests that Beatty intentionally kept the 5th BS at arm's length because he didn't want them sharing in the glory of what he did not doubt would be a resounding BCF victory (Roskill, *Admiral of the Fleet Earl Beatty*, 155). This line of thought is suggested by a remark by

Captain Walter Cowan of *Princess Royal* at the beginning of the Run to the South, to the effect that the 'damned 5th Battle Squadron is going to take the bread out of our mouths'; Roskill finds it plausible that Beatty was of like mind, and so deliberately did not order Evan-Thomas to join the battle cruisers during their approach.

Certainly Beatty thought his ships superior to their German counterparts; after the Dogger Bank action, he wrote to Jellicoe that

> Their [i.e., the Germans'] 11-in. [shell] is no good, seldom burst and the effect when they do is very local. The 12-in. is serious, but not to be compared to our 13.5. Their guns are good, calibration too close, gun laying excellent, but the projectile no good, and I am sure we can stand a lot of it . . . (Beatty to Jellicoe, undated, but late January or early February 1915; reproduced in *Jellicoe Papers*, 1:131).

The idea that Beatty believed the BCF to be decisively superior to Hipper's 1st Scouting Group is further reinforced by his well-known comment after the Dogger Bank that

> I had made up my mind that we were going to get four [i.e., the four German battle cruisers], the lot, and four we ought to have got. There is no blinking it, we had them beat. Another half hour would have done it . . . (Roskill, *Admiral of the Fleet Earl Beatty*, 114).

So there is no doubt that Beatty believed his ships were superior to their German counterparts. But whether he deliberately delayed ordering the 5th BS to join him in order to win a resounding victory without their help is speculation – intriguing, but impossible to prove one way or the other.

3. Jellicoe states that these signals sent by Flight-Lieutenant F J Rutland ('Rutland of Jutland' forever after) and Assistant Paymaster G S Trewin were 'received on board *Lion* at 3.30 pm' (Jellicoe, *Grand Fleet*, 320); however, other authorities state that, whilst they were received in *Engadine*, that ship's efforts to pass them along to both *Lion* and *Barham* via signal lamp were unsuccessful. The published 'Harper Record' quotes a report from *Engadine*:

> Attempts were made to pass these signals to LION by searchlight, but this could not be done as apparently she had already opened fire on the enemy. An attempt was also made to pass them through BARHAM, but this failed for the same reason. (Cmd. 2870: Harper, *Reproduction of the Record of the Battle of Jutland*, 19.)

Worth noting is that Rutland's aircraft, a Short 184 (No. 8359) still exists and is owned by the Imperial War Museum, and at time of writing is on display at the Fleet Air Arm Museum in Yeovilton, UK (www.fleetairarm.com).

CHAPTER IV

THE BATTLE CRUISER ACTION FROM 3.40 PM TO 4.40 PM

35. When the action began the British Battle Cruiser Force was on a course ESE, going 25 to 26 knots in the process of forming a line of bearing NW;[1] the 9th Flotilla were taking up position ahead, and the 13th just before the starboard beam. The 2nd Light Cruiser Squadron were with the *Lion*, the *Nottingham* and *Dublin* some three miles off on her port bow making to the southward to get ahead, and the *Southampton* and *Birmingham* a couple of miles before the beam to starboard; the *Galatea* with the 1st and 3rd Light Cruiser Squadrons were away to the North-West almost out of sight[2] making to the eastward after the enemy; to the northward were the enemy light cruisers some 11 miles off, coming down at full speed on a South-Easterly course to rejoin their battle cruisers (Diagram 7).

The opening range has been variously estimated, and was probably about 14,300 yards.[3]

---

[1] The signal for the line of bearing was made at 3.45 and ships were probably on this line by 3.48 or 3.49.

Editor's note: This is an altogether too optimistic assessment of the time required for this manoeuvre; see the Chapter IV Endnote for a discussion of Beatty's opening moves.

[2] NNW, 15 to 16 miles.

[3] There are wide differences between the gun ranges of the various ships until 3.55 pm, when they agree fairly well. The opening range of 14,300 is obtained by laying back the known runs of both squadrons to 3.50 pm.

Editor's note: Campbell has the Germans opening fire first at 3.48pm, at a range of circa 16,000 yards. Both sides overestimated the ranges, *Lützow*'s opening range being 16,800 yards, while *Lion* and *Tiger* used 18,500. (All figures from Campbell, *Jutland*, 39).

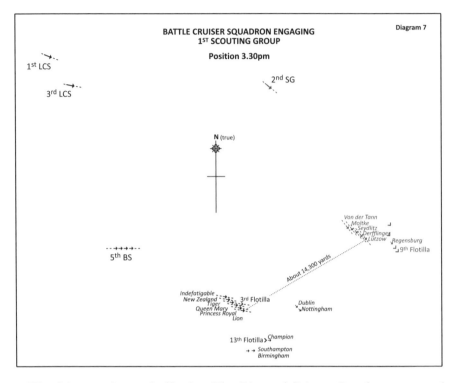

The firing was hot and effective. The *Lion* and *Princess Royal* concentrated at first on the *Lützow*[4] while the Germans fired at their opposite numbers.[5] Great rippling sheets of flame came from the enemy's guns, and the ships were quickly surrounded with mountainous columns of water and huge fountains of spray.

Hitting soon became general: the *Lion* was hit twice about 3.51, one shot exploding forward on the inboard side of the 4 in. armour and the other forward on the upper deck, causing many casualties among the 4 in. guns' crews; the *Tiger* was hit on the forecastle and then on the port side of X turret, breaking the armour but leaving the gun mounting uninjured; then again on the roof of

---

[4] *Lion* opened on *Lützow*; *Princess Royal* first on *Lützow*, later on *Derfflinger*; *Queen Mary* on *Seydlitz* at first, then on *Derfflinger*; *Tiger* and *New Zealand* on *Moltke*; *New Zealand* at 3.57 on *Von der Tann*. *Derfflinger* was unengaged for a time till the *Princess Royal* shifted to her. On the German side, *Lützow* on *Lion*, and stuck to her through the action; *Derfflinger* on *Princess Royal* at first, then *Queen Mary* (and blew her up); *Seydlitz* on *Queen Mary*; *Von der Tann* possibly on *Tiger* up to 3.56, then on *Indefatigable* (sank her).

[5] *Editor's note*: Not stated is the fact that there were mistakes in the distribution of fire of the battle cruisers: *Queen Mary* should have engaged *Derfflinger*, not *Seydlitz*, and as a result, *Derfflinger* was able to shoot undisturbed.

Q turret, knocking off the central sighting hood but leaving the turret in action.[6] Information as to the hits obtained on the enemy is naturally less detailed, but the *Princess Royal*'s third salvo hit the *Lützow*.[7]

The *Lion* by 3.54 had altered course some four points to starboard parallel to the enemy, and the squadron was now running SSE[8] at a range of about 13,000 yards. The 9th Flotilla was making strenuous efforts to get ahead to a position favourable for attack, and its smoke was interfering with the fire of the *Tiger* and *Princess Royal*.

The *Lion* shortly afterwards received her heaviest blow. A shell struck Q turret, entered the gun-house and burst over the left gun. Nearly all the guns' crews were killed and all the men in the working chamber killed or severely wounded. Major Harvey, RMA,[9] the officer of the turret, was severely wounded but was able to pass the word down to close the magazine doors and flood magazines, a precaution which saved the ship and won him a Victoria Cross in death.

A fire started in the wreckage of the turret and about 20 minutes later a charge slid back from the gun and fell into the well. The fire caught it and spread to the charges in the gun-cages, then down the main trunk to the charges there. It gathered into a great flash of flame which passed right up and down and through the turret, penetrating up the escape trunk into the switchboard compartment and killing instantly all there. Their bodies and clothes were not burnt and where they had screened their faces with their hands, their skin was not even singed. It reached the doors of the magazines but they were closed.

It was now close on four o'clock. A large barque[10] with all sail set was lying

---

[6] It jammed the wires of the gun cages, reducing the right gun to secondary loading, and 'wooded' the telescopes, reducing the turret to percussion firing by elevation and bearing from director. Two men were killed and the midshipman mortally wounded; Fawcett and Hooper, *Fighting at Jutland*, 83.

[7] *Editor's note*: Actually, it was *Queen Mary* who scored the first hit for the RN, on *Seydlitz* at 3.55 pm. She would hit her target once more, and (probably) *Lion* hit *Lützow* at about 4 pm. These were the only four made by the British battle cruisers until 4 pm, when in the same period the Germans made about 15 hits (Campbell, *Jutland*, 41).

[8] Scheer makes the German course SSE (German IV).

[9] *Editor's note*: An obvious typographical error in the original has him as 'Hervey' – a check of the 1914 *Navy List* has a Royal Marine Major Francis J. W. Harvey, but no Hervey. That same *Navy List* registers him under the Royal Marine Light Infantry, and not the RMA. Interestingly, Winston Churchill also uses the spelling 'Hervey' (*The World Crisis, 1916-1918*, vol. 3, part I, 128): more evidence of his use of the *NSA* as a source.

[10] *Editor's note*: Gordon suggests that this was the Norwegian barque *Candace* (*Rules of the Game*, 111 n.35).

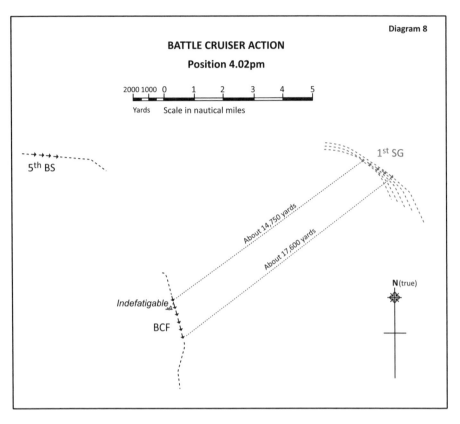

Diagram 8

BATTLE CRUISER ACTION

Position 4.02pm

becalmed between the two fleets. The *Princess Royal* had shifted her fire to the *Derfflinger*, and the two were hotly engaged. The *Derfflinger* received a hit in one of her casemates which did a great deal of damage,[11] and shortly afterwards hit the *Princess Royal*,[12] putting her Argo tower and main control out of action till 4.16 pm.

The squadrons were gradually coming round to the southward and the range was beginning to increase (Diagram 8).

The *Von der Tann* was maintaining a steady fire on the *Indefatigable*. Shortly after four o'clock a salvo of three shots fell on the latter's upper deck in line with the after turrets and evidently penetrated the interior; an explosion followed and she fell out of line, sinking by the stern. Another salvo struck her near the fore turret; a second explosion followed, and she turned over and disappeared. In the roar and crash of the battle her loss passed almost unobserved by some of the ships ahead. Meanwhile, the 5th Battle Squadron had been coming up

---

[11] Von Hase (I.D. 1220), 25; Austrian Naval Mission Report, August 4, 1916.

[12] At 3.56 *Derfflinger* was firing at 11,500 m. (12,600 yards).

astern at full speed. They were still some seven or eight miles astern of the Battle Cruiser Squadron, but shortly after four o'clock[13] their guns were beginning to range on the rear of the enemy's line. The *Barham* opened fire at 19,000 yards,[14] and made a signal to concentrate in pairs on the rear ships. It was some time, however, before their fire became effective,[15] for the light was difficult, the targets constantly obscured, and often only the flashes of the enemy's guns could be seen; but the *New Zealand* could see the splashes of other guns falling round the enemy, and knew that the *Barham*'s squadron was coming into action. Torpedo tracks were stated to have been seen about this time, one passing under the *Princess Royal* and another missing the *Lion*, but these reports must be regarded as supposititious.[16]

By 4.05 the range had increased to nearly 20,000 yards, and at 4.12 the Battle Cruiser Squadron altered course to the SE to close the enemy: the *Lion* now came under a heavy fire, and was hit several times, but no important damage was done, though several fires were started and a number of men were killed and wounded by a shell bursting on the mess deck.

The 13th Flotilla had been ordered to attack and was beginning to draw ahead, though the attack did not exercise any influence on the battle till 4.30 pm. Before it had begun to develop the squadron was to suffer another heavy loss. The *Queen Mary* was now firing steadily at the *Derfflinger*[17] and had twice straddled her, obtaining a hit each time on her opponent, who was firing in reply with a slowly decreasing range.[18] But at 4.26 pm a plunging salvo pitched

---

[13] *Warspite* (s) 4.00; *Warspite* (r) 4.02; *Valiant* (r) 4.01; R.A., 5th Battle Squadron (r), 4.06; *Barham* (r) 4.11.

[14] *Editor's note*: Although Campbell (*Jutland*, 46) agrees with this figure, Andrew Gordon (*Rules of the Game*, 113–14) provides evidence that the 5th Battle Squadron may not have squandered their long-range advantage, actually opening fire at about 23,000 yards.

[15] *Editor's note*: This is not quite correct; firing at *Frankfurt*, *Barham* straddled with her third salvo, the first falling a mere 300 yards short. She opened fire on *Von der Tann* at 4.08 pm, scoring a hit one minute later (Campbell, *Jutland*, 44, 49). Admiral Hipper would later describe these as having 'produced an excellent impression'. This may be a case of the *NSA*'s downplaying the role of the 5th BS's contributions to this phase of the battle.

[16] See *Official Despatches*, 132, 148, 257, 451. These are stated in two reports to have passed from starboard to port, i.e. from West to East, and were attributed to submarines, but Scheer definitely states that none took part in the action. Harper (p. 20) thinks it possible that the torpedoes were fired by the *Moltke*, which fired four torpedoes at this time; but the *Moltke*'s torpedoes were 19.7 in., and the latest Mark carried in 1916 was G**, 28½ knots, with a maximum range of 11,250 yards. To reach the British line would have required a range of something like 18,500 yards and a speed of well over 30 knots.

[17] Von Hase (I.D. 1220), 27.

[18] At 4.25, 200 yards a minute, Von Hase. Von Hase gives time of salvo as 4 hrs. 26 min. 10 secs. and range as 13,200 m. (14,400 yards). Harper V gives 15,500 yards.

on the *Queen Mary* abreast of Q turret; a dazzling red flame leapt up in the forward part of the ship, accompanied by an explosion and a mass of black smoke. The *Tiger* passed her to port, the *New Zealand* to starboard. Her stern was high in the air with the propellers revolving. Men were crawling out of the after turret and great masses of paper were blowing out of the after hatch. Suddenly the entire ship was rent by a terrific upheaval and disappeared in a gigantic pall of smoke which rose 1,000 ft. in the air.[19] A rain of debris fell on the deck of the *Tiger* as she passed through the dreadful cloud, but hardly a fragment of the ship remained afloat. She had gone down leaving only 17 survivors to be picked up later by the *Laurel* and *Petard* (Diagram 9).

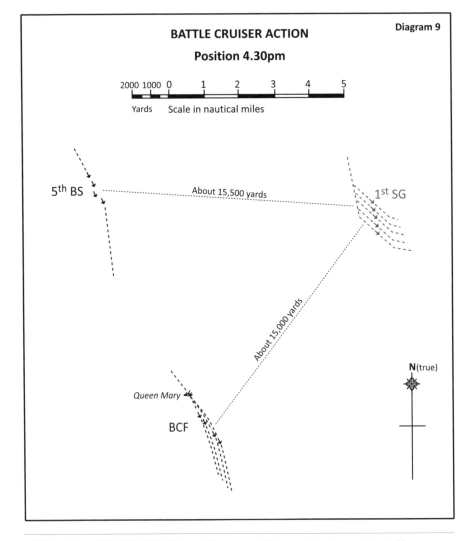

[19] Von Hase, 101 (I.D. 1220), 28, and Fawcett and Hooper, *Fighting at Jutland*, 30.

This was the second blow which had befallen the squadron within half an hour, but the squadron continued its course undismayed till 4.30 pm, when a destroyer action began to develop and to occupy the water between the lines.

The Destroyer Attack

36. Shortly after 4 o'clock Admiral Beatty had ordered Captain Farie in the *Champion* (13th Flotilla) to attack the enemy.[20] The Flotilla,[21] with the exception of the *Obdurate*, was then almost a mile on the starboard and disengaged beam of the *Lion*; on her engaged side were six destroyers of the 9th Flotilla,[22] which had been ahead when the squadron turned to South-East, and since the beginning of the action had been making strenuous efforts to recover that position, steaming hard about half a mile on the port beam, receiving the splash and splinter of some of the shorts', and causing considerable interference with their smoke.[23] The *Obdurate*, too, which had become detached from the 13th Flotilla, was with them on the engaged side. They had gradually drawn level with the *Tiger*, when they were ordered about 4.10[24] to clear the range, and, turning to port, took station astern, with the exception of the *Morris* and *Moorsom*, which went further ahead, and continued their course on the engaged side.

At 4.15,[25] the *Champion* gave the order to attack, and the flotilla, increasing to full speed and led by the *Nestor* (Commander E.S. Bingham), drew ahead of the *Lion*. But before they crossed her track, they met a momentary check; the *Nottingham*, hitherto on the *Lion*'s engaged side, crossed her bows about 4.21 and ran through the line of destroyers ahead of the *Petard*, forcing its rear to turn astern of her and parting them from the van. The foremost portion, consisting of the *Nestor*, *Nicator*, *Nomad*, *Narborough* and *Pelican*, went on at full speed, crossing the *Lion*'s track about a mile ahead of her, and steered for a favourable position to attack the enemy, who could be seen some eight miles off to the North-East with his destroyers coming across to meet the attack. Precisely how and when the *Narborough* and *Pelican* became detached is doubtful, but they evidently did not follow the *Nestor*, and being unable to open

---

[20] Signal is timed 4.09, and was evidently made by wireless and visual. It was passed by *Princess Royal* as *Lion*'s main W/T was out of action. *Champion* (r) 4.15; *Nicator* (r) 4.15; *Nestor* shortly after 4 pm.

[21] *Champion*, Captain (D), *Nestor*, *Nomad*, *Nicator*, *Pelican*, *Narborough*, *Petard*, *Nerissa*; also *Turbulent* and *Termagant*, detached from 10th Flotilla.

[22] *Lydiard*, *Liberty*, *Landrail*, *Laurel*, *Morris*, *Moorsom*.

[23] *Official Despatches*, 132 (*Lion*); 148 (*Princess Royal* at 3.59), 155 (*Tiger* at 3.51).

[24] *Lion* (s), 4.09, also 4.20; *Lydiard*, (r) 4.30.

[25] 4.15, *Champion* (r); 4.20, *Pelican* (r); 4.15, Von Hase; 4.15, *Nicator* (r); 4.30, *Nerissa* (r).

fire on the advancing destroyers, and not finding an opportunity to attack, turned back to join the *Champion*. The *Petard*, with her three destroyers, after clearing the *Nottingham* and supported by the *Moorsom* and *Morris* from the engaged side, was making approximately East-South-East to attack.

Hipper saw the attack developing and launched his 9th Flotilla against it, supported later by the *Regensburg* and a portion of the 2nd Flotilla.

The destroyers rapidly covered the distance between the lines, and by 4.30 the two forces were well within range[26] engaging each other with an energetic fire.

By 4.40[27] the *Nestor* found herself on the starboard bow of the enemy and turned some 14 points to attack on a North-Westerly course. They now came under a heavy fire from the destroyers and the battle cruisers, and the *Nomad* was hit by a shell which burst in the engine-room, killing the Engineer-Lieutenant-Commander, and brought her to a dead stop.

The *Nestor* and *Nicator* each fired two torpedoes at about 6,000 yards, but the *Lützow*[28] had turned away and the torpedoes probably ran harmlessly past. The *Petard* had turned to attack immediately after the *Nestor*, and had fired her first torpedo at V.27, the leading German destroyer, which she probably hit, and three others at the second or third cruiser (*Derfflinger* and *Seydlitz*), at a range of about 7,000 yards.

By this time two of the German destroyers, V.29 and V.27, which had been badly hit, were sinking.[29] The remainder had fired twelve torpedoes[30] without a hit, and after rescuing the crews of their sinking vessels were now racing back to the shelter of their squadron.

The *Nerissa*, astern of the *Petard*, saw the enemy turn sixteen points to a Northerly course, and turning with the *Turbulent* and *Termagant* to a Southerly

---

[26] 6,000 yards at 4.32 pm, according to Harper V.

[27] Harper V; *Nestor* says 4.30 pm.

[28] At 4.28, 4.33 and 4.36 probably to open the range.

Editor's note: Lützow also fired a torpedo, at *Tiger*, at 4.34 pm. *Seydlitz* seems to have been *Nicator's* target (Campbell, *Jutland*, 51).

[29] The *Petard* probably hit one with a torpedo. Scheer, *Germany's High Seas Fleet*, 144, states they were hit by heavy calibre shell, but the *Tiger* is the only ship that reports firing on them (*Official Despatches*, 155). V.27 was the leader of the 17th Half-Flotilla.

Editor's note: Campbell (*Jutland*, 50) notes that *Petard* torpedoed V.29, V.27 being disabled by shell hits in the engine room. The latter would be sunk by gunfire from V.26 after her crew were taken off.

[30] Scheer, *Germany's High Seas Fleet*, 144. None of them seems to have reached the British line except a couple mentioned by the *Barham* and even in their case the time seems uncertain (*Official Despatches*, 193).

course to attack, fired two torpedoes at 7,000 yards,[31] and then shaped course to rejoin the *Champion*.

The turn away of the enemy at 4.45 pm had frustrated the *Nestor*'s attack, but Commander Bingham was determined to press it home. Turning with the *Nicator* to an Easterly course, he followed him up under a heavy fire. Reaching a position abeam of the *Lützow* at a distance which, according to Von Hase,[32] was 'devilishly close', she fired her third torpedo at 3,000 to 4,000 yards, then turned to make back. By this time the enemy Battle Squadron could be seen to the southward, and the *Nicator* fired her third torpedo at the second ship. The destroyer recall was flying,[33] but the gallant *Nestor* was not to reach home. The *Regensburg*, appearing from behind the squadron, opened a heavy fire on her, and succeeded in getting two shots into her boilers, reducing her speed to 17 knots with the enemy Battle Fleet drawing nearer and nearer. The Captain of the *Petard* (Lieutenant-Commander E.C.O. Thompson), seeing his leader disabled, closed and offered him a tow. But minutes were precious. Every moment brought the enemy nearer, and Commander Bingham, loath to involve another in his impending fate, refused the offer, and watched him turn westward and make off. The *Nestor* soon came to a full stop. The *Nomad* was lying equally helpless a mile or so away. The latter was visibly sinking. Both Commanders could see that a storm of fire must break on them in a few minutes, and both made shift to strike a last blow by firing their remaining torpedoes at the approaching Battle Fleet. The *Nestor*'s crew gave three cheers for the *Nestor*, and sang a verse of 'God Save the King'. The Carley rafts were launched, and the wounded got on to them.

As the High Sea Fleet approached, an overwhelming fire was opened, which sank both boats in a few minutes; the crews were picked up by enemy destroyers as they passed.

The destroyer attack was over. Boldly led by Commander Bingham, it had exercised a temporary influence on the battle. Eleven destroyers had attacked; two had been lost on each side;[34] ten torpedoes had been fired at the battle cruisers, and ten at the approaching Battle Fleet,[35] and one at a destroyer. No

---

[31] *Official Despatches*, 235. This implies the enemy on an approaching course, but Harper V makes the enemy on an opening course on a NE bearing.

[32] Von Hase, 144.

[33] *Lion*, 4.43 pm.

[34] *Nomad* and *Nestor* (British); V.27 and V.29 (German).

[35] A = at battle cruisers; B = at Battle Fleet; C = at destroyers. *Nestor* 3 A, 1 B; *Nomad* (when stopped) 4 B; *Nicator* 2 A, 1 B; *Petard* 1 C, 3 A; *Nerissa* 2 A; *Turbulent* unknown; *Termagant* 0; *Narborough* and *Pelican* did not attack; *Morris* 0; *Obdurate* 0; *Moorsom* 4 B. Total 10 A, 10 B, 1 C = 21. Hits 1 (V.27). Torpedoes fired by Germans = 12; hits, nil.

hits were made on the enemy's big ships,[36] but the attack had thrown out the fire of his heavy guns.[37]

All this time while the destroyers were firing at one another in between the lines, the thunder of the heavy guns had continued over their heads. At 4.33 the fire of the *Lion* and *Princess Royal* forced the *Lützow* to turn away.[38] She was badly hit and on fire, and she did not resume her Southerly course till 4.49 pm.[39]

The increasing range threw out the German fire, and for ten minutes[40] the *Derfflinger* did not fire a single round from her big guns, mainly owing to the smoke of the destroyer action raging between the lines, partly also to the fire of the 6 in. guns[41] throwing out the control. As the British destroyers approached, the German ships could also see the 5th Battle Squadron coming up,[42] and began zigzagging to throw out their fire. At 4.49 the destroyer attack was spent, and the *Lützow* turned to a Southerly course. The van of the High Sea Fleet was in sight, and at 4.53 Admiral Hipper turned to starboard and took station some 7 miles ahead of it. His ships were all in a condition to renew the action.[43]

Chapter IV endnote

Beatty's handling of his ships in the opening phases of the battle cruiser action has recently been criticised by John Brooks (Brooks, *Dreadnought Gunnery and the Battle of Jutland*, 232–8). Basing his analysis on a close study of rangefinder readings, signals, reports and eyewitness accounts, Brooks goes beyond the long-standing controversy over Beatty's handling of the 5th BS – his handling of the 2nd BCS was equally dilatory. He observes that '. . . in the forty-five

---

[36] Scheer, *Germany's High Seas Fleet*, 145 and note *infra*.

[37] *Editor's note*: Von Hase would note 'numerous' hits from the destroyers' guns on *Derfflinger*, though they had no real effect (*Kiel and Jutland*, 166–7). The British destroyers did in fact score one torpedo hit on *Seydlitz* – usually credited to *Petard*, but Campbell (*Jutland*, 56) suggests that it may have been *Turbulent*.

[38] *Editor's note*: It was the threat of destroyer torpedoes which caused the German battle cruisers to alter course, not BCF gunnery (see Marder, *FDSF*, 3:69 and Campbell, *Jutland*, 51).

[39] Course at 4.20, S; 4.28, SE by S; 4.33, ESE; 4.36, E.

[40] From 4.36 to 4.45, Von Hase, 103.

[41] *Editor's note*: To be precise, all the German battle cruisers had a secondary battery of 15cm (5.9in) 45 calibre guns.

[42] Von Hase (I.D. 1120) 28.

[43] The damage done to the German battle cruisers in this phase of the action was considerable, but German information on the point is not conclusive. The *Lützow* was badly hit and on fire about 4.30 pm. Von Hase distinctly mentions three hits on the *Derfflinger* and says that the enemy (the *Queen Mary*) shot splendidly (I.D. 1220, 25, 27). The *Moltke* had only four hits, and all of these were on the starboard side. At least two out of the *Von der Tann*'s four hits were also on the starboard side. Five or six of the hits on the *Seydlitz* were on the starboard side, one of which was a hit on No. 4 turret by a 13.5 shell at about 15,310 yards which necessitated the turret being abandoned, and which was possibly *Queen Mary*'s about 4 pm.

minutes since *Galatea* had reported "smoke as though from a fleet", Beatty had taken no steps to form his line or even concentrate his forces' (Brooks, 234).

The sequence of events runs as follows: *Galatea* signalled her sighting of 'smoke as though from a fleet' at 2.39 pm, but it was only at 3.34 that Beatty ordered the 2nd BCS (*New Zealand* and *Indomitable*) to form up astern of *Lion* and the 1st BCS (*Princess Royal*, *Queen Mary* and *Tiger*); since the 2nd BCS was still two miles off *Lion*'s port bow, this required the squadron to follow an S-shaped path. At 3.45 Beatty ordered his ships to form a line of bearing to the NW, in order to keep clear of the smoke of the leading ships; this manoeuvre probably took about seven minutes – not the three or four minutes suggested by the *Appreciation* – an estimate based on information from Captain Peter Grindal, RN (Brooks, 275 n.31). Thus when the Germans opened fire at 3.47 Beatty's ships were still in the process of assuming their fighting formation, and four of his six ships probably could fire with their forward turrets only. Moreover, it was the midst of changing formation, at 3.46, that Beatty issued a fire-distribution order – which was missed by *Tiger* and *New Zealand*, perhaps because all these signals were made by flags alone while a lot was going on. As a result, the BCF began the action with little more than half its available gun-power. Even worse, since the ships were still manoeuvring, they could not aim their guns properly.

These problems – confused or belated signals and the apparent carelessness in handling squadrons – plagued Beatty throughout the battle cruiser action. Beatty's tactics, which involved frequent course changes that imposed high closing or opening rates on his fire-control teams, hindered the gunnery of the BCF, which proved less than adequate even when the visibility conditions are taken into account. Brooks concludes: 'Beatty's gunnery defeat in the Run to the South was due primarily to the consequences of his tactics, compounded by the inefficiency of his battlecruisers' gunnery' (Brooks, 284).

There are, of course, no hints of any of this in the *Naval Staff Appreciation*.

CHAPTER V

GERMAN BATTLE FLEET IN SIGHT. THE ACTION FROM 4.40 PM TO 5.40 PM

37. The *Southampton* was the first to see the enemy Battle Fleet. She was two or three miles ahead of the *Lion* and sighted an enemy cruiser at half-past four. Following it to the South-East she sighted the head of the enemy Battle Fleet three minutes afterwards, and immediately flashed the signal, 'Battleships South-East' to the *Lion*. This was followed by a more detailed report five minutes later,[1] and the *Champion*, who had also sighted them, sent in a signal at the same time.[2] The signalled positions of both the *Southampton* and *Champion* were considerably[3] out, which must be attributed partly to the awkward and ponderous method then in vogue for translating latitude and longitude into a code form. These errors[4] did not affect Admiral Beatty, for both ships were only a few miles off, and before the *Champion*'s signal got through, and probably before he himself had seen the *Southampton*'s second report,[5] the enemy Battle Fleet was in sight from his own flagship. It was the first time it had been seen since that momentous hour when the war began, and with Jellicoe's Battle Fleet hurrying down only 50 miles away, the door of a great opportunity seemed at last to be on the point of opening.

---

[1] Senior Officer, 2nd Light Cruiser Squadron, to Commander-in-Chief, Senior Officer Battle Cruiser Forces. Have sighted enemy Battle Fleet bearing approximately SE. Course of enemy North. My position Lat. 56° 34' N, Long. 6° 20' E, 1638. Received *Lion* (w), 4.40; *Iron Duke*, 4.35; *New Zealand*, 4.38; *Barham*, 4.40.

[2] Course of enemy Battle Fleet is ENE single line ahead. Van, Dreadnoughts. Bearing of centre SE. My position 56° 51' N, 5° 46' E, 1630. *Champion*'s time of origin 1630 is evidently a mistake for 1638. The *Southampton* was ahead of the *Champion* and her brief signal at 4.33 bears all the stamp of a first report.

[3] *Champion*'s is about 12 miles to northward of actual position, *Southampton*'s about 13¼ miles 98° from actual position, according to Harper V.

[4] The effect of these errors in the Commander-in-Chief's view of the situation will be dealt with in the next Chapter.

[5] *Lion* received *Champion*'s signal at 4.47; *Southampton*'s at 4.40 pm.

Two of Admiral Beatty's ships[6] had been lost, but if Scheer could be brought within range of the thunderbolt coming down on him from the North-West, their loss would be amply avenged and would bulk small in the disaster menacing him.

Scheer's appearance probably came as something of a surprise, for only a few hours before, Admiral Beatty had seen an intercepted signal from the Admiralty to the Commander-in-Chief stating that directionals placed the

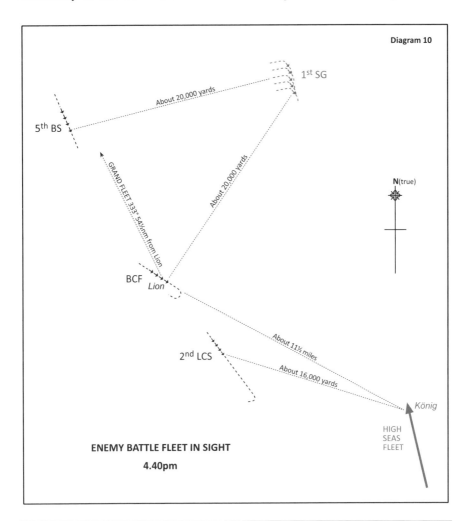

[6] There appears to be little doubt that the destruction of the *Queen Mary* was caused by shell-fire igniting charges in the turret or working chamber, the flash from which was conveyed down the trunk to the handing room and magazine. If the danger from this cause had been more fully appreciated, the risk could have been decreased and the ship would probably have come through the battle in safety. It is uncertain whether the loss of the *Indefatigable* was due to the same cause or whether a shell pierced her armour and burst in the vicinity of the magazine.

enemy flagship in the Jade at 11.10 a.m. and they were sighted some 180 miles from it at half-past four. They were now plainly visible. The head of their line was some 11½ miles off to the South-East, and the signal went up to turn 16 points to starboard, followed almost immediately by the destroyer recall[7] (Diagram 10). Hipper's battle cruisers were some ten miles off to the north-eastward when the *Lion* turned.

Scheer Sights Beatty's Squadron

38.   Scheer's fleet,[8] which had just appeared, consisted of the 3rd, 1st and 2nd Squadrons, numbering 16 modern battleships and 6 pre-Dreadnoughts. In the van was the 5th Division comprising the newest and strongest ships of the *König* class. With the Battle Fleet was the 4th Scouting Group of 5 light cruisers, the *Rostock* with the 3rd, 5th, and 7th Flotillas, and the 11th Half Flotilla, 38 destroyers in all. He had received the news of the British battle cruisers at 3.25 pm and at 4.05 had altered course to North-West and increased to 15 knots. At 4.20 he had shaped course West, hoping to pass to southward of the British and catch them between two fires, but news arrived shortly afterwards of the presence of British battleships, and, fearing the position of the 1st Scouting Group might become critical, he altered course again to North.

At 4.32 he sighted the ships in action some 15 miles off[9] to the NW. His fleet was at this time in line ahead steering North at 15 knots with ships 2½ cables and squadrons 3,500 metres (1.9 miles) apart, screened by light cruisers and torpedo craft.

At 4.45 pm he increased to 17 knots and altered course by divisions, leaders together to NNW, going on to full speed about 4.55 pm. The *Regensburg* with the 3rd Flotilla and 1st Half Flotilla were a couple of miles on the starboard beam of the leading squadron, while the 7th and 5th Flotillas were on the starboard beam[10] of the 1st Squadron. Hipper had seen the *König* coming up,

---

[7] Signal to alter course 4.40 pm; 4.43 destroyer's recall.

[8] 1st Squadron, 1st Division: *Friedrich der Grosse* (flag), *Ostfriesland*, *Thuringen*, *Helgoland*, *Oldenburg*; 2nd Division: *Posen*, *Rheinland*, *Nassau*, *Westfalen*; 2nd Squadron, 3rd Division: *Deutschland*, *Hessen*, *Pommern*; 4th Division: *Hannover*, *Schlesien*, *Schleswig-Holstein*; 3rd Squadron, 5th Division: *König*, *Grosser Kurfurst*, *Kronprinz*, *Markgraf*; 6th Division: *Kaiser*, *Kaiserin*, *Prinzregent Luitpold*.

[9] Scheer's report, *Official Despatches*, 592. *Lion* was then N 39 W 15½ miles from *König*; the 2nd Light Cruiser Squadron was then 12 miles from *König*, and was probably the ship first sighted. Cf. 4.33, when *Southampton* sighted the enemy.

[10] *Official Despatches*, German VI, Diagram 1.

and he now turned 16 points and took station about 7 miles ahead of her.[11] It was 4.50 when Von Hase in the *Derfflinger* told his guns that the 3rd Squadron was coming up. The *König* and her proud sisters seemed to them the harbingers of victory and they were burning to win fresh laurels. But the day was not over yet.

39. When the *Lion* turned at 4.41 pm the *Southampton*, a couple of miles ahead of her, gallantly held on for a time to get a better view of the enemy fleet, but at 4.45 came under a heavy fire at about 13,000 yards, which forced her to turn and follow the Battle Cruiser Squadrons now some five miles off to the North-West. Salvos were falling around her for some time sending torrents of spray over the bridge and the navigator, whose time was wholly taken up with zigzagging to avoid them. She kept the enemy Battle Fleet in sight, however, and between 4.38 and 5 pm sent to the Commander-in-Chief three reports whose value was unfortunately diminished by errors and discrepancies of position.

The 5th Battle Squadron still on a Southerly course was now rapidly closing Beatty's battle cruisers. When the action commenced it found itself seven miles on the *Lion*'s port quarter,[12] and though the *Barham* and *Warspite* opened fire on the 2nd Scouting Group about 4 pm[13] and drove them to the eastward, it was not till ten minutes later that they were able to range on the German battle cruisers.[14] The enemy replied at 4.21 and straddled the *Barham*, hitting her a few minutes later, but doing no serious damage. The fire had then slackened and tended to become intermittent owing to decreasing visibility. To the South-East the light was growing steadily worse and the enemy battle cruisers were gradually becoming merged in a grey background, illuminated fitfully by the flashes of their guns, while to the South-West our own destroyers silhouetted against a clear horizon showed that the squadron presented a good target to the enemy.[15] The range, however, was too great for him and his fire was intermittent and desultory. At 4.40 pm when the enemy destroyers attacked, Rear-Admiral Evan Thomas had made a signal to turn two points away, which was apparently

---

[11] Harper V makes Hipper's 16 point turn at 4.46 pm and puts them seven miles apart at 4.51; Scheer's diagram, German V, makes them turn at 4.48 pm. Von Hase's track and the revised track makes the turn at 4.53 pm.

[12] Harper V.

[13] *Barham* (r), 3.58 at 17,000 yards; *Warspite*, 4.02; *Valiant*, 4.01.

[14] *Barham* on *Von der Tann* at 19,500, 4.11; *Warspite*, 4.14; *Malaya* on *Von der Tann* at 18,500, 4.15.

[15] *Barham* (r), *Official Despatches*, 193-199; *Malaya* (r), ibid., 217.

carried out about 4.46.[16] By this time the *Lion* was returning at full speed on a
Northerly course. She was soon on the port bow of the *Barham* with a signal
flying to the 5th Battle Squadron to turn 16 points[17] in succession.[18] She passed
about two miles off on the port hand about 4.53 and the 5th Battle Squadron
turned to starboard shortly afterwards.[19] They had hitherto seen nothing of the
German Battle Fleet, but as the *Warspite*, the rear ship of the line, turned, she
sighted it, and the *Barham* saw it, too, to the SSE as she steadied on a Northerly
course. Her turn had been delayed, and the *Lion* was now some three or four
miles off on the starboard bow.

Course at 1645 to Join the Commander-in-Chief

40. When the *Lion* turned at 1645 she had to draw the enemy back to the
Main Fleet, and the relative position of the two flagships was therefore a
question of primary importance. At 4.45 Admiral Beatty sent a signal to the
Commander-in-Chief reporting the enemy Battle Fleet bearing SE and giving
his own position in Lat. 56° 36' N, Long. 6° 04' E[20] This signal was made

---

[16] *Valiant* (r).

[17] *Lion* (s), 4.48.

[18] *Editor's note*: Andrew Gordon argues that the 4.48 time cited was the time the signal was
hoisted, but was not made executive (i.e., hauled down) until about 4.54, which is the real reason
for Evan-Thomas' delay in turning (Gordon, *Rules of the Game*, 129–40). If so, this would be
another example of *Lion*'s sloppy signalling organisation, usually attributed to his flag-lieutenant,
Ralph Seymour.

[19] Harper V makes them turn at 4.56; *Barham* (r), 4.53; *Warspite* (r), 4.56; *Valiant* (r), 4.57;
Malaya (r), 4.57.

[20] (a) 'Have sighted enemy's Battle Fleet bearing SE. My position Lat. 56° 36'N, Long. 6°
04'E, 1645' (*Official Despatches*, 453); (b) *Lion* (s): 'Flag to *Princess Royal*. Report enemy's Battle
Fleet to Commander-in-Chief bearing SE, 1645'; (c) *Barham* (w). *Princess Royal* to Commander-
in-Chief, urgent, 1645. To Commander-in-Chief from Senior Officer, Battle Cruiser Force: 'Have
sighted enemy Battle Fleet bearing SE 96. F. V. 63, received 5.10 pm'; (d) *Benbow* (s): 'W/T
1645, urgent. Battleship ? Number of enemy ships 26–30, bearing SSE. Course SE. 96 F. V. 63,
received 5.08'; (e) *Iron Duke* (s) has '1645. 26–30 battleships, probably hostile, bearing SSE,
steering SE. 96 F. V. 63, received 5.05 pm'; (f) *Marlborough* (w) and (s) *Princess Royal* to
Commander-in-Chief, Senior Officer, Battle Cruiser Force to Commander-in-Chief: 'Have
sighted enemy's Battle Fleet, bearing approximately SE. My position 96 F. V. 63. 1645, received
5.08 pm'; (g) *Minotaur* (s). Senior Officer, Battle Cruiser Force, to Commander-in-Chief: 'Have
sighed the enemy's Battle Fleet bearing SE. 96 F.V. 63'. The errors apparently originated in the
Benbow, which was acting as 'stand by' ship on 'S' wave. The signal does not appear to have been
received on main W/T in the *Iron Duke*. Note: *Official Despatches*, 453, in giving the
Commander-in-Chief's version, omits the *Lion*'s position, which he undoubtedly received.

Editor's note: The notation '96 F.V. 63', which appears in several of the signals transcribed
above, seems to indicate where the ship's position was to be inserted; in the *Official Despatches*,
this notation is replaced by the latitude and longitude of the reporting ship.

correctly by the *Princess Royal*, and taken in correctly by some of the ships of the Grand Fleet, but in the form in which the flagship received it at 5.05 pm it made the enemy steering SE. This error did not affect the *Lion*'s position, which got through correctly, so that by 5.05 pm the Commander-in-Chief knew where the *Lion* was, or thought she was.[21] The next question is the position of the Commander-in-Chief as known to the *Lion*. The last position made by the Commander-in-Chief placed him at 3.15 in 57° 50' N, 4° 15'E, proceeding SE by S at 19 knots. This signal, sent at 3.26 and received about 3.38 pm,[22] was what the *Lion*'s navigator had to work with at 4.45 pm, and it made the Commander-in-Chief at 1645 in 57° 30' N, 4° 56½' E, that is, 66 miles 325° (N 22 W) from the *Lion*.

On the basis of these figures the course to join him would have been N 14 W; the course steered was Northerly,[23] governed probably by the necessity of keeping in touch with the enemy battle cruisers and covering the destroyers of the 13th Flotilla returning from their attack.

The Run to the North, 4.45 pm to 5.35 pm

At 4.45 pm the enemy battle cruisers bore from the *Lion* some nine miles North-East, and their Battle Fleet about ten miles South-East.[24]

Three or four minutes later fire was re-opened by the *Lion* for a few minutes, and by 4.50 all the battle cruisers except the *New Zealand*, which could not get the requisite elevation of her guns, were in action again at a range of over 18,000 yards.[25] The enemy replied with a heavy fire, and succeeded in obtaining a few more hits.

The *Lion* was hit by two shells, one of which went through the upper deck and exploded on the inboard side of the 4 in. armour, the port side, and another wrecked the galley and caused many casualties amongst the gun crews. A fire, too, which had been smouldering in Q turret ignited the charges still in the trunks and killed all the magazine and shell room parties below, but the

---

[21] The *Lion*'s signalled position is six miles 277° (or approximately WNW) from Harper's.

[22] *Iron Duke* (s), 3.34; *Minotaur* (s), 3.38; *Lion* (w/e), 3.38; *Barham* (s), 3.39; *New Zealand*, 3.35; *Falmouth* (s), 3.37.

[23] In Harper V, North; *Lion* (r) North; Harper (text, 23), merely says a 'Northerly course'; *New Zealand* (log), 4.50 pm, N by W.

[24] The revised track makes them 9¼ miles N. E. and 10¼ miles S E by E.

[25] Salvos were fired by the *Lion* at 4.48, 4.49, 4.50½, 4.52½ at the (?) *Von der Tann*. Then no more till 4.57½, 4.58½, 5.00½, then five between 5.01½ and 5.04 (*Lion* T.S. record). It would appear that fire was re-opened about 4.50 on the battle cruisers still steering a Southerly course till about 4.53. The enemy's turn with the resulting smoke and confusion threw out the British fire. Then about 4.58 they were again visible and fire was re-opened till about 5.08 pm, when the enemy was lost sight of in mist and smoke.

magazine doors were closed, and the squadron was saved from another disastrous explosion.

The increased range and decreased visibility rendered the fire much less effective, and the rear ships of the German battle cruisers may have been firing at the 5th Battle Squadron, for neither the *Tiger* nor the *New Zealand* received a single hit.[26]

At 5 pm the *Lion* altered course to NNW, to establish her junction with the Commander-in-Chief (Diagram 11[27]). The visibility was becoming worse and worse. Earlier in the day light mists had been driving down, but the enemy battle cruisers now became obscured in mist and could barely be seen. The conditions were peculiarly unfavourable to the British, for the mist only extended to the eastward; to the westward all was clear, and they themselves were silhouetted against a sharp yellow horizon.

By this time all the light cruisers had joined up, and were in visual touch. The 1st Light Cruiser Squadron and *Galatea* had been sighted at 5 pm on the starboard bow. They had lost sight of the *Lion*'s squadron at 3.45 pm, and followed the 2nd Scouting Group to the eastward for a time; then turning to the SE had come down practically along the track of the 1st Scouting Group, and at 5 pm had sighted the battle cruisers on the starboard bow coming North. As Admiral Beatty turned to the NNW, they shaped a converging course to the north–westward to take station ahead of him.

The 3rd Light Cruiser Squadron (*Falmouth*), a couple of miles to the northward of the *Galatea*, followed suit. The 2nd Light Cruiser Squadron (*Southampton*), which held on for a time when the *Lion* turned at 4.45, was gradually coming up on her port quarter, but was still some five miles off.

The *Onslow* and *Moresby* (13th Flotilla), who had been helping the *Engadine*, came down from the northward about this time, and, finding themselves between the lines on the enemy's bow, closed to make an attack. The *Onslow* was driven off by the 2nd Scouting Group, but the *Moresby*, at 5.10, managed to fire a torpedo at the *Kronprinz*[28] at about 8,000 yards without effect.

The *Lion* could now see all her cruisers, and some 3½ miles astern of her was the 5th Battle Squadron. Its two leading ships, the *Barham* and *Valiant*,

---

[26] *Editor's note*: At 4.44 the German battle cruisers had been ordered to fire on the 5th BS (Campbell, *Jutland*, 55). When the battleships were masked by Beatty's battle cruisers, the German ships shifted their fire to the latter.

[27] *Editor's note*: The 5th BS was more likely on the BCF's starboard quarter (see Gordon, *Rules of the Game*, 405), not the port quarter, as indicated in Diagram 11.

[28] The third ship of the Dreadnought line; *Moresby* (r), *Official Despatches*, 238.

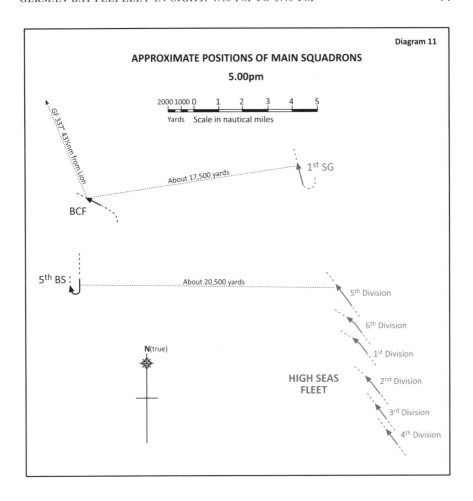

Diagram 11

APPROXIMATE POSITIONS OF MAIN SQUADRONS

5.00pm

2000 1000 0   1   2   3   4   5

Yards   Scale in nautical miles

GF 337° 43½nm from Lion

1st SG

About 17,500 yards

BCF

5th BS

About 20,500 yards

5th Division

6th Division

1st Division

N(true)

HIGH SEAS
FLEET

2nd Division

3rd Division

4th Division

were engaging the battle cruisers; its rear ships, the *Warspite* and *Malaya*, the enemy's Battle Fleet. It will be remembered that the 5th Battle Squadron had held on for a mile or two at 4.50, when the Vice-Admiral signalled to it to turn. This brought it under a heavy fire from the *König*, and the leading division of the Battle Fleet.[29] The *Barham* had hardly turned when she was hit by a heavy shell which went through the glacis the starboard side forward, and burst on the main deck, wrecking the auxiliary wireless, putting her wireless set out of action, and causing heavy casualties among the W/T staff and medical parties. The flash passed up to the battery deck, starting a serious cordite fire in S.2

---

[29] *Editor's note*: The Dewars are correct here. Although Campbell (*Jutland*, 98) denies that the German battleships were firing at the 5th BS during their turn, this does not seem to be supported by the evidence (see Gordon, *Rules of the Game*, 141–6, 614–19).

casemate, which put the guns' crew out of action. Three other hits were received, but the damage done by them was less serious.[30]

The *Valiant* was engaged intermittently with the *Derfflinger* on the Northern course, and not only escaped injury but seems to have obtained two or three hits.[31]

The *Warspite* was heavily hit, and most of the hits she received seem to have been in this phase of the action.[32] One of the first hits went through the side armour on the boys' mess deck, bursting in a 'terrific sheet of golden flame, stink and impenetrable dust',[33] and starting all the fire brigade souvenir hunting. Another blew in the side aft and began to flood the steering compartment. Another burst in the captain's lobby reducing it to a state of indescribable wreckage. Further forward, X turret was hit and water was flooding through a hole in the side and going down the engine room supply trunk. Another took away the engineer's office.

The *Malaya*, too, suffered severely. She herself was firing at the *König*,[34] but the leading German Division concentrated on her with the evident intention of disabling her and making her fall behind, and at one time salvos were falling round her at the rate of six a minute. At 5.05 the enemy had her range and forced her to haul out to port, and for the next 20 minutes she was constantly straddled. At 5.20 two shells struck her below the water line, one of which burst on impact and made a rent in both inner and outer bottoms, flooding the wing compartments[35] and giving her a list. At 5.30 pm another shell penetrated the forecastle deck the starboard side, and bursting inside the starboard battery, wrecked it, starting a fire, and causing 102 casualties. The 5th Battle Squadron in this phase of the action suffered severely, and its apparent inability with a speed of 25 knots[36] to escape from the *König* class, which were credited by the Intelligence Division with only 20.5, gave rise to an exaggerated idea of the

---

[30] The main wireless feeder and action feeder were both severed.

[31] Von Hase, 109.

[32] Probably eight or nine out of the 13. The *Warspite*'s dramatic turn at 'Windy Corner' seems to have led to an exaggerated estimate of the damage received there.
Editor's note: Here, too, the *NSA* account is probably accurate: it seems likely that *Warspite* was hit several times during this phase of the action, and not twice as recorded by Campbell (*Jutland*, 130).

[33] Fawcett and Hooper, *Fighting at Jutland*, 139.

[34] *Malaya* (r), *Official Despatches*, 218.

[35] At Station 98. Projectile Committee Report, 1917, 72.

[36] *Editor's note*: The best speed of the *Queen Elizabeth*s is occasionally called into question, in part because Jellicoe himself (Jellicoe, *Grand Fleet*, 330) makes it sound as if the 5th Battle Squadron wasn't capable of much more than 23 knots. In fact, as designed, the ships were intended to make 25 knots, and most could touch this speed under the right conditions. Raven

König's speed, and led the Commander-in-Chief not only to think that the information supplied by the Intelligence Division was wrong, but to the more general conclusion that all German ships possessed a speed much in excess of their nominal design.[37] The explanation, however, is simple. The 5th Battle Squadron was going at least 24 knots up to 5 pm, and the *König* just over 20: the superior speed of the former was never really in doubt. The maintenance of the range was due not to the latter's speed, but to the fact that the *Barham* and *König* were steering on converging courses.[38] Had the *Barham* turned away, she would quickly have opened the range, but her course had to be governed by considerations of covering the Battle Cruiser Force and of joining the Grand Fleet. Only for a short time[39] did she turn to a parallel course and she never turned right away, for this would have delayed her junction with the Grand Fleet. The *Lion* had turned in ample time, but the three or four minutes that the *Barham* held on to the southward after passing the *Lion* meant an appreciable difference of bearing between the *König* and *Barham*.[40] At 5 pm the *Barham* increased to 25 knots and at 5.13 turned to NW for seven or eight minutes. By 5.26 the shots were becoming fewer and fewer and the action was gradually broken off. The whole force was speeding to the northward to join the Commander-in-Chief (Diagram 12).

To the German battle cruisers this phase of the action was as disappointing as the first had been full of promise.[41]

Their guns were outranged, and Von Hase in the *Derfflinger* confined himself to firing single rounds from one turret. The British battle cruisers were disappearing in mist and smoke, and it was to little purpose that at 5.21 Admiral Scheer ordered Hipper to 'pursue', for his ships could do no more than 25

---

and Roberts (*British Battleships of World War Two*, 27) show *Warspite* managing 24.65 knots, and *Malaya* hitting 25 knots, but these were not true measured-mile trials. In July 1916 *Barham* did venture out on to a measured mile, displacing 32,252 tons – well over her designed load displacement – and reaching only 23.91 knots. Much depended on their displacement, and how long it had been since their bottoms were last cleaned, but overall the squadron can be considered capable of managing 24 to 24.5 knots, under most circumstances.

[37] Commander-in-Chief's despatch, June 18, 1918, para. 4, *Official Despatches*, 2; also in Jellicoe, *Grand Fleet*, 330: 'The fact that the 5th Battle Squadron was unable to increase its distance . . . comes as an unpleasant surprise. It is quite evident that all German ships possess a speed much in excess of that for which they are nominally designed'.

[38] From 5.00 to 5.08 *Barham*'s course N 16 E, *König*'s NNW; between 5 pm and 5.42 the *Barham*'s mean course was N by W, *König*'s NW by N.

[39] Between 5.12 pm and 5.20 when range opened 1,400 yards; Harper VIII.

[40] About seven degrees. About 1,200 yards, too, in distance – little enough at 22,000, but still something.

[41] Von Hase (I.D. 1220), 30.

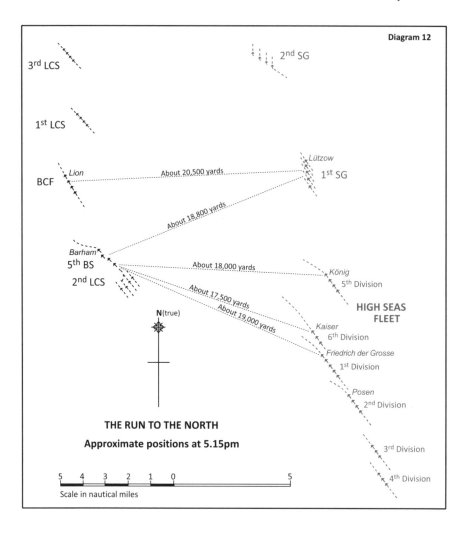

Diagram 12

3rd LCS

2nd SG

1st LCS

Lützow

Lion   About 20,500 yards   1st SG

BCF

About 18,800 yards

Barham
5th BS   About 18,000 yards   *König*
                                                                    5th Division
2nd LCS
                              About 17,500 yards
                                                          HIGH SEAS
                          About 19,000 yards   **FLEET**
N(true)
                                                       Kaiser
                                                        6th Division

                                                     Friedrich der Grosse
                                                        1st Division

                                                     Posen
                                                        2nd Division

THE RUN TO THE NORTH

Approximate positions at 5.15pm
                                                        3rd Division

5   4   3   2   1   0   5
                                                        4th Division
Scale in nautical miles

knots while the British appeared to be 'romping'[42] away at 28 knots. They
turned their guns on the 5th Battle Squadron, but found that the British were
able to keep them under fire at ranges too great for the 12 in. guns to reply –
conditions which evoked a sense of depression and anxiety and kept their nerves
constantly on the stretch.[43]

Von Hase states that the salvos pitched well together with a maximum spread
of 400 or 500 yards, but they fell at very irregular distances. Due perhaps to the
depressing conditions emphasised by Von Hase or to a reduction of their speed
by damage, the 'pursuit' ordered by the German Commander-in-Chief does

---

[42] '*Lief uns spielend*', Von Hase, 109.
[43] Von Hase, 110.

not seem to have been very ardently performed, for their own diagram credits them with a speed of only about 22 knots.[44]

The State of the Battle Cruiser Force

In the lull between 5.10 pm and 5.40 pm Admiral Beatty may have found time to review the state of his force. Their speed had not been reduced. Of the ships that were left, the *Lion* had suffered most heavily and Q turret was out of action; the *Tiger* was making water in a wing compartment aft, which had been penetrated by a shell, but the damage was not serious.[45] The *New Zealand* had not been hit.

The state of the 5th Battle Squadron was equally satisfactory. Both the *Barham* and the *Malaya* had suffered severe casualties in their 6 in. batteries, and the *Warspite* had been heavily hit but none of them were seriously damaged, their turrets were all in action, their engines were intact, and the *Valiant* had not been hit.[46]

Every minute, too, was bringing them nearer and nearer to the Main Fleet, and the Vice-Admiral could look forward with confidence to a renewal of the action.

---

[44] Harper VIII gives them 20 to 21 knots.

[45] *Tiger* had flooded Q magazine. These details were not known to the Senior Officer, Battle Cruiser Force, till later.

[46] Hits received up to 5.40 pm on Southerly and Northerly courses (from report of Projectile Committee, 1917):

	Southerly	Northerly		Southerly	Northerly
Lion	10	2	*Barham*	2	4
Princess Royal	2	0	*Valiant*	0	0
Tiger	4	0	*Warspite*	3 (a)?	5 (a)
New Zealand	0	0	*Malaya*	3	4

(a) Approximate estimate only

CHAPTER VI

COMMANDER-IN-CHIEF'S VIEW OF THE SITUATION, 2 PM TO 5 PM

41. Leaving the Battle Cruiser Force hastening northward, we must turn to the doings of the Battle Fleet and look at the situation from the point of view of the Commander-in-Chief. At 2 pm he was, according to the *Iron Duke*'s reckoning, still some 20 miles from his rendezvous,[1] proceeding quietly at 15 knots,[2] and, in view of the Admiralty signal[3] which located Scheer's flagship in the Jade, probably not in any immediate expectation of an encounter. The first sign of the enemy came from the *Galatea* at 2.20 pm, and the two other signals made by her in the next quarter of an hour confirmed the first report. It was clear that enemy light forces of some sort were at sea, and at 2.35 the Commander-in-Chief ordered the Fleet to raise steam for full speed.[4]

From this time up to 5.35 pm reports fall into three series:

Series I.	-	(1 hour 15 minutes) From 2.20 pm to 3.35 pm, ten reports of enemy cruisers.
Series II.	-	(19 minutes) 3.40 pm to 3.59 pm, six reports of enemy Battle cruisers.

---

[1] N 40 W, 20 miles from the rendezvous. The *Iron Duke* was actually in Lat. 57° 54½' N, Long. 3° 52' E, or 4½ miles ahead of her reckoning.

[2] *Editor's note*: This was an economical speed for his destroyers. For example, the *Acasta* class had a radius of action of about 2,750 nautical miles at 15 knots, but a mere 620 when at full power. March, *British Destroyers*, 124.

[3] Admiralty to Commander-in-Chief, 1235, see *supra*.

[4] *Official Despatches*, 443 gives a signal at 2.15 pm, Commander-in-Chief to cruisers: 'My course SE by S at 3 pm. Raise steam for full speed with all despatch'. This appears only in *Iron Duke*'s (s[1]) and (s[2]), and in the latter it has evidently been inserted by a different hand. It seems very doubtful whether it was ever actually made.

Editor's note: The published 'Record of Messages' states: 'Time of despatch shown was logged in *Iron Duke* but records cannot be found of such a signal at the time stated in any other ship's log'. What is important is the 2.35 signal from Jellicoe to the entire Fleet: 'Raise steam for full speed and report when ready to proceed'; *Official Despatches*, 443.

This is followed by an interval of 45 minutes.

Series III. – (15 minutes) 4.45 pm to 5 pm, six reports of enemy battleships.

This is followed by an interval of 30 minutes.

Each of these series falls naturally into a group by itself, and as it is justifiable to assume that each group gave rise to a fresh view of the situation, each will be considered separately.[5]

The reports up to 3 pm indicated clearly the presence of light cruiser forces in the vicinity of 57° N, 6° E, and at 3.10[6] the cruisers were ordered to take station 16 miles ahead of the Battle Fleet, but owing to their insufficient speed they never attained anything like that distance, and were actually only some four or five miles ahead when the *Black Prince* sighted the *Falmouth* coming North at 5.35 pm.

On receipt of these reports the Commander-in-Chief made a signal to prepare for action, opened his columns[7] to manœuvring distance of a mile, increased speed to 19 knots,[8] and shortly after 3.30 pm made his 3.15 position to the Senior Officer, Battle Cruiser Force.[9] His view of the situation at this time is reflected in a signal made at 3.30 to the 3rd Sub-Division and Commodore (F), stating that enemy cruisers were being chased to the North and should be in touch with our cruisers[10] by 4 pm.

Up to 3.30, then, the encounter appeared as an affair of light cruisers, and in view of the Admiralty signal of 1235 the Commander-in-Chief possibly did not expect it to develop into anything more.[11]

---

[5] For Summary of Reports of Enemy received, see Appendix F. For full text of signals, reporting enemy light cruisers from 2.20 to 3.35 pm, from *Galatea, Falmouth, Lion, Nottingham* and Admiralty, see *Official Despatches*, 444–6.

[6] *Marlborough*, (s) 3.07 pm.

[7] *Official Despatches*, 446, 316: *Iron Duke* (s¹), 3.20; *Benbow* (s), 3.16; *Marlborough* (s), 3.15.

[8] *Official Despatches*, 446, 3.18: *Benbow* (s), 3,20; *Iron Duke* (s¹), 3.25 pm.

Editor's note: 'Manoeuvring distance' meant that the columns were now separated by a distance equal to the length of each column of four battleships, which would allow the fleet to deploy into single line by a single 90° turn to port or starboard of the leading ships of each column, with the following ships turning in succession as they came up to the turning point. This was an 'equal speed' deployment, so-called because the ships would maintain a uniform speed throughout; it was the quickest form of deployment, taking only about four minutes to form line of battle.

[9] Position 3.15 pm, Lat. 57° 50' N, Long. 4° 15' E. Course SE by S, 19 knots, 1526: *Official Despatches*, 447, 3.27; *Iron Duke* (s¹), 3.27; *Iron Duke* (s²), 3.34; *Iron Duke* (w/e), 3.34; *Minotaur* (s), 3.38; *Benbow* (s), 3.36; *Marlborough* (s), 3.36; *Lion* (s), 3.38.

[10] *Official Despatches*, 449. By 'our cruisers' the Commander-in-Chief evidently meant the 3rd Battle Cruiser Squadron, 20 to 25 miles ahead.

[11] Compare the signal to destroyers at 3 pm to bank fires in boilers not required for 21 knots, followed at 3.22 by orders to raise steam for full speed; *Official Despatches*, 445, 447.

42. In the course of the next half hour, however, the situation began to harden. At 1540 an important signal came in from Beatty reporting five battle cruisers North-East of him, and between that time and four o'clock six signals were received.[12]

By the *Iron Duke*'s reckoning, the *Lion* at 3.35 pm, when she sighted the enemy, bore S 16° E, 60 miles from the Commander-in-Chief.

The positions given in the *Lion*'s signals were not reconcilable with her speed on a straight course, but the mean of these positions showed that somewhere about Lat. 56° 52' N, Long. 5° 31' E,[13] she was engaging the enemy battle cruisers on an ESE course.

At 3.55 pm an important signal arrived: Beatty was engaged. Speed was increased at 4 pm to 20 knots, and a few minutes[14] later the *Invincible* and the 3rd Battle Cruiser Squadron were sent off at full speed to support him (Diagram 13).

The *Invincible* was then some 25 miles from the *Iron Duke*, four and a half points on her port bow.[15] Her normal position was 20 miles ahead of the Battle Fleet, but at 3 pm she had been rather ahead of her station,[16] and when the *Galatea* signal came in at 3.08 pm stating the enemy light cruisers had altered course NW she had shaped course ESE at 22 knots to intercept them. Then came the *Galatea*'s signal at 3.44 pm saying the enemy had turned South and Rear-Admiral Hood had altered at 3.45 pm to S 26 E. Quarter of an hour later he received the order to support Admiral Beatty. Beatty's latest position was that made at 1550,[17] which made him at 4 pm about 48 miles S by W, steering in a South-Easterly direction, from the *Invincible*, and as the latter had no margin of speed, she could not hope to overtake or intercept him. Rear-Admiral Hood accordingly steered SSE in the hope of getting in touch – a happy course which was to disconcert the enemy and give Scheer an entirely false impression of the tactical situation.

After 4 o'clock the reports shut down, and for three-quarters of an hour the Commander-in-Chief received no news of the situation. He was evidently somewhat anxious about it, for at 4.15[18] he asked Rear-Admiral Evan-Thomas

---

[12] *See* Appendix F. For text of signals reporting enemy battle cruisers and light cruisers from *Lion*, *Galatea* and *Falmouth*, see *Official Despatches*, 449, 450.

[13] Harper V makes *Lion* at the mean of these times (3.45 pm) in Lat. 56° 53½' N, Long. 5° 27½' E, only two miles from the above position.

[14] *Official Despatches*, 451; *Iron Duke* (s¹), 1604; *Marlborough* (s), 4.12; *Benbow* (s), 4.14.

[15] Rear-Admiral Hood signalled his position shortly after 4 pm in Lat. 57° 39' N, Long. 5° 35' E.

[16] S 64 E (i.e., on port bow), 25 miles from *Iron Duke* at 3 pm.

[17] 56° 53' N, 5° 31' E.

[18] *Barham* (s), 4.24, reply 1630.

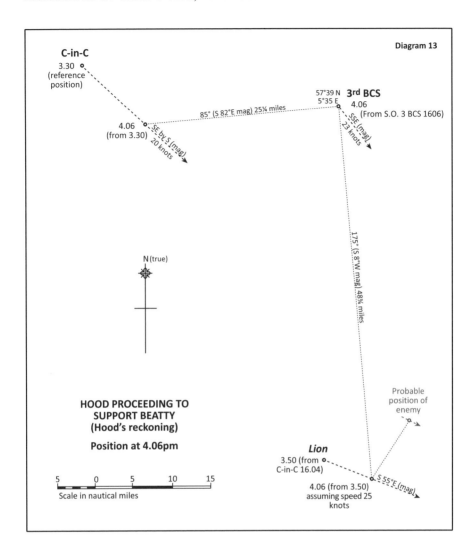

Diagram 13

C-in-C
3.30
(reference position)

57°39 N
5°35 E
3rd BCS
4.06
(From S.O. 3 BCS 1606)

85° (S 82°E mag) 25¼ miles

4.06
(from 3.30)
SE by S (mag)
20 knots

SSE (mag)
23 knots

N (true)

175° (S 8°W mag) 48¾ miles

HOOD PROCEEDING TO
SUPPORT BEATTY
(Hood's reckoning)

Position at 4.06pm

Probable
position of
enemy

Lion
3.50 (from
C-in-C 16.04)

4.06 (from 3.50)
assuming speed 25
knots

S 55°E (mag)

5   0   5   10   15
Scale in nautical miles

if the 5th Battle Squadron was in company with Beatty's force, and received a reply in the affirmative.

Commander-in-Chief Hears of Enemy Battle Fleet

43. It was now 4.30, and there was no indication of the enemy Battle Fleet appearing on the scene, but in the next quarter of an hour the whole situation underwent a dramatic change. For the first time in the war, the enemy's Battle Fleet was reported in sight. The first token of it was a signal from the *Southampton* reporting a cruiser to the South-East, followed by a definite report of the enemy Battle Fleet made at 4.33 pm, and a more detailed report at 4.38

pm with one from the *Champion* at the same time, and then five more reports[19] between 4.40 and 5 pm.

These seven signals contained very considerable discrepancies. The *Champion*'s position made her a long way off the *Southampton*,[20] and the *Southampton*'s 1638 position was 8 miles from her 1630 position, giving her a speed of 60 miles an hour. Her next signal was very little better, and made her go 6 miles in eight minutes, a speed of 45 knots.

Shortly afterwards a signal came in from the *Lion*, made at 4.45 pm, which would have cleared up the confusion had it been correctly taken in. Unfortunately it became mutilated, probably in the *Benbow*,[21] and as received by the Commander-in-Chief, reported the enemy to be steering South-East. Then at 5 pm came a signal from the Admiralty giving the enemy's position accurately at 4.09 pm, and then a final signal from the *Southampton*, concluding an admirable series unfortunately marred by faulty positions.

It is possible to reconstruct the work of an Intelligence Officer in the *Iron Duke*. A glance at the *Lion*'s signal as received in the *Iron Duke* would show that it had been mutilated, for it spoke of '26 to 30 battleships'. The course, therefore, could be rejected,[22] for all the other signals agreed on a Northerly or North-Westerly course. Then again the *Southampton*'s last signal at 5 pm was probably the most correct of her series, and as she had been asked to check her first signal she would make an effort to get her position right. Working the positions up to 5 pm (the *Lion*'s with a Northerly course), the Admiralty's 5 pm position places the enemy 8½ miles 272° from the *Southampton*'s at 5 pm, and the *Lion*'s position falls between them about 5 miles to the southward.

The mean of these three positions at the centre of the triangle would place the enemy Battle Fleet at 5 pm in 56° 34' N, 6° 11½' E, which is actually only a few miles from the actual position of the *Friedrich der Grosse*[23] (Diagram 14).

It was clear, at any rate from these signals, that the enemy Battle Fleet was coming North, and at 4.50 pm the Commander-in-Chief informed the Admiralty that a fleet action was imminent. The opportunity, which Sir Arthur Wilson had in the early days of the war rightly regarded as a dream,[24] had come.

---

[19] See *Official Despatches*, 452–4.

[20] *Champion*'s signal position was 17½ miles N 30 W of *Southampton*'s.

[21] *See* para. 40 (footnote) *supra*, p. 74 n. 20.

[22] It was rejected, for at 4.47 pm the *Iron Duke* signalled 'Enemy's Battle Fleet coming North'.

[23] Revise of track places the *Friedrich der Grosse* in 56° 36' N, 6° 08' E, or 3 miles 324° from above.

[24] 'The dream of most Naval Officers seems to be a great sea fight in which . . . we are to . . . crush the Germans at one blow. This, however, is only a dream'. M.03177, Sir A. Wilson's Minute 722/11/14, Commander-in-Chief's letter of October 30, 1914.

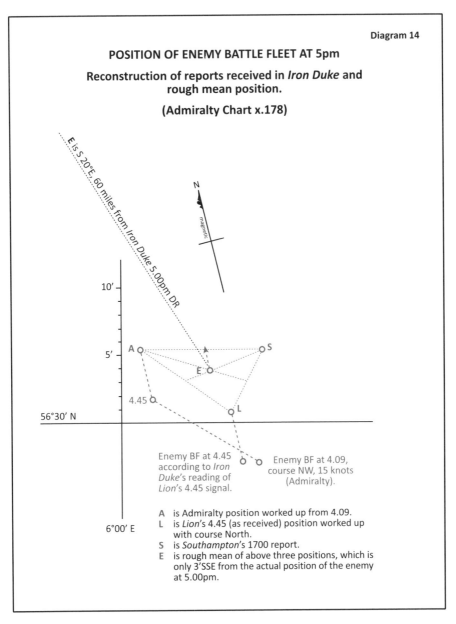

Diagram 14

POSITION OF ENEMY BATTLE FLEET AT 5pm

Reconstruction of reports received in *Iron Duke* and rough mean position.

(Admiralty Chart x.178)

Enemy BF at 4.45 according to *Iron Duke*'s reading of *Lion*'s 4.45 signal.

Enemy BF at 4.09, course NW, 15 knots (Admiralty).

A   is Admiralty position worked up from 4.09.
L   is *Lion*'s 4.45 (as received) position worked up with course North.
S   is *Southampton*'s 1700 report.
E   is rough mean of above three positions, which is only 3'SSE from the actual position of the enemy at 5.00pm.

A minute later the message charged with such tremendous issues was received at Whitehall. From the War Registry the pink sheets passed rapidly on their way – to the First Lord, the First Sea Lord, and the Chief of the War Staff, to the Directors of the two great Divisions of Operations and Intelligence, to Sir A.K. Wilson too. The whisper passed down the corridors. In Room 40 the enemy's battle signals were already coming in. A bustle began to run through the dockyards and up the East Coast. At all the ports, tugs and docks were ordered to be held in readiness, and Commodore Tyrwhitt was ordered to complete with fuel in readiness to relieve light cruisers and destroyers. The signal crossed a message from him stating that he was proceeding to sea,[25] and he was recalled.

At 5.13 the Commander-in-Chief made his position to the Senior Officer, Battle Cruiser Force.[26] This was evidently his 5 pm position,[27] but as no time was mentioned in the body of the signal, the *Lion* probably gave it the time of origin, in which case the *Iron Duke* would appear to be 13 minutes (or 4 miles) behind the Commander-in-Chief's reckoning. This in itself would not be serious, but in conjunction with other cumulative errors of reckoning, would throw out the *Lion*'s bearing of the *Iron Duke*.

From 5 pm to 5.30 there was silence for half an hour. No reports came in. The Battle Fleet was ready to deploy: its guns were manned, and every man was at his station. The mists had come down, and the columns were becoming grey and ghostly.

---

[25] *Official Despatches*, 454.

[26] *Official Despatches*, 454. 'My position Lat. 57° 25' N, 5° 12' E, steering SE by S, 20 knots 1713'.

[27] Position at 5 pm 57° 24' N, 5° 12' E, Commander-in-Chief's despatch. *Official Despatches*, 12.

CHAPTER VII

COMMANDER-IN-CHIEF IN TOUCH WITH BATTLE CRUISER FORCE, 5.35 PM TO 6.15 PM

44. The phase which follows between 5.35 and 6.15 pm is one of great importance, but of some complexity. All the forces were converging, and four encounters, all more or less coincident, require to be borne in mind. First, touch is made between Beatty's cruisers and those of the Main Fleet: secondly, Beatty renews the engagement with Hipper; thirdly, the *Chester* comes into action from the North-East with the 2nd Scouting Group, and is supported by the 3rd Battle Cruiser Squadron; fourthly, an engagement develops between the *Defence* and *Warrior* ahead of the British Battle Fleet and the light cruisers of the 2nd Scouting Group.

In the *Lion* as she sped northward, the last news of the *Iron Duke*'s position was received about 5.20 pm.[1] This signal was timed 1713 and gave the Commander-in-Chief's position as Lat. 57° 25' N, Long. 5° 12' E. This was actually his position at 5 pm, but as no particular time was given, the time of origin (namely 5.13) was probably attached to it, which would make the *Iron Duke* about 333° 30½ miles off[2] at 5.35 pm.

The *Lion* altered course at this time[3] to NNE apparently with the two-fold intention of renewing the engagement with Hipper and of striking the cruiser screen[4] which had been spread ahead of the Battle Fleet in accordance with the instructions contained in the Grand Fleet Battle Orders (Diagram 15).

---

[1] *Official Despatches*, 454 gives 5.16, but signal logs of Battle Cruiser Force are all later; *Iron Duke* (s[1]), 5.16; *New Zealand* (w), 5.19; *Falmouth* (w), 5.20; *Princess Royal* (w/e), 5.21.

[2] Beatty's despatch, *Official Despatches*, 135, gives the estimated position of the Grand Fleet as N 16 W or 331°.

[3] Harper, 5.35; Beatty's track, 5.30; Brock (r), 5.35.

[4] The course to strike the cruiser screen 10 miles ahead would have been about 6° (N 18 E).

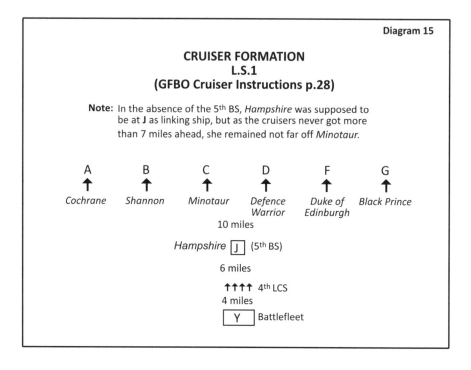

Diagram 15

CRUISER FORMATION
L.S.1
(GFBO Cruiser Instructions p.28)

Note: In the absence of the 5th BS, *Hampshire* was supposed to
be at **J** as linking ship, but as the cruisers never got more
than 7 miles ahead, she remained not far off *Minotaur*.

A	B	C	D	F	G
↑	↑	↑	↑	↑	↑
Cochrane	Shannon	Minotaur	Defence Warrior	Duke of Edinburgh	Black Prince

10 miles

Hampshire [J] (5th BS)

6 miles

↑↑↑↑ 4th LCS
4 miles

[Y] Battlefleet

The Commander-in-Chief in his dispatch[5] says that 'it was apparent on meeting that the reckoning of the Battle Cruiser Fleet was about 12 miles to the eastward of the *Iron Duke*'s reckoning'. This was the cumulative effect of a series of three errors (Diagram 16):

(a) Firstly, the *Iron Duke*'s position by reckoning at 5.13 pm was 4.3 miles (13 minutes at 20 knots) ahead of the position given to the *Lion*. This was due to the omission of a specific time in the *Iron Duke*'s signal of 1713.

(b) Secondly, the *Iron Duke*'s real position was 4½ miles ahead (that is, to south-eastward) of her reckoning.

(c) Thirdly, the *Lion* was actually some 6¾ miles to westward of her reckoning.

Contact with the enemy, however, did not depend entirely on the *Lion*'s reckoning, but on the position assigned to the enemy at 5 pm from the series of reports culminating at that time, in which the *Lion*'s reckoning was only a single factor. It would be interesting to know what was the assumed position of

---

[5] *Official Despatches*, 16.

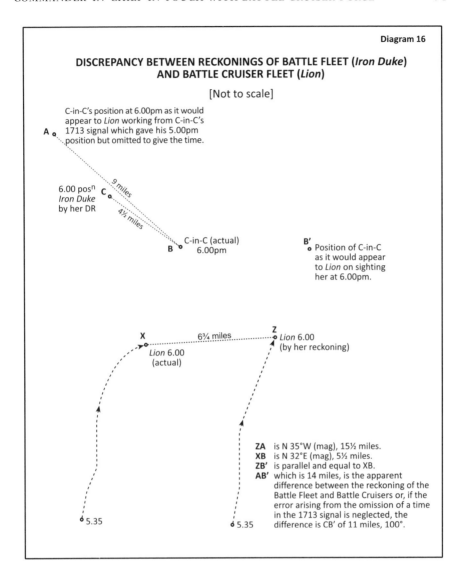

Diagram 16

**DISCREPANCY BETWEEN RECKONINGS OF BATTLE FLEET (*Iron Duke*)
AND BATTLE CRUISER FLEET (*Lion*)**

[Not to scale]

C-in-C's position at 6.00pm as it would appear to *Lion* working from C-in-C's 1713 signal which gave his 5.00pm position but omitted to give the time.

A

6.00 pos^n *Iron Duke* by her DR   C

9 miles

4½ miles

C-in-C (actual) 6.00pm   B

B' Position of C-in-C as it would appear to *Lion* on sighting her at 6.00pm.

X   6¾ miles   Z *Lion* 6.00 (by her reckoning)

Lion 6.00 (actual)

ZA is N 35°W (mag), 15½ miles.
XB is N 32°E (mag), 5½ miles.
ZB' is parallel and equal to XB.
AB' which is 14 miles, is the apparent difference between the reckoning of the Battle Fleet and Battle Cruisers or, if the error arising from the omission of a time in the 1713 signal is neglected, the difference is CB' of 11 miles, 100°.

5.35   5.35

the enemy at 5 pm, but there is no mention of this in the Commander-in-Chief's despatch.[6]

---

[6] If the enemy were assumed to maintain a Northerly course from the *Lion*'s report at 1645, he would have been approximately ahead at 6.30 pm. On the other hand, the Admiralty 1700 position would make him on the starboard bow at 6.15 pm.

Renewal of Engagement with Hipper at 5.40 pm

45. At 5.25 pm Admiral Beatty ordered his force to prepare to renew the action; quarter of an hour later the ships of the 1st Scouting Group were seen again dimly through the mist, and fire was reopened at 14,000 yards. The *Lion* and the *Princess Royal* opened on the *Lützow*, the *Tiger* on the *Seydlitz*, and the *New Zealand* on the *Derfflinger*. Hipper came under a heavy fire and things went badly with him: the setting sun was in his eyes and it was becoming more and more difficult to range and spot. The *Lützow* was heavily hit about 5.50 and her main and auxiliary wireless were put out of action. Hipper could stand it no longer, and at 5.53 turned to the eastward and withdrew.[7] He had entered what really amounted to a trap. To the North-West was the Battle Fleet; to the West, Beatty and the 5th Battle Squadron; to the eastward, Rear-Admiral Hood and the 3rd Battle Cruiser Squadron were rushing down ahead of him. He had not gone far before he heard Hood's guns ahead of him engaging the 2nd Scouting Group and turned accordingly to SE at 6.04. But he had barely gone a mile when he saw the *Shark*'s little flotilla coming out to attack. Like Von Ingenohl on December 16 he thought the British Main Fleet must be behind her and that a big torpedo attack was menacing him. He decided to retire on the Battle Fleet and at 6.07 turned to SW.

The 3rd Battle Cruiser Squadron comes into Action

46. In the meantime, while Beatty was hammering the *Lützow*,[8] the *Chester*, *Canterbury* and 3rd Battle Cruiser Squadron away to the eastward[9] had come into contact with the enemy. Since 4 pm the *Invincible* with the 3rd Battle Cruiser Squadron had been hurrying down to Beatty's support, with the *Chester* about six miles off a point or two abaft her starboard beam, and the *Canterbury* about 5 miles ahead. At 5.30 the sound of gunfire was heard to the south-westward; flashes of guns could be seen through the mist, and the *Chester* ran down to investigate. This was the roar and flash of Hipper's guns engaging

---

[7] Beatty (r), 'hauling gradually to the north-eastward'. Von Hase indicates that Beatty's reappearance greatly disconcerted them 'by completely outflanking us in spite of our utmost speed. Admiral Beatty executed a brilliant manœuvre ... compelling us to alter course, bringing us at length into a position where we were completely encircled by the British Battle Fleet'; Von Hase (I.D. 1220), 30. For the effect of the sun and the hit on the *Lützow*, see Scheer's Report, *Official Despatches*, 593.

[8] *Editor's note*: Campbell (*Jutland*, 134) notes that *Lützow* was hit five times during the 'Run to the North' – four of them being 15in shells from the 5th BS. The damage to *Lützow*'s wireless was caused by two hits at 5.25 pm. One hit at 5.45 pm was probably from *Princess Royal*, and caused minor damage.

[9] Harper VIII, 21 miles East.

the 5th Battle Squadron, and as the *Chester* came down she sighted at 5.36 pm a three-funnelled cruiser with one or two destroyers[10] showing dimly on the starboard bow. This was one of the 2nd Scouting Group under Rear-Admiral Boedicker, probably in a quarterly formation,[11] two or three miles to the north-eastward of Hipper on a North-Westerly course.[12] The *Chester* turned West to bring her guns to bear, but this course laid her open to attack by the destroyers now on her port bow, and she turned North bringing the enemy well abaft the port beam. As she turned she saw two more cruisers. They opened fire about 5.40, and the *Chester* replied at a range of about 6,000 yards[13] (Diagram 17).

She was almost immediately smothered in a hail of fire. Within five minutes three guns were disabled, a number of her men were killed and wounded, and the after gun only was left in action. But Rear-Admiral Hood had heard the firing, and at 5.37 pm had turned the 3rd Battle Cruiser Squadron round to the North-West. He was now on the *Chester*'s starboard bow coming up at full speed, and at 5.55 his 12 in. guns crashed out a reply to Boedicker and checked his relentless pursuit.

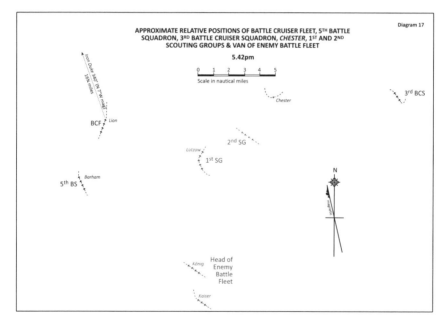

APPROXIMATE RELATIVE POSITIONS OF BATTLE CRUISER FLEET, 5TH BATTLE SQUADRON, 3RD BATTLE CRUISER SQUADRON, *CHESTER*, 1ST AND 2ND SCOUTING GROUPS & VAN OF ENEMY BATTLE FLEET

Diagram 17

5.42pm

---

[10] 12th Half-Flotilla accompanying 2nd Scouting Group.
[11] Scheer's diagram, *Official Despatches*, German IV.
[12] Scheer, N 26 W.
[13] Harper VII, 7,500 yards.

The *Chester*, badly damaged, crossed the *Invincible*'s bows and was safe. She had been under fire for 19 minutes: her guns and fire control system were badly damaged,[14] and she had suffered severe casualties, but the engines and boilers were intact, and she was able to steam. She remained to north-eastward of the 3rd Battle Cruiser Squadron, and afterwards took station astern of the *Minotaur* and 2nd Cruiser Squadron.

The alteration of the 3rd Battle Cruiser Squadron to the north-westward at 5.37 brought the *Canterbury* astern and was followed by her. About 6 pm she sighted two light cruisers on her port bow coming down on a Southerly course ahead of the enemy battle cruisers. She thereupon altered course about 14 points to port and engaged the light cruisers, which were then firing at the *Shark* and *Acasta*. The enemy turned away at 6.20, and the *Canterbury* then proceeded to the northward and joined the 3rd Light Cruiser Squadron.

This sudden appearance of heavy ships to the north-eastward fell on Boedicker like a thunderbolt. A mist was hanging over the sea, and it was impossible to make out the full extent of the British strength. He turned sharply to the South-East,[15] fired three torpedoes at the enemy, and reported them by wireless to Admiral Scheer,[16] leading the latter to think that the British Main Force had appeared to the North-East.

In spite of the fog and poor visibility, the *Wiesbaden* and *Pillau* were badly hit, the former was put out of action, and Boedicker found himself in a nasty predicament. Heavy ships were ahead and Beatty's Squadron astern, but the German 12th Half Flotilla and the 9th Flotilla were close at hand, and recognizing the gravity of the situation, pushed boldly to the front and attacked. By this time the *Wiesbaden* had set smoke boxes alight and was enveloped in a dirty white screen. The 3rd Battle Cruiser Squadron left her and passed on to the north-westward. Nine or ten German destroyers were forging ahead of the 2nd Scouting Group, and the *Shark* and *Acasta* could be seen pushing boldly out to make an attack.

---

[14] Three guns disabled, after control destroyed, electrical circuits damaged, holes in armour, two holes above armour, slight damage to two boilers from splinters, number of small steam pipes shot away. The casualties were 76 (30 killed, 2 died of wounds, 32 seriously and 12 slightly wounded), among them, the Commander, Charles Stuart Forbes, and Jack Travers Cornwell, Boy 1st Class, who gained the V.C. (Captain Robert Lawson's report of June 5, 1916, in M. 05150/1916).

Editor's note: Boy First Class John Cornwell remains the youngest V.C. winner in the Commonwealth. The gun which he served is now in the Imperial War Museum.

[15] Scheer's diagram, *Official Despatches*, German V, S 23 E. *Indomitable* (r) 'turned 16 points'.

[16] Scheer *Germany's High Seas Fleet*, 151.

It was 6.04[17] when the *Invincible* turned to the westward, steering for the sound of the guns or possibly to keep the light cruisers under fire. As she drove on, heading now towards Jellicoe and the Main Fleet, Beatty's Squadron came in sight on the port bow making to the eastward, and almost simultaneously the tracks of torpedoes could be seen coming from the direction of the enemy's light cruisers. The *Invincible* stopped and turned sharply to starboard.[18] The *Indomitable* and *Inflexible* turned too, and the torpedoes ran harmlessly past. The *Lion* was rapidly approaching from the westward, and Rear-Admiral Hood shaped on a course S 50 E to take station ahead of him. Five miles to the westward the Battle Fleet had begun to deploy. To the south-eastward the guns of the German destroyers could be heard engaging the *Shark*.

The *Shark*'s Attack, 5.50 pm

The *Shark* was leader of four destroyers,[19] acting as a screen to the 3rd Battle Cruiser Squadron, and when the *Invincible* turned to the north-westward to help the *Chester* she left the *Shark* on her port quarter. Lieutenant-Commander Loftus Jones in the *Shark* saw the 3rd Battle Cruiser Squadron open fire, and saw the enemy light cruisers turn to the south-eastward on his port bow, and at once pushed out to attack.

This was not the first time he had shown himself a bold and resolute leader. On the morning of the Scarborough raid (December 16, 1914) with only four destroyers[20] (one of them badly damaged), he had followed an enemy cruiser so stoutly to the eastward as to create the impression that a great force was behind him, inducing the Commander-in-Chief, Admiral Von Ingenohl, to turn back with the whole High Sea Fleet from a position[21] where he was advancing on Beatty and the 2nd Battle Squadron. He was now to repeat his exploit in a larger arena on a greater day.

On the port bow two or three light cruisers could be seen with the *Regensburg* and nine or ten destroyers, and the *Shark*, followed by the *Acasta*, *Ophelia* and *Christopher*, altered course to West to engage them supported by the fire of the

---

[17] This turn is not mentioned in the *Indomitable* or *Inflexible* reports, but appears in the *Indomitable*'s track; *Official Despatches*, Plate 13.

[18] Large quantities of steam were issuing from her exhaust, and she hoisted the Disregard, then hauled it down and went on at full speed. *Indomitable* (r). The cause of this action remains obscure. She certainly was not hit. The torpedoes were probably fired by the 12th Half-Flotilla and the 9th Flotilla.

[19] *Shark*, *Acasta*, *Ophelia* and *Christopher*, of the 4th Flotilla.

[20] *Shark*, *Acasta*, *Spitfire* and *Hardy* (damaged).

[21] This was not known at the time, but is now evident from German reports. (Naval Staff Monograph No. 8, C.B. 1552, 11.) This was the 'lost opportunity' which Von Tirpitz lamented so bitterly.

3rd Battle Cruiser Squadron. She fired a torpedo at the *Regensburg*,[22] then as she turned to go back, came under a heavy fire.

The pipes to her oil suction were damaged; she was forced to ease down, and finally brought to a stop. Her fore steering gear was shot away. Another shot blew away the foremost gun and she lay helpless in the water. The *Acasta* (Lieutenant-Commander John O. Barron), which had been with her on the morning of the Scarborough raid, stood stoutly by her now and offered to help, but was told by the Captain 'not to get sunk for him', and withdrew badly damaged and holed fore and aft. At this moment the *Canterbury* appeared, and drew the light cruisers off to the southward, giving the *Shark* a short respite. But soon afterwards several destroyers, probably of the 9th and 6th German Flotillas, came up and opened a heavy fire on her. The after gun was hit and all its crew killed, but the midship gun remained in action. The Captain's leg was shot off at the knee, but he continued to encourage his men, and even gave orders for a new ensign to be hoisted to replace one that was shot away. Right up to the end her single gun was firing;[23] then a destroyer came up and fired two torpedoes at her, one of which hit her near the after funnel. She took a heavy list and sank.[24]

The *Acasta*, trying to help her, had been holed fore and aft, but was still in action, and at 6.12 pm could see the battle cruisers of the 1st Scouting Group coming up again on a North-Easterly course.[25] She fired her foremost tube at them at about 4,500 yards, and hit the *Seydlitz*, then crawled off badly hit in the engine-room, with her steering gear shot away.[26]

---

[22] *Editor's note*: Spelt 'Regensberg' in the original.

[23] It possibly accounted for V.48, which belonged to the 3rd Flotilla, and was a total loss before 6.35 pm.

Editor's note: Campbell (*Jutland*, 162) credits *Shark* with hits on S.32 as well as one on V.48 which disabled her. It was S.54 which torpedoed *Shark*.

[24] A stoker Petty Officer had tied a lifebelt round Commander Jones, and as the ship sank got him on to a Carley raft. There a few hours later he succumbed from exhaustion, and the remaining survivors were picked up by the Danish S.S. *Vidar*. Commander Loftus Jones was awarded a posthumous V.C. (M. 011160/1916.)

[25] *See* para. 45, Hipper had turned to NE again at 6.12 pm.

[26] The torpedo hit on the *Seydlitz* was on the starboard side, and was received in the day action. The only attack on this side was that of the 13th Flotilla at 4.30 pm and of the *Acasta* (4th Flotilla) between 6.12 and 6.18. In the former, torpedoes were fired by the *Petard* (3), the *Nicator* (2) and the *Nestor* (2), but in view of Scheer's statement that none of the torpedoes hit (Scheer, *Germany's High Seas Fleet*, 145) they must be ruled out. The attacks by the *Moresby* and *Onslow* later are not admissible, for both fired at the port side and the former at the Battle Fleet. There remains only the *Acasta*, which fired a torpedo at the leading enemy battle cruiser at about 4500 [yards] when she attacked with the *Shark* and saw an explosion; *Official Despatches*, 307. The *Ophelia* attacked too, but fired at the port side.

Editor's note: *Acasta* actually fired at *Lützow* and missed *Seydlitz* was torpedoed at 4.57, probably by *Petard* or (less probably) by *Turbulent* (Campbell , *Jutland*, 80, 83, 117).

The *Ophelia*, which had been driven off for a time, saw the battle cruisers alter course to the southward to engage the 3rd Battle Cruiser Squadron, and attacking at full speed fired a torpedo at them as they came north.

The attack had borne good results. In its first stages it gave Hipper the impression that the Main Fleet was ahead of him, which induced him to turn to the South, and when he came North again the *Seydlitz* fell a victim to the *Acasta*'s torpedo.[27]

The *Defence* in Action, 5.47 pm to 6.16 pm

47. The period between 5.40 and 6.15 pm, when two great Battle Fleets were about to enter the arena, appears at first as a confused picture of mist and battle smoke, but out of it the various cruiser forces begin to emerge clearly enough. Beatty's guns begin to speak first, renewing the engagement with Hipper, and a little earlier[28] the *Chester*, 10 miles or so to the eastward, comes into action with Boedicker and the 2nd Scouting Group, then a mile to the eastward of Hipper. The *Lützow*, heavily hit by the *Lion* and *Princess Royal*, turns to the eastward, a bold push by the *Onslow* at this juncture perhaps contributing something to this result.[29]

The 2nd Scouting Group engaging the *Chester* suddenly finds itself under fire from the *Defence* and *Warrior* in the North-West. The *Chester* almost simultaneously turns to the north-eastward, and the 2nd Scouting Group, glad to escape from the *Defence*'s fire, follows her in hot pursuit.

A few minutes later Boedicker finds the *Invincible* and 3rd Battle Cruiser Squadron barring his path, and is forced to the south-eastward, leaving the *Wiesbaden* disabled and out of action – the *Shark*'s attack, with what he fancied might lie behind it, contributing to this result.

Hipper hears the crash of the *Invincible*'s guns, sees the *Shark*'s attack, thinks he is facing the Main British Fleet, and at 6.07 pm turns to the SW to close the German Battle Fleet. As soon as he sights it three or four miles to the westward

---

[27] 'At 5.55 we turned East, and at 6 pm, as the enemy destroyers launched their attack, the entire Battle Cruiser Squadron turned together on a Southerly course'. Von Hase (I.D. 1220, 31). Harper X has SE by S at 6.04 and SW at 6.07. Scheer, *Official Despatches*, (German Plan V), has S 24 E then SW.

[28] Beatty's renewal of engagement may be taken as at 5.41. The *Chester* came into action about 5.38.

[29] Scheer and Von Hase both mention a destroyer attack at 5.40 pm (Scheer (r), *Official Despatches*, 593; Von Hase (I.D.), 31; Scheer, *Germany's High Seas Fleet*, 140). This appears to be a magnified account of the *Onslow*'s attack. (Beatty's despatch, *Official Despatches*, 135; Tovey (r), *Official Despatches*, 227). The 1st Light Cruiser Squadron were ordered to make a torpedo attack, and increased speed to do so, but it did not materialise.

of him, he turns[30] and resumes his course to the North-East, giving the *Acasta* a chance to get her torpedo home. This represents the general trend of events up to the moment when the 1st Cruiser Squadron comes prominently on the scene.

As early as 5.47,[31] the *Defence* and *Warrior*, then about five miles ahead of the *Iron Duke*, sharp on her starboard bow,[32] had caught a glimpse of the 2nd Scouting Group, and turning three points to port opened fire at long range. As it disappeared in the mist Sir Robert Arbuthnot evidently decided to chase, and at 6 pm turned south-eastward to do so. By this time the *Wiesbaden*, crippled by the 3rd Battle Cruiser Squadron, was crawling slowly back to the westward, hoping perhaps to find cover behind the advancing Battle Fleet. Scheer had heard from Boedicker of her plight and had altered course two points to port to help her.[33] But it was too late. The *Defence* saw her at 6.05 and opened fire.[34] She was hit by the second salvo and brought to a stop.

Rear-Admiral Sir Robert Arbuthnot, evidently determined to put her out of action and prevent her using torpedoes, altered course to starboard[35] across the head of the advancing Battle Fleet and came rushing down on her at full speed. Impatient to get into action he pressed across the bows of the *Lion*; he was only 5,500 yards from his target, and had turned to starboard to bring his whole broadside to bear, when he found himself facing a more terrible foe. Hipper's squadron, after turning to the South-West away from the 3rd Battle Cruiser Squadron, was coming up again on a North-East course. Von Hase saw the *Wiesbaden* terribly disabled and hidden in smoke, on fire fore and aft with shell after shell crashing into her.[36] Seized with fury, and evidently regarding the plucky little *Onslow* as her tormentor, he fired a salvo at her and she turned

---

[30] At 6.12 pm.

[31] *Duke of Edinburgh* (r) 5.50, *Hampshire* (r) 5.47, *Warrior* (r) 5.47, 'observed 4 points on starboard bow, three and possibly four enemy light cruisers' (*Official Despatches*, 291). The range was then 9½ miles. The *Defence* and *Warrior* each fired three salvos, but the initial damage to the *Wiesbaden* seems to have been done by the 3rd Battle Cruiser Squadron at a range of about 5 miles.

[32] Harper VII, 17° on *Iron Duke*'s starboard bow. Since 4.40 pm the *Defence* and 1st Cruiser Squadron had been steering SE (in towards *Iron Duke*) in order to close *Minotaur* on account of decreasing visibility. *Duke of Edinburgh* (r), *Official Despatches*, 286.

[33] Scheer, *Germany's High Seas Fleet*, 151.

[34] *Warrior* (r), *Official Despatches*, 291.

[35] Harper X, 6.10; *Warrior* mentions this turn at 6.01 (possibly for 6.10), *Official Despatches*, 291. *Duke of Edinburgh*'s track chart, *Official Despatches*, Plate XI (a), also give 6.10 pm.

[36] Von Hase saw a light cruiser (evidently the *Onslow*) firing on her and apparently did not at first see the *Defence*. The *Onslow* engaged the *Wiesbaden* at 6.05 and fired 58 rounds at 2,000 to 4,000 yards. 'I was struck by a big shell amidships'; *Official Despatches*, 227.

away in a cloud of escaping steam, managing, however, to fire a torpedo at the battle cruiser line, another at the *Wiesbaden*[37] and two more at the advancing Battle Fleet. Then through the mist and smoke Von Hase saw the *Defence*, but in the very act of training his guns on her, she was struck by two salvos from the *Friedrich der Grosse* or *Lützow*[38] in quick succession.[39] One hit her aft and a big red flame flashed up and died away; another hit her forward. A huge furnace flared into flame under her fore turret and she blew up with a terrific explosion, leaving only a huge pillar of smoke to mark the place of Arbuthnot's proud flagship. The *Warrior* too, behind her, came under a heavy fire[40] from Hipper's ships and the head of the approaching Battle Fleet. Another five minutes and she would almost certainly have suffered the same fate. But just at the critical moment the *Warspite* with her helm jammed turned between her and the enemy, drawing off their fire, and she managed to get away safely to the westward.

The movements of the *Black Prince* are obscure during this phase of the action.[41] She reported battle cruisers bearing South at 5.42 pm[42] and the *Duke of Edinburgh* saw her turn about 12 points to port at that time.[43] She was probably the armoured cruiser sighted later by the *Warrior* about 4 miles astern of the Battle Fleet.[44]

The *Duke of Edinburgh*, endeavouring to follow the *Defence*, found herself unable to cross the head of Beatty's squadron and withdrew to the eastward.

---

[37] This may have hit.

Editor's note: *Onslow* fired 58 rounds of 4in at *Wiesbaden* and a torpedo which probably hit aft. She also fired a torpedo at the German battle cruisers at a range of ca. 8,000 yards, which missed (Campbell, *Jutland*, 116).

[38] Harper, 6.19; *Warrior* (r), 6.19; *Colossus*, 6.19; *Malaya*, 6.20 pm. Scheer says the *Friedrich der Grosse*. Von Hase thought it was the *Lützow*. Von Hase, 31; Scheer, *Germany's High Seas Fleet*, 153; *Warrior* (r), *Official Despatches*, 291.

[39] *Editor's note*: *Defence* was the target of 12in gunfire from *König* and *Lützow* (who also fired a torpedo), plus secondary battery (5.9in) from *Seydlitz*, *König* and several other German battleships, some of which also turned their big guns on her. Credit is usually given to *Lützow*, but one of the other capital ships may have been responsible (Campbell, *Jutland*, 152–3, 181).

[40] Hit 15 times by 11 in. shell (evidently from the *Von der Tann*). Very severe damage was done by a heavy shell which struck the waterline on the port side and entered the engine room, bursting as it passed through the middle line bulkhead.

[41] *Editor's note*: *Black Prince* was lost with all hands during the night, and thus there are gaps in what is known about her movements during the battle.

[42] *Official Despatches*, 456 gives this signal as 'enemy battle cruisers', but *Iron Duke* (s[1]), also *Marlborough* (s), has 'battle cruisers', and the Commander-in-Chief assumed them rightly to be Beatty's squadron (Jellicoe, *Grand Fleet*, 344).

[43] *Official Despatches*, 286.

[44] *Official Despatches*, 292.

The *Defence*'s attack was no doubt inspired by a keen and praiseworthy impatience to get to close quarters, but in the circumstances must be regarded as unnecessary and unsound. Though the *Lion*'s target may not have been visible, she was evidently in action with heavy ships. The attack forced the *Lion* off her course, threw out the fire of her squadron, and made them lose sight of their target in the cruiser's smoke.

Contact between Battle Fleet and Battle Cruiser Force

48. It was 6.19 pm when the *Defence* disappeared in a cloud of flame and spray and smoke, and the fleet had already begun to deploy at 6.15. But here it is necessary to retrace our steps and review the information on which the Commander-in-Chief's action was based.

As the enemy's Battle Fleet approached, it was of the utmost importance for the Commander-in-Chief to get a reliable bearing of it as soon as possible – a point emphasised in the Grand Fleet Battle Orders,[45] which also laid special stress on the importance of visual contact in view of the possibility of errors in reckonings arising in wireless reports.

The best position to keep in touch with the enemy Battle Fleet was astern of the 5th Battle Squadron, and this position was taken up by the *Southampton*. She hung doggedly on to the enemy under fire, and though her reports were somewhat marred by mistakes and discrepancies in reckonings, they show that she had a clear conception of her task and did her best to fulfil it. But wireless reports alone were not sufficient. A visual chain had to be established as rapidly as possible. But though the importance of visual touch had found recognition in print, it is clear that it had not received sufficient attention in practice, and it is legitimate to assume that the enormous development and extension of wireless had induced a neglect of the tactical importance of this aspect of visual signalling. The *Falmouth* and the *Black Prince* were in touch at 5.33 pm (Diagram 18); but the former was some 9 miles ahead of the *Southampton*, and probably not in visual touch with her, and the latter was some 13 miles from the *Iron Duke* and not in visual touch.

The 5th Battle Squadron had been in sight of the enemy's Battle Fleet, and might well have made a report, when it was lost to sight at about 5.25 pm.[46]

The *Barham*'s wireless was out of action, and the *Malaya*, silhouetted against

---

[45] Section XXII, paras. 6 and 20, Vol. III, folio 320, 322 in Training and Staff Duties Division collection.

Editor's note: See the Chapter VII Endnote for the complete text of the relevant section of the GFBOs.

[46] *Barham*, 5.25; *Valiant*, 5.24 (very indistinct); *Malaya*, 5.30 (nearly obscured).

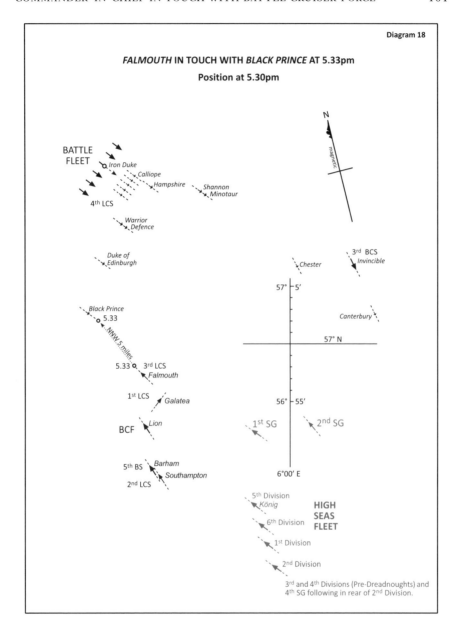

a clear horizon, had received heavy punishment, but the *Valiant* certainly was in a position to make a report, and the fact that not a single report was sent in by the 5th Battle Squadron, which was the squadron nearest to the enemy, clearly shows that its importance to the Commander-in-Chief had not been sufficiently appreciated.

Contact Signals 5.35 pm to 6.14 pm

49. The series of signals made at this time must be viewed in a very different light from those made between 4.45 and 5 pm. The conditions were much more difficult. Two great fleets were approaching one another wrapped in mist and with only a limited time to make the most momentous decisions.

Positions had to be rapidly plotted, and there was no time available to check or confirm them, but a considerable amount of information did come in which is contained in a series of 12 signals received between 5.35 and 6.14 pm, beginning with one from the *Southampton* and ending with one from the *Lion*[47] (Diagrams 18 and 19).

The first seven of these signals were what the Commander-in-Chief probably had to work with at 5.50, and though in the pressure then prevailing, there must have been little time to check and compare them, their general effect in conjunction with the previous series ought to have been to place the enemy sharp on the *Marlborough*'s bow about 14 miles off at 6 pm. Evidently they were getting very near, and at 5.55 pm.[48] the Commander-in-Chief asked the *Marlborough* what she could see, and received a reply about 6 pm that Beatty's battle cruisers bore SSW three to four miles, and were steering East. The thunder of heavy guns could be heard from ahead right round to the starboard beam, and it must have been a matter of great difficulty to form a clear picture of the situation.

At 6 pm the *Lion* could be seen from the *Iron Duke* SW, about five miles off, steering East, and the Commander-in-Chief decided to take ground to southward.[49] His intention as given later[50] was 'to clear up the situation', but the movement, slight in itself, had a distinct tactical significance which merits examination. Here a short digression is necessary. A clear distinction can be drawn between what may be called a direct deployment by a single turn of divisions to NE by E at right angles to the line of advance, and a deployment on the wing in the direction of the line of advance. The time occupied by the former would have been four minutes, by the latter twenty-two. Now the Commander-

---

[47] *See* Appendix F.

[48] *Iron Duke* (s[1]), 5.55; *Marlborough* (s), 6 pm. The *Lion* had been in sight from *Marlborough* since 5.45 pm.

[49] *Editor's note*: It was at 6.01 that Jellicoe sent the signal 'Where is Enemy's B.F.' [battle fleet]? to Beatty by signal lamp. At this moment the German battle fleet was not in sight from the *Lion*, so she responded at 6.06 with the signal 'Enemy's B.C.s [battle cruisers] bearing SE'. But this did not provide Jellicoe with the information he needed to determine his deployment course, so at 6.10 he again asked where the enemy's battle fleet was. Almost at the same time, *Lion* caught a glimpse of Scheer's force, and at 6.14 she signalled: 'Have sighted Enemy's battle fleet bearing SSW.' (*Official Despatches*, 457–8).

[50] Jellicoe, *Grand Fleet*, 346.

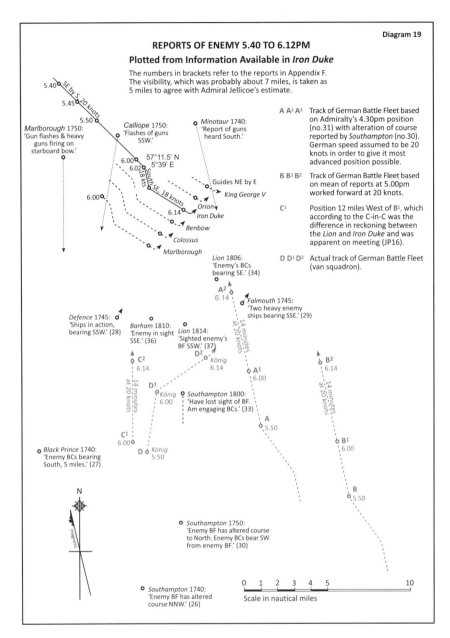

Diagram 19

REPORTS OF ENEMY 5.40 TO 6.12PM

Plotted from Information Available in *Iron Duke*

The numbers in brackets refer to the reports in Appendix F.
The visibility, which was probably about 7 miles, is taken as
5 miles to agree with Admiral Jellicoe's estimate.

5.40 SE by S 20 knots

5.45

5.50

Marlborough 1750:
'Gun flashes & heavy
guns firing on
starboard bow.'

Calliope 1750:
'Flashes of guns
SSW.'

Minotaur 1740:
'Report of guns
heard South.'

6.00
6.02 South SE 18 knots
57°11.5' N
5°39' E

Guides NE by E
King George V

6.00

Orion
6.14
Iron Duke

Benbow

Colossus

Marlborough

Lion 1806:
'Enemy's BCs
bearing SE.' (34)

A² 6.14

Falmouth 1745:
'Two heavy enemy
ships bearing SSE.' (29)

Defence 1745:
'Ships in action,
bearing SSW.' (28)

Barham 1810:
'Enemy in sight
SSE.' (36)

Lion 1814:
'Sighted enemy's
BF SSW.' (37)

D²

C² 6.14
König 6.14

D¹
König 6.00

Southampton 1800:
'Have lost sight of BF.
Am engaging BCs.' (33)

A¹ 6.00

14 minutes at 20 knots

B² 6.14

A 5.50

C¹ 6.00

D König 5.50

B¹ 6.00

14 minutes at 20 knots

Black Prince 1740:
'Enemy BCs bearing
South, 5 miles.' (27)

B 5.50

N magnetic

Southampton 1750:
'Enemy BF has altered course
to North. Enemy BCs bear SW
from enemy BF.' (30)

Southampton 1740:
'Enemy BF has altered
course NNW.' (26)

A A¹ A²   Track of German Battle Fleet based
on Admiralty's 4.30pm position
(no.31) with alteration of course
reported by *Southampton* (no.30).
German speed assumed to be 20
knots in order to give it most
advanced position possible.

B B¹ B²   Track of German Battle Fleet based
on mean of reports at 5.00pm
worked forward at 20 knots.

C¹   Position 12 miles West of B¹, which
according to the C-in-C was the
difference in reckoning between
the *Lion* and *Iron Duke* and was
apparent on meeting (JP16).

D D¹ D²   Actual track of German Battle Fleet
(van squadron).

0 1 2 3 4 5 10
Scale in nautical miles

Note
The format and 'content' of the signals in the original diagram, which were inconsistent, have
been harmonised in the interests of clarity, using Appendix F as a reference.

in-Chief had evidently expected to meet the enemy right ahead, which would
have required only a turn of divisions to NE by E, and the fleet would have been
deployed. But if the enemy were found on the starboard bow, a turn to NE by E
would not be enough. For a direct deployment the line of bearing of the guides

would have to be thrown forward to an angle at right angles to the enemy's bearing, that is to E by N.[51] But the same object could be obtained without altering the bearing of the guides by altering the bearing of the enemy, and bringing him right ahead by moving the fleet to the southward. Herein lies the tactical significance of the alteration of course to South at 6.02 pm, and it is not without interest to consider the probable effect of continuing the movement. Had the fleet continued for ten minutes on a South course, and then turned back for five minutes to SE by S – the converse of what it actually did – it would have found itself in a suitable position for direct deployment on a NE by E course, which would have brought all its guns into action in four minutes. On the other hand, it would have run the risk of superior fire on the heads of its columns and of an inferior horizon. Whether this actually was the Commander-in-Chief's intention must remain doubtful, but hardly had the column turned to South than the sound of heavy firing indicated the close proximity of the enemy's heavy ships, and the *Lion* signaled[52] that the enemy's battle cruisers bore South-East. The *Southampton*'s 5.50 pm signal, according to Lord Jellicoe[53] added now to the perplexities of the situation. The *Lion*'s signal made the enemy battle cruisers bear about S by E from the *Iron Duke*, but the *Southampton*'s report placed them SW from his Battle Fleet, which tended to make the German Battle Fleet some seven miles or so to the south-eastward.[54] In the Commander-in-Chief's mind, however, the conviction was gradually shaping itself that he would strike the enemy's Battle Fleet on a bearing sharp on the starboard bow,[55] and in these circumstances he turned back to a SE course and ordered all destroyers to take up position No. 1 for battle.[56]

Meanwhile, the *Barham* had sighted Scheer's battleships SSE at 6.10 and ordered the *Valiant* to pass the news by wireless. The Commander-in-Chief received it at 6.14 pm[57] and almost simultaneously a signal came in from the *Lion* reporting them in sight SSW (Diagram 20). These two reports tended to

---

[51] The Commander-in-Chief evidently had this in mind (cf. Jellicoe, *Grand Fleet*, 345). To alter the bearing of the guides to ENE would have taken 15 minutes and to E by N 20 minutes.

[52] At 6.06 pm.

[53] Jellicoe, *Grand Fleet*, 347.

[54] The discrepancies in the *Southampton*'s previous series of signals would lead, however, to the rejection of any statement which seemed improbable.

[55] Jellicoe, *Grand Fleet*, 346.

[56] *See* p. 126, *infra*, footnote 30.

Editor's note: The signal to the destroyers came at 6.08; position No. 1 meant that three flotillas were to take station on the port wing of the battle fleet, in expectation of a deployment to port; one flotilla was to take up a position on the starboard wing, to guard the rear of the battle fleet after deployment (GFBOs, Destroyer Instructions, 50).

[57] *Iron Duke* (s[1]), 6.14 pm. Lord Jellicoe says 6.15 in *Grand Fleet*, 347.

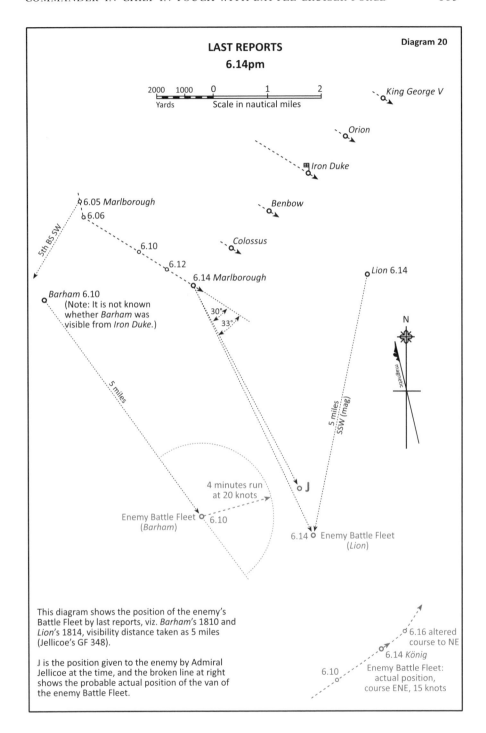

LAST REPORTS
6.14pm

Diagram 20

This diagram shows the position of the enemy's Battle Fleet by last reports, viz. *Barham*'s 1810 and *Lion*'s 1814, visibility distance taken as 5 miles (Jellicoe's GF 348).

J is the position given to the enemy by Admiral Jellicoe at the time, and the broken line at right shows the probable actual position of the van of the enemy Battle Fleet.

place the enemy thirty to forty degrees on the *Marlborough*'s bow,[58] and there appeared to be danger of deployment on the starboard wing column involving it in action with the German Battle Fleet before the movement could be completed, and exposing the Battle Fleet to destroyer attack.

These were the considerations which passed through the Commander-in-Chief's mind. He decided to deploy to port on a SE by E course, and the signal for deployment went up – Equal Speed Pendant C.L.[59] It was made by flags and wireless at fifteen minutes past six.[60]

Chapter VII Endnote

Section XXII of the Grand Fleet Battle Orders specified how enemy sighting reports were to be distributed and underscored the necessity for accurate reporting based on relative positions of the enemy and the Commander-in-Chief:

6. Ships having to make a report of sighting or of movements of the enemy must pass the message to the Admiral as well as their own senior officer.

In addition, senior officers of squadrons, or captains of ships acting independently must be most careful to ensure that the adjacent senior officers receive all information obtained by ships of their squadron respecting the enemy.

Attention is called to the vital necessity of indicating the *position*, based on the Commander-in-Chief's reference position, in all reports of the enemy; unless this is given, officers not in visual touch can make no use of the signal, for ordering movements of other squadrons or ships and the most serious consequences may follow.

20. When the two battlefleets are comparatively close to one another the position of the reporting ship as given in the usual Emergency W/T Signal is not a sufficiently accurate guide upon which the Admiral can base his tactics, since a few miles difference in latitude or longitude of estimated positions may make all the difference in distance.

It is therefore necessary that the screening cruisers should be linked to the battlefleet by other vessels which are in certain visual touch with both.

---

[58] Jellicoe, *Grand Fleet*, 348, Diagram I, 30° on *Marlborough*'s bow, seven miles; Harper X places enemy seven miles 25° on *Marlborough*'s bow at 6.15, on a course N 40 E (mag.). Scheer's diagram makes the course of the German Battle Fleet N 68 E (mag.) from 6 pm to 6.16 pm, then N 45 E; *Official Despatches*, German Plan V.

[59] General Signal Book 1915, p. 17, 32.

[60] *Official Despatches*, 6.15; *Iron Duke* (s¹), 6.16; *Iron Duke* (s²), 6.14; *Marlborough* (w), 6.13; *Marlborough* (s), 6.15; *Benbow* (s), 6.16; *Falmouth* (s), 6.15 pm.

CHAPTER VIII
REMARKS ON
THE DEPLOYMENT AT 6.15 PM

50. While the *Defence* was pressing forward impatiently to attack the *Wiesbaden*, the Battle Fleet had begun to deploy. Beatty's squadron had passed its right wing, and was now steering ESE some two miles ahead of its centre. There can be little doubt that Beatty in steering an Easterly course had the German Battle Fleet in view, and expected the Battle Fleet to deploy more or less behind him. The signal flying, however, was for deployment on the left wing, and the whole line began to move away. If the object of deployment is to bring all guns to bear at an effective range, that object does not appear to have been fulfilled, for the fleet when deployed, under the prevailing conditions of visibility, was not at effective range.[1] What were the circumstances, then, which militated against its full and complete fulfilment?

The key to the question seems to lie in a consideration of the course on which the Commander-in-Chief expected to deploy.[2] This is more or less implied in the statement that he expected to meet the enemy fleet approximately ahead.[3]

This means that as soon as the divisions turned at right angles to the course, the fleet would have found itself in four minutes in line of battle. But if the enemy were located on a bow or beam bearing, the line joining the centres would shift in that direction and alter the initial direction of deployment. The fact that Beatty was to westward of his expected position probably gave rise to the assumption that the enemy were to the westward too. At about 6.00 there

---

[1] *Editor's note*: See the Chapter VIII Endnote for a discussion of the *Appreciation*'s handling of Jellicoe's deployment.

[2] It is hardly necessary to say that if the order of battle is to be single line, deployment should be at right angles to the line joining the centre or prospective centre of the two fleets, when in line of battle within effective range. See *Notes on Tactical Exercises, Home Fleet, 1909-1911*, Admiral Sir William May. This is in book form, issued September 19, 1911.

[3] Jellicoe, *Grand Fleet*, 343. On the basis of reports from *Southampton* between 5 and 6 pm and Beatty's signal of 1645.

was great uncertainty as to the position of the enemy's fleet, and the idea was gaining ground that they would be sighted on the bow. This meant that the line of bearing of the centres had shifted to the south-ward (clock-wise), and called for the line of bearing of the guides to be thrown forward to about E by N.[4]

But there appeared to be no time for this. To throw forward the line of bearing of the guides would have taken nearly a quarter of an hour.[5] On the other hand, it was possible to bring the enemy once more ahead on his expected bearing by moving the fleet to the southward. This was possibly the intention of the Commander-in-Chief's alteration of course to South at 6.02. The enemy's new position was to southward of the expected line of bearing, but by taking ground to the southward he would again be brought ahead and the bearing of the guides would still hold good (Diagram 21).

The fleet had barely been four minutes on this course when an impression arose that the enemy was close at hand, and, as the disposition was an unsuitable one for deployment,[6] the Commander-in-Chief reverted to a SE course. Then the *Barham*'s and *Lion*'s signals came in, and by giving them a visibility of only five miles, it looked as if the enemy was only some five miles[7] off, and might emerge at any moment out of the mist just before the *Marlborough*'s beam. There appeared to be no time to lose. The fleet must deploy at once. In these circumstances the Grand Fleet Battle Orders had announced an intention of deploying on the wing nearest the enemy,[8] which was probably what Admiral Beatty expected. But the fire of the 1st Scouting Group and the general uncertainty gave rise to the idea of the High Sea Fleet being close at hand, and of the *Marlborough* being 'severely handled' before the battle line could be formed. The risk of German destroyers, too, attacking the line during deployment made it appear 'suicidal', and the supposed position of Scheer's Battle Fleet appeared to give him the advantage of a considerable overlap over the starboard wing column. This would necessitate the *Marlborough* altering course to port, and would introduce a bend in the line of deployment.[9] For

---

[4] The idea of throwing forward the guides naturally occurred to the Commander-in-Chief, and he says: 'The information (received up to 6 pm) had not even been sufficient to justify me in altering the bearing of the guides'; Jellicoe, *Grand Fleet*, 345, also *Official Despatches*, 16.

[5] With a difference of speed of ten knots between wing columns.

[6] It would involve a clumsy turn unless the Commander-in-Chief decided to deploy to the southward and engage on opposite courses.

[7] The actual distance was about seven miles.

[8] 'In low visibility, if the enemy is sighted near the beam and bearing and time do not permit of re-disposing the guides, line of battle will usually be formed on the wing column nearest the enemy'; GFBO, Section VI, para. 4.

[9] Jellicoe, *Grand Fleet*, 350.

Diagram 21

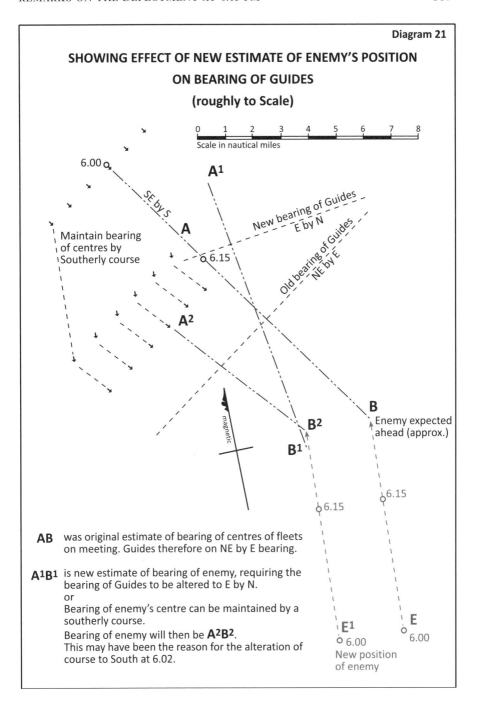

SHOWING EFFECT OF NEW ESTIMATE OF ENEMY'S POSITION
ON BEARING OF GUIDES
(roughly to Scale)

Scale in nautical miles

6.00

A^1

SE by S

A

New bearing of Guides
E by N

Old bearing of Guides
NE by E

Maintain bearing
of centres by
Southerly course

6.15

A^2

magnetic

B

B^2

Enemy expected
ahead (approx.)

B^1

6.15

6.15

AB   was original estimate of bearing of centres of fleets
on meeting. Guides therefore on NE by E bearing.

A^1B^1 is new estimate of bearing of enemy, requiring the
bearing of Guides to be altered to E by N.
or
Bearing of enemy's centre can be maintained by a
southerly course.
Bearing of enemy will then be **A^2B^2**.
This may have been the reason for the alteration of
course to South at 6.02.

E^1 E
6.00   6.00
New position
of enemy

these reasons the Commander-in-Chief decided to deploy on his port wing on a SE by E course, though it is difficult to see why the fleet should not have deployed on the course it was steering, namely, SE, which would have reduced the range by at least 1,200 yards,[10] when its reduction was an important tactical consideration.

51. So far as a deployment on the starboard wing was concerned, the risks of torpedo attack were in reality not very great. The enemy's destroyers were considerably to leeward of their line, and made no attempt to attack at this time.[11] The German 9th Flotilla and 12th Half-Flotilla were already busily engaged with the *Shark* and the 3rd Battle Cruiser Squadron, and on the British side the 3rd and 4th Light Cruiser Squadrons and the 12th Flotilla were available for counter-attack. If the Germans could launch an attack, there was no reason why we should not do the same.

The risk to the *Marlborough* and wing column from the enemy's gun fire was less conjectural, but in the light of later events cannot be regarded as excessive. It is true that she could not have continued very long on her course at the time. She would either have had to turn at once to ESE or, failing this, to alter course about four points to port not later than 6.21,[12] at a range of about 10,000 yards. The former would have resulted in a nasty 12 point turn at the point of deployment. This would have been inconvenient but not impracticable. The latter course would have given the enemy a certain amount of overlap, but on the other hand he would be bound himself to turn and introduce a similar bend in his own line. Assuming, also, that he turned away (as he actually did) immediately he found himself in action with the whole British Battle Fleet, he would have had to do so under a heavy fire, and it would have been a much easier matter to see and follow him (Diagram 22). The 5th Battle Squadron, too, was between the *Marlborough* and the enemy, in a position to take its place at the head of the line and to afford her valuable support.

From the Commander-in-Chief's point of view, however, a deployment on the starboard wing column appeared to involve some degree of risk to the *Marlborough* and 1st Division, and it was on the grounds of overlap that the Commander-in-Chief rejected it. But the disadvantages of deploying on the

---

[10] At 6.33. The bearing would have been brought before the beam, but the bearing was not so important as the range.

[11] *Editor's note*: Hindsight provides a view not given to the commander on the spot. Jellicoe did not know where the German torpedo boat flotillas were; the last news he had of them was a signal from *Southampton* at 4.48 which did indeed place them 'on both wings and ahead' of the German fleet; *Official Despatches*, 453.

[12] Lord Jellicoe in his diagram in the *Grand Fleet* allows another minute.

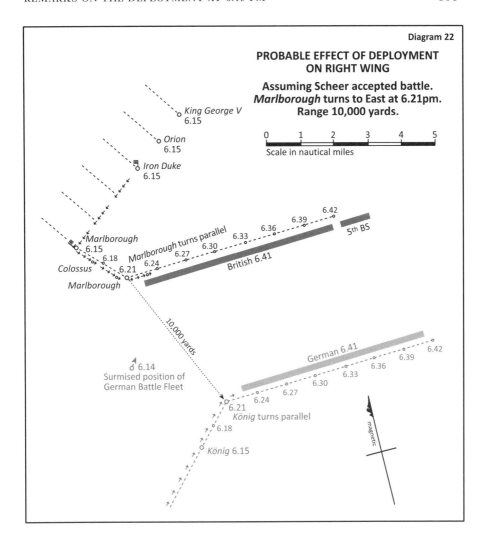

Diagram 22

PROBABLE EFFECT OF DEPLOYMENT ON RIGHT WING

Assuming Scheer accepted battle. *Marlborough* turns to East at 6.21pm. Range 10,000 yards.

Note

The 'start position' of Jellicoe's flagship *Iron Duke* was omitted in the original diagram, and has been inserted here in the interests of clarity.

port wing were almost equally evident. It diminished the risk, but it also diminished the chance of a decisive action. It inevitably increased the range of deployment by at least two or three miles, a very serious increase when the visibility was not much more than five.[13]

---

[13] Five miles; Jellicoe, *Grand Fleet*, 348.

In fact it might be regarded as almost a last resource in the face of imminent danger.

Was there no alternative method? The supposed bearing of Scheer's Battle Fleet was about 30° before the *Iron Duke*'s beam, or roughly S 15 W. The correct course for deployment was therefore about E by S. Now, in the mist of uncertainties, one thing was certain and could be clearly seen. Beatty's flag was there, ahead of the fleet, steering almost the identical course required, pointing out to the Battle Fleet the direction in which to deploy. The *Iron Duke* had only to steer eastward towards the *Lion* and order the fleet to deploy on the Commander-in-Chief. This would have at once withdrawn the right wing from danger, and at the same time deployed the fleet at effective range. But the Equal Speed Pendant was designed for deployment on a wing column only,[14] a limitation which precluded the Commander-in-Chief from using it for any deployment between the five-mile front of the columns. The requirements of the case could, however, have been fully met by an older and simpler signal, namely a Forming and Disposing Signal, which would have enabled line ahead to be formed on the *Iron Duke* in the order of divisions in which distinguishing signals were shown.[15] This was an entirely practicable movement; the fleet was not under fire; the signal was an old signal, well known to all the leaders of divisions, and there can be little doubt that it would have brought the fleet into action without undue risk at effective range. It is not possible, however, to say whether the idea of forming single line ahead in this way actually occurred to the Commander-in-Chief, and in default of any reference to it,[16] it may be inferred that it did not. All that can be said is that the movement was possible and did not entail undue risk. Deployment on the port wing no doubt carried with it lesser risk, but it increased the range of the enemy by at least 4,000 yards

---

[14] General Signal Book, 1915, page 18: 'Hoisted superior to alphabetical flags directs the column nearest the bearing shown to alter course in succession to the point of compass indicated, and the remaining columns to alter course, leading ship together, the rest in succession, so as to form astern of the leading column, maintaining the speed of the fleet'.

[15] Forming and Disposing Signal. General Signal Book, 1915, page 70. 'The ship and columns are to form in the sequence of their numbers, or in the order in which their Distinguishing Signals may be shown on the side the formation is directed by the signal'. To avoid reducing speed, which might be thought risky in view of the contemporary fear of the submarine, the 1st and 2nd Divisions could each have made two 16-point turns to port in succession (see diagram), with a short interval in between. A Forming and Disposing Signal would have taken the form of 1 Pendant A with flags 3, 4, 5, 6, 2, 1 inferior. The rest would have been left to the initiative of leaders of divisions. An apparent disadvantage would have been interference with fire while getting into position, but the only ships which actually fired on a NE by E course were those of the 6th Division, whose fire would not have been affected.

[16] Nothing is said on this point in Jellicoe, *Grand Fleet*.

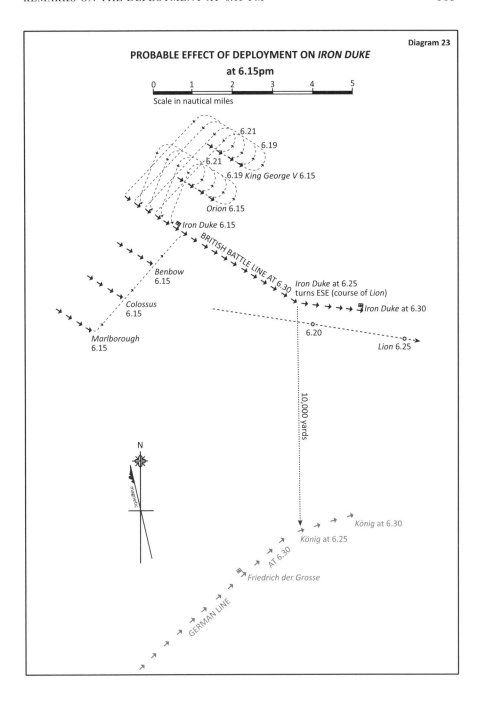

Diagram 23

PROBABLE EFFECT OF DEPLOYMENT ON *IRON DUKE*

at 6.15pm

Scale in nautical miles

at a time when every 1,000 yards of range was of value, and every ten minutes of daylight was beginning to weigh in the scale of victory[17] (Diagram 23).

The lesson which remains seems to be that in mist and uncertainty we should cast aside preconceptions, leave much to initiative, and follow what can be seen. But time pressed. The signal to deploy on the port wing went up. The fleet turned, and began to move out of effective range.

Chapter VIII Endnote

The Dewars' discussion of Jellicoe's deployment is one of the most biased sections of the *Appreciation*; it ignores its advantages while emphasising all its disadvantages. In doing so, moreover, it employs a good deal of *ex post facto* knowledge that was unavailable to Jellicoe at the time.

To begin with, the Dewars define the object of deployment as being 'to bring all guns to bear at an effective range', but this was not the object generally accepted by tacticians of the day. In fact, the general view was that deployment should occur *before* reaching gunnery ranges, as Admiral Sir Arthur Wilson noted in 1901:

> These battles [i.e., exercises] confirmed my opinion that the safest rule for taking a fleet into action is to form single line [i.e., deploy] roughly at right angles to the bearing of the enemy *before coming within effective range*, and then alter course together as necessary (Wilson's report, 4 October 1901, in 'Combined Manoeuvres Mediterranean and Channel Fleets, 1901', 60; TNA: ADM 1/7506; emphasis added).

Fifteen years later, Jellicoe's Grand Fleet Battle Orders voiced the same idea: 'I shall probably deploy . . . at a range of about 18,000 to 20,000 yards so as to be in a favourable position for opening fire in good time . . . In weather of good visibility, the range should be between 15,000 and 10,000 yards. . . ' (*Jellicoe Papers*, 1:244). Thus the GFBOs clearly indicate that Jellicoe would deploy 3,000 to 5,000 yards beyond gunnery range, because the key purpose of deployment was to gain a tactical advantage before opening fire. By redefining the purpose of deployment, the Dewars are able to declare that Jellicoe failed to achieve the object of deployment.

This leads to the question of whether or not Jellicoe obtained a 'favourable position'. Marder notes (*FDSF*, 3:105–6) 'three mighty advantages' to Jellicoe's deployment on the port wing column:

1. It crossed Scheer's 'T';
2. It placed the Grand Fleet between Scheer and his line of retreat to either the Heligoland Bight or the Skagarrak;
3. It gave the British fleet the advantage of the best light.

Nor were these advantages the result of lucky accident. For example, it was often assumed in exercises that the High Seas Fleet would retreat to the eastward – towards Heligoland (See, for example, 'Exercises carried out on 13-14 June', 8 July 1915; Grand Fleet Orders; TNA: ADM 137/2020) and Jellicoe made provision for this in the Grand Fleet Battle Orders:

---

[17] *Editor's note*: Churchill's discussion of the deployment, and especially the supposed advantages of deploying on the centre column, is clearly based on the Dewars' account; see *The World Crisis, 1916-1918*, vol. 3 part 1, 148–9.

The direction of deployment may . . . be governed by the desire to fight a decisive action before the enemy can return to his own waters . . . under some circumstances . . . it would be our object to get to the eastward to intercept the enemy . . . (GFBOs, XXIV; TNA: ADM 116/1343).

The deployment certainly placed Jellicoe between Scheer and his bases, a fact which greatly discomfited him.

As for obtaining the best light, this also was no accident. Before the deployment Jellicoe had asked Dreyer, his flag captain, to take rangefinder readings to determine in which direction the light was best; the answer was that it was 'best to the southward, and as the sun sank lower, to the westward' (Marder, *FDSF*, 3:102). This aspect of the deployment is only belatedly acknowledged by the *Appreciation*: 'Admiral Jellicoe's choice of a southern horizon seems to have been fully justified' (Chapter IX, Section 59). Jellicoe knew that Scheer was somewhere to the west of his own position; he also knew that the High Seas Fleet was advancing in line-ahead formation; this meant that Jellicoe would almost certainly cross his 'T'.

To these may be added a fourth: Long before the deployment was complete, Scheer was exposed to the fire of the maximum number of British ships, for he was charging head-on into what was essentially an envelopment; had it not been for the smoke interference caused by the battle cruisers' unavoidable passage between the Grand Fleet and the Germans, much more damage would undoubtedly have been inflicted on the leading German ships during the first battle fleet encounter.

If all this is so, one point raised by the Dewars still remains: 'it is difficult to see why the fleet should not have deployed on the course it was steering, namely, SE, which would have reduced the range by at least 1,200 yards, when its reduction was an important tactical consideration'. But there is an answer, and the Dewars should have been aware of it, since they quote the signal at issue. According to the signal book, the equal-speed deployment signal

directs the column nearest the bearing shown to alter course in succession to the point of compass indicated, and the remaining columns to alter course, leading ship together, the rest in succession, so as to form astern of the leading column, maintaining the speed of the fleet.

The critical phrase is 'the column nearest the bearing shown'. Since the fleet was already steering SE, had the signal ordered deployment on a course of SE neither wing would have been 'nearest' the deployment course. This was an oversight in the signal book – the situation arising at Jutland had simply not been imagined. In fact, Jellicoe initially did order a deployment course of SE, but his fleet signal officer, Commander A.R. Woods, realising the ambiguity of such a signal, suggested: 'Would you make it a point to port, Sir, so that they will know it is on the port-wing column?' (Dreyer, *Sea Heritage*, 146–7.) Jellicoe accepted this modification. Hence the course of SE by E.

As for the use of *ex post facto* knowledge to condemn Jellicoe's deployment, two examples may be cited:

1. So far as a deployment on the starboard wing was concerned, the risks of torpedo attack were in reality not very great. The enemy's destroyers were considerably to leeward of their line, and made no attempt to attack at this time (Section 51).
2. It is noted that the 5th BS sustained 'very little damage' when it was manoeuvring off the starboard wing of the fleet, which 'tends to show that a deployment on the right wing would not have involved excessive risk' (Section 56).

These facts are used to show that Jellicoe was wrong to deploy on the port wing, despite the fact that Jellicoe did not know that the German destroyers were not in a position to attack; his last information was that the destroyers were 'on both wings and ahead' of the High Seas Fleet (signal from *Southampton*, sent at 4.48 pm; *Official Despatches*, 453). Had they maintained these positions, some of them would certainly have been well placed to make torpedo attacks on the right wing as the British fleet deployed. Likewise, the fact that the 5th BS sustained relatively little damage could not have been known to Jellicoe at the time; moreover, one of *Malaya*'s officers believed that the damage inflicted on the squadron at this time was slight because 'no time was lost in straightening out the muddle' at the 'Windy Corner' (Fawcett and Hooper, *Fighting at Jutland*, 129). Deployment on the right wing would have been a much more protracted affair, and consequently the Germans might have scored many more hits.

Certainly his erstwhile enemies endorsed Jellicoe's decision. Admiral von Trotha, Scheer's Chief of Staff at Jutland, was 'emphatic that Jellicoe acted rightly' (Marder, *FDSF*, 3:105). The German official history also held that a starboard deployment would have been a bad idea from the British perspective:

> One must agreed with the British leader that had he acted in this way [deployment to starboard] he would in fact have led his ships into a position which would have been only too welcome to the German Fleet (quoted in Marder, *FDSF*, 3:105).

In the end, even Herbert Richmond, a good friend of Kenneth Dewar and a sometimes harsh critic of Jellicoe, agreed that the deployment was a good one after discussing the battle with Sir Julian Corbett, the official historian (Hunt, *Sailor-Scholar*, 115).

More recent historians have also approved Jellicoe's decision to deploy on the port wing. We can close the discussion with the opinions of two great historians of the First World War. First, Stephen Roskill:

> Rivers of ink have been spilt over the question of whether [Jellicoe's] was the best deployment, but nearly all students of the battle – except the brothers Captain A C and Vice-Admiral K G B Dewar . . . and Churchill (who accepted the Dewars' opinion uncritically) – agree that it was by far the best manoeuvre possible . . . (Roskill, *Admiral of the Fleet Earl Beatty*, 169).

Roskill's great colleague and rival Arthur Marder was even more emphatic:

> Lacking this information [i.e., the 'bearing on which the enemy would come into view'], Jellicoe's deployment decision was little short of miraculous (Marder, *FDSF*, 3:108).

THE FIRST HALF HOUR, 6.15 PM TO 6.40 PM

52. The two fleets about to engage constituted the most tremendous array of naval force in the history of the world, but the German Fleet, formidable as it was, could not compare with the British in numbers, speed, or gun power. Admiral Jellicoe as he deployed could count on 28 Dreadnoughts and 9 battle cruisers,[1] while Scheer could muster only 16 Dreadnoughts, 6 pre-Dreadnoughts, and 5 battle cruisers. In speed the British Fleet was markedly superior. Its slowest battleship could do 20 knots, and the 5th Battle Squadron formed a homogeneous squadron of four very powerful ships capable of steaming 24 to 25 knots. On the German side Scheer's fastest battleship could only go 21 knots,[2] while his 6 pre-Dreadnought ships of the *Deutschland* class could only steam 16 knots,[3] and their slow speed and poor armament made them a source of grave anxiety to the German Commander-in-Chief.

The British superiority in gun-fire was still more marked. Admiral Jellicoe's Battle Fleet mounted 272 heavy guns against Scheer's 200. This superiority in numbers was greatly enhanced by an overwhelming superiority in size, for the British Fleet mounted 48 15 in., 10 14 in., 110 13.5 in. and 104 12 in. against the German 128 12 in. and 72 11 in., representing a potential British broadside of 317,900 lb. against the German 157,672. The superior weight of the battle cruisers broadside was equally pronounced. The British mounted 32 13.5 and

---

[1] Including *Queen Mary* and *Indefatigable*, of whose loss the Commander-in-Chief was unaware.

[2] *Editor's note*: German dreadnoughts of the *Kaiser* and *König* classes were designed for 21 knots, but were capable of achieving greater speeds when forced: *Kaiser* herself seems to have managed 23.4 knots (at 55,187 shp, almost double the designed 28,000 shp!) when forced (Gröner, *German Warships*, 1:26). British Intelligence was apparently aware of these higher speeds achieved on the measured mile, as well as the designed 21 knots (*German Warships of World War I*, 12).

[3] *Editor's note*: Their designed speed was 18 knots.

40 12 in.[4] against the German 16 12 in. and 28 11 in., or a broadside of 78,800 lb. against 32,268.

In torpedoes the strength of the two fleets was more equal.[5] The British mounted 382 21 in. tubes to the German 362 19.7 in. On the other hand, the Germans mounted more short range torpedoes than their opponent, but in a day action these were not likely to be effective. Such were the comparative strengths in terms of gun and torpedo power of the two fleets.

Formation of German Fleet

53. When the British Battle Fleet turned to deploy at 6.15, the *König*, which was leading the enemy's line, bore about S 16 E, seven miles from the *Marlborough*. She was on an ENE course,[6] and behind her were the six ships of Rear-Admiral Behneke's 3rd Squadron. Then came the *Friedrich der Grosse*, Scheer's flagship, followed by the eight ships of the 1st Squadron. At 6.16 the *König* turned to NE, and the position at 6.19 is shown in Diagram 24.

Preliminary Firing

54. As the British Battle Fleet turned to deploy at 6.15, a few enemy salvos fell round the centre and rear divisions,[7] and the ships of the *Marlborough*'s division could see vessels of the *Kaiser* or *Helgoland* class looming indistinctly and intermittently through the mist. The *Wiesbaden* could be seen through its smoke screen some five miles off, and became the first target for a number of ships.[8] With the exception of the *Marlborough* and 5th Battle Squadron, few ships were firing as the fleet proceeded NE by E.[9] Even after turning to SE by E, fire was impeded by mist and intervening smoke, and did not become general till about 6.25.

The Battle Cruisers

55. When the Battle Fleet started to deploy, the battle cruisers were already two or three miles ahead, steaming at full speed on an Easterly course. They

---

[4] Including *Queen Mary* and *Indefatigable*.

[5] For detailed figures see Chapter XI.

[6] German VI, Scheer's diagram No. 4.

[7] *Iron Duke, Hercules* and *Revenge*.

[8] *Hercules, Collingwood, Vanguard, Iron Duke, Superb, Canada, Monarch, Conqueror, Thunderer* and *Barham*. The smoke screen was evidently effective, for she managed to survive till 7 pm. Some 13 ships fired about 30 salvos at her, and the *Onslow* fired a torpedo, which very possibly hit.

[9] The *Marlborough* opened fire at 6.17 at a *Kaiser* class battleship at a range of 13,000 yards and fired seven salvos in four minutes. The *Barham* opened fire about 6.14 and the *Valiant* reports a range of 19,000 yards and very good visibility at 6.17. Her time is apparently two or three minutes fast; *Official Despatches*, 207.

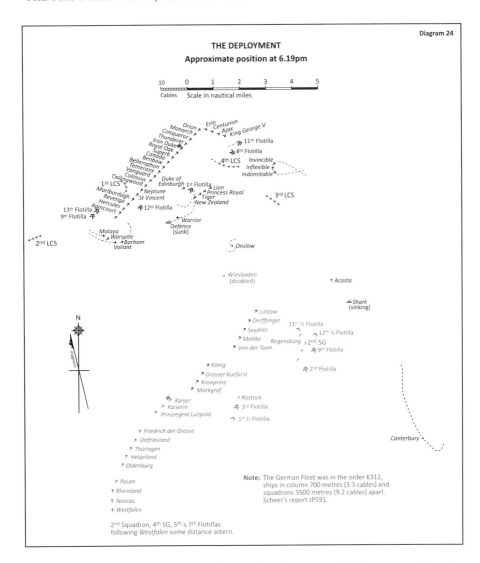

Diagram 24

THE DEPLOYMENT

Approximate position at 6.19pm

Cables   Scale in nautical miles

Note: The German Fleet was in the order K312, ships in column 700 metres (3.3 cables) and squadrons 3500 metres (9.2 cables) apart. Scheer's report JP591.

2nd Squadron, 4th SG, 5th & 7th Flotillas following *Westfalen* some distance astern.

presented a tremendous picture of speed and power, with the scars of battle plainly visible. The guns of one of the *Lion*'s turrets were gazing blankly out on the disengaged side, and a long trail of smoke was pouring from a shell hole in her side. They were engaging the enemy to the southward,[10] when the *Defence* and *Warrior* crossed their bows, and coming down their engaged side fouled the range and shut out the target for a time (Diagram 25). A few miles off on the port bow the 3rd Battle Cruiser Squadron could be seen approaching on a

---

[10] Probably about 12,000 yards off, about 30° before the *Lion*'s starboard beam. *Princess Royal* reports a range of 13,000 yards at 6 hrs. 16 mins. 40 secs. *Tiger* 15,000 yards at 6.17; *New Zealand* (battleship) 17,000 yards at 6.19.

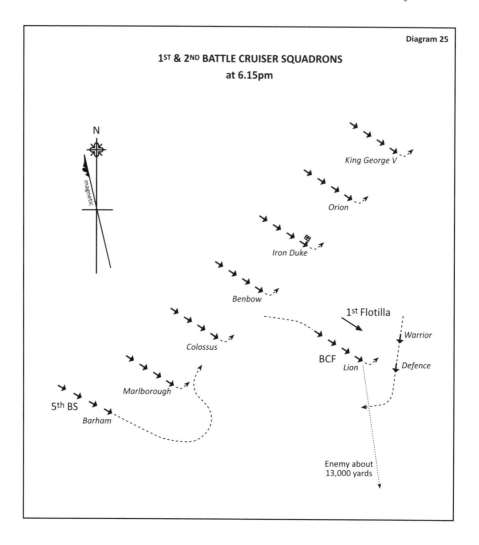

1ST & 2ND BATTLE CRUISER SQUADRONS
at 6.15pm

Diagram 25

Note
The names of the column guides have been inserted for clarity.

Westerly course, and Admiral Beatty altered course to port[11] towards them, ordering Rear-Admiral Hood to take station ahead. Admiral Hood's ships had just been manœuvring to avoid torpedoes fired by the 12th Half Flotilla and 9th

---

[11] About 6.17.

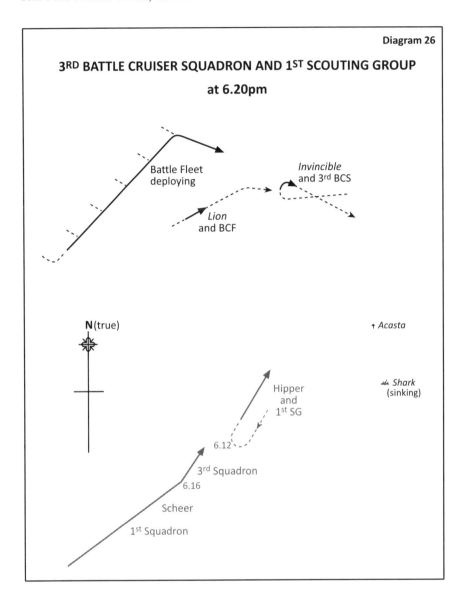

Flotilla about 6 pm.[12] He now turned in a masterly manner ahead of Beatty to a South-Easterly course. Away to the southward, Hipper was returning on a North-Easterly course, and a few minutes later the engagement commenced which was to prove so fateful to the *Invincible* (Diagram 26).

---

[12] These flotillas had gone out to cover the turn away of the 1st Scouting Group and 2nd Scouting Group at 5.55. The tracks of about five torpedoes were seen by the 3rd Battle Cruiser Squadron. The *Invincible* turned to starboard about 6.15, the *Indomitable* to starboard, the *Inflexible* to port to avoid them.

The 5th Battle Squadron

56. Leaving the 3rd Battle Cruiser Squadron just before their guns open at 6.21 on Hipper's ships, we must look at the 5th Battle Squadron turning up in the rear of the battle line. When Admiral Evan-Thomas first sighted the *Marlborough* shortly after 6 pm,[13] he decided to take station ahead of her, evidently regarding her as the head of the line till he saw the fleet beginning to deploy. When the deployment commenced, the *Barham* had reached a position a mile or so on the *Marlborough*'s starboard beam, and as she could not follow Beatty's squadron, now some 3½ miles ahead of her, without masking the fire of the battle line, Admiral Evan-Thomas decided to take station in rear. To do this he had to make a wide turn to port, reducing his range to about 10,000 yards, and the fact that this was done with very little damage to the squadron tends to show that a deployment on the right wing would not have involved excessive risk.[14]

Three of his ships turned in safety, but the *Warspite* was not so fortunate. About 6.20, just as the *Barham* was turning to the northward, she was closing the *Malaya* and 20° port helm was given her.[15] The steering engine was working badly at the time, probably due to a heated thrust bearing and the helm being put over too quickly for the speed of 25 knots, bent the telemotor gearing and the helm jammed.[16] The ship swung round to starboard, just shaving the *Valiant*'s stern, and neither helm nor engines would bring her head back to port. She continued to swing round and was coming under a heavy fire[17] when Captain Phillpotts, making a virtue of necessity, went full speed ahead, and continued the compulsory turn to starboard. A mile or so to the eastward, the *Defence* had just disappeared in a black pall of smoke, and the *Warrior*, badly damaged with her bridge wrecked, and the fate of the *Defence* menacing her every moment, was drawing close, making to the westward under heavy fire.

---

[13] At 6.06 pm; Jellicoe, *Grand Fleet*, 351.

[14] *Editor's note*: See the Chapter IX Endnote for descriptions of the German fire concentrated on the 5th BS.

[15] The account of her movements is not clear. The R.A. [Rear-Admiral] 5th Battle Squadron (*Official Despatches*, 194) says the turn was made without signal, but the signal logs contain the signal at 6.18, 'Turn in succession 16 points to port'. Her movements can be best accounted for on the assumption that she put her helm over with the *Barham*, and then gave hard-a-port helm to get back into line again. The helm jammed and she went right round shaving the stern of the *Valiant*.

[16] *Editor's note*: *Warspite* would also have steering difficulties later in her career: On 18 August 1917, while steaming in the North Sea, her steering jammed; on 8 March 1937, during post-reconstruction trials, her helm jammed again; and again in July 1937 during further trials (Roskill, *HMS Warspite*, 144, 164, 165).

[17] *Warspite* (r) gives the closest range as 12,000 yards (*Official Despatches*, 203).

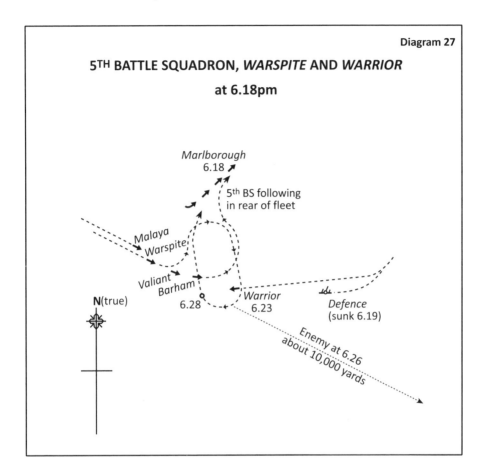

Diagram 27

5TH BATTLE SQUADRON, *WARSPITE* AND *WARRIOR*

at 6.18pm

The *Warspite*'s turn carried her right round the *Warrior*, and drawing off the enemy's fire gave the latter a respite of five or six minutes, which probably saved her from immediate destruction.[18] After making a complete turn to starboard under heavy fire,[19] the *Warspite* regained control of her helm and followed the *Barham* to the northward (Diagram 27).

At 7 pm she was about half a mile off the *Malaya* when it was discovered that the helm was again out of order, and she withdrew out of action to the North-West.[20] She did not return to the fleet. She had received 13 hits, one of which

---

[18] Captain Molteno attributed the movement to chivalry, but the *Warspite*'s report mentions only the vagaries of a stubborn telemotor.

[19] Between 6.18 and 6.28.

[20] One report states that the second steering engine had been connected up with 15 degrees port helm (Fawcett and Hooper, *Fighting at Jutland*, 147). At 8.30 she was some 30 miles to northward of the *Barham*, and at 8.50 asked for the position of the Battle Fleet and was ordered by the Rear-Admiral 5th Battle Squadron to proceed to Rosyth.

had opened the wings and appeared to threaten the engine-room bulkheads. The engines, however, were not damaged, and all the turrets were in action. On her way home she was able to increase to 19 knots and to 22 knots, and to full speed when attacked by a submarine. The 5th Battle Squadron remained in rear of the fleet for the rest of the day, proceeding at 15 to 17 knots, throwing away all the money, foresight and ingenuity which had been spent in equipping it with a speed of 25 knots.[21]

The Light Cruisers and Destroyers

57. The movements of the light cruisers and destroyers were largely governed by the Deployment Diagram, though, in the case of the 2nd Light Cruiser Squadron and 3rd Light Cruiser Squadron, this consideration was rightly subordinated to the exigencies of keeping in touch with the enemy. This diagram (to be found in Grand Fleet Battle Orders)[22] was based on the conception of the fleet in single line engaging the enemy on a parallel course, and various lettered positions were allotted to the cruiser squadrons and flotillas (Diagram 28).

Its disposition provided for a total of four light cruiser squadrons[23] and five flotillas ahead of the Battle Fleet or on its engaged bow. Its limitations are now fairly obvious. It stopped at 6.33 when the battle had scarcely begun: it was based on the battle beginning in a particular way, and on its continuing in a way which the enemy would do his utmost to avoid.

At about 6.15 pm the position of the Light Cruiser Squadrons was approximately as in Diagram 29.

---

[21] According to GFBO the normal position of the 5th Battle Squadron was 1½ miles on the engaged bow of the leading ship, but in the case of a deployment 'away from Heligoland' it was to be in rear. The expression was indefinite. For instance, suppose the German Fleet bearing North of Heligoland to deploy to the East (more or less the conditions of Jutland), is the deployment towards or away from Heligoland?

Editor's note: GFBO Section V 'Orders for the 5th Battle Squadron':

> 5. When practicable, on or shortly before deployment, the Commander-in-Chief will order the 5th Battle Squadron to take station either at the van, forming part of the fleet, or as a fast division some 4 to 5 miles ahead of it, or at the rear.
>
> . . .
>
> 11. The Rear-Admiral [commanding the 5th BS] must be most careful to avoid having his ships between the two battlefleets when fire is opened, or in such a position that the smoke of his ships hampers the fire of our battlefleet. This caution is particularly necessary if the 5th Battle Squadron is proceeding towards our van.

[22] GFBO, December, 1915, 41.

[23] Inclusive of the 5th Light Cruiser Squadron and 10th Flotilla from Harwich.

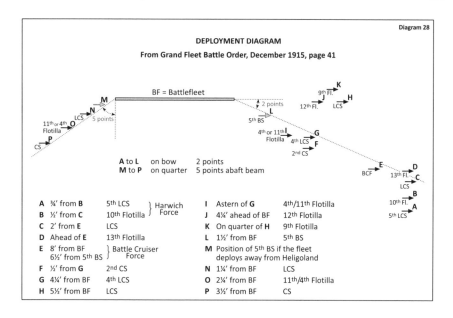

Diagram 28

DEPLOYMENT DIAGRAM

From Grand Fleet Battle Order, December 1915, page 41

A to L	on bow	2 points
M to P	on quarter	5 points abaft beam

A	¾′ from B	5th LCS	Harwich Force	I	Astern of G	4th/11th Flotilla
B	½′ from C	10th Flotilla		J	4¼′ ahead of BF	12th Flotilla
C	2′ from E	LCS		K	On quarter of H	9th Flotilla
D	Ahead of E	13th Flotilla		L	1½′ from BF	5th BS
E	8′ from BF 6½′ from 5th BS	Battle Cruiser Force		M	Position of 5th BS if the fleet deploys away from Heligoland	
F	½′ from G	2nd CS		N	1¼′ from BF	LCS
G	4¼′ from BF	4th LCS		O	2¼′ from BF	11th/4th Flotilla
H	5½′ from BF	LCS		P	3½′ from BF	CS

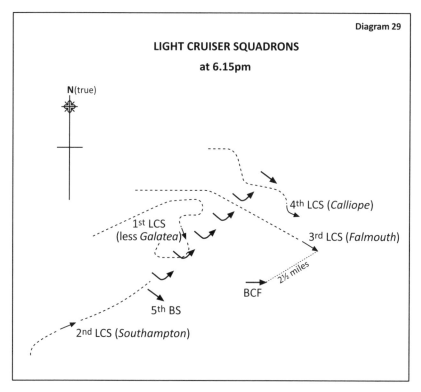

Diagram 29

LIGHT CRUISER SQUADRONS

at 6.15pm

Note

The flagship of the 1st LCS, *Galatea*, experienced a breakdown in a forced draught fan shortly before, and was lagging behind.

The 1st Light Cruiser Squadron, which had been two miles ahead of the *Lion* at 6 pm, got entangled for a time in the lines of the Battle Fleet,[24] then, leaving the *Galatea* behind, went on at full speed round the disengaged side of the fleet. The *Falmouth* and 3rd Light Cruiser Squadron were well ahead[25] of the Battle Fleet just before deployment, keeping in touch with the enemy. As the fleet deployed, they engaged the *Wiesbaden* to the southward,[26] and the *Falmouth* fired a torpedo at her at 5,000 yards. The movements of the 4th Light Cruiser Squadron were simple enough. In a position immediately ahead of the Battle Fleet, it was more easily able to conform to its movements, and forming line ahead just before deployment,[27] took station on the disengaged bow of *King George V*. The *Southampton* and 2nd Light Cruiser Squadron were some distance away all this time. When the deployment commenced they were some 7½ miles behind the *Lion*, and passing 'Windy Corner'[28] at 6.25, went on towards the deployment point.

All this time the 3rd Light Cruiser Squadron, and behind it the 4th Light Cruiser Squadron, were ahead of the Battle Fleet, and up to 6.25 pm were in a favourable position to repel any torpedo attack which the enemy might make. In the movements of the 2nd and 3rd Light Cruiser Squadrons at this time can be discerned a definite intention to keep in touch with the enemy,[29] but the destroyers seem to have been governed only by the idea of taking station on the Battle Fleet. The position of the flotillas on deployment is shown in Diagram 30.

Shortly after 6 pm[30] the Commander-in-Chief had ordered destroyers to take up No. 1 disposition. The 4th, 11th and 12th Flotillas[31] were ahead of the Battle Fleet. On the port beam of the *Lion* was the 1st Flotilla, unable to get ahead because of the *Lion*'s speed: the *Fearless*, their leader, had fallen behind; so, too,

---

[24] Between 6.07 and 6.21; it turned sharp round between the 4th and 5th Divisions at 6.07 and passed astern of the 4th. The *Galatea*'s speed was reduced to 16 knots by a breakdown in the port forced draught fan.

[25] About three miles ahead of the *Orion*.

[26] At 10,000 to 7,000 yards.

[27] At 6.10 pm.

[28] A name given in the fleet to the point nearest the enemy where the *Marlborough* turned at 6.15.

[29] The 3rd Light Cruiser Squadron (*Falmouth*) from 6.24 to 6.32, and 2nd Light Cruiser Squadron (*Southampton*) from 6.40 to 7 pm.

[30] At 6.08 pm No. 1 disposition was divisions in line ahead disposed abeam with leaders ahead.

[31] The 4th Flotilla, ahead of the 2nd Battle Squadron, was 12 in number. With the 3rd Battle Cruiser Squadron: *Shark* (sunk), *Acasta* (disabled), *Ophelia*, *Christopher*. With the 2nd Cruiser Squadron: *Owl*, *Hardy*, *Midge*. The 11th Flotilla, ahead of 4th Battle Squadron, 16 in number. The 12th Flotilla, ahead of the 1st Battle Squadron, 15 in number. (*Mischief* with 2nd Cruiser Squadron.)

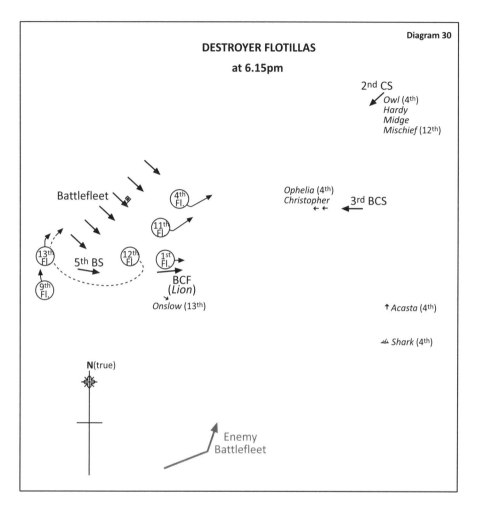

DESTROYER FLOTILLAS

at 6.15pm

Note
The flotilla number of *Onslow* is missing from the original, and has been inserted for completeness.

had the 13th Flotilla:[32] the 9th and 10th, led by the *Lydiard*, had dropped to the port beam of the 5th Battle Squadron at 6 pm.[33]

When the fleet deployed, the 4th and 11th Flotillas turned to port and proceeded to take station ahead of the line: the 12th turned and took up its position in rear on the engaged side. The 13th and 9th did the same on the disengaged side and remained there during the action.

---

[32] Only five ships with the *Champion*, viz.: *Narborough*, *Obdurate*, *Petard*, *Pelican*, *Nerissa*. The *Turbulent*, *Termagant* and *Nicator* were with the *Lydiard* and 9th. The *Onslow* and *Moresby* were on the engaged side of the *Lion*. The *Nestor* and *Nomad* had been sunk.

[33] *Lydiard*'s diagram, *Official Despatches*, Plate 22.

As the battle cruisers passed the head of the Battle Fleet, the destroyers of the 1st and 12th Flotillas began to run through one another's lines, and several had to stop and go astern to avoid collision.[34] Salvos were falling round them, and the *Attack* was hit by the nose of an 11 in. projectile.

The lines were in some confusion at this juncture, and for a short time destroyers were so busy getting out of one another's way that they had little time to think of the enemy.

The disposition of the flotillas was too cramped, but this was a temporary drawback, and the confusion had certainly straightened out by 6.30 pm. After deployment the policy adopted seems to have been one of passivity. The flotillas appear merely to have attached themselves to the Battle Fleet, and did not even conform to the Deployment Diagram. Between 6.35 and 7.10 pm the Germans were allowed to make three separate attacks[35] on the fleet: two of them were made by only two and three boats respectively, which were left to do what they liked between the lines.

The flotillas might have attacked the enemy Battle Fleet at this time, but this was more or less precluded by the Battle Orders, which made the defence of the Battle Fleet their primary duty. It remained for them to defend the Battle Fleet against destroyer attack. This could only be done by pushing out towards the enemy and keeping the line of approach under observation. That is why the Deployment Diagram placed them on the engaged side. Had half a flotilla pushed boldly out on the course followed in safety by the *Falmouth*,[36] they would almost certainly have encountered and driven back the German attacks, one of which possibly accounted for the *Marlborough*.

There was no lack of initiative in destroyers working independently,[37] but the flotillas as a whole seemed to wait for orders. Only two attacks were made on the enemy fleet in the day action: one by the 13th, ordered by the Vice-Admiral, Battle Cruiser Fleet, at 4.15, when the *Nestor* and *Nomad*, *Nicator* and *Petard* made their brave and resolute attack; and the other independently by the *Shark* and her gallant little flotilla, which sent a torpedo into the *Seydlitz*.[38]

---

[34] *Faulknor, Obedient* and several others (Fawcett and Hooper, *Fighting at Jutland*, 130, 131).

[35] About 6.35: G.88, V.73, S.32. About 6.55: V.73, G.88. About 7.05: three boats of 3rd Flotilla and three others.

[36] The *Falmouth* followed a course about 4,000 yards on the engaged side and actually engaged the enemy's battle cruisers without being hit, but by 6.35 she was far past the point where the German flotillas attacked.

[37] E.g., the *Moresby* and *Onslow*.

[38] *Editor's note*: As noted on p. 96, *Seydlitz* was probably torpedoed by *Petard*, not one of *Shark*'s flotilla.

There was nothing to prevent the 13th and 9th Flotillas, which were in rear on the disengaged side, putting on speed and encircling the fleet to take up station ahead, but they did not attempt to do so. This lack of initiative must have been closely associated with their system of training and command, though it may partly be attributed to the defensive policy assigned to them.

The Battle Fleet

58. The Battle Fleet after deployment was only occasionally in action, and its actual firing was confined to two intervals of about quarter of an hour each: the first immediately after deployment when the fleet was in line ahead, commencing about 6.25 and lasting till about 6.40; the second on the Southerly course, commencing abut 7.10 and lasting till about 7.25. The *Iron Duke* was one of the first to fire; she turned to SE by E at 6.21,[39] and opened fire on the *Wiesbaden* two minutes later, but it was not till 6.30 that she found a suitable target in the form of a ship of the *König* class, and gave it nine salvos and saw six hits.[40] For the first twenty minutes the firing was limited to about one-third of the fleet, the ships firing with any effect on the enemy's Battle Fleet at this time numbering less than a dozen;[41] but in spite of smoke and poor visibility considerable punishment was certainly inflicted between 6.25 and 6.35 on the leading ships of the German line.[42] At 6.26 the Commander-in-Chief reduced speed to 14 knots in order to let the battle cruisers get ahead.[43] The signal did not get through quickly, and bunching and overlapping began to occur,[44] with the result that two or three ships found their fire masked.[45] It was probably accentuated by the numerous small craft moving close to the lines, but gradually the line straightened out, and the deployment may be regarded as completed at 6.42.[46]

---

[39] Jellicoe's plan, *Official Despatches*, Plate 7A.

[40] *Editor's note*: Campbell (*Jutland*, 187–8) credits *Iron Duke* with 7 hits on *König* (CPC) and *Monarch* with one APC, all striking within a few minutes either side of 6.35 pm.

[41] *Iron Duke* (9 salvos), *Hercules* (7 salvos), *Marlborough* (7), *Revenge*, *Colossus*, *Neptune*, *Barham* (3), *Orion* (4), *Monarch* (3), *Conqueror* (3), *Thunderer* (3).

[42] Forty-two salvos are reported at the 3rd Squadron between 6.16 and 6.40. It received 25 hits altogether, and it is reasonable to attribute at least one half of them to this period.

Editor's note: Only *Markgraf* was hit (probably by *Orion* at 6.35) and she also received damage from a near miss (Campbell, *Jutland*, 193).

[43] Jellicoe, *Grand Fleet*, 352: the battle cruisers were then on the starboard beam of the *King George V*, going 25 knots.

[44] The *Marlborough* had to reduce to 8 knots and the *St. Vincent* had to stop. The 5th Division was still bunched at 6.32.

[45] *Neptune* (6th Division) by *St. Vincent* (5th Division) at 6.32; *Thunderer* and *Conqueror* (2nd Division) by *Iron Duke* (3rd Division).

[46] Jellicoe, *Grand Fleet*, 353 says 6.38, but the *Valiant* did not turn till 6.40.

The German Fleet

59. At 6.27 the *König* coming up on a NE course turned to East, probably induced to do so by the thunder of the guns on her starboard bow.[47] The 1st Squadron had apparently turned together to the northward about 6.24.[48]

Just at this time the poor visibility evidently led Admiral Jellicoe to think of closing the range, and he hoisted a signal to alter course by sub-divisions to SSE.[49] This would have been a difficult movement to accomplish. Half the fleet only had deployed, and including the 5th Battle Squadron there were still some fourteen ships to turn.[50] The British Fleet was therefore in the form of an L open to the SSE, and a turn by sub-divisions in that direction would have resulted in an L with twelve sub-divisions steering out of it (Diagram 31). The disadvantages of such a formation were quickly seen and the signal was negatived, but it indicated an appreciation of the necessity for closing the range. Admiral Jellicoe's choice of a southern horizon seems to have been fully justified, for the Germans do not seem to have seen the British line, and their fire at this time was apparently directed against Beatty's battle cruisers. Half of the British fleet was firing by now,[51] but the enemy's reply was ineffective,[52] and no British battleship was hit.

The Loss of the *Invincible*

60. While the Battle Fleet was deploying a fierce engagement had developed to the south-eastward between Admirals Hipper and Hood. As the *Invincible* turned to south-eastward at 6.20, Hipper's battle cruisers could be seen approaching from the southward,[53] and turning to a parallel course, they opened fire about 6.23[54] (Diagram 26). The advantage at first lay with the 3rd Battle Cruiser Squadron and several heavy projectiles crashed into the

---

[47] The 3rd Battle Cruiser Squadron engaging the 1st Scouting Group.

[48] *Editor's note*: *König* and the 3rd Squadron turned together onto 32° at 6.15 pm, and subsequently returned to a line-ahead formation on 55° and then 77°. The 1st Squadron and Fleet Flagship, *Friedrich der Grosse*, were steering 32° by 6.18. At 6.35, when *König* was being fired on by *Iron Duke*, she gradually altered course to starboard, generally following Hipper's battle cruisers (Campbell, *Jutland*, 149).

[49] Not in *Iron Duke* (s[1]); *Benbow* (s), 6.29.

[50] The turning point was probably occupied at 6.27 by the *Benbow* or one of her division.

[51] Mean time of opening fire was 6.27½.

[52] 'Our ships were not seriously under fire', Sturdee (r), *Official Despatches*, 122. 'The 3rd sub-division was never under fire', Duff (r), *Official Despatches*, 124.

[53] Bearing about S 15 W.

[54] Von Hase says they engaged 'Dreadnoughts' to the N.E., but as he speaks of the *Invincible* as a 'Dreadnought' it is clear that the 3rd Battle Cruiser Squadron is meant.

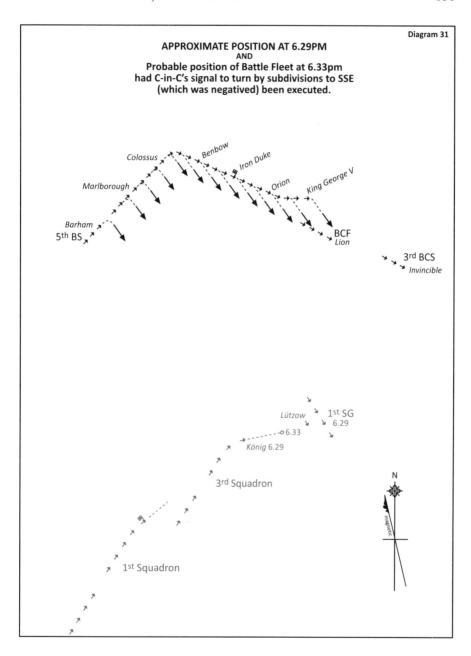

APPROXIMATE POSITION AT 6.29PM
AND
**Probable position of Battle Fleet at 6.33pm
had C-in-C's signal to turn by subdivisions to SSE
(which was negatived) been executed.**

Diagram 31

Derfflinger. But at 6.31[55] the veil of mist lifted for a few minutes. Von Hase in the *Derfflinger* saw a 'Dreadnought' sharply silhouetted before him steaming at full speed on a parallel course. He trained rapidly on her and gave a range of 9,000 metres (9,876 yards). The salvo went over and he came down 100. The

---

[55] Von Hase says 6.29.

next salvo had two shorts and two hits. The third fell on Q turret and again was witnessed the tremendous tragedy of a great ship disappearing beneath the waves.

Several big explosions took place in rapid succession; masses of coal dust issued from the riven hull; great tongues of flames played over the ship; the masts collapsed; the ship broke in two, and an enormous pall of black smoke ascended to the sky. As it cleared away the bow and stern could be seen standing up out of the water as if to mark the place where an Admiral lay.[56]

The action continued for a few minutes, but Hipper's squadron had evidently suffered severely, for at 6.35 it turned sharply away to the westward.

Scheer's Turn Away at 6.35 pm

61. The position at this time is shown in Diagram 32. The *König* and Behneke's 3rd Squadron after turning at 6.27 had continued for some six minutes on an Easterly course. Behneke, in the *König*, then turned to the South-East, mistaking the guns of the 3rd Battle Cruiser Squadron on his port bow for the British Main Fleet. The 1st Squadron seems to have turned together at the same time to ENE, bringing them once more in line with the 3rd. The *König* had only been a few minutes on her new course when Scheer, evidently falling into the same mistake as Behneke and influenced by Hipper's turn away at this time,[57] decided to withdraw, and made a signal for the whole fleet to turn 16 points together to the westward.

The manœuvre was not a simple one, for it involved a turn together of 16 ships with a kink of not less than two points at two places in the line.[58] But this swing round of the whole fleet on a curved line had been constantly practised by Scheer in manœuvres and it now stood him in good stead. The line turned,[59] and, followed by the battle cruisers, drew off to the westward.

---

[56] Von Hase (I.D. 1220), 32; picture of the explosion in Fawcett and Hooper, *Fighting at Jutland*, 244. Six survivors (two officers and four men) were picked up by the *Badger* (1st Flotilla) at 6.40 pm.

Editor's note: Surveyed immediately post-war, *Invincible*'s position was determined to be 57° 03' 15.0" N, 06° 07' 45.0" E. In 1991, an expedition set off to find some of the Jutland wrecks, and the mean position of the centre of the wreck was noted as 57° 03' 47.3" N, 06° 07' 11.0" E (correspondence from Warrant Officer Robert Myers, Expedition Leader).

[57] Scheer says 'that the battle cruisers were forced to turn away so sharply that at 6.35 I was obliged to make a battle turn of 16 points to starboard, altering course to West'.

[58] A kink of about four points at the 3rd or 4th ship (*Kronprinz* or *Markgraf*) and of some two points at the last ship of the 3rd Squadron, the *Prinzregent Luitpold*. Scheer's diagram V, German Plan VI.

[59] To about S 60 W.

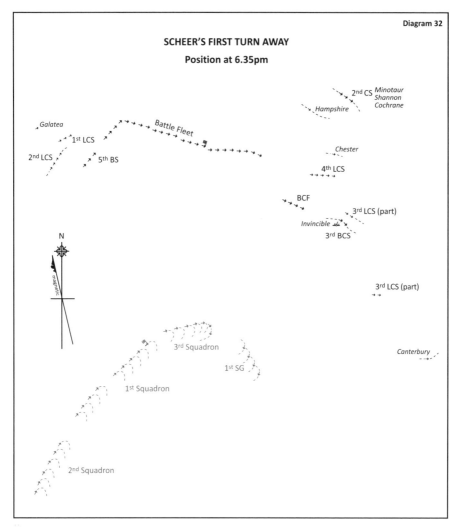

Diagram 32

SCHEER'S FIRST TURN AWAY

Position at 6.35pm

Note
Lützow is missing from the original. She would have been between the 3rd Squadron and the 1st Scouting Group.

As Scheer turned, the 3rd Flotilla was sent out to attack to the North-East, but the slackening of the British fire led Commodore Michelson,[60] the Senior Officer (T), to think that it was being launched 'into a void', and he recalled it. It came back after raising a smoke screen to cover the turn of the fleet, but two of its boats, G.88 and V.73, went on in company with S.32 of the 1st Flotilla, and

---

[60] *Editor's note*: Spelt 'Nichelsen' in the original. In fact, it was Commodore Andreas Michelson whose pendant was flown in *Rostock*.

fired six torpedoes, four of which passed close to the *Princess Royal* and *Tiger*.[61]
This was one of the critical moments of the action, and Scheer's manœuvre
was almost precisely similar in its main features to that which he performed
three-quarters of an hour later at 7.15. It bears all the marks of a preconcerted
design. The prospect of meeting the British Fleet must often have presented
itself to the German Commander-in-Chief. A fight on parallel courses with a
fleet greatly superior in gun power was out of the question. There was only one
course to pursue – to turn away – and in each case the same manœuvre is
repeated. A flotilla attacks, a smoke screen is thrown up, and the fleet turns away
altogether.

The withdrawal of the German Fleet from its precarious and difficult
position must be ascribed to the British Fleet deploying outside the range of
practical visibility, and to the lack of an immediate tactical answer to Scheer's
move. To ensure a continuance of the action the British Fleet had to turn at
once to a course between SW and SSW.[62] No reply was forthcoming, and in the
thickening mist and smoke the enemy was lost to sight, and a lull ensued which
gave Scheer a short and much needed respite.

Chapter IX Endnote

Although the *Appreciation* asserts that the 'very little damage' sustained by the 5th Battle
Squadron as it turned under the guns of the High Seas Fleet as the Grand Fleet deployed shows
'that a deployment on the right wing would not have involved excessive risk', in fact the squadron
was subjected to an intense barrage of German gunfire and it is fortunate for the British (and
indicative of the difficulties inherent in concentrating the gunfire of several ships onto the same
target) that so few ships were hit. One of *Malaya*'s officers would record:

> . . . it is indeed extraordinary that so few hits were obtained, considering the number
> and proximity of the shells that fell amongst us . . . (Fawcett and Hooper, *Fighting at Jutland*,
> 124–6).

It was this officer's opinion that it was the short duration of the 'muddle' which prevented more
damage from occurring. Furthermore, Evan-Thomas' report would state:

---

[61] Scheer (r); Scheer, *Germany's High Seas Fleet*, 154; *Tiger* (r) states that they 'developed a
very heavy smoke screen' at this time.

[62] Reference to Diagram 33 will show that if the 5th Battle Squadron, followed by the 6th, 5th,
and 4th Divisions had led round to the south-westward and proceeded at full speed to the
northward of the enemy fleet, whilst the battle cruisers, followed by the 1st, 2nd and 3rd
Divisions, had carried out a similar movement to the southward, the rear of the High Sea Fleet
would have been enveloped and exposed to an overwhelming concentration. Nor would the
danger of torpedoes have been great, for the fleet could break up into divisions and thus reduce
the target very considerably. But an attack of this kind was outside the scope of the Grand Fleet
Battle Orders, which were based on the principle of the Battle Fleet working as one large unit
in a single line.

During this turn ships came under a heavy fire from the enemy's leading battleships, but the shooting was not good and very few hits were made (*Official Despatches*, 192).

Barham's Captain wrote:

The leading enemy Battle Squadron ('Königs') seeing this [turn], opened a terrific fire on the turning point, and 'Barham' was surrounded by a hailstorm of splashes . . . (*Official Despatches*, 200).

Captain Woollcombe of *Valiant* reported:

As H.M. Ships 'Defence', 'Warrior' and 'Black Prince' came within range of the enemy, they received a concentrated and extremely hot fire; the shot were falling at regular intervals, grouped in salvoes, forming a danger zone of from 1,000 to 1,500 yards (*Official Despatches*, 208).

All of this suggests that, had the Grand Fleet deployed on the right wing, it would have been subjected to a very hot fire indeed, and the longer time required to complete the manoeuvre (involving as it would have two turns for most of the fleet – the first turn to get in line behind *Marlborough*'s division, and then a turn to get onto a course parallel to the Germans) would have given the High Seas Fleet a chance to punish the British severely before turning away for an unimpeded escape toward the southeast (see Diagram 22).

CHAPTER X

THE SECOND ENGAGEMENT AND SCHEER'S TURN AWAY. THE TURN TO SOUTH-EAST AND SOUTH

62. By 6.40 the deployment was almost complete and the line was straightening out. It was evident that the enemy had turned away, and at 6.42 the Commander-in-Chief made a signal to alter course by divisions to South-East[1] (Diagram 33). Course was altered at 6.44 but the turn of one point towards the enemy was not sufficient to meet the circumstances of the case. Had the fleet turned at once to South, which was done ten minutes later, the effect would have been more pronounced, and the 1st Scouting Group, when it returned at 7.15 pm, would have come under a crushing fire from the 5th and 6th Divisions at a range of under 8,000 yards.

The only objection to a Southerly course was the risk of torpedo attack, which could have been greatly reduced by the flotillas moving out on the exposed flank, but in any case had to be accepted if the action was to be decisive. A lull ensued in the firing, and for eleven minutes the fleet moved to the South-East. The 4th Light Cruiser Squadron had crossed the track of the fleet at 6.33, and now took station ahead of the *King George V*.[2]

The *Lion* by this time had reached a position some 3½ miles ahead[3] of the *King George V* and was steering SE. The 3rd Battle Cruiser Squadron was a mile off on her starboard bow. Far away to the westward, astern of the Battle Fleet, was the *Southampton*. She had just reached the point of deployment where the long file of ships had followed one another in succession to SE by E.

---

[1] Lord Jellicoe in Jellicoe, *Grand Fleet*, 356 says 'without signal'; *Iron Duke* (s[1]), 6.42; *New Zealand*, 6.42; *Marlborough* (w/e), 6.41; *Benbow* (s), 6.40.

Editor's note: Commander-in-Chief to Dreadnought Battlefleet and attached cruisers: 'Divisions separately alter course in succession to SE, preserving their formation'. This is noted as being sent at 6.44 in the *Official Despatches*, 460.

[2] It came too close, and the *King George V* had to alter course to starboard at 6.51 to avoid a collision.

[3] At 6.44, 10° on *King George V*'s engaged bow.

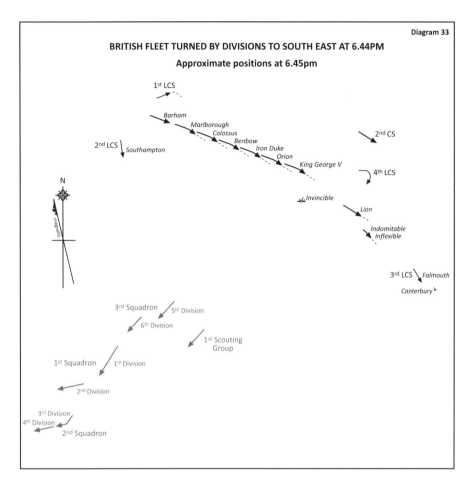

Diagram 33

BRITISH FLEET TURNED BY DIVISIONS TO SOUTH EAST AT 6.44PM

Approximate positions at 6.45pm

There she saw the enemy turn away, and to keep them in view, ran boldly down to the southward and south-eastward. At 7 pm she signalled their bearing and course to Admiral Beatty,[4] and though the importance of the signal was subsequently diminished by the re-appearance of the enemy, it deserves to be remembered as a fine example of light cruiser work. She then turned, and as the British Fleet was now coming down on a southerly course to the eastward of her, passed to the northward and astern of it.

The Commander-in-Chief did not receive the *Southampton*'s report till 7 pm and had already ordered the fleet to alter course to South.[5] Whilst this signal was being made the only German torpedo to hit in the action got home

---

[4] 'Enemy Battle Fleet steering ESE. Enemy bears SSW, number unknown. My position Lat. 57° 02' N, Long. 6° 07' E'. Received *Iron Duke* 7 pm.

[5] *Benbow* (s), 6.52; *Iron Duke* (s[1]), 6.50; *Marlborough* (s), 6.52 executive, 6.53; *New Zealand* (s), 6.55; *Iron Duke* (r) mentions altering course to S 8 E at 6.51; *Official Despatches*, 53.

on the *Marlborough*. The probability is that it was fired by the *Wiesbaden*. The explosion flooded the Diesel and hydraulic engine rooms: one of the boiler rooms began to flood and the ship listed seven degrees, but she was able to continue in the line and to maintain a speed of 17 knots. In 'A' boiler room the rising water quickly put out the fires on the starboard side, but the stokers working in water up to their knees continued with the greatest coolness to keep the port boilers going.[6]

At about 6.55 Scheer had sent three or four destroyers to save the crew of the *Wiesbaden*. On their way V.73 and G.88 seized the opportunity of firing four torpedoes at the 5th Battle Squadron. It is just possible that one of these may have hit the *Marlborough*, but it would have had to be fired about 6.44, which does not agree with Scheer's time. The turn to South at 6.55, which brought the fleet into a quarter line formation of divisions in line ahead with guides bearing roughly SE by E (Diagram 34), is one of the noteworthy movements of the action, for it brought the fleet back again into divisions. It had taken nearly half an hour to deploy, and had only been deployed about quarter of an hour when a divisional formation was resumed leaving the *Marlborough*'s division more exposed to attack than it was at 6.15, when its position caused the Commander-in-Chief to deploy away from the enemy. This resumption of a divisional formation indicates that the fleet was too large to manœuvre as a single whole, and that a more flexible tactical system was required in which the Commander-in-Chief, after indicating the point of attack, would have left the squadron commanders free to support and assist each other in carrying out his wishes.[7]

---

[6] At 2 am the ship had to reduce to 12 knots.

[7] *Editor's note*: This statement was considered by Captain Vernon S H Haggard, the Director of Training and Staff Duties, to be 'one of the most noteworthy misrepresentations in the whole work'. He went on to say:

> In the first place, the obvious way for the line of battle to be closed upon the enemy was by divisions, as was, indeed, laid down in the [Grand Fleet] battle orders. The turn to south was not made to resume a divisional formation but to close the enemy, and the C-in-C has already been severely criticised for not closing the enemy. The single line is alleged to be wrong and to turn into divisions is alleged to be wrong.
>
> As the enemy was out of sight, the MARLBOROUGH's division was not left 'more exposed to attack that [*sic*; than] it was at 6.15', nor can any stretch of the imagination support the contention that to close the enemy by divisions (obviously the most handy and seamanlike method) 'indicated that the fleet was too large to manoeuvre as a single whole' (University of California, Irvine, Langston Library, Microfilm M 000147).

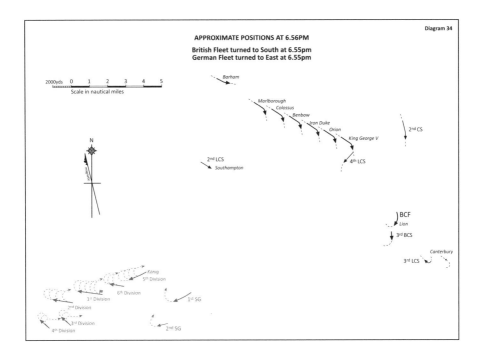

Scheer's Turn to the Eastward at 6.55

63. The enemy meanwhile was retiring on a Westerly course. His formation was apparently a loose divisional formation.[8]

The lines were reversed, and the *Westfalen* was leading with the *König* bringing up the rear. The 2nd Squadron was a mile or so to the south-westward on a North-Westerly course, conforming to the movements of the 1st Squadron. Some three or four miles to the south-eastward of the *König* was the 1st Scouting Group in a far from happy state.

The *Lützow* was badly down by the bows listing heavily with enormous volumes of smoke pouring out of her forecastle; she hauled out of the line and steamed slowly off on a Southerly course.[9] At 7 pm Admiral Hipper left her and headed in a destroyer for the *Seydlitz*, signalling to Captain Hartog of the *Derfflinger* to assume command till his flag was transferred.

The *Derfflinger* herself was in a bad way. The masts and rigging were badly cut up and the wireless sending apparatus out of action. Two armour plates had been torn off the bows, leaving a huge hole open to the sea. A danger of another sort now confronted her. The torpedo nets aft had been shot away and were trailing over the port propeller, threatening every moment to foul it and

---

[8] *Official Despatches*, German Plan VI, diagram 6.
[9] German Plan V shows her out of the line at 6.30 pm.

bring the engine to a stop. But the enemy were no longer in sight. The ship was stopped; the crews of the two turrets, all to perish within an hour, swarmed out, and, working like madmen, cut away the nets.

At 6.55,[10] when about 13 miles SW of the *Iron Duke*, the German Battle Fleet was swung round 16 points together to an Easterly course. It was now heading straight into the centre of the arc formed by the British Fleet. In a few minutes the leading squadron and battle cruisers would be threatened with envelopment and the concentrated fire of practically the whole Grand Fleet. The High Sea Fleet seemed to be rushing headlong to destruction. The motives for this manœuvre which are given in Scheer's book and despatches should be accepted with reserve. He explains that it was too early to take up night cruising order. The British could follow, and by compelling him to fight, force him to adopt a particular course of action under enemy pressure. The initiative would pass into their hands, and they would be able to cut off his retreat from the Bight. There was only one way to avoid this: by advancing regardless of consequences, and sending all destroyers to the attack. A bold offensive would upset Admiral Jellicoe's plans for the rest of the day, and, if the blow fell heavily, facilitate the German retreat during the night. It would give an opportunity, too, for a last effort to save the *Wiesbaden*, or at least rescue her crew.[11] His intention was more probably to slip past the rear of the British Fleet, but in any case his hazardous movement escaped the crushing counter-attack that it deserved.

British Movements from 6.55

64. Meanwhile, the British Battle Fleet was pursuing its way to the south in divisions line ahead one mile apart, disposed approximately SE by E. At 7.05 the Commander-in-Chief had altered course three points to starboard (to SW by S), in order to close the range,[12] but he had only been on this course a few

---

[10] Harper X, 6.57; Scheer's despatch and book, 6.55.

[11] The Austrian Naval Attaché's report (June 17, 1916) quotes Scheer as saying that 'The fact is, I had no definite object. I made the first advance because I thought I ought to assist the *Wiesbaden* and because the situation was quite obscure to me, for I saw nothing of the *Lützow* and received no W/T reports. I soon saw that the leading ships were coming under an overwhelming fire and that I could not risk the fleet on the *Wiesbaden*'s account. When I noticed that the British pressure had quite ceased and that the fleet remained intact in my hands, I turned back under the impression that the action could not end in this way, and that I ought to seek contact with the enemy again'. Von Trotha, the Admiral's Chief of Staff, is reported on the same authority to have said jocularly that if an Admiral had brought about such a position at manœuvres he would be relieved of his command.

[12] Jellicoe, *Grand Fleet*, 360; not mentioned in Commander-in-Chief's despatch.

minutes when a submarine was reported,[13] and hostile destroyers were seen approaching from the SW. The Commander-in-Chief thereupon turned back to South[14] with the two-fold object of turning on the submarine, and being ready for any manœuvre that might be required.[15] This alteration turned the fleet away from the enemy just when pursuit to the westward was vitally important. If the German Fleet had not returned on its own initiative at 6.55, this turn to the South might have meant the end of the battle. Neither the report of a submarine nor the sighting of a few destroyers appear to justify such a proceeding. No manœuvre was necessary except to close the enemy.

The disadvantages of a cut-and-dried plan of deployment were now painfully evident. When the fleet turned into divisions, the conditions of the Deployment Diagram fell away. The direction from which a torpedo attack might be expected was now the area ahead of the *Marlborough*. Her division was the most exposed, while that of the *King George V*, about five miles further away, was the safest and least exposed. If the function of the flotillas was to protect the Battle Fleet, it appears that the 12th, 13th and 9th should have pushed up on the *Marlborough*'s engaged quarter, whilst the 4th Light Cruiser Squadron, the 11th and 4th Flotillas, should have taken up a position on her bow without orders at 6.55. The 4th Light Cruiser Squadron could easily have done so. It had crossed ahead of the *King George V* at 6.51, and it required a speed of only 24 knots to reach a position two miles ahead of the *Marlborough* by 7.06 It would probably not have been able to stay there long, for at 7.12 the enemy battle cruisers would have forced it away, but it would have continued in a better position to deal with the flotillas later on. Nor need it have gone far, for Hipper's ships almost immediately came under a terrific fire, and could have done nothing to the 4th Light Cruiser Squadron. This view is upheld by the cases of the *Falmouth* and *Yarmouth*, which engaged the same squadron between 6.24 and 6.32 with entire immunity at 8,000 yards when it was occupied only with the fire of the 3rd Battle Cruiser Squadron. But the Commodore was apparently still thinking of the Deployment Diagram, and was maintaining station on the *King George V*.[16]

---

[13] Jellicoe, *Grand Fleet*, 360. The *King George V* at 7 pm reported a submarine ahead of the *Iron Duke* and the *Duke of Edinburgh* (then about 3½ miles on the port bow of the *Iron Duke*), reported a submarine at 7.01 two points on her own port bow. The reports could not have referred to the same submarine, but as there was no submarine in the vicinity the point need not be laboured.

[14] Harper, 7.09; *King George V*, 7.09; *Revenge*, 7.10; *Iron Duke*, 7.07; Commander-in-Chief's despatch, 7.10.

[15] Jellicoe, *Grand Fleet*, 361. The Commander-in-Chief's despatch mentions only the approach of a flotilla of destroyers.

[16] *See* signals, 4th Light Cruiser Squadron, between 7.08 and 7.22; *Official Despatches*, 463 and 464.

Editor's note: For convenience, the signals referred to are given in Chapter X Endnote 1.

The tendency to turn away at 7.10, and later at 7.22, would probably have been diminished if the flotillas had moved out in this direction, but the defensive rôle assigned to them was an exceedingly difficult one to fulfil satisfactorily. They did not know how long the divisional formation was to be maintained, they were probably unacquainted with the general tactical situation, and may not even have known the direction in which the German Fleet had retired.

Admiral Beatty, however, appreciated the significance of the new formation, for he made a signal to the 3rd Battle Cruiser Squadron (then a mile or so ahead), to take station astern, and turned at 6.54 to allow him to do so, then shaped course SW by S to cross the line of the advancing Battle Fleet.[17]

The Engagement, 7.12 pm to 7.20 pm (Diagram 35)

65. The Battle Fleet had hardly turned to South when the *Hercules*, the third ship in the *Marlborough*'s division, sighted the *Seydlitz* to the south-westward, and at the same moment the *Colossus* in the next division saw the *Derfflinger* coming out of the mist. There were the German battle cruisers clearly visible on a South-Easterly course at a range of less than 10,000 yards. Two or three miles further off, Scheer's battleships could be seen. He was returning in line ahead, the *König* leading at the head of the 3rd Squadron, with the *Friedrich der Grosse* and the 1st Squadron following behind. The *Hercules* opened fire on the *Seydlitz* and the *Colossus* on the *Derfflinger*, and hits were obtained by both after a few salvos. The *Marlborough*'s guns came into action at the same time,[18] followed at 7.15 by those of the battle cruisers, and the guns of practically the whole fleet joined in. The mist cleared for a few minutes and the *Derfflinger* and *Seydlitz* came under a tremendous fire.[19] In the former, a 15 in. shell went through the armour of C turret and burst. The flames passed to the working chamber and ignited four charges, and then to the handing room, setting four

---

[17] *Editor's note*: There is a telling omission in the *NSA* at this point: the circling of Beatty's battle cruisers at circa 7.05. It is hinted at in Diagram 34, but you'll note that the text makes no mention of it – this was one of the key items that Beatty did his best to suppress in the Harper Narrative. All evidence points to a lack of attention on the bridge of *Lion* (Captain Chatfield had gone below) as a course change was made, the end result being *Lion* and the rest of the BCF making a complete 360° turn.

[18] The *Marlborough* says she was firing at a *Markgraf* class at 10,200.

[19] The *Derfflinger* from the **Revenge*, **Colossus*, **Neptune*, **Benbow* and *Superb*; the *Seydlitz* from **Hercules*, **Revenge* and **Barham*, *Agincourt*, **Collingwood*, *Bellerophon*, *Royal Oak* and *Lion*. The **Valiant* and **Malaya* at the *Von der Tann* at 10,400. The *Orion* was firing at 19,000 yards, *Monarch* about 18,000, and *Centurion* probably at *Lützow*. (Asterisks denote probable hits.)

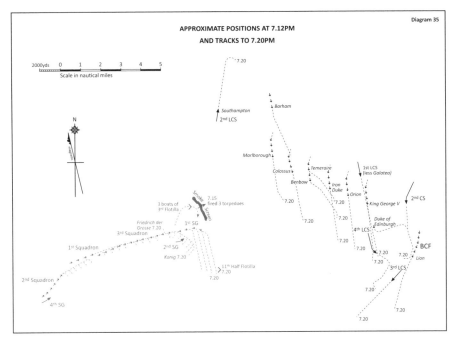

Diagram 35

APPROXIMATE POSITIONS AT 7.12PM
AND TRACKS TO 7.20PM

more on fire. But they burnt only, and did not explode. Of the 78 men in the turret, 73 perished. Another 15 in. shell struck the roof of D turret,[20] went through it, and burst inside with terrible effect. The flash set fire to a number of cartridges, and great tongues of flames went roaring skyward from both the after turrets – like two ghastly funeral torches.[21] Another shell struck the conning tower, tearing huge pieces out of the armour, and another burst under the bridge.[22] The visibility was all in favour of the British. The British ships were barely visible: the red flashes of the guns were all that could be seen. In the *Derfflinger* only A turret remained in action, and got in two hits on the *Colossus*;[23] one entered the foremost superstructure and burst on the port side

---

[20] This corresponds with the *Benbow*'s report; *Official Despatches*, 120.

[21] Von Hase (I.D. 1220), 35.

[22] It is highly probable that the *Derfflinger* would have shared the fate of the *Queen Mary* if it had not been for experience gained during the Dogger Bank action, when a shell which ignited charges in the *Seydlitz*'s after turret wiped out two complete turrets' crews. Double asbestos flaps were fitted subsequently, and alterations were made in the stowage of ammunition. Curiously enough a shell hit the *Seydlitz* in almost exactly the same place at Jutland, but only caused a few casualties.

[23] *Colossus* (r) states that they were hit by the second ship (i.e., *Seydlitz*). These were the only hits received in the Battle Fleet during the action.

Editor's note: Other than the ships of the 5th BS, *Colossus* was indeed the only British battleship to be hit that day. Campbell (*Jutland*, 218) gives the credit to *Seydlitz*, not *Derfflinger*.

of the lower gun deck, firing ten boxes of ready use cordite but only slightly wounding two or three men; the other hit the port signal deck without bursting; a third burst short, abreast of the fore bridge, wrecked the starboard searchlight, damaged the chart and signal house, and severely wounded three men. The guns of the 5th Battle Squadron were also in action. The ships in the British port wing divisions were firing too, but at a considerably greater range.[24]

The *Iron Duke* had opened fire on the battleships[25] as early as 7.13 at a range of 15,400 yards, shifting to the battle cruisers at 7.20. Some 2½ miles ahead[26] of the British Battle Fleet, Admiral Beatty's battle cruisers were also firing.[27]

This heavy burst of firing lasted for about six minutes,[28] and was for the German battle cruisers the most critical part of the action. It had hardly begun when Hipper went alongside the *Seydlitz* to transfer his flag, but finding her wireless shot away, and a couple of thousand tons of water in her,[29] he proceeded to the *Moltke*. As he got alongside, the intensity of the British fire redoubled, the captain dared not stop,[30] and Hipper was left to wander about in his destroyer for a time.

As soon as Scheer realised that he was facing the Main British Fleet, he turned his Battle Fleet to the westward, and ordered the battle cruisers and flotillas to attack in order to cover his retreat. As no attempt was made to follow, the Battle Fleet was soon freed from a most dangerous situation.

A few minutes later he ordered the battle cruisers to manœuvre off the enemy's van, whereupon they also turned to the westward. It was now eighteen minutes past seven.

Scheer's and Von Hase's explanations of this phase differ. The former pictures the whole German Fleet advancing, with the battle cruisers and flotillas attacking as fiercely as possible in order to force the British into a second battle. The object is attained, and the fleet withdraws to the westward at 7.17 pm. Von Hase, on the other hand, indicates that the High Sea Fleet suddenly found itself in a trap, practically surrounded, and that the advance

---

[24] The *Vanguard* (4th ship in the 4th Division) and *Thunderer* (4th in 2nd) did not open fire.

[25] The *Monarch* (2nd ship in 2nd Division) and *Marlborough* also state definitely that they were firing at battleships.

[26] About a point on *Orion*'s port bow.

[27] *Editor's note*: The Germans were on the receiving end of a torrent of shells from the battlefleet. See Chapter X Endnote 2 for a complete enumeration of hits scored at this time.

[28] From 7.14 to 7.20.

[29] From the torpedo (probably the *Acasta*'s).

Editor's note: As noted in Chapter IX, Section 57, Campbell (*Jutland*, 80) credits this torpedo hit not to *Acasta*, but to *Petard* or, less probably, *Turbulent*.

[30] Von Hase (I.D. 1220), 37. The time was probably about 7.15.

of the battle cruisers and flotillas was intended to extricate the Battle Fleet.[31] Scheer's own signals[32] show that the order to the battle cruisers to attack was made after the British opened fire, and there is little doubt that Von Hase's account is the more correct of the two. What might have been a disastrous blunder was by a stroke of luck turned to Scheer's advantage, and he is naturally inclined to ascribe the agency to himself. The probable explanation of his end-on advance is that he badly miscalculated the position of the Main British Fleet, and was endeavouring to pass astern of it in order to overcome the unfavourable light conditions which were so seriously handicapping the firing of his Battle Fleet, or to slip past and make for home. He may also have hoped to cut off the 5th Battle Squadron and some battle cruisers, which he thought were some distance astern of the Main Fleet.[33] The impression that the British Fleet was far enough to the South to enable him to pass astern about 7 pm, would arise from the fact that the 3rd Battle Cruiser Squadron and *Shark*'s Flotilla had been mistaken for part of the Main Fleet when they attacked the 1st and 2nd Scouting Groups from the north-eastward about 5.55 pm.[34] If this were the case, it should be some consolation to know that these gallant attacks prepared a situation which, if it had been taken advantage of, should have led to the annihilation of the German Fleet.

The Torpedo Attacks

66. Although the German flotillas did not succeed in hitting anything, they played a decisive part in this encounter. As early as 7.05, destroyers ahead of the battle cruisers had come under fire. This was a small attack made by half a dozen boats,[35] including three of the 3rd Flotilla. The *Colossus* was the first to

---

[31] 'Meanwhile the Commander-in-Chief had realised the danger to which our fleet was exposed. The van of our fleet was shut in by the semicircle of the enemy. We were in a regular death trap. There was only one way to escape from the unfavourable tactical situation: to turn the line about and withdraw on the opposite course. Before everything we must get out of the dangerous enemy envelopment. But this manœuvre had to be carried out unnoticed and unhindered. The battle cruisers and destroyers had to cover the movements of the fleet. At about 7.12 pm the Commander-in-Chief gave the fleet the signal to turn about on the opposite course and almost at the same time sent by wireless to the battle cruisers and destroyers the historic order: "Attack the enemy". . . . At 7.18 pm. we received a wireless signal from the Commander-in-Chief: "Manœuvre off the enemy van".' – Von Hase.

[32] German Plan VI.

[33] *Ibid.*

[34] *See* page XXX.

[35] Three boats of the 3rd Flotilla, possibly supported by some of the 1st Half-Flotilla. Scheer, *Germany's High Seas Fleet*, 154, shows six torpedoes fired, of which G.88 fired two and V.73 one. The *Neptune* reports six to eight boats, the *Hercules* six; Scheer, *Germany's High Seas Fleet*, 153.

see them approaching on the starboard bow and opened fire with 12 in. and 4 in. By 7.10 they were about two points before the beam of the 5th and 6th Divisions, and in the next minute or two fire was opened by several ships and Admiral Sturdee hoisted the 'preparative' and turned the 4th Division two points away. Three or four torpedoes were seen approaching about this time and the *Neptune* had to alter course to avoid one.[36] By this time the enemy battle cruisers were in sight, and the thunder of their engagement had begun. The Commander-in-Chief now signalled to the 1st Battle Squadron[37] (*Marlborough* and *Colossus*) to form astern of the 4th Battle Squadron, probably with the intention of withdrawing them from their exposed position on the flank. The 5th Division (*Colossus*) appears to have turned to port about 7.15 and the 6th Division (*Marlborough*) about 7.12,[38] which brought the 1st Battle Squadron into a ragged sort of line ahead steering about SSE. Admiral Sturdee, too, turned into line astern of the 3rd Division[39] about this time, bringing the 4th Battle Squadron into line ahead behind the *Iron Duke*'s division, steering approximately South. While the engagement with the battle cruisers was at its height, the Commander-in-Chief evidently decided to re-form single line ahead, for he signalled to the 2nd Battle Squadron to take station ahead,[40] and a few minutes later ordered them to proceed at utmost speed, and he himself reduced to 15 knots to expedite the movement. But he had hardly done so when he ordered the 2nd Battle Squadron to alter course four points to port together, which had the effect of annulling, for a time at least, the signal to form ahead.

At 7.22 pm, when the engagement with the battle cruisers was drawing to a close, the fleet was disposed as in Diagram 36.

A second torpedo attack was now developing, and as early as 7.16 the *Royal Oak* had opened a vigorous fire on destroyers on the starboard beam. This was made by the 6th and 9th Flotillas attached to Hipper's Squadron, and as Scheer turned away, a dense smoke screen rose from them, and drifted down towards the British Fleet, effectually obscuring the German battleships from view.

Some six destroyers pressed on to attack and came under a heavy fire at

---

[36] *Colossus* one at 7.08 (missed astern), *Agincourt* one at 7.08 (missed astern), *Neptune* three (two of which possibly identical with *Colossus* and *Agincourt* reports) at 7.10. These torpedoes were probably fired about 7 pm.

[37] At 7.12 pm.

[38] *Marlborough*'s Track Chart. There is no signal record of this turn in *Marlborough*'s signal log.

[39] Sturdee (r), *Official Despatches*, 122, 'The attack was soon repelled . . . and the division ordered to turn back to the course of the fleet, forming astern of the 3rd Division'.

[40] At 7.16 and 7.18 to proceed at utmost speed; Commander-in-Chief reduced to 15 knots at 7.20.

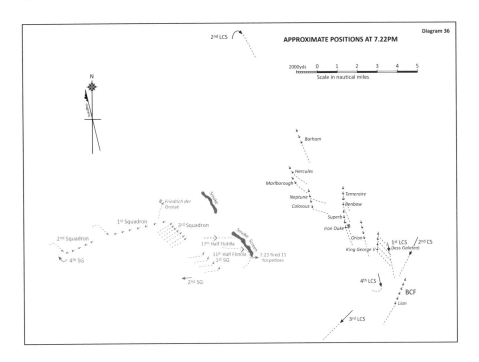

ranges of 11,000 to 8,000 yards from the ships of the 1st and 4th Battle Squadrons, particularly the *Royal Oak*, *Iron Duke*, *Benbow*, *Agincourt*, *Marlborough* and *Temeraire*.[41] It was now twenty-two minutes past seven. The destroyers could be seen approaching 10,000 yards off, and the Commander-in-Chief decided to turn away. The signal went up for the fleet to turn two points away to SSE, and the 4th Light Cruiser Squadron was at last ordered to attack. Some doubt arose as to whether a two-point turn was sufficient, and a few minutes later, at twenty-five minutes past seven, the signal was made to turn away another two points[42] (Diagram 37). The 4th Light Cruiser Squadron and a half flotilla of the 11th Flotilla were moving out to attack, but the enemy flotilla already seemed to be breaking up and two of its boats showed signs of being hit. It had fired some 21 torpedoes,[43] of which at

---

[41] 7.16, *Royal Oak* (6 in.), on starboard beam; 7.18, *Agincourt* (6 in.) 7.19; *Marlborough*, starboard bow, 11,000 yards; 7.20, *Vanguard* (12 in.); *Temeraire* (4 in.), before starboard beam, 9,000 yards; 7.24, *Iron Duke*, (6 in.), green 115°, 10,000 yards; *Benbow*, 7.27; *Tiger* (6 in.); 7.31, *Hercules* (12 in.).

[42] *Official Despatches*, 7.25; *Barham* (s), 7.25; *King George V* (s), 7.25; *New Zealand* (w), 7.25; *Benbow* (s), 7.26; *Iron Duke* (s¹), 7.27.

[43] Scheer's Diagram 7, German Plan VI; 17 Half-Flotilla fired 10 torpedoes at 7.25; 11th Half-Flotilla 11 at 7.23.

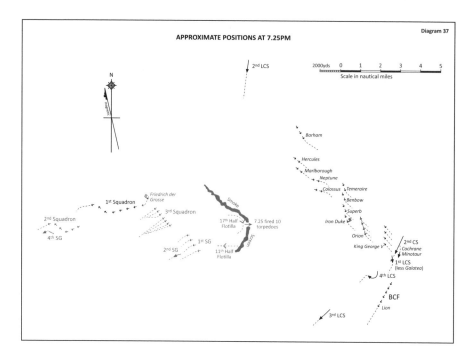

the most 11 reached the British line, about 7.35.[44] The *Marlborough*, as leader of the flank division, was again the favourite target and had to alter course to avoid three torpedoes which passed ahead and close astern. The *Revenge* and *Agincourt* in the same division had to do the same.

By this time the 4th Light Cruiser Squadron had got away to the south-westward and was firing at a portion of the 3rd Flotilla. This proved an entirely effective counter, for as soon as the German destroyers sighted the light cruisers they turned hastily away, and the only one to see the Battle Fleet was S.32 of the 1st Half Flotilla, who apparently attacked independently and fired one or two torpedoes at the *Marlborough*'s division at 9,000 metres range.[45]

At 7.32, only ten minutes after it had moved out to attack, the Commander-

---

[44] *Marlborough*, three at 7.33; *Revenge*, one at 7.35 (and one probably identical with *Marlborough*); *Agincourt*, two at 7.35; *Colossus*, one at 7.35; *Collingwood*, one at 7.35 (and one probably identical with *Colossus*); *Inflexible*, one; also *Revenge*, at 7.45. Total reports, 13; torpedoes, 11. Lord Jellicoe (Jellicoe, *Grand Fleet*, 361) mentions 20 torpedoes, but he is probably quoting Vice-Admiral Burney's figure of 21 (*Official Despatches*, 67), which gives the total number of tracks seen by the 1st Battle Squadron since 6.45 (viz.: at 6.45 - 1; 6.55 to 7.00 - 3; 7.15 - 5; 7.35 - 10; 7.45 - 2; total 21). *Neptune*'s report (*Official Despatches*, 90) of three tracks seems to refer to the 7.15 attack. The six tracks seen by *Calliope* (*Official Despatches*, 296) when moving out to attack are evidently identical with those reported by the Battle Fleet.

[45] Scheer says one, but *Revenge* reports two torpedoes at 7.45 pm.

in-Chief signalled to the 4th Light Cruiser Squadron not to go too near the enemy Battle Fleet.[46] It thereupon retired and again took station on the *King George V*. The German 5th Flotilla advanced a little later, but sighted only some destroyers of the British 11th Flotilla and made no attack.[47] No exceptional dash was displayed by the enemy in these attacks, nor were they pressed home with any great persistency,[48] a result which must be attributed to the intensity of the fire of the 1st and 4th Battle Squadrons, especially of the *Iron Duke* and *Royal Oak*. The actual German losses were not excessive. One destroyer was sunk by a hit from a 12 in. shell,[49] and two were badly hit.[50]

67. This was the culminating attack of the German flotillas. Between six and half-past seven they had launched a series of six attacks at the British Battle Fleet,[51] and the important part they played in the tactics of the German Fleet bears a striking contrast to the comparative inactivity of the British flotillas. It is not enough to say that the Grand Fleet Battle Orders had laid down defence as their primary task, for up to 7.35 not a single flotilla had taken up its station where defence was chiefly required. The fact is, the idea of a battle on the British side had never got beyond the conception of an action on parallel courses. It was only correct to tie the destroyers down to a defensive task, if their defence was the counterpart of a vigorous offensive by the Battle Fleet. The attacking power of the British destroyer flotilla had been sacrificed to the idea of defending the Battle Fleet, but at the supreme moment when the Battle Fleet required protection to enable it to return to the westward, the flotillas were on its disengaged side in a position where they were useless for attack and powerless to defend. When one considers the serious damage inflicted on the enemy in the brief half hour that firing lasted, there can be little doubt that another half an hour within effective range would have ensured the beginning of a decisive victory. Scheer's use of his flotillas is a striking confirmation of the principle that an offensive is the best defensive. In his attacks on the Battle Fleet he lost only one destroyer and entirely dislocated the British offensive.

---

[46] *Editor's note*: Exactly that: 'Do not go too near Enemy's battlefleet' (*Official Despatches*, 464).

[47] *Editor's note*: At this point, Beatty has pencilled in his copy of the *NSA* the words 'Attack was over' opposite the first two sentences of this paragraph.

[48] Rear-Admiral A. L. Duff (r); *Official Despatches*, 125.

[49] S.35, of 18th Half-Flotilla, by *Iron Duke* or *Vanguard* (7.20) or *Bellerophon* or (less probable) *Collingwood* (7.35).

[50] S.52 and S.36, of 17th Half-Flotilla, were hit by one heavy, one medium and two light shells.

[51] At 6 pm 12th Half-Flotilla and 9th Flotilla at 3rd Battle Cruiser Squadron; at 6.35 3rd Flotilla go out and are recalled, but three boats attack; about 6.50 T.B.D.s are sent out to help *Wiesbaden*, and V.73 and G.88 fire four torpedoes at 5th Battle Squadron; 7.10, six boats attack the 1st Battle Squadron; 7.35, main attack by 9th and 6th Flotillas; 7.25, 3rd and 5th go out.

Remarks on Scheer's Second Turn Away

68. According to all accepted ideas, Scheer's advance at 6.55 pm should have led to the annihilation of the High Sea Fleet. His battle cruisers, already severely damaged, were practically unsupported, within 10,000 yards of a large portion of the British Battle Fleet; the 3rd Squadron was also in a very dangerous situation, and the 1st and 2nd were not in a position to offer much help. Even the light conditions which prevented the Germans from seeing anything but the flash of their opponent's guns were in favour of the British. To say that the Grand Fleet had to turn away from the German flotillas does not fully explain the uninterrupted retreat of the German Fleet, for their attacks only lasted a short time. From 7.15 to 8 pm the movements of the British Battle Fleet seem to have been mainly directed to getting back into single line as if nothing could be done until it were again ranged according to the Deployment Diagram. Thus the tendency to cling to a formal and preconceived system of tactics again recurs as a cause of failure in the history of sea warfare.[52]

Was it necessary at this stage to preserve the unity of the Battle Fleet? Was it not preferable to break up that long inarticulate line and for each division or sub-division to press forward independently at utmost speed to the westward, supporting each other in the envelopment and destruction of the German Fleet? If the Battle Fleet had proceeded in this direction, one half to the northward and the other half to the southward of the German line, led by the 5th Battle Squadron and Battle Cruiser Fleet respectively, the fate of the High Sea Fleet would probably have been sealed. But the idea of attack was lacking, and the High Sea Fleet withdrew in safety whilst the British Battle Fleet was struggling to free itself from the rigidity of its own formation. When one surveys the mass of signals made at this stage of the battle, a new light shines on the words of old Sir Charles Geary: 'Now, my dear Kempy, do, for God's sake, my dear Kempy, oblige me by throwing your signals overboard and make that which we all understand, 'Bring the enemy to close action'.[53] The mass of

---

[52] For analagous examples see 'Executive Command and Staff', *Naval Review*, 1913, 229. Also 'A Fighting Instruction', *Naval Review*, 1915, 185.

Editor's note: The full title of the first citation is 'The Executive Command and Staff in Naval Warfare' (3 parts), authored by Kenneth Dewar. 'A Fighting Instruction' was written by Herbert Richmond.

[53] On the Channel Fleet meeting what was thought to be a hostile fleet in 1780. Kempenfelt was Geary's, the Commander-in-Chief's, Flag Captain. Barrow's *Life of Howe*, 141.

Editor's note: The reference is to Sir John Barrow, *The Life of Richard Earl Howe K.G., Admiral of the Fleet, and General of Marines* (London: John Murray, 1838). Note that the Admiral's name was Sir Francis, not Charles, Ceary.

signals which was such a feature of British tactics at Jutland was bad in principle and practice. In war, the only real basis of action is the sympathy arising from the mutual grasp of a clear tactical idea. Instead of numberless signals to alter course so many points, to steer such and such a course, to go so many revolutions or to take up such and such a bearing, all that is necessary in most cases is some such signal as to cut off the van division, attack the rear, etc. Training and mutual co-operation should do the rest.

To make effective use of a large fleet attended by scores of light craft required a great deal of concentrated thought; this thought was not available; no provision had been made for it. The result was that the tactics of the Battle Fleet entirely broke down. To attempt to gloss over its deficiencies or to justify its tactics between 6.35 and 8 pm means nothing less than the negation of the battleship and of Battle Fleet tactics. The turns made at 7.22 and 7.25 increased the range by about 3,500 yards,[54] and the small number of torpedoes that reached the British lines indicates that no very great risk would have been involved in maintaining the course of the fleet.[55] But this alone would have been far from sufficient. Merely to continue a Southerly course was useless, for, to effect anything, the fleet had to turn to the westward or south-westward and adopt tactics of active pursuit. But this it could not do, for it had been accepted that there was no real counter, and that the difficulties were insuperable.[56] In turning, too, by divisions to South, the Battle Fleet had got itself into a radically bad formation, bad for attack and bad for defence. But at 7.20, as at 6.15, the Battle Cruiser Fleet indicated the course to take. It was making to the south-westward with the 3rd Light Cruiser Squadron.

Position at 7.35 pm (Diagram 38)

69.   The two turns away and the individual manœuvring to avoid torpedoes had brought the fleet into a ragged and irregular disposition. The German

---

[54] In the case of the *Marlborough* which altered only two points, the range of the torpedo was increased by less than 1,500 yards.

[55] *Editor's note*: This statement ignores the fact that, because the turns increased the distance the torpedoes had to travel, they were near the end of their runs and, moving slowly, were relatively easy to avoid. For example, at about 7.35 the destroyer *Oak* observed a torpedo 'cross the track of our ships, about 200 yards ahead of "Iron Duke", Torpedo was travelling slowly' (*Official Despatches*, 54, 300).

[56] Commander-in-Chief's Despatch (*Official Despatches*, 3). Jellicoe, *Grand Fleet*, 405.
Editor's note: See Annexe III, paragraph 10, for the relevant portion of Jellicoe's despatch.

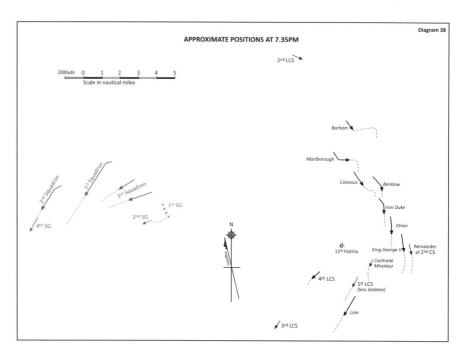

Diagram 38

APPROXIMATE POSITIONS AT 7.35PM

destroyers had retired, and at 7.35[57] the Commander-in-Chief made a signal to alter course to S by W and form single line ahead.

By that time the absence of light cruisers and destroyers in the direction of the enemy had been partly remedied. The 4th Light Cruiser Squadron and 11th Flotilla had moved out to the westward and the fleet could have turned at once to SW. There was still an hour and a half of daylight,[58] and had the fleet altered course to the south-westward behind the battle cruisers and increased speed it would probably have come into action about 8.30 pm. At 7.30 the *Lion*, which was about six miles to the south-westward, sent an important signal to the Commander-in-Chief stating that the enemy bore NW by W 10 to 11 miles. This was received in the *Iron Duke* at 7.40, and at 7.42 the Battle Fleet altered course to SW (Diagram 39).

The day was drawing to a close. Admiral Beatty could still see the enemy, but the Battle Fleet behind him was drawing no nearer. Doubts evidently began to rise in his mind as to the possibility of renewing the action that day; the only hope of doing so lay in pressing hotly to the westward, but alone and unsupported he could not engage the whole of Scheer's Battle Fleet.

---

[57] Then on a SE course proceeding at 15 knots since 7.20.
[58] Sunset at 8.07 GMT, but it was still light enough for firing at 9 pm.

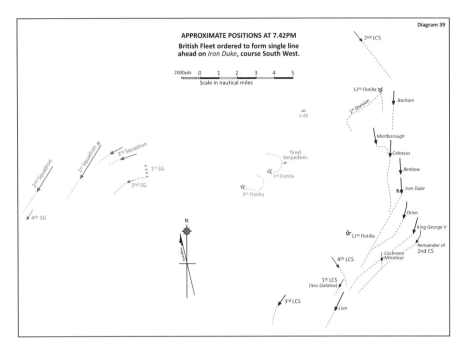

Note
In the original diagram the flags denoting the two fleet flagships were omitted. They have been inserted here for clarity and for consistency with the other diagrams in the sequence.

At 7.45 he made a signal by searchlight to the *Minotaur*[59] telling her to inform the leading British battleship that the enemy bore NW by W course about SW, evidently in the hope that the 2nd Battle Squadron would shape course at full speed to the SW by W to support him. He followed this at 7.47 by a signal to the Commander-in-Chief: 'Submit that the van of the battleships follow me; we can then cut off the whole of the enemy's fleet', and a few minutes later altered course W by S to close the enemy.

The signal was passed by wireless and searchlight, and reached the *Iron Duke* at 7.54. The *Calliope* and 4th Light Cruiser Squadron had been recalled by this time,[60] and were taking up their previous station on the starboard bow of the *King George V*. The 2nd Battle Squadron was gradually hauling round to South-West to get ahead of the *Iron Duke*. By 8 pm it was in position, and the Battle Fleet was once more in single line ahead on a South-West course.

[59] Between *Lion* and *King George V*; signal was passed to *King George V*, and on to Commander-in-Chief. Received in *Iron Duke* at 7.59.

[60] At 7.40. Took station on *King George V* about 7.50 pm.

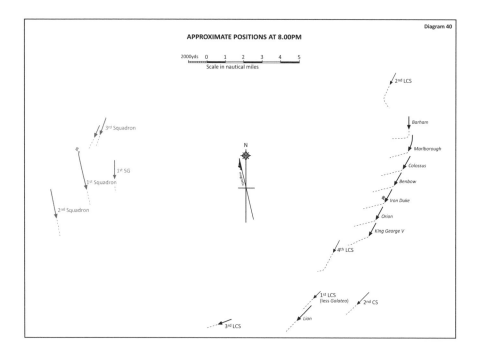

Turn to West at 8 pm (Diagram 40)

The Commander-in-Chief now decided to turn towards the enemy and the fleet altered course to West by divisions[61] and increased to 17 knots.[62] But it was now 8 o'clock; three-quarters of an hour had passed since Scheer turned away and he was already some 15½ miles off. The chance of dealing a serious blow at the German Fleet before dark was slipping rapidly away. The peculiar light conditions had been all in favour of the British, and would have resulted in the infliction of serious losses on the enemy with little or no risk[63] from his guns had battle been joined.

---

[61] At 7.59 Lord Jellicoe (*Grand Fleet*, 367) states that enemy battleships were observed to westward, that is on starboard bow of *Iron Duke* at this time, and implies that this was the cause of the turn. The only mention of the enemy at this time is in *Royal Oak*'s report (*Official Despatches*, 99), which states that at 7.44 enemy ships were faintly visible on the starboard quarter. These were probably the destroyers of the 3rd Flotilla.

[62] *Editor's note*: The text of Jellicoe's signal was: 'Divisions separately alter course in succession to West preserving their formation. Speed 17 knots'. Time of despatch 8 pm (*Official Despatches*, 467).

[63] As actually happened at 7.15. During the firing at 7.15, and later at 8.20, the Germans were only able to see the flashes of the British guns, and could not distinguish the ships. Scheer's report of the 7.15 action: 'These ships suffered very severely, as they were able to distinguish little more of the enemy than the flash of his salvos'. And of the action at 8.20 with Beatty's battle cruisers: 'Only the flashes of the enemy could be seen. The ships which were already seriously damaged received further hits without being able to reply to the fire seriously'.

The Battle Cruiser Fleet at this time was some 6 miles WSW from the *King George V*, and was no longer in sight. The 3rd Light Cruiser Squadron and 1st Light Cruiser Squadron were with the *Lion*,[64] and at 8 pm Admiral Beatty ordered them to sweep to the westward and locate the head of the enemy line before dark.[65]

Scheer's Movements

70. Meanwhile Scheer after steering to the westward for a short time had gradually brought his fleet round to South. All his ships were with him, and the *Lützow*, in spite of the hammering she had received, had rejoined her squadron, and reported that she could go 15 knots.[66] He now knew from the reports of his flotillas that he was confronted with the whole British Battle Fleet,[67] and expected that every effort would be made to force him to the westward by attacks in force during the remaining hours of daylight, and by destroyer attacks at night so as to ensure bringing him to action at dawn the next day. The situation was one of extreme peril, for an action the next day might involve the practical annihilation of his fleet. His only hope lay in warding off the British encirclement. If he could reach Horns Riff by break of day he might still win through and escape the net closing around him. Every four miles he was forced to the westward meant half an hour further from Horns Riff. Scheer, it must be granted, was a man of quick appreciation and of bold and rapid decision. He decided to make straight for Horns Riff in close order during the night maintaining his course regardless of attack. The 2nd Flotilla and 12th Half Flotilla were sent to the eastward to give notice of the British approach, and all flotillas were ordered to be ready to attack during the night, though this might leave him bereft of destroyers in the battle impending the next day.

Shortly after 8 o'clock his whole fleet was proceeding South at 16 knots. The 1st Squadron was leading,[68] with the 3rd Squadron a mile or so behind; a couple

---

[64] The 3rd Light Cruiser Squadron (*Falmouth*) was about five miles West of the *Lion*; the 1st Light Cruiser Squadron (*Inconstant*) a mile or so astern of the *Lion*.

[65] *Editor's note*: Beatty's signal was: 'Sweep to the Westward and locate the head of the Enemy's line before dark'. It wasn't until 8.14 that the Senior Officer of the 3rd LCS was able to pass it to his ships (*Official Despatches*, 467).

[66] Scheer, *Germany's High Seas Fleet*, 159.

[67] *Editor's note*: At 5.25 pm Scheer received the following signal from the senior officer, 5th Flotilla: 'According to statements of prisoners from destroyer Nomad, there are 60 large ships in the vicinity, including 20 modern battleships and 6 battle cruisers' (Tarrant, *Jutland*, 281; note that the High Seas Fleet was keeping German summer time, two hours in advance of GMT, so this signal is timed at 7.25 pm).

[68] In line ahead reversed, with the *Westfalen* leading.

of miles on the starboard bow of the *Westfalen* was the 2nd Squadron[69] trying to get ahead, with the 4th Scouting Group a mile or so ahead of it. On the port bow as the 1st Scouting Group, with the 2nd Flotilla and 12th Flotilla away to the eastward. The British Fleet he knew must be some 12 to 15 miles to the South-East.[70]

The fleets were now converging, and at 8.05 the *Calliope* sighted smoke to the WNW. Five minutes or so later the *Castor* sighted destroyers and ordered the 1st Division of the 11th Flotilla to attack.[71] This was the German 12th Half Flotilla or possibly the German 2nd Flotilla pushing down to the south-eastward (Diagram 41).

By 8.15 twelve of them could be seen, and Commodore (F) informed the Commodore, 4th Light Cruiser Squadron, who promptly proceeded with the *Calliope*, *Comus* and *Constance*[72] to his support.

Quarter of an hour had passed since Admiral Beatty's signal asking for the 2nd Battle Squadron had been received in the *Iron Duke*, and the Commander-in-Chief now ordered the 2nd Battle Squadron to follow him.[73] This signal was presumably the answer to Admiral Beatty's signal of 7.47 but it struck no note of urgency. Did the Commander-in-Chief intend the 2nd Battle Squadron to proceed at utmost speed, or merely to follow in the direction of the Battle Cruiser Fleet? In any case, the Vice-Admiral, 2nd Battle Squadron, took no action in the matter. He did not detach himself from the fleet, nor did he even increase speed. He may have been uncertain of the position of the Battle Cruiser Fleet, or he may have regarded the Westerly course as equivalent to following the *Lion*.[74] But he made no effort to get the *Lion*'s position from the *Minotaur*, which was in sight of the *King George V* at 8.10, and could have passed the bearing and distance of the *Lion* just as she passed to the *Lion* the bearing and distance of the *King George V*.[75] It is true that the actual effect of following the *Lion* at 8.10 would probably only have been to reduce its distance at 8.30 from 6½ to 5 miles, but this was not known to the Vice-Admiral, 2nd Battle Squadron, at the time. The *Lion*'s signals were obviously urgent, and on

---

[69] Presumably *Schleswig-Holstein* leading, then *Schlesien*, *Hannover*, *Pommern*, *Hessen*, *Deutschland*.

[70] The *King George V* bore from the *Westfalen* approximately ESE about 15 miles.

[71] *Ossory*, *Martial*, *Magic*, *Minion*, *Mystic*, *Mons*, *Mandate*, *Michael*.

[72] The 1st Division of the 4th Light Cruiser Squadron.

[73] At 8.14, logged in *King George V* as received at 8.07 pm.

Editor's note: '2nd B.S. follow our Battle Cruisers' (*Official Despatches*, 468). The time of receipt in *King George V* is possibly a mistake for 8.17.

[74] Vice-Admiral 2nd Battle Squadron omits any reference to the incident in his report.

[75] At 8.15.

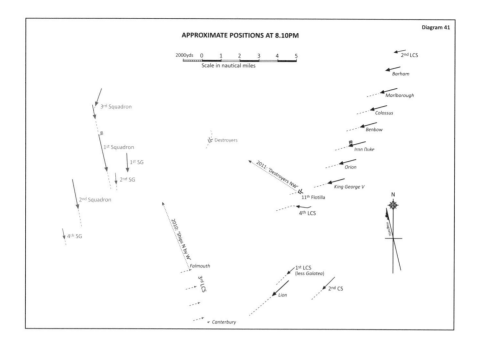

APPROXIMATE POSITIONS AT 8.10PM

Diagram 41

Scale in nautical miles

Note
The name *Canterbury* has been added to the original. *Canterbury* did not belong to the 3rd
Light Cruiser Division, but was one of the cruisers attached to the Grand Fleet.

receipt of the Commander-in-Chief's signal his course was plain. It was to
proceed at full speed to support Admiral Beatty without a moment's delay.[76]
This he did not do.

71. At quarter past eight the 3rd Light Cruiser Squadron were on their way
to the westward[77] when they sighted five light cruisers W by N steering to the
south-westward. This was the 4th Scouting Group ahead of the 2nd Squadron,
and the 3rd Light Cruiser Squadron opened fire at 9,600 yards, altered course
to South, and increased to 25 knots[78] (Diagram 42).

Almost simultaneously the *Calliope*, three or four miles to the eastward of the
Falmouth, opened fire on a half flotilla of enemy's [*sic*] destroyers which was

---

[76] Half an hour later – at 8.40 pm, after the Battle Cruiser Force had been in action – the
Vice-Admiral 2nd Battle Squadron asked Admiral Beatty for his position and course, and
signalled that the was following him; but he remained with the fleet and informed the
Commander-in-Chief a few minutes later that the battle cruisers were not in sight.

[77] Spreading on a line of bearing South; Rear-Admiral 3rd Light Cruiser Squadron gives
time of sighting at 8.18.

[78] *Falmouth* (s), 8.14, course south; 8.17, opened fire; 8.19, speed 25 knots.

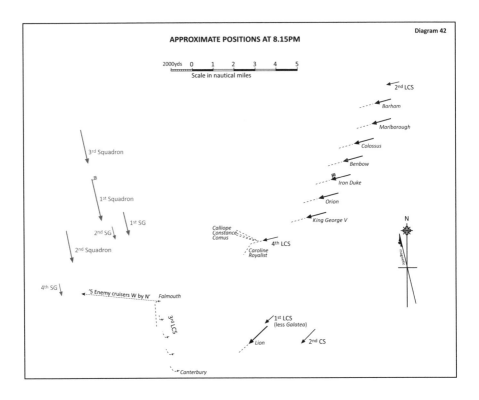

steering SSW towards the Battle Cruiser Fleet, and proceeded to chase them at full speed to the NW.[79] Two engagements now began to develop – one five miles ahead of the Battle Fleet between the *Calliope*[80] and the 12th Half Flotilla, the other six or seven miles to the south-westward of the Battle Fleet between Beatty's Battle Cruisers and the head of the enemy's fleet.

The destroyer attack never developed, and only two torpedoes reached the Battle Fleet.[81] When the enemy destroyers saw the light cruisers, they turned and ran, and the *Calliope* and her cruisers followed at full speed. The chase lasted only five minutes. At 8.26 the enemy's Battle Fleet suddenly loomed out of the mist to the westward about 8,000 yards off. The enemy opened fire,[82] but the *Calliope* held on for a minute or two and fired a torpedo at 6,500 yards range at the leading ship of the *Kaiser* class,[83] then turned to fall back on the Battle

---

[79] Commodore (r), 8.18, opened fire on enemy's destroyers – Signal, 8.18, utmost speed.
[80] *Calliope, Comus,* and *Constance.*
[81] *Agincourt* and *Benbow* saw tracks at 8.25 and 8.27.
[82] At 8.28.
[83] At 8.30. Probably the *Prinzregent Luitpold.*

Fleet.[84] As she retired, she came under heavy fire from two *Kaisers* and a *Helgoland*. Shots were falling thick round her and she was hit five times,[85] but got safely back with all her ships.

While the *Calliope* was driving off the enemy destroyers, the thunder of the battle cruisers' guns had broken out again to the southward. The *Falmouth* making to the westward had sighted the 4th Scouting Group ahead, and opened fire. Admiral Beatty had turned at once[86] to the sound of the guns and almost immediately sighted the enemy's battle cruisers to the north-westward.[87]

Beatty's squadron opened fire, and a short, sharp encounter followed which lasted ten or fifteen minutes (Diagram 43), the last time big ships were to engage during the war.[88] The enemy were on a Southerly course with the *Derfflinger* leading,[89] and the battleships of the *Deutschland* class were in sight as well. The *Tiger* was apparently the first to open fire,[90] and the ranges varied from 9,000 to 13,000 yards at this time.[91]

The *Lion* led gradually round to the South-West,[92] and the enemy altered to the westward.

The sudden outburst of firing from the South-East had taken them by surprise. Dusk was falling and they could see little more that the flashes of the British guns. It may be doubted whether the *Seydlitz* opened fire; the *Lützow* almost certainly was not in a position to do so; the *Derfflinger* had only her two

---

[84] *Editor's note*: *Calliope* does not appear to have signalled this intelligence to anyone.

[85] One 4 in. gun was hit, and all the crew except the sight-setter were killed; a second shell disabled another 4 in. gun; a third burst in the after dressing station. Total casualties were 10 killed and 23 wounded.

[86] 8.17. Course West.

[87] *Princess Royal* reports sighting them at 8.18, green 60°, 12,000 yards.

[88] *Editor's note*: This is not strictly speaking true, as the British raid into the Heligoland Bight, 17 November 1917, would see the battle cruisers *Glorious* and *Courageous* in action, and *Repulse* taken under fire by the German battleships *Kaiserin* and *Kaiser*. It was, however, little more than a skirmish, and like Jutland itself, not one of the Royal Navy's finer moments.

[89] Von Hase (I.D. 1220), 38. The *Lützow* may have been with them, for *New Zealand* (r) mentions five ships.

[90] *Tiger*, 8.21, at three-funnelled battleship. *Princess Royal*, 8.22; *Lion*, 8.23.

[91] Ranges, 8.18, *Princess Royal*, green 60°, 12,000 yards; 8.19, *Princess Royal*, 10,000; 8.20, *New Zealand*, third ship, 13,000; 8.21, *Tiger*, 7,900; 8.22, *Princess Royal*, 9,400; 8.22½, *Tiger*, 8,400; 8.24, *New Zealand*, third ship, 11,500; 8.25, *New Zealand*, 10,400; 8.25¼, *Princess Royal*, 9,625; 8.26, *New Zealand*, 9,200; 8.27, *Tiger*, 9,600; 8.26, *New Zealand*, 9,100; 8.31, *Tiger*, 10,300 (straddle); *Princess Royal*, 9,500 (three-funnelled ship); 8.32, *Tiger*, 11,100 (straddle); *Official Despatches*, 387 *et seq.*

[92] Courses, 8.17, West, 17 knots; 8.21, WSW; 8.25, SW by W; 8.28, SW.

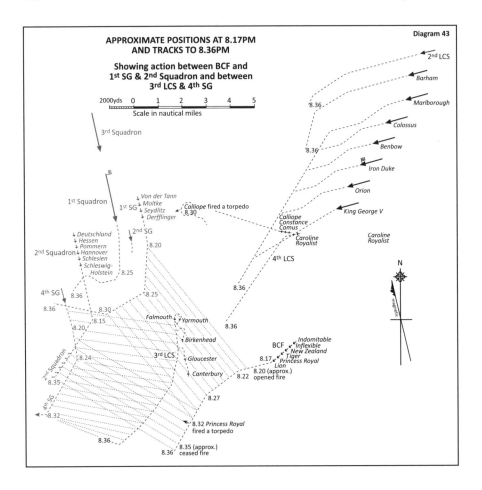

Note

German sources state that the lead ship of the 2nd Squadron at this stage of the battle was not *Schleswig-Holstein* but *Hannover*. Throughout the battle Rear-Admiral Mauve appears to have adopted a 'double-headed' arrangement of his two three-ship divisions, with the divisional flagships at the head and the tail of the formation.

foremost turrets in action, and this was quickly reduced to one by a shot[93] which glanced off the armour, bent the rail of the turntable and jammed the turret. Help came from an unexpected quarter. Rear–Admiral Mauve's squadron of old *Deutschland*s were ahead of the fleet, and now came into action. They turned to westward ahead of the 1st Scouting Group, and Hipper's sorely tried

---

[93] Probably from *Lion* or *Princess Royal*. The *Princess Royal* engaged leading ship (*Derfflinger*) – then the 2nd Squadron; the *New Zealand* and *Indomitable* the third ship (probably *Moltke*). The *Tiger* seems to have been in action with three-funnelled battleships all the time.

squadron took refuge behind them. As the three-funnelled ships came into view, the British battle cruisers shifted their fire to them.[94] The *Princess Royal* was hit[95] about this time but sustained no serious damage. The German battle cruisers undoubtedly received further injuries (one of them turned away on fire), and in the 2nd Squadron, the *Schlesien*, *Schleswig-Holstein* and the *Pommern* were hit.[96]

Torpedoes were used towards the end of the action, the *Princess Royal* firing one at 8.32, and a few minutes later the track of one was seen crossing the *Inflexible*'s bows – probably fired by the 2nd Scouting Group about 8.24.

About 8.29 the enemy turned to the westward and disappeared in the mist and deepening twilight.

While the battle cruisers were firing, the *Falmouth* and 3rd Light Cruiser Squadron had been following a Southerly course between the lines engaging the light cruisers of the 4th Scouting Group. At 8.30, when the enemy turned away, the *Falmouth* followed them to the North-West, losing sight of them in the mist about 8.40.[97]

The Battle Fleet turns to South-West

72. At 8.15, when the two fleets were again coming into contact, the British Battle Fleet was in divisions steering West, with the *King George V* on the port wing and guides of columns bearing SW. The *Calliope* was two or three miles sharp on the bow of the *King George V*. The *Lion* was out of sight six miles to the SW, and the *Falmouth* about nine miles to the westward.[98]

A few minutes later the guns of the *Calliope* and the 4th Light Cruiser Squadron opened on enemy destroyers,[99] and firing could be heard away to the westward.[100] Touch had evidently been regained, and at 8.21 the Commander-

---

[94] *Princess Royal*, at 8.31; *Tiger* had been firing at them the whole time.

[95] *Princess Royal* (r); *Official Despatches*, 149, about 8.32.

[96] Each received one hit. The 2nd Squadron were in reversed order, viz., *Schleswig-Holstein*, *Schlesien*, *Hannover*, *Pommern*, *Hessen*, *Deutschland*.

Editor's note: According to Campbell (*Jutland*, 264), *Lion* took a hit from the 5.9in secondary guns of Hipper's battle cruisers, and it was *Posen* which hit *Princess Royal*. In turn, *Lion* hit *Derfflinger*; *New Zealand* and *Princess Royal* hit *Seydlitz* (5 hits in total); *Pommern* was hit by one shell from *Indomitable*, and *New Zealand* scored a damaging hit on *Schleswig-Holstein*.

[97] *Falmouth* (r), 8.38.

[98] From *King George V*.

[99] Firing could be seen from *Royal Oak* at 8.17 pm. *Calliope* opened fire at 8.18. Commodore (F) reported enemy destroyers NW to Vice-Admiral, 2nd Battle Squadron, at 8.14, but report did not reach Commander-in-Chief until 8.26.

[100] The *Falmouth* opened fire at 8.17 pm.

in-Chief altered course to WSW two points away from the enemy.[101] By this time the flash of Beatty's guns could be seen to the SW, and course was altered again to West at 8.25. The *Calliope* could be seen under fire three or four miles ahead.[102] No enemy ships were actually in sight,[103] but the Commander-in-Chief decided to form single line ahead to the south-westward. At 8.28 the signal was made to alter course to SW, bringing the fleet into line ahead. The enemy's Battle Fleet was then some seven miles to the westward right ahead of the *Iron Duke* before she turned. The battle cruisers could still be heard engaged to the South-West.

8.30 to 9 pm

The encounter with the Battle Cruiser Fleet was the last engagement between heavy ships, but for over an hour the two fleets were little more than six miles apart, and a constant succession of reports was coming in.[104] The action with Beatty had forced Hipper's battle cruiser and Mauve's pre-Dreadnoughts seven or eight miles to the westward – no inconsiderable matter in itself when every four miles in that direction meant half an hour further from Horns Riff – and Scheer now brought the 1st and 3rd Squadrons down between them and the British Battle Fleet (Diagram 44).

On the British side, there was ample evidence to place the enemy about seven or eight miles to the westward. The 4th Light Cruiser Squadron were two or three miles on the *Iron Duke*'s starboard bow, returning to their station at the head of the fleet; and at 8.30 the *Comus* could be seen firing, and in answer to a signal from the *Iron Duke* reported that she was firing at the enemy's Battle Fleet to the westward.[105] Admiral Beatty's guns were now silent, but at 8.40 pm he reported the enemy ten or eleven miles to the north-westward.[106]

---

[101] *Editor's note*: This is palpably unfair to Jellicoe; Diagrams 42 and 43 show that *Calliope* and her squadron were about 45° off *Iron Duke*'s port bow. A turn to port would bring the battlefleet down in support, and open the arcs of fire to starboard.

[102] *Royal Oak*: 'Hit observed on starboard quarter of *Calliope*' (*Official Despatches*, 99); *Benbow*: 'Heavy firing heard right ahead' (*Official Despatches*, 354).

[103] There is only one Battle Fleet report of sighting the enemy Battle Fleet at this time. *Iron Duke* (B turret) reports 'nine heavy ships ahead' at 8.25½ pm (*Official Despatches*, 60).

[104] *Editor's note*: It was not really a 'constant succession of reports': see Annexe IV for a complete list of reports from 8 pm to midnight.

[105] At 8.38 pm.

[106] At 8.40 pm *Lion* to Commander-in-Chief. 'Enemy battle cruisers and pre-Dreadnoughts N. 34° W, distant 10 to 11 miles steering SW.' Received in *Iron Duke* 8.59. The *Lion* gave her position as 56° 40' N, 5° 50' E about six miles NE of her actual position, but her relative position was known.

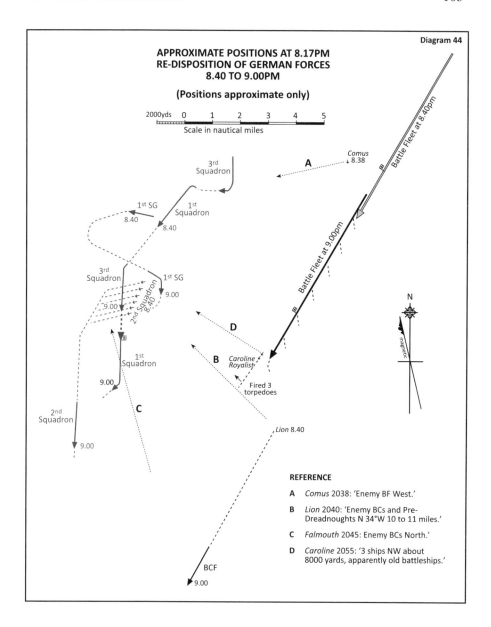

APPROXIMATE POSITIONS AT 8.17PM
RE-DISPOSITION OF GERMAN FORCES
8.40 TO 9.00PM

(Positions approximate only)

Diagram 44

2000yds 0   1   2   3   4   5
Scale in nautical miles

REFERENCE

A   *Comus* 2038: 'Enemy BF West.'

B   *Lion* 2040: 'Enemy BCs and Pre-
Dreadnoughts N 34°W 10 to 11 miles.'

C   *Falmouth* 2045: Enemy BCs North.'

D   *Caroline* 2055: '3 ships NW about
8000 yards, apparently old battleships.'

Half an hour had elapsed since the Commander-in-Chief ordered the 2nd
Battle Squadron to follow the Battle Cruiser Fleet, and it was only now, at 8.40
pm, that the Vice-Admiral, 2nd Battle Squadron, asked Admiral Beatty his
position, and added that he was following him – a statement only correct in the
sense that the Battle Fleet was following, for the 2nd Battle Squadron had
remained with the Battle Fleet the whole time.

When the 1st Division of the 4th Light Cruiser Squadron[107] had gone out to drive off the 13th Half Flotilla at 8.16, the 2nd Division, consisting of *Caroline* and *Royalist*, had remained behind keeping a couple of miles or so ahead of the *King George V* and they now got into touch with the enemy. At 8.45 the *Caroline* sighted three enemy battleships NW,[108] and the *Falmouth* at the same time reported enemy battle cruisers North, going WSW, but as the latter was out of sight and her position uncertain, the report was probably discounted.[109]

Five minutes later the *Caroline* reported the battleships she had seen to the *King George V*[110] and ordered the *Royalist* to attack with torpedoes.

The dusk was now deepening but it was still light, and the Vice-Admiral, 2nd Battle Squadron, somewhat unaccountably mistook the ships for our battle cruisers[111] and negatived the attack.[112]

The *Caroline* replied that the ships were evidently enemy battleships (which was corroborated by the *Castor* at 9.15) and made an attack.[113]

The enemy opened fire on them, but the *Caroline* fired two torpedoes and the *Royalist* one, all without result. The *King George V* still remained convinced

---

[107] *Calliope, Constance, Comus.*

[108] *Calliope* (r) says NNW, but 4th Light Cruiser Squadron track chart (*Official Despatches*, 12a) says 305°; the report also says they were pre-Dreadnoughts.

[109] The *Falmouth* was then about 7½ miles W of the *Royalist*. She reported her position as 56° 42' N, 5° 37' E, but as her reckoning was about five miles North-East of the *Iron Duke*'s, her report would place the enemy battle cruisers about nine miles NW of *Iron Duke* instead of about eight miles West.

[110] At 8.55 three ships NW about 8,000 yards – apparently old battleships.

[111] Vice-Admiral, 2nd Battle Squadron (r), states that he was certain the vessels on the starboard beam were our battle cruisers. The *Lion* was then about six miles ahead of him. It is possible that the Vice-Admiral, 2nd Battle Squadron, saw the 1st SG and mistook them for our battle cruisers, or may have been misled by the *Falmouth*'s position. It is hardly possible that the *Deutschland* class could be mistaken for them. *King George V* made the 'negative' at 9.06 pm.

Editor's note: This mistake in identification shows that in fact the position of the BCF was uncertain. The report of Vice-Admiral Jerram, commanding the 2nd BS, states that 'The Navigating Officer of my Flagship, who has just come from the battle-cruiser fleet, was also certain that they were ours, and saw them sufficiently clearly to give their approximate course . . .' (*Official Despatches*, 108).

[112] *Editor's note*: Although he immediately after signalled *Caroline*: 'If you are quite sure attack'; both this signal and the preceding negative are timed at 9.06 (*Official Despatches*, 471). In his report, Jerram said: 'I do not know whether an attack was made. If they were enemy ships and no attack was made, the fault is mine, and not that of "Caroline"' (*Official Despatches*, 109).

[113] It seems to have been made before it was negatived.

that they were our battle cruisers and reported them as such to the Commander-in-Chief.[114]

There could be little doubt then at 9 pm that the enemy were about 7 miles to the westward going in a South-Westerly direction. Their van had engaged the Battle Cruiser Fleet; their rear had fired on the *Calliope*; they had been fired at by the *Comus*, never lost to sight by the *Falmouth*, attacked by the *Caroline* and *Royalist*, fired at by the *Benbow*,[115] and mistaken by the *King George V* for our own battle cruisers.

Meanwhile the *Southampton* and 2nd Light Cruiser Squadron a couple of miles on the starboard quarter of the fleet had not been idle. Enemy destroyers[116] had twice pushed up to the starboard quarter of the fleet. Two had been engaged and driven off at 8.30, and just before nine they made a more determined attack on the 5th Battle Squadron, and were again met by the fire of the *Southampton*'s squadron and driven off.[117]

Chapter X Endnotes

1. The signals from Senior Officer, 4th Light Cruiser Squadron to his ships (as recorded in *Official Despatches*, 462–4):

7.08	–	Alter course together three points to starboard.
7.09	–	Alter course together three points to port.
7.11	–	Alter course together four points to port.
7.12	–	Alter course together eight points to starboard.
7.12	–	[to HMS *Constance*] Get astern of me.
7.16	–	Alter course together four points to starboard. Admiral intends to proceed at 18 knots.
7.22	–	Alter course together eight points to port.
7.22	–	Admiral intends to proceed at 20 knots.
7.27	–	Admiral intends to proceed at 25 knots.

[114] At 9.05. The enemy fired a star shell about 9.15 which ought to have sufficiently indicated their nationality, but the *King George V* did not amend her previous report.

Editor's note: The Royal Navy was not equipped with starshell at Jutland. In July 1916, it would be noted that 'Efforts are being made to obtain star shell for our own use' (Grand Fleet Gunnery and Torpedo Orders, Number 167, 17 July 1916; TNA: ADM 137/293).

[115] *Benbow* turret [*sic*] fired at 9.04, probably at 1st Squadron.

[116] Probably of the German 2nd Flotilla.

[117] *Editor's note*: The captain of *Valiant* thought that they were firing on a submarine which was imagined at 8.56 pm (Captain Woollcombe's Report, *Official Despatches*, 210).

At about 7.15 the light cruisers were on the starboard quarter of *King George V*, when the 2nd Battle Squadron turned together to port and continued on a roughly SE course. By 7.25, Commodore C. E. Le Mesurier's 4th LCS would be well south (i.e., ahead) of the battleships and travelling on a diverging course. After deployment, the GFBOs had the 4th LCS stationed between the battleships and battle cruisers, on the engaged side: during the quarter hour between 7.15 and 7.30, the track of the light cruisers was indeed consistent with their trying to take station as per the deployment diagram. The authors of the *NSA* are suggesting that the 4th LCS would have been better placed had they ended up to the NW of where they were at 7.30. Perhaps; nevertheless, they were well positioned at 7.30 (well to the SE of the German fleet) for striking West or Southwest. Unfortunately, those orders were never given.

2. Campbell (*Jutland*, 218–46) lists the following hits between 7.00 and 7.45, most occurring before 7.30 – note that none were scored by the battle cruisers:

Lützow	–	Five 13.5in, shared between *Monarch* and *Orion*.
Derfflinger	–	Five 15in from *Revenge*: one of these hits was the only time a British shell penetrated thick armour and burst inside, while another merely passed through the fore funnel without exploding.
	–	Five 12in from *Colossus*.
	–	One 12in from *Collingwood*.
	–	Two 15in from *Royal Oak*, both passing through plating too thin to trigger the fuze.
	–	One 12in from *Bellerophon*.
Seydlitz	–	Two 12in HE from *Hercules*.
	–	Two 12in APC from *St Vincent*.
	–	One 15in from *Royal Oak*.
Von der Tann	–	One 15in from *Revenge*.
König	–	One 13.5in from *Iron Duke*.
Grosser Kurfürst	–	Three 13.5in hits from *Marlborough*.
	–	Four 15in hits from *Barham* and/or *Valiant*.
Markgraf	–	One 12in hit from *Agincourt*.
Kaiser	–	Two 12in hits from *Agincourt*.
Helgoland	–	One 15in hit from (probably) *Valiant* or *Barham*.
Wiesbaden	–	An unknown number (three?) of 13.5in from *Marlborough*.
S.35	–	Two (?) 13.5in from *Iron Duke*.
G.86	–	One near miss, from an unknown battleship.

CHAPTER XI
PROCEEDINGS DURING THE NIGHT

General View of Situation

73. The position of the two fleets at 9 pm[1] is shown in Diagram 45. The British Battle Fleet is in single line ahead, course SW, speed 17 knots,[2] with the battle cruisers about eight miles ahead, also steering SW 17 knots. The 2nd Light Cruiser Squadron is at the rear of the battle line: the *Calliope*, *Constance* and *Comus* of the 4th Light Cruiser Squadron at its head on the port bow of the *King George V*, with the *Royalist* and *Caroline* on the starboard side. The 1st Light Cruiser Squadron[3] and 3rd Light Cruiser Squadron are on the starboard side of the Battle Cruiser Force with the 2nd Cruiser Squadron[4] on its starboard

---

[1] It was still light at 9 pm; *Official Despatches*, 74, *Hercules* (r): '9.05 pm, weather misty; visibility two to five miles'. *Official Despatches*, 289: *Duke of Edinburgh* (r): '10 pm, too dark for long-range firing; went to night defence stations'. *Official Despatches*, 297: '9.05 pm, *Caroline* and *Royalist* engaged with enemy's battleships at four miles range'. *Official Despatches*, 284: '8.45 pm.' *Shannon* reports *King George V* in sight at five miles range.

Editor's note: The quotes from the *Official Despatches* are essentially correct, but it is worth repeating the full 9.05 extract from the Diary of the 4th Light Cruiser Squadron:

9.05-9.10 *Caroline* fired two torpedoes and *Royalist* fired one torpedo at enemy, mean range 8,000 yards. Enemy opened fire on *Caroline* and *Royalist*, also on *Comus* – rejoining *Caroline*. Latter and *Royalist* turned away.

Also relevant is the report of the Gunnery Officer of *Shannon* (Lieutenant-Commander F.W. Bennett), stationed in the foretop of the armoured cruiser – note that *Shannon* did not signal the range/bearing of *King George V*:

At 8.45 pm – *King George V* again sighted bearing NNE. Visibility had again improved and her range was estimated at 10,000 yards.

[2] The 6th Division (*Marlborough*, *Revenge*, *Hercules* and *Agincourt*) and 5th Battle Squadron were slightly astern of station.

[3] Less *Galatea*.

[4] Plus *Duke of Edinburgh* and *Chester*.

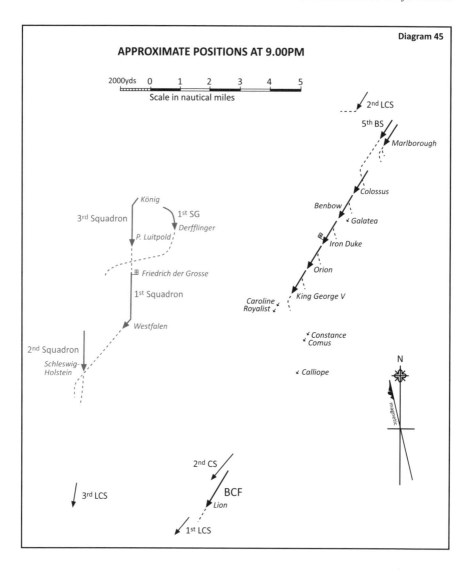

quarter. The *Galatea*[5] is on the port side of the Battle Fleet making for the head of the line. The 4th and 11th Flotillas, with the *Castor* (Commodore F), are ahead and the 9th, 10th, 12th and 13th Flotillas at the rear of the battle line. The 1st Flotilla is in company with the battle cruisers.

[5] At 6.07 pm *Galatea*'s speed had been temporarily reduced to 18 knots by damage to forced draught fan.

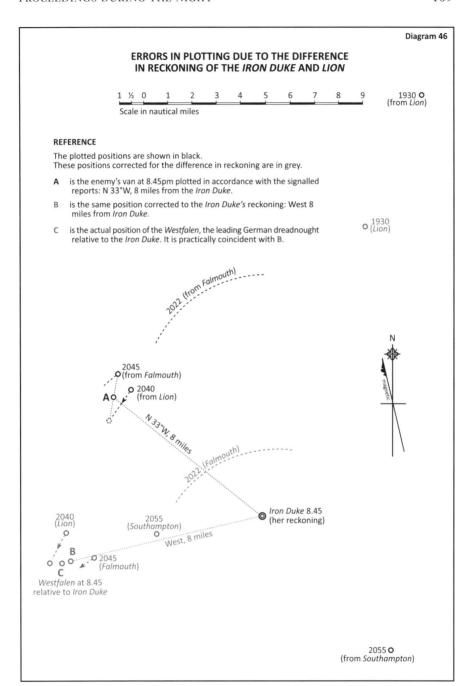

Diagram 46

**ERRORS IN PLOTTING DUE TO THE DIFFERENCE
IN RECKONING OF THE *IRON DUKE* AND *LION***

1 ½ 0   1   2   3   4   5   6   7   8   9
Scale in nautical miles

REFERENCE

The plotted positions are shown in black.
These positions corrected for the difference in reckoning are in grey.

A   is the enemy's van at 8.45pm plotted in accordance with the signalled
   reports: N 33°W, 8 miles from the *Iron Duke*.

B   is the same position corrected to the *Iron Duke's* reckoning: West 8
   miles from *Iron Duke*.

C   is the actual position of the *Westfalen*, the leading German dreadnought
   relative to the *Iron Duke*. It is practically coincident with B.

1930 ○
(from *Lion*)

1930
○ (*Lion*)

2022 (from Falmouth)

N

magnetic

2045
○ (from *Falmouth*)

○ 2040
(from *Lion*)

A ○

N 33°W, 8 miles

2022 (Falmouth)

Iron Duke 8.45
(her reckoning)

2040
(*Lion*)
○

2055
(*Southampton*)
○

West, 8 miles

B
○ ○ ○
C
○ 2045
(*Falmouth*)

Westfalen at 8.45
relative to *Iron Duke*

2055 ○
(from *Southampton*)

The German 1st and 3rd Squadrons are approximately W by N 6 miles[6] from the *Iron Duke*, in single line, steering South by West, the van led by the *Westfalen*.

The 2nd Squadron and 4th Scouting Group are on the 1st Squadron's starboard bow, also steering South by West, and on the port quarter is the 1st Scouting Group.

The enemy Battle Fleet was not sighted from the Battle Fleet after 7.59 pm,[7] but, as explained in Chapter X, the Commander-in-Chief could have had no doubt[8] of their approximate position at 9 pm.

If the High Sea Fleet had not been so close, the difference between the reckoning of the *Iron Duke* and the Battle Cruiser Fleet would have made its location difficult. In Diagram 46 the reports of the *Lion*, *Falmouth* and *Southampton* between 7.30 and 9 pm are plotted so as to emphasise this point. But if the actual position of the Battle Cruiser Fleet had not been known,[9] the Battle Fleet might have been misled by these signals. The whole service of tactical scouting depends on synchronizing the reckoning of detached forces to that of the Battle Fleet. Although an opportunity for this occurred between 6.10 and 6.35, and again between 7.10 and 7.35 pm, when the *Lion* was in sight of the *Iron Duke*, and although great stress was laid on this particular point in the Battle Orders,[10] it was not done.[11]

---

[6] *Editor's note*: Written 6' in the original. Miles is obviously the unit. This usage occurs several times in the latter part of the *Appreciation*, and has been replaced by the word 'miles' without being noted.

[7] Jellicoe, *Grand Fleet*, 367, states that enemy battleships were sighted to westward on the starboard bow at 7.59 pm. Lieutenant-Commander Calvert in *Iron Duke*'s turret saw nine heavy ships ahead at 8.25 (*Official Despatches*, 60), but this was an individual observation. The *King George V* sighted enemy battle cruisers, which she at first mistook for British, about 9.05 pm. They fired at the 4th Light Cruiser Squadron, and it is probable that they were observed by other ships in the Battle Fleet.

[8] *Editor's note*: In the published Admiralty 'Narrative' this was softened slightly to: 'the Commander-in-Chief could have had *little* doubt . . .' (*Narrative of the Battle of Jutland*, 67; emphasis added).

[9] The battle cruisers had been in sight of the Battle Fleet until about 7.35 pm. Their course and speed were reported at 7.40 pm, and the flashes of their guns were seen from the Battle Fleet at 8.20. The 2nd Cruiser Squadron, too, was in sight of both Battle Fleet and battle cruisers until 8.15 pm. Lord Jellicoe says that during this period he assumed the *Lion* to be five or six miles ahead of the van of the Battle Fleet; Jellicoe, *Grand Fleet*, 366.

[10] GFBO, XXII, para. 6: 'Attention is called to the vital necessity of indicating the position based on the Commander-in-Chief's reference position in all reports of the enemy; unless this is done, officers not in visual touch can make no use of the signals . . . and the most serious consequences may arise'.

[11] Reference positions were made at 0.40 pm and 9.48 pm, the former by visual and the latter by wireless, but the Battle Cruiser Fleet was not in sight at either time.

State of the Two Fleets

74. The day was over and it was possible to survey the situation. As a result of the fighting the British had lost the *Queen Mary*, *Indefatigable* and *Invincible*. The *Lion* and *Princess Royal* had each one turret out of action, but the battle cruisers were otherwise ready and fit to renew the action. The *Warspite* was returning to Rosyth, and the guns' crews of the *Malaya*'s secondary battery had suffered heavy casualties, but with these exceptions the steaming and fighting qualities of the 5th Battle Squadron were practically unimpaired. In the Battle Fleet the speed of the *Marlborough* had been slightly reduced, and the *Colossus* had five men wounded, but for all practical purposes it was as fit for action as on the day it left harbour. The *Defence* and three destroyers[12] had been sunk, and the *Warrior* and three destroyers disabled.

On the German side, the *Lützow* and *Seydlitz*, two of their most powerful battle cruisers, were incapable of renewing the action; the former had received about 40 large calibre hits, and the latter 24 besides having been torpedoed. Nor was the *Derfflinger* much better off; she had 3,400 tons of water on board, and only one turret and two 5.9 in. guns fit for action.[13] There remained only the *Von der Tann* and *Moltke*, and the latter had one turret out of action.[14] The battleships had not suffered so severely as the battle cruisers, but the powerful 3rd Squadron had lost some of its fighting value.[15] The *König*'s fore part was flooded, and she had been hit by ten large projectiles, whilst the *Grosser Kurfurst*, *Markgraf* and *Kaiser* had received 15 hits between them. The 1st and 2nd Squadrons had escaped with little damage, but the *Wiesbaden* and four torpedo boats[16] had been sunk.

Although the absolute losses were heavier on the British than the German side, the actual result was to increase the relative superiority of the British battle cruisers. Four modern and five older British battle cruisers had originally been opposed to four modern and one older: but now at the end of the day the British had three modern and three older battle cruisers fit for action against only one modern and one older – the *Moltke* and *Von der Tann*.

Editor's note: At 6.10 – five minutes before the deployment signal was hoisted – Jellicoe was anxiously awaiting information as to the location of the German battle fleet; the period between 7.10 and 7.35 included the second engagement with the High Seas Fleet and the attack by German destroyers. These were hardly the times for broadcasting reference positions!

[12] *Nestor*, *Nomad* and *Shark* sunk. *Acasta*, *Onslow* and *Defender* disabled.

[13] Von Hase.

[14] *See* Appendix D for hits on German ships.

[15] Scheer's Report; *Official Despatches*, 598.

[16] V.27, V.29, V.48 and S.35.

To the Commander-in-Chief the situation may have appeared in a still more favourable light, for he did not know the full extent of the British losses, and was spared any anxiety as to the *Queen Mary* and *Indefatigable*. He knew only that the *Invincible*[17] had been sunk and that the *Marlborough*'s speed had been reduced to 17 knots.[18]

It was not till the next day that he learnt of the fate of the *Queen Mary* and *Indefatigable*.[19]

The loss of the *Defence*, too, must have been known; and the *Warrior* had reported both engines disabled at 8.37 pm. No reports had been made to the Commander-in-Chief as to destroyer casualties, and he would only be aware of those that came under his immediate notice.[20]

For an estimate of the state and efficiency of the German Fleet, the Commander-in-Chief could rely on his own observation. On the two occasions when the Battle Fleet was in effective range of the enemy, the latter's ships were seen to be repeatedly hit and to be incapable of effective reply. The *Iron Duke* herself had one of the *König* class under an accurate fire from 6.30 to 6.37 pm, and she was not even fired at in return. The Commander-in-Chief had also seen the three torpedo attacks made by the enemy flotillas at 7.10, 7.25 and 8.15 pm driven off without difficulty, and two German boats destroyed. Only one ship on the British side had been hit by a torpedo, and she was still in the line fit for action. So far, then, as the Commander-in-Chief could judge of the situation, he could look forward with confidence to a renewal of the battle. The gunnery of the Grand Fleet appeared to be undoubtedly superior to that of the enemy, and the threat of the torpedo had proved less serious than was anticipated.

The fighting had also revealed the mind and intentions of the German Commander-in-Chief in a very definite and satisfactory manner. He had turned away in every encounter with the Battle Fleet, and it was clear that his one idea was to avoid action and return to harbour.

---

[17] *Official Despatches*, signal made at 7.3 pm.

[18] *Official Despatches*, signal made at 7.49 pm.

[19] 'I was unaware of the loss of the *Queen Mary* and *Indefatigable* until the morning of June 1'; Jellicoe, *Grand Fleet*, 328. The Commander-in-Chief seems to have mistaken the *Indomitable* and *Inflexible* for the *Queen Mary* and *Indefatigable*, for on meeting the Battle Cruiser Forces the next morning he asked Beatty at 5.55 am what he knew of the movements of the *Indomitable* and *Inflexible*, though these two ships were actually with the Battle Cruiser Forces and in sight of the *Iron Duke*. At 11.04 am the Commander-in-Chief asks: 'When did the *Queen Mary* and *Indefatigable* go?'

[20] Probably only the *Acasta*.

Editor's note: Although Jellicoe wouldn't have known, most of his light cruiser and destroyer torpedoes remained unfired: only about 31 had been expended in the day action (TNA: ADM 186/586, 'Analysis of Torpedo Firing in the Battle of Jutland').

The Problem before the Commander-in-Chief

75. The Commander-in-Chief decided very rightly not to fight a night action, and the problem now before him was to intercept the enemy in daylight before he reached the shelter of his shore defences.[21]

This problem resolved itself into two main aspects – the danger of minefields and the probable route of the enemy. Reference to Diagram 47 will show that minefields offered no real obstacle above the latitude of 55° N, whilst South of it only British minefields stood in the way of the pursuit of the German Fleet via the Horns Riff route. But the position of these was known;[22] they could be regarded in the same light as shoal water, and there was even a possibility of driving the German Fleet towards them. The latest information as regards German minefields was contained in HF 005 of May 25, 1915.[23]

There was next the question of Scheer's probable route. These were limited to four – the Kattegat and the three channels which the Germans kept regularly swept in the Bight in response to British minelaying. Return via the Kattegat was unlikely. Scheer was 344 miles from the Little Belt, and a choice of this route would give the British a whole day to chase and renew the action. The channels or 'ways' kept swept in the Bight were three in number – one past the Ems along the Frisian coast, one radiating to the North-West from Heligoland, and one by Amrum Bank and Sylt to Horns Riff.[24] These 'ways' were known at the Admiralty and their general direction had been communicated to the Commander-in-Chief.

---

[21] *Editor's note*: It is significant that the Dewars, despite their very aggressive philosophy, agree that it was not wise for the Grand Fleet to fight a night action. The simple fact is that the RN was neither equipped nor trained to fight in darkness, and that the risks from German torpedo craft far outweighed any possible gain. This is one of the many lessons that the RN took to heart, and the next war would find it well prepared for night fighting.

[22] *Editor's note*: It must be remembered that the *exact* positions of the minefields would have been uncertain, as was the exact position of the Grand Fleet itself.

[23] Mining Memorandum HF 005 of May 25, 1915, stated that a German minefield was reported to exist from a position 10 miles 258° from Heligoland towards a gas buoy in 53° 52' N, 7° 15' E, and probably beyond that buoy towards Baltrum Island (Lat. 53° 44' N, Long. 7° 33' E). It went on to say that 'the waters between Heligoland and the northern end of the above line are believed to be mined, with a swept channel through. A black conical buoy is reported in 53° 52' N, 7° 8' E. Vessels should not pass to eastward of a line drawn 33½° from this buoy. A German minefield is reported to exist in the area formed by a parallelogram, two of whose adjacent sides are drawn 20 miles 253° and 7 miles 153° from Lat. 53° 56' N, 6° 56' E'.

(NOTE. *The above fields are in the Ems to Nordeney and Nordeney to Heligoland areas.*)

[24] See Diagram 47.

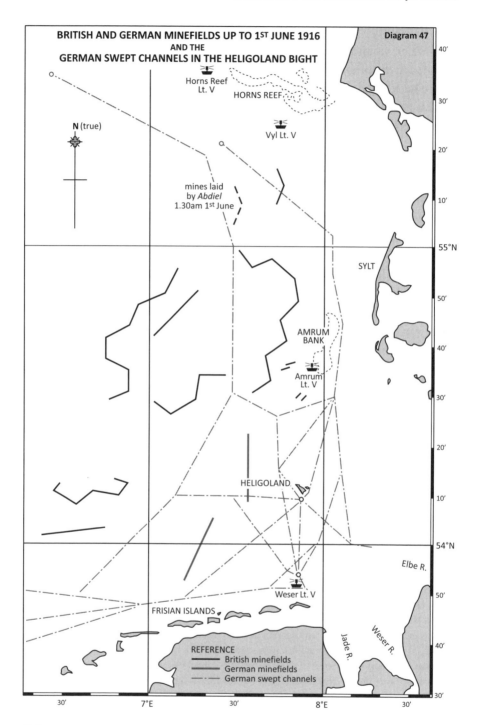

BRITISH AND GERMAN MINEFIELDS UP TO 1ST JUNE 1916
AND THE
GERMAN SWEPT CHANNELS IN THE HELIGOLAND BIGHT

Diagram 47

Horns Reef
Lt. V

HORNS REEF

N (true)

Vyl Lt. V

mines laid
by *Abdiel*
1.30am 1st June

55°N

SYLT

AMRUM
BANK

Amrum
Lt. V

HELIGOLAND

54°N

Elbe R.

Weser Lt. V

FRISIAN ISLANDS

REFERENCE
—— British minefields
—— German minefields
—·— German swept channels

Jade R.

Weser R.

30'   7°E   30'   8°E   30'

Note
The Amrum and Weser light vessels were not marked on the original diagram. They have
been added for clarity.

The Ems route was improbable, for it was long and round about. Heligoland and Horns Riff were the most likely,[25] and Horns Riff the more probable of the two.

At the Admiralty there were very distinct indications that the Heligoland route was not in use. The routine signals made in the Bight were intercepted daily and decoded in Room 40,[26] and the minesweeping signal in force on May 28 appeared to rule out the Heligoland route.[27] There is, however, no trace of this important piece of information having been communicated to the Commander-in-Chief, and it seems probable that it never reached him. This must be regarded as a serious omission, for the Commander-in-Chief, at 9 pm, was evidently thinking both of the Ems and Heligoland routes.[28]

At the same time it was obviously unsound to rely wholly on assumption. The enemy might have made for the Kattegat, and definite arrangements ought to have been made and orders issued for keeping in touch with him during the night.

A glance at the chart[29] will show that a favourable position for intercepting a fleet making for either Horns Riff or Heligoland was about 10 miles to the south-westward of the Horns Riff Light, for the shallow water made the passage of large ships to the eastward of the Light extremely improbable. From Scheer's 9 pm position to a point 10 miles[30] to the South-West of Horns Riff was 90 miles. Allowing some delay in getting round the British Fleet, and crediting his fleet with an average speed of 16 knots,[31] he could not get there before 3 am, half an hour after daylight.[32] The British Fleet was nearer and could go at least two knots faster than the German. It was imperative to prevent the High Sea Fleet slipping past unobserved, and the Grand Fleet had only to keep in

---

[25] See Diagram 48. From Scheer's 9 pm position to Sylt via Horns Riff was 142 [miles]. To Heligoland via the Heligoland way was 175 miles.

[26] Room 40 at this time was not under the Director of the Naval Intelligence Division. Special intelligence was not sent regularly to the Commander-in-Chief till August, 1917.

[27] German message, decoded 7.16 pm, May 28, 1916: 'The way from Horns Riff East of Amrum Bank is free of mines, and also the way to the Ems from 31 epsilon (54° 3' N, Long. 5° 15' E) and 61 epsilon (53° 33' N, 5° 45' E), area 7-147 beta (54° 33' N, 7° 45' E) is suspected of mines. Mines were found in 117 beta area 7 (54° 27' N, Long. 7° 15' E)'. The suspected area and the one in which mines were found fouled Scheer's return route via Heligoland.

[28] Commander-in-Chief's despatch, *Official Despatches*, 21: 'Should be favourably placed to intercept the enemy should he make for his base by steering for Heligoland or towards Ems'.

[29] See Diagram 48.

[30] *Editor's note*: This and the next number were written as 10' and 90' in the original text.

[31] The German 2nd Squadron could not steam more than 16 knots, and some of his ships were known to be damaged.

[32] Cf. *Shannon* '2.45 am, *Lion* in sight bearing South six miles'; *Colossus*, '2.15 am, "general quarters"'; *Lizard* '2.30 am, Zeppelin six to seven miles away'; *Fearless*, 'When daylight broke . . . and . . . at 2.45 am.'

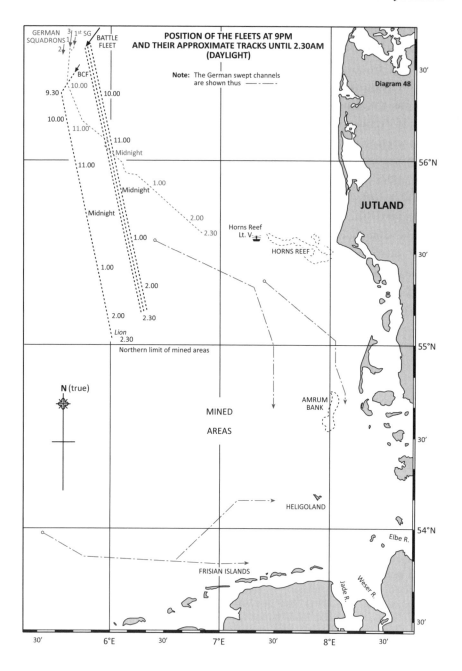

touch with it in order to force it to fight at daylight. By 11 pm there could have been no further doubt as to its destination.[33] Its destination was Horns Riff.

---

[33] *Editor's note*: See the Chapter XI Endnote for Jellicoe's rebuttal to the Dewars' interpretation, as published in the 'Admiralty Narrative'.

Narrative of Proceedings

76. At 9.01 pm the Battle Fleet was turned by divisions to South, speed 17 knots. The Commander-in-Chief states: 'I was loath to forego the advantage of position which would have resulted from an Easterly or Westerly course, and I therefore decided to steer to the southward, where I should be in a position to renew the engagement at daylight, and should also be favourably placed to intercept the enemy should he make for his base by steering for Heligoland or towards the Ems and thence along the North German coast'.[34] The reasoning is difficult to follow, for the course ordered by the Commander-in-Chief was on the direct line to the Ems, and if it were continued during the night the fleet must find itself at dawn (2.30 am) 43 miles to the south-westward of Horns Riff and 25 miles to the westward of Scheer's direct course to Heligoland,[35] in either case much too far off to force him to action. The course decided on left the enemy fleet free to retreat by Horns Riff, the Kattegat, or Heligoland, unless it were merely intended as a temporary measure pending further information of the enemy's movements. At about 9.05 pm the *King George* V sighted the enemy's battle cruisers bearing West-North-West, but mistook them for British, reporting them to the Commander-in-Chief as such, and negativing a signal of the *Caroline* to attack with torpedoes. The *Castor* and 11th Flotilla were also ready to attack, but apparently owing to the lack of support from the Battle Fleet did not do so. Meanwhile, the enemy battle cruisers turned away to starboard, and some enemy battleships opened fire on the *Caroline* and *Royalist*. The former fired one torpedo and the latter two, but without result. A good opportunity of dealing a final blow at the already beaten German battle cruisers was thus missed, and the whole incident shows a grave lack of tactical co-operation, which must be partly attributed to a rigid and inelastic system of command. Here was the Battle Fleet within effective range of the enemy, offering a good opportunity of dealing one final blow before dark. But the Battle Fleet did not recognise the enemy. It mistook him for Beatty's battle cruisers, which were really eight miles ahead. Surely it was the business of the 2nd Cruiser Squadron to keep it better informed. It mustered six ships[36] lying between the *King George V* and the *Lion*, actually in sight of both until about 8.15 pm.[37] Though it was of vital importance to maintain continuous and clear visual communication, this force remained concentrated and apparently thought only of maintaining its deployment position on the quarter of the battle

---

[34] Commander-in-Chief's dispatch; *Official Despatches*, 21.
[35] *See* Diagram 48.
[36] The 2nd Cruiser Squadron accompanied by *Duke of Edinburgh* and *Chester*.
[37] *Shannon* (r); *Official Despatches*, 280.

cruisers.[38] Its true function was lost in blind obedience to the letter of the deployment diagram. Similarly the van of the Battle Fleet seems to have thought only of maintaining station on the Commander-in-Chief. It neither pressed forward in support of the battle cruisers nor did it endeavour to maintain visual touch with them by means of the 2nd Cruiser Squadron.

At 9.17 pm the Battle Fleet assumed the second organisation (vide Appendix B) and formed divisions in line ahead columns one mile apart, disposed abeam to port from the *King George V*. The *Marlborough*'s sub-division[39] was by this time two to three miles astern of station, with the 5th Battle Squadron between it and the Main Fleet. The object of the closer formation was to ensure the divisions remaining in sight of each other during the night and prevent ships mistaking each other for enemy vessels.[40] At 9.27 pm the destroyer flotillas were ordered to take station astern five miles. Admiral Jellicoe states that it was intended to provide the Battle Fleet with a screen against torpedo attack, and also to give them a chance of attacking the enemy's heavy ships should they also be proceeding to the southward. But this was not communicated to the destroyers, and not a word was told them of the formation and disposition of their own fleet nor of the position and probable course of the enemy. To tell a flotilla merely to take station astern was worse than nothing at all. It was a justification of inactivity. It was equivalent to telling a brigade to march on a certain road and await further orders. At 9.30 pm the Battle Cruiser Fleet altered course to South, speed 17 knots. The *Lion* now bore about 13 miles West-South-West from the *Iron Duke*, maintaining this position during the night. No instructions were issued as to the Commander-in-Chief's intentions, but Beatty states that he considered he would be carrying out the Commander-in-Chief's wishes by turning to the course of the fleet so as to ensure that the enemy did not regain his base by passing round the Southern flank of the fleet.[41]

77.   Meanwhile Scheer had also been disposing his fleet for the night. He had ordered the officers commanding the 1st and 2nd Torpedo Divisions to launch

---

[38] *Minotaur* (r). 'It was now decided that the place for our squadron was on the quarter of the Battle Cruiser Squadron, which would be in conformity with the plan of the deployment'; *Official Despatches*, 272.

[39] *Marlborough, Revenge, Hercules* and *Agincourt*.

[40] Commander-in-Chief's dispatch; *Official Despatches*, 21.

[41] Beatty (r); *Official Despatches*, 139.

Editor's note: It was at 9.32 pm that *Lion* asked *Princess Royal* (via flashing lamp) 'Please give me challenge and reply now in force as they have been lost'. It has long been suggested that the Germans saw this and that is how they knew the RN's secret recognition signals, although Gordon disagrees (*Rules of the Game*, 481 n.22).

all flotillas to the attack during the night,[42] and they had therefore distributed them over the various sectors where the British were expected to block the passage to Horns Riff. At 9.14 pm Scheer ordered the Main Fleet to proceed in, course SSE ¼ E, speed 16 knots. The 1st Squadron, which had scarcely been in action, was at the head of the line, followed by the 3rd Squadron, both being in reverse order with the *Westfalen* leading, and at 9.29 pm the 2nd Battle Squadron was directed to take station astern of the 3rd Squadron.[43] At the same time the battle cruisers were placed in the rear, but as the *Lützow* had been left behind and the *Seydlitz* and *Moltke* were proceeding independently, only the *Derfflinger* and the *Von der Tann* actually took up this position. The 2nd Scouting Group covered the van and the 4th Scouting Group the starboard side.

The two fleets were now converging on one another; at about 10.15 pm the 2nd Scouting Group came in contact with the *Castor* and 11th Flotilla, which were on the starboard quarter of the British starboard wing division and a short action ensued.[44]

By 10 pm the *Marlborough*'s sub-division was about four miles astern of station, and at 10.03 the 5th Battle Squadron turned 16 points to starboard to regain station on her, resuming its course at 10.12 pm. As the *Marlborough* was then seen to be going very slowly, the Rear-Admiral, 5th Battle Squadron, increased speed to take station on the Main Fleet.

---

[42] The decentralisation of command practised in the High Sea Fleet is illustrated by the orders to the torpedo flotillas. At 7.16 pm the Commander-in-Chief directed the 2nd Torpedo Division (*Regensburg*) to launch the 2nd, 6th, and 9th Flotillas to night attack. The latter thereupon issued the necessary orders allocating each flotilla to a definite sector, and at 8.26 he reported them advancing through these sectors to the Commander-in-Chief. At 8.12 the Commander-in-Chief issued further instructions to the 1st Torpedo Division (*Rostock*) and 2nd Torpedo Division (*Regensburg*) to launch all flotillas to night attack. Whereupon the Officer Commanding 1st Torpedo Division (*Rostock*) ordered the 2nd Torpedo Division (*Regensburg*) to allocate his flotillas independently, and then proceeded to divide his own flotillas over the sectors left vacant by the 2nd Torpedo Division. In each case the *Rostock* kept the flotillas informed of the position of the Main Fleet, and at 10.32 pm, without any instructions from the Commander-in-Chief, he warned all flotillas to be off Horns Riff at 2 am, leaving it to their discretion to return round the Skaw if necessary. At 1.15 am (the *Rostock* being out of action) we find the *Regensburg*, again without instructions from the Commander-in-Chief, ordering all flotillas to assemble at the head of the 3rd Battle Squadron, owing to the delay in reaching Horns Riff.

[43] Commander-in-Chief to High Sea Fleet: '2nd Battle Squadron behind 3rd. All large cruisers in the rear. 2nd Scouting Group ahead. 4th Scouting Group to starboard'.

[44] Details of destroyer actions during the night are given in the next chapter, see p. XXX.

At 10.05 pm *Abdiel* received orders from the Commander-in-Chief to lay mines in accordance with instructions which had been previously issued.[45] The work was completed by 2.04 am, and the *Abdiel* returned to Rosyth.

78. In the meantime the 2nd Light Cruiser Squadron, which it will be remembered was astern of the 5th Battle Squadron at 9 pm, had moved over to westward of the Battle Fleet.

About 10.30 pm,[46] when approximately seven miles on the starboard quarter of the *King George V*, five ships steering in the same direction appeared on the starboard beam. This was the 4th Scouting Group. They suddenly switched on searchlights and concentrated a heavy fire on the *Southampton* and *Dublin*. The action was brief and fierce. The *Southampton* was extensively damaged about the upper deck and suffered very heavy casualties. The *Dublin*, which was hit on the forebridge, lost touch with the squadron and did not rejoin until 10 am next day. The enemy ships were also frequently hit, and the *Frauenlob* was sunk by a torpedo fired from the *Southampton*. After the action was over, the 2nd Light Cruiser Squadron altered course to the eastward and took station astern of the Battle Fleet with the idea of screening it against torpedo attack.[47] In taking up this position the *Birmingham* had to alter course to avoid the two rear ships of the 5th Battle Squadron and, becoming separated from the *Southampton*, took station astern of the rear ship of that squadron. This movement of the 2nd Light Cruiser Squadron right through the area where its own flotillas were placed to attack the enemy is open to criticism. Destroyer officers are not likely to accept the responsibility of instant attack unless they are positive that the ships attacked are not their own. Dispositions and instructions for the night should therefore be communicated to all vessels as a matter of routine, and the mere fact that destroyers are ordered to attack in a certain area should be sufficient warning for other craft to keep clear. Unfortunately it must be admitted that in these matters the staff work in the Grand Fleet was inferior to that of its opponents. The German flotillas were allotted definite areas in which to attack, and they were informed of the

---

[45] For position of minefield *vide* Diagram 47.

[46] Times are somewhat conflicting. *Southampton* (r), 'at 10.20 squadron was engaged'; *Birmingham* (r), 'about 10.15'; *Dublin* (r), 10.40, 'sighted enemy vessels on starboard beam'. Scheer states the *Frauenlob* was hit by a torpedo at 10.45 pm.

[47] The Commodore, 2nd Light Cruiser Squadron, explains his action in taking station astern of the Battle Fleet by saying that he did not know what protection had been provided against torpedo attack; *Southampton* (r), *Official Despatches*, 177.

formation of their cruiser squadrons, and the position of the Main Fleet was communicated to them periodically.

The signal reporting the *Southampton*'s engagement did not reach the Commander-in-Chief until 11.38 pm,[48] but the gun flashes and searchlights were seen by the whole Battle Fleet.[49] As the scene of the engagement was about four points abaft the starboard beam, it must have been apparent even at that early hour that the course of the Grand Fleet was rapidly opening the enemy's path to Horns Riff. At 10.41, just as this action was finishing, the Commander-in-Chief received information of the greatest importance from the Admiralty. It read: 'German Battle Fleet ordered home at 9.14 pm, battle cruisers in rear course SSE ¾ E,[50] speed 16 knots'.[51] This course, laid off from the position of the German Fleet at 9 pm as given in the Admiralty's 10.23 signal, passed some 9 miles SW of the Horns Riff Light Vessel, and could have left no further doubt that the High Sea Fleet was returning to its base by this channel (Diagram 49).

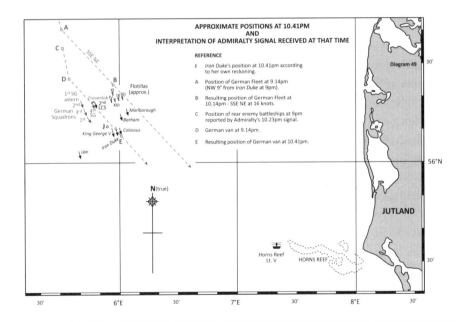

[48] The *Southampton*'s wireless had been shot away, but at 11.30 she ordered the *Nottingham* to report the action.

[49] Practically every battleship's report mentions gun flashes and searchlights on the starboard quarter at about 10.30 pm, and the *Royal Oak* and *Vanguard* report seeing ships silhouetted against the searchlights.

[50] Cf. Appendix G, Nos. 25 and 27.

[51] *Editor's note*: Beatty thought this sentence, and each of the next two paragraphs, as being important: he highlighted them in the margins, the last paragraph in the green pencil he frequently used.

If the Commander-in-Chief really desired to intercept the German Fleet, his course was now clear; without risking a night action he had only to turn his fleet to a parallel course and increase speed to 18 knots.[52] This would have brought him to a favourable position to cut off the High Sea Fleet at daylight, and the danger of torpedo attack would not have been increased one whit.

But the fleet continued on its course. Nothing was done, and as it proceeded South there commenced a series of destroyer actions,[53] which, gradually working round from the starboard to port quarter, pointed a great guiding finger direct to Horns Riff. Astern of the British Battle Fleet the flash of guns, the gleam of searchlights, the sudden glare of explosions and the great torches of flame rising from burning destroyers marked the route along which the German Fleet was escaping as surely and unmistakably as the compass in Scheer's flagship.

79. About 10.50 pm the German 7th Flotilla[54] sighted British destroyers, and these were reported by the *Rostock* to the German Commander-in-Chief.[55] This report, combined with one from Neumünster,[56] repeating the British Commander-in-Chief's order to his flotillas to take station 5 miles astern of the Battle Fleet, probably gave Scheer a fairly accurate idea of the relative positions of the two fleets at this time. In any case, at 11 pm he altered course to SE ½ S – two and three-quarter points to the eastward[57] – evidently to give the High Sea Fleet a little more room as it crossed the track of its opponent. The *Rostock* and 7th Flotilla were not unobserved by the British, for at 10.35 pm the *Garland* reports sighting a cruiser of the *Graudenz* class, and at 10.50 the *Porpoise* and *Unity* sighted three enemy destroyers approaching from the starboard quarter. Neither of these reports were passed on to the Commander-in-Chief.

It was 11.30 pm when the German Fleet struck the 4th Flotilla, and a heavy fire was opened on the latter's van, probably by the 2nd Scouting Group, supported by the *Rostock* and 1st Squadron. The *Tipperary* was set on fire

---

[52] *Editor's note*: Again, see the Chapter XI Endnote for Admiral Jellicoe's rebuttal.

[53] These are described in detail in Chapter XII.

[54] This flotilla had been ordered at 8.40 pm to advance from Lat. 56° 35' N, Long. 5° 30' E, through a sector SE, to S by E.

[55] 'Enemy destroyers in Lat. 56° 3' N, Long. 5° 55' E, course S high speed'.

[56] Neumünster to German Commander-in-Chief, 10.10 pm: 'Destroyers have taken up position five sea miles astern of the enemy Main Fleet'.

Editor's note: Although Jellicoe's signal to his destroyers was intercepted and decyphered by Neumünster, Scheer apparently was not aware of this information until he had returned to harbour, so it could not have affected his decisions during the night after the battle (Campbell, *Jutland*, 297).

[57] *Official Despatches*, German Plan VII.

forward and completely disabled, the *Broke* was seriously damaged, the *Spitfire* collided with the *Nassau*, and the *Sparrowhawk* was disabled by collision with the *Broke*. On the German side the *Elbing* was rammed and disabled by the *Posen* and the *Rostock* was torpedoed. The remainder of the flotilla made off to the eastward, then turned again to the South, and ignorant of the course of the German Fleet inevitably struck it again at about midnight, and the *Fortune* and *Ardent* were both sunk by gunfire.

During this action, the *Pillau* and *Frankfurt* became separated from the Main Fleet. Following a more Northerly course they were kept informed of Scheer's position and rejoined shortly after daylight. The 13th Flotilla heard the firing and made off to the eastward.

At 0.10 am the *Black Prince*, which had lost touch with the fleet when it deployed and was apparently following it up, found herself within 1,600 yards of the rear ships of the German 1st Squadron. A tornado of fire was opened on her from the *Thuringen* and *Ostfriesland*. She burst into flames and sank with a terrific explosion in four minutes. At about 0.25 am the head of the German line, by this time well on the port quarter of the British Fleet, cut through the end of the line formed by the 9th and 10th Flotillas and stragglers from the 13th. A heavy fire was opened on them and the *Turbulent*, the last of the line, was sunk. There can be no possible doubt that these engagements were seen by the Battle Fleet, and several ships saw the firing commencing on the starboard quarter and gradually working round to the port quarter.[58] The Commander-in-Chief's idea that no enemy ships were seen by the Battle Fleet during the night[59] probably arose from the fact that no reports of the enemy were received from the Battle Fleet.

80. At 11.30 pm the *Birmingham*, then astern of the 5th Battle Squadron, observed two large enemy ships switch on their searchlights. She took them for battle cruisers,[60] and at once reported them bearing North-East and steering South: her D.R. position placed them a long way to the northward of their true

---

[58] *Hercules* (r): 'From 10.15 pm to 12.30 am (June 1) five separate engagements seem to have occurred . . . On the first occasion searchlights were observed, and attack bore NW by W. The attack gradually worked round the stern to N by E.' (*Official Despatches*, 74). *Colossus* (r): '10.35 pm, firing starboard quarter; 11.40, rapid and continuous firing for 15 minutes right astern'. *Superb* (r): '10.13, much firing on starboard quarter; 11.30 and 11.43, firing observed right astern; 0.25 am, ditto on port quarter' (*Official Despatches*, 81, 307). The *Revenge, Thunderer, Temeraire, Vanguard, Barham, Malaya, Valiant, Agincourt, Active* and *Boadicea* all report sighting enemy ships at various times between 10.15 pm and 0.30 am, and the *Malaya* actually identified one of the *Westfalen* class as leading the German line during the attack on the 4th Flotilla.

[59] Commander-in-Chief's dispatch; *Official Despatches*, 22.

[60] They were probably battleships of the German 1st Squadron.

position, but the report clearly confirmed the passage of German ships across the rear of the British Fleet.

At 1.48 am the Commander-in-Chief received another message from the Admiralty to the following effect: 'Position of the *Lützow* at midnight 56° 26' N, 5° 41' E, course S, speed 7 knots, damaged. All German submarines are being hurried from German ports to attack. One flotilla returning round Skaw'.[61] This signal did not convey the exact sense of the German original, and tended to exaggerate the submarine danger, for the Order apparently applied only to the 3rd Submarine Half Flotilla and to U.67 and U.51.[62]

At 1.55 am the Vice-Admiral, 1st Battle Squadron, reported to the Commander-in-Chief that the *Marlborough* was obliged to ease to 12 knots. She thereupon hauled out of line, and at about 3 am the Vice-Admiral transferred his flag in the *Fearless* to the *Revenge*. Shortly afterwards the Commander-in-Chief ordered the *Marlborough* to the Tyne, the *Fearless* accompanying her as escort. The *Revenge*, *Hercules* and *Agincourt*, which had continued their course, were 12 miles astern of the fleet at daylight, and if the action had been renewed would have experienced difficulty in rejoining. At midnight they had crossed the enemy's track only 4½ miles ahead of him, with the British Battle Fleet 7½ miles away, and the situation which would have arisen had an action ensued is an interesting subject for conjecture. The German Fleet was greatly superior, but it certainly would not have escaped scatheless; the 5th Battle Squadron, which had crossed within two miles of the enemy Battle Fleet at about 11.15 pm, was only three miles away, and would almost certainly have been dragged into the fight, and a situation might have arisen which would have compelled the Commander-in-Chief either to turn and force an action or face very serious losses to the 6th Division and 5th Battle Squadron.

---

[61] The paraphrase in *Official Despatches*, 477 hardly conveys sense of original message. *Editor's note*: The paraphrase referred to reads:

At 1.48 am the Admiralty informed the Commander-in-Chief that enemy submarines were apparently coming out from German ports, and that a damaged enemy ship, probably *Lutzow*, was in Lat. 56° 26' N, Long. 5° 41' E at Midnight (*Official Despatches*, p. 477).

[62] From Heligoland NIC to Arcona, time group 2150 (7.50 pm): '3rd Submarine Half-Flotilla, 3rd of 4th Submarine Half-Flotilla (U.67). Heligoland NIC for 2nd of 2nd Submarine Half-Flotilla (U.51). Submarines ready for service and U.67 at once to advance North. At 6 am report position. Officer Commanding Submarines' (Room 40 Records Signal 20438, Vol. 897).

Editor's note: The meaning of the abbreviation 'NIC' is obscure. Since it is also used for the Neumünster deciphering station in Appendix G, message 12, it might stand for 'Naval Intelligence Centre' or something similar.

By 1.45 am the enemy fleet had worked right round to the port quarter and were sighted by the 12th Flotilla, led by the *Faulknor*. This was reported to the Commander-in-Chief, the *Faulknor* giving her position as 10 miles astern of the 1st Battle Squadron.[63] There is no trace of this signal having been received in the *Iron Duke*. At 2.10 am the 12th Flotilla carried out an organised attack and succeeded in torpedoing the *Pommern*, which blew up with a terrific explosion and the loss of all hands. At 2.35 am, just as it was getting light, the *Champion*, after making to the eastward, was returning to the southward in company with the *Obdurate* and *Moresby* of the 13th Flotilla,[64] and the *Marksman* and *Maenad* of the12th, when they sighted the German 2nd Squadron at about 4,000 yards. They were unobserved by the enemy, but the *Champion* appears to have turned away again, leaving the *Moresby* to make an attack without support. She fired one torpedo and evidently sank the German destroyer V.4.

81. Meanwhile the fleet was approaching the end of its fruitless journey to the South. At 2.15 am the Commander-in-Chief signalled that single line would be formed on a Northerly course at 2.30 am, and at 2.22[65] he ordered the various detached squadrons to conform and close. The *King George V* led round to North at 2.39 am, and the Battle Fleet, less the *Marlborough*'s division, formed line ahead on her in the 5th Organisation.[66] The Commander-in-Chief states that: 'I deemed it advisable to disregard the danger from submarines due to a long line of ships and to form line of battle at once in case of meeting the enemy Battle Fleet before I had been able to get in touch with my cruisers and destroyers'. The battle cruisers and 5th Battle Squadron altered course to the North a few minutes after the Battle Fleet.[67]

But it was now too late to bar the way to Horns Riff, for the *Iron Duke* was 33 miles and the Germans only 12 miles away from it.[68] It was not too late, however, to make an effort to intercept stragglers and to harass their retreat. No effort was made to do so, and it is impossible to resist the conclusion that the Commander-in-Chief had abandoned any idea of renewing the action, for the

---

[63] He appears to have been further away, probably about 30 miles NNE of the *Iron Duke*.

[64] The remainder of the flotilla had joined up with the 9th and 10th Flotillas.

[65] Priority: 'My position 2.30 am, Lat. 55° 07' N, Long. 6° 21' E, altering course North, conform and close'.

[66] *See* Appendix B.

[67] For position at 2.45 am, *see* Diagram 50.

[68] From position A in the diagram, 10 miles SW of Horns Riff.

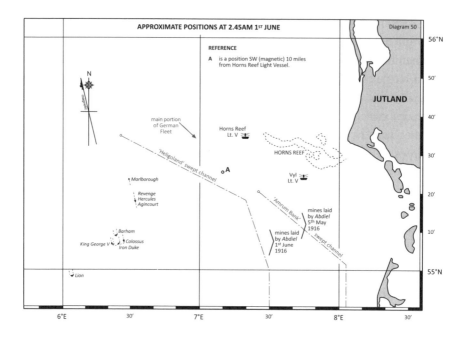

Northerly course of the fleet was now taking it almost directly away from the enemy's line of retreat.[69]

Beyond the avoidance of a night action, it is difficult to trace any definite purpose in the British movements during the night. No instructions were issued as to the Commander-in-Chief's intentions, no organised attempt was made to obtain information of the enemy's movements, and when definite intelligence from the Admiralty supplied absolute confirmation of the enemy's course, nothing was done to intercept him.

This is the darkest part of the battle. The question of deployment and the question of turning away from torpedo attack are points which belong to the sphere of tactics, but the question of pursuing the enemy was a very different one. It was an irredeemable charge which was not done.[70]

The official despatches throw no light on the subject, but Lord Jellicoe states[71] that when he decided to steer to the southward, it had been his intention

---

[69] *Editor's note*: This is patently unfair – Jellicoe (*Grand Fleet*, 384–5) points out that his fleet, especially the destroyers, was scattered, and that it was necessary to regroup before renewing the action. The delay prevented him from steering straight for Horn Reef, as had been his original intention. By the time the Grand Fleet had sorted itself out (the 5th BS would only be in station ahead of the 2nd BS after 3.30) Jellicoe was aware that the High Seas Fleet had gotten behind the shelter of the German minefields.

[70] *Editor's note*: This paragraph, and the one before, were also highlighted in Beatty's copy of the book.

[71] Jellicoe, *Grand Fleet*, 385.

to close Horns Riff at daylight, but the scattered state of the fleet next morning prevented his doing so.

This, however, would not have solved the problem, for course had to be altered to the eastward not later than about 0.30 am in order to intercept the High Sea Fleet. If this had been done the various squadrons and flotillas could have been concentrated within supporting distance of the Battle Fleet at daylight. But no one was told the intentions of the Commander-in-Chief nor the disposition of the fleet, nor the position and course of the enemy. Course South, speed 17 knots, were the only instructions issued.

82. At 3.15 am the *Indomitable* and some of the 3rd Light Cruiser Squadron opened fire on a Zeppelin which was observing the movements of the Battle Cruiser Force. At 3.20 am the Commander-in-Chief received information from the Admiralty that five light cruisers and 13 destroyers from Harwich had been ordered to join his Flag. At 7 am the Commander-in-Chief ordered four of these to screen the *Marlborough*. The remainder did not join the fleet, as the Commander-in-Chief informed the Admiralty at 4 pm that they were not required. At 3.30 am the *Champion*, accompanied by the *Obdurate*, *Moresby*, *Marksman* and *Maenad*, sighted four enemy destroyers steering in opposite directions. The latter fired two torpedoes and the *Champion* appears to have opened fire with her 6 in. guns, but although in greatly superior force no attempt was made to follow the enemy boats, which would have been an easy prey, for they were returning to their base with 1,250 survivors of the *Lützow*.

At 3.29 am a final signal came from the Admiralty informing the Commander-in-Chief that at 2.30 am the German Main Fleet was in Lat. 55° 33' N, Long. 6° 50' E, course SE by S, 16 knots. This placed it 17 miles from Horns Riff Light and 23 miles from the Grand Fleet at that time.

At 3.42 the Battle Fleet altered course to West and reduced to 15 knots, heavy firing having been heard to the westward.[72] It turned again to North and increased again to 17 knots at 3.52 am.

Meanwhile the battle cruisers were also steering in a Northerly direction at 20 knots to regain visual touch with the Battle Fleet. At 4.07 the Vice-Admiral ordered his light cruisers to spread to the westward to locate the enemy. Thus, five hours after the Commander-in-Chief had received definite information of the enemy's course[73] to the south-eastward, Beatty still was in ignorance of it,

---

[72] Presumably the Battle Cruiser Force engaging a Zeppelin at 3.20 am.

[73] 10.41 pm, Admiralty to Commander-in-Chief. 'German Battle Fleet ordered home at 9.14, battle cruisers in rear, course SSE ¾ E, speed 16 knots'.

and imagined him to the westward.[74] The battle cruisers had been too far ahead to observe the route of the High Sea Fleet as indicated by the destroyer actions, and the Admiralty cypher signals were not received in the *Lion*.[75] The *Birmingham*'s report of sighting hostile battle cruisers at 11.30 might have given Beatty a hint, but their course had been received by him as WSW instead of South, an error which tended to support the idea that the British battle cruisers were still between the enemy and his base.

The failure to sift and promulgate information during the night indicates a practical breakdown in the staff organisation. It is a mere truism to say that intelligent co-operation is impossible if subordinate commanders are not informed of the general situation, but unfortunately these truisms turn out to be astoundingly true.

There is little more to be told. At 4.10 am the *Dublin* sighted some enemy vessels steering a Southerly course, one of which appeared to be a light cruiser. This may have been the *Regensburg*, which had turned back to escort the destroyers bringing in the survivors of the *Lützow*, one of which had been hit in the engine room.[76] It was the last occasion on which the ships of the opposing fleets sighted each other.

At 4.13 am the Battle Fleet formed divisions in line ahead columns disposed abeam to starboard with the 5th Battle Squadron three miles ahead.

At 4.40 am the Commander-in-Chief informed the Senior Officer, Battle Cruiser Force, that the enemy fleet had returned to harbour and told him to try and locate *Lützow*, but omitted to mention the position given in the Admiralty's 1.48 am message.

At 4.45 am the battle cruisers altered course to East to close the Battle Fleet and turned up astern at 5.10 am, and at 5.40 increased to 20 knots and proceeded to sweep out an area to the South and south-eastward.

Meanwhile, the Battle Fleet also swept out an area to the southward of the scene of the action, and at noon it was in Lat. 56° 20' N, Long. 5° 26' E. It only remained to return to harbour.

The Battle Fleet, which had put to sea full of hope and ardour, superior to the foe in numbers and gunpower, at least his equal in discipline, individual

---

[74] *Editor's note*: Jellicoe also clearly believed that the High Seas Fleet was somewhere to the west, as proved by his signal at 2.15 am signal ordering line of battle to be formed at 2.30 – he wanted to be prepared for immediate action in case the enemy was close by as the day dawned.

[75] *Lion*'s wireless was shot away. The *Princess Royal* received signals addressed to Vice-Admiral, Battle Cruiser Force, but not the Commander-in-Chief's signals.

[76] Possibly during the short encounter with the *Champion* at 3.30 am.

skill and courage, returned home with two killed and five wounded. It had never been seriously in action.[77]

The enemy meanwhile had swept right across the stern of the fleet during the night.[78] At dawn his ships were still 16 miles from Horns Riff and scores of glasses swept the horizon anxiously for the British Fleet which they fully expected to see. To their surprise and intense relief it was not there. The way lay open and the battle cruisers were ordered to proceed in at 3.24 am. The *Seydlitz* did not reach Horns Riff till 4 am and it was still doubtful if she could get home. She was ultimately beached the next day at the entrance to the Jade steering stern first and drawing 42 ft. of water. The Battle Fleet arrived at Horns Riff at 3 am and Scheer waited for the *Lützow*, which he had not heard of. At 3.30 came the news that she had been abandoned. At 3.38 am the fleet was reformed[79] with a submarine screen, but the three British submarines posted off Vyl Light did not sight the enemy.[80] One misfortune still awaited them. The *Ostfriesland* struck a mine at 5 am, and had to be escorted back by tugs.[81] By 6.30 all danger of pursuit by the Grand Fleet was over, though the *König* drawing 34½ ft. could not pass the Amrum Bank channel till 9.30 am.

Interception of German Signals

83. It will have been noted that the meeting of the two fleets was directly due to the interception of enemy signals, and that during the battle both Admirals

---

[77] *Editor's note*: A very biased statement! Although the Battle Fleet itself was only engaged for a short while, it's worth looking at the ammunition expenditure and hits obtained (based on Campbell, *Jutland*, 346–7, 355): the 24 Grand Fleet battleships (1st through 6th Divisions) fired 1,539 shells from their main batteries and scored 57 hits (3.70 per cent hitting rate). The 5th BS: 1,099 rounds of 15in expended, 29 hits scored (2.64 per cent); 1st and 2nd BCS (approximately – the expenditure from the lost ships is of course unknown) 1,469 shells fired for 21 hits (1.43 per cent); 3rd BCS (*Invincible*, *Inflexible* and *Indomitable*), 373 rounds, 16 hits (4.29 per cent). Despite limited opportunity and poor gunnery conditions, the main fleet was the source of 35.13 per cent of the heavy calibre gunfire, and scored 46.34 per cent of the hits obtained by the British fleet.

[78] Eleven miles astern at midnight.

[79] '2nd Scouting Group astern, 4th Scouting Group ahead. Officer Commanding, 1st Torpedo Division, "distribute TBs for submarine protection, 2nd Squadron proceed in"'.

Editor's note: The Germans called their destroyers 'torpedo boats', hence the abbreviation 'TBs' in the translated signal.

[80] E.50, E.26 and D.1 had orders to spread on a line 270°, 4, 12 and 20 miles respectively from Vyl Light Vessel.

Editor's note: The British submarines, which had departed from Harwich in the early evening of 30 May, were under orders to remain submerged until 2 June – thus they had no way of knowing that the battle had occurred (Marder, *FDSF*, 3:190–1).

[81] This was one of the mines laid by the *Abdiel* on 5 May 1916.

were receiving from London and Neumünster at least a portion of their opponents' signals. The general effect of this factor on the strategy of the Grand Fleet has been dealt with in Chapter I (p. 16), but it has also an important tactical aspect.

Appendix G (p. 233) gives the more important German signals as decoded at the Admiralty between May 30 and June 1, and a comparison between them and those passed on to the Commander-in-Chief[82] shows that this priceless talisman of intelligence was not fully utilised.

Three of the German signals (Nos. 25, 28 and 32), made between 9.06 pm and 10.32, indicated clearly that Horns Riff was the destination of the High Sea Fleet. Only one of these – No. 25 – was transmitted to the Commander-in-Chief at 10.41. Nos. 27, 31, 37 and 38, which gave Scheer's course at 9.46 pm, 10.32 pm, 11.30 pm and 11.36 pm respectively, were not passed on. Of three signals, Nos. 35, 43 and 45, fixing the position of the High Sea Fleet at 11 pm, 12.30 am and 2.30 am respectively, only No. 45 was transmitted at 3.29 am.[83] It is true that No. 25 (received in the *Iron Duke* at 10.41 pm) was enough for the purpose, but the Commander-in-Chief might justifiably complain that other signals of great importance, confirming the enemy's destination and giving his position and course at various times during the night, were not sent to him.

Precisely what happened at the Admiralty is obscure, but we know that between 10.41 pm and 3.30 am information of vital importance remained gazing blankly upwards from an Admiralty table whilst the fate of the war hung in the balance.[84]

The special intelligence branch (Room 40) was not attached to the Intelligence Division at this time, and this truly peculiar organisation may partly explain the failure to make full use of it. The Room was not open to the officers of the German Section (Section 14) nor to the German Movements Section (Section E). Co-operation with the German Section would have been enormously useful to Room 40,[85] and Room 40 could have supplied the German Section with priceless information, but they were not allowed to work in

---

[82] These will be found amongst the signals in *Official Despatches*, Appendix II.

[83] *Editor's note*: The original text has this as 3.29 pm, but this is an obvious misprint (see *Official Despatches*, 484).

[84] This cannot be regarded as an exaggeration, for had the Grand Fleet cut Scheer off from Horns Riff, there can be little doubt that it would have been able to inflict a disastrous defeat on the German Fleet.

Editorial note: For a detailed examination of the organisational problems that hindered the use of 'special intelligence', see Hines, 'Sins of Omission and Commission'.

[85] The special intelligence personnel was installed in Room 40, Old Building.

conjunction, though the German Section had actually translated the early codes in use in Room 40. The case of E.1 Section was precisely similar. E.1 dealt with the movements of German submarines on the basis of British and neutral sources. All reports of ships attacked and reports of sighting and attacking German submarines came to E.1, and were duly plotted and recorded there. Room 40, on the other hand, obtained its information from German sources, and knew nothing of British reports. It took in the submarines' signals and knew their identity and time of departure. E.1 followed their track across the ocean so far as British reports could give it, but the two sections were not allowed to work in conjunction.[86] It was not till July, 1917, that Room 40 became a section of the Intelligence Division; it was not till September, 1917, that the German section and submarine movements section were given access to it; and it was not till December, 1917, that Room 40 and E.1 became sub-sections of the same section.[87]

Enough has now been said to show that at the time of Jutland a policy of secrecy, amounting to an absolute obsession, was maintained. Vitally important information, instead of being sent out as a matter of course, was only sent to the Chief of the War Staff and Director of Operations, who passed or did not pass it on. The defects of the system are obvious. The section that is responsible for such information was the only section able to 'vet' it in the light of continuous and cumulative intelligence.[88] It was clearly the function of the Intelligence Division to keep the Commander-in-Chief supplied with information as to the movements of the High Sea Fleet, and this it did not do because its function had been withheld.

Chapter XI Endnote

Some of the more damaging statements made in the *Naval Staff Appreciation* concern Jellicoe's arrangements for the night of 31 May and what he should have known regarding the enemy's intentions. Jellicoe defended his decisions in his comments on the 'Admiralty Narrative', the expurgated version of the *Naval Staff Appreciation* that was published in 1924. Since this section of the 'Narrative' is virtually identical to the corresponding section of the *Appreciation*, we have

---

[86] The prohibition was a real and not a nominal one. The only channel of communication was through the Director of the Intelligence Division himself, which was a very different thing from the sections coalescing. This policy of secrecy was accepted quite as a matter of course, the enormous handicap it offered to staff work being apparently ignored.

[87] The H.S. operations of October, 1917, in which three submarines were destroyed, was the direct consequence of E.1 using Room 40 material. E.1 was also able to construct the German squared chart of the Atlantic by combining British reports of attacks with German signals, which led directly to the destruction of U.154. Room 40 and Section E.1 became Sections 25a and 25b of the Intelligence Division under a single head.

[88] *See* Birch and Clark for an interesting exposition on this point.

an opportunity to compare the Dewars' criticisms to Jellicoe's defence. (The text below is taken from the Admiralty's *Narrative of the Battle of Jutland*, 111–13; references to the pagination and section numbers in the original 'Admiralty Narrative' have been adjusted to reflect those of the *NSA*, and the punctuation has been modernised. A few editorial notes have been added in [square brackets].)

IX. Pages 181–2, hardly convey correct impression.

The information at the disposal of the Commander-in-Chief regarding the position of the High Sea Fleet, and the deductions to be drawn from that information as to the route which the Fleet would follow, are given below:

At 9.41 pm the Commander-in-Chief heard from Sir David Beatty that at 9 pm the enemy bore N by W from *Lion* and was steering WSW. As he had signalled the distance of the German ships at 8.40 pm as 10 to 11 miles, the same distance would be assumed at 9 pm. The position assigned to the *Lion* in this signal did not agree with that signalled by Admiral Jerram in the *King George V* at 9.05 pm, and as the *Lion* and *Iron Duke* were at that time both in sight from the *King George V*, the position of the *Lion* with reference to the *Iron Duke* given by Admiral Jerram, would naturally be accepted as accurate, instead of that given by Sir David Beatty. The Commander-in-Chief could not, of course, know that the Vice-Admiral, 2nd Battle Squadron, mistook other vessels for our Battle Cruisers.

Taking the *Iron Duke*'s position at 9 pm as Lat. 56° 39' N, Long. 5° 42' E, (i.e., the position worked back from her signalled 9.45 position; *Official Despatches*, 474), the German Battle Cruisers at 9 pm would be in about Lat. 56° 47' N, Long. 5° 24' E, steering WSW, and the Admiralty 9 pm position signalled at 2158 would be rejected in favour of this information. The Admiralty position was obviously incorrect, since it placed the enemy 10 miles ahead of the *Iron Duke* at 9 pm. The difference in position of the enemy at 9 pm between the Admiralty report and that of the *Lion* (worked out from the position assigned to the *Lion* by the *King George V*) is 14 miles. As, however, the *Lion* was reporting Battle Cruisers, which were presumably in the van, and the Admiralty was reporting the rear ship of the enemy's fleet, the actual difference was much greater. The *Lion*'s position, as signalled by Sir D. Beatty at 9 pm would also obviously be rejected in favour of that given by Admiral Jerram, since Sir D. Beatty placed the *Lion* in the position which I knew the *King George V* was in.

The Admiralty signal of 2241 is the next information.

The deduction to be drawn from the Admiralty message depended largely on the time that it was assumed that the course SSE ¾ E was adopted. If it was considered at the time that the course was steered at 9.30 pm it would take the High Sea Fleet 8 miles off the Horn Reef Light Vessel, or 16 miles off if the WSW course was maintained till 10 pm. As a matter of fact, it appears from Scheer's diagram No. VII. (*Official Despatches*) that the SSE ¾ E course was not adopted till after 9.30 pm. Course was also altered to starboard soon after 10 pm, probably as a result of the attack by the *Castor*. In any case, however, other reports received at about the same time made it appear that the enemy would make for a more westerly approach to his base. I refer to the 2330 and 2240 reports from the 2nd Light Cruiser Squadron, already mentioned, the 2240 report from the Commodore F and the gun flashes that were seen, star shell explosions seen, and the sound of gun-fire heard from the *Iron Duke* between 10 pm and midnight. The 2330 report gave the course of the enemy Battle Cruisers as South, i.e., following us, and indicated that a SSE ¾ E course was not being followed. The evident signs of destroyer fighting in rear, at a long distance astern lead me to think that our T.B.D.'s [Torpedo Boat Destroyers] were in action with enemy T.B.D.'s and supporting light cruisers, and I considered that the effect of such fighting would be to turn the enemy to the northward or westward, even if he had originally intended to take the passage by the Horn Reef. Very possibly the reason which caused Von Scheer [*Editor's note*: Scheer declined the title of nobility offered by the Kaiser, and so was never a 'von'] to hold to his course for the Horn's Reef in face of our destroyer attacks was that he was informed by a German shore station (which had apparently intercepted my 9.15 pm signal to the destroyers to take stations 5 miles astern of the Battle Fleet), that my destroyers were so placed, and this gave him a clue to the course and position of the British Battle Fleet once he came in contact with our destroyers [*Editor's note*: As indicated in note 56, Scheer did not receive this signal until the next morning]. I do not know whether he had also been informed of my signalled course, but as the above incident shows that the code was compromised, it is quite possible that he had been so informed, and therefore knew that he was safe in steering to cut across the rear of the British Fleet. An explanation of the above should be given as it explains Scheer's movements and his tenacity in adhering to his course in spite of the destroyer attacks.

It should be realised that implicit reliance could not be placed on 'Intercepts'. I could not assume, for instance, that because the High Sea Fleet steered a course SSE ¾ E at some time between 9 and 10 pm, that this course would be maintained until I received information from the Admiralty to the contrary. I could not expect that any but a small proportion of Scheer's signals would be intercepted. It was only possible to get those made on 'Power'. It is easy after the event, with full knowledge from both sides, to make correct assumptions.

Experience earlier in the day had shown that one might be misled if trusting too much to Intercepts, e.g., the different courses assigned to the enemy by the Admiralty and the *Southampton*.

CHAPTER XII
DESTROYER ACTIONS DURING THE NIGHT

The British destroyer flotillas played such an important part in the night operations that it is necessary to devote a separate chapter to their proceedings.

11th Flotilla

84. At about 10.15 pm the *Castor* and 11th Flotilla,[1] which were on the starboard quarter of the Battle Fleet, came in contact with the 2nd Scouting Group. The two leading German cruisers opened fire on the *Castor*, obtaining several hits and wounding 23 men. The *Castor* replied with her 6 in. guns and fired one torpedo. The *Magic* and *Marne* also fired torpedoes, but the remainder of the destroyers did nothing; some were blinded by the flash of the guns, and others were under the impression that the attacking ships were British.[2] This uncertainty as to the identity of enemy ships, with its natural consequence of hesitation and delay, was a characteristic feature of nearly all the night actions on the British side, and must be largely ascribed to the fact that the destroyers were given no information whatever as to the general disposition of the British squadrons, or the position of the enemy fleet and its probable course.[3]

---

[1] Consisting of *Kempenfelt, Ossory, Mystic, Morning Star, Magic, Mounsey, Mandate, Minion, Marital, Milbrook, Moon, Marne, Manners, Michael* and *Mons*. Individual reports from the vessels of this flotilla cannot be traced, and the only information available is that given by ships' logs and Captain (D); *Official Despatches*, 303.

[2] *Castor* (r), *Official Despatches*, 304: 'It is unfortunate that this element of doubt existed in the minds of the Captains of the Destroyers as to whether the ships were enemy, as a good opportunity of firing torpedoes was lost'.

[3] *Editor's note*: This is quite true. Other than Jellicoe's signal at 9.27 'Destroyers take station astern of battlefleet five miles', and a wireless to the Commodore of Flotillas (10.46) asking if he was engaging enemy destroyers, no intelligence or orders were sent to the British destroyers. Of course, other than three signals from the Captain (D) of the 12th Flotilla in *Faulknor* (which

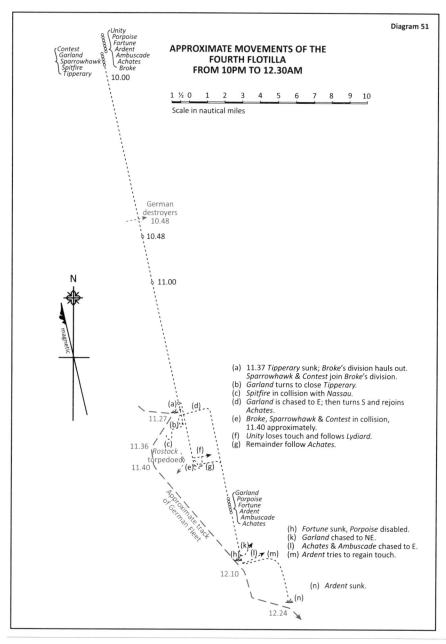

Diagram 51

APPROXIMATE MOVEMENTS OF THE FOURTH FLOTILLA FROM 10PM TO 12.30AM

Unity
Porpoise
Fortune
Ardent
Ambuscade
Achates
Broke
10.00

Contest
Garland
Sparrowhawk
Spitfire
Tipperary

Scale in nautical miles

German destroyers 10.48

10.48

11.00

N
magnetic

(a) 11.37 *Tipperary* sunk; *Broke*'s division hauls out. *Sparrowhawk* & *Contest* join *Broke*'s division.
(b) *Garland* turns to close *Tipperary*.
(c) *Spitfire* in collision with *Nassau*.
(d) *Garland* is chased to E; then turns S and rejoins *Achates*.
(e) *Broke*, *Sparrowhawk* & *Contest* in collision, 11.40 approximately.
(f) *Unity* loses touch and follows *Lydiard*.
(g) Remainder follow *Achates*.

(a)
(d)
11.27
(b)
(c)
11.36
Rostock torpedoed
11.40
(f)
(e)
(g)

Approximate track of German Fleet

Garland
Porpoise
Fortune
Ardent
Ambuscade
Achates

(h) *Fortune* sunk, *Porpoise* disabled.
(k) *Garland* chased to NE.
(l) *Achates* & *Ambuscade* chased to E.
(m) *Ardent* tries to regain touch.

(k)
(h)
(l)
(m)

12.10

(n) *Ardent* sunk.

(n)

12.24

weren't received in *Iron Duke*, see below), none of the flotillas bothered signalling what they saw back to Jellicoe.

However, it may well be that Jellicoe didn't expect to get much information from his destroyers, nor were they in turn expecting much from him. Keith McBride has pointed out that destroyers were not expected to maintain a W/T listening watch when in company with the fleet (see McBride's letter in *Mariner's Mirror*).

At 10.45 pm the flotilla again fell in with the 2nd Scouting Group, and after exchanging a few rounds the enemy was lost to sight.

At 0.15 am the *Castor* reports sighting an enemy torpedo boat and firing on her at point blank range.

At 8.40 am the 11th Flotilla rejoined the Battle Fleet and formed a submarine screen.

4th Flotilla (Diagram 51)[4]

85. At about 9 pm, when the 4th Flotilla was in screening station ahead of the 2nd Battle Squadron, the *Garland* engaged four enemy destroyers, which fired two torpedoes and made off at high speed to the westward. On being ordered to take station astern of the fleet 5 miles, the flotilla turned 16 points and passed through the lines. At 9.50 it was in two columns, led by *Tipperary* and *Broke*, and at 10 pm single line ahead was formed, course South, speed 17 knots. No instructions had been issued as to the duties of the flotilla during the night, and the formation adopted was equally unsuitable for attack or defence. It was right in the path of the High Sea Fleet, which was rapidly converging on a South-South-Easterly course, and ran into it an hour or so later without any effort to find or avoid it.

At 10.35 pm the *Garland* reported to the Captain (D) a cruiser of the *Graudenz* class bearing W, course S, speed 17 knots, whilst at 10.50 the *Porpoise* and *Unity*, the rear ships of the line reported three enemy destroyers[5] approaching from the starboard quarter. Other suspicious vessels[6] were apparently sighted after 11 pm, but the flotilla continued its course as if the enemy fleet was the last thing it expected to meet.

A rude awakening was at hand. At 11.30[7] searchlights blazed out suddenly on the starboard beam of the flotilla, and three enemy ships[8] poured a heavy fire

---

[4] Consisting of *Tipperary* (Captain D), *Spitfire*, *Sparrowhawk*, *Garland*, *Contest*, *Broke*, *Achates*, *Ambuscade*, *Ardent*, *Fortune*, *Porpoise* and *Unity*.

[5] Probably of German 7th Flotilla.

Editor's note: Campbell (*Jutland*, 279), confirms the German ships sighted by *Garland* as being the German 7th Flotilla.

[6] The surviving executive officer of the *Tipperary* states that the enemy ships were sighted about 20 minutes before they opened fire, but their identity was in doubt. The *Sparrowhawk* reports that 'about 11.30, vessels were sighted on the starboard quarter overtaking the flotilla, and apparently steering the same course . . . When the leading ship was abreast of the *Tipperary* she switched on searchlights'. As the *Sparrowhawk* was third ship in the line an appreciable interval must have elapsed between sighting these vessels and the moment of attack.

[7] *Achates*, *Sparrowhawk*, *Unity*, *Ambuscade*, *Spitfire* and *Champion* (13th Flotilla), 11.30. *Garland*, 11.28. *Nassau* reports ramming a destroyer 11.31. *Broke*, 11 pm.

[8] Probably the 2nd Scouting Group.

on the head of the line, quickly disabling the *Tipperary* and setting her on fire forward.[9] The subsequent movements of the flotilla are shown in Diagram 51. The *Spitfire*, second ship in the line, fired two torpedoes and claims to have hit a four-funnelled cruiser.[10] She then turned to the westward to reload, apparently under the impression that there was a British flotilla in that direction, and on again steering towards the *Tipperary* suddenly found herself close to what she thought were two cruisers. These were ships of the German 1st Battle Squadron. The *Spitfire* opened fire on the *Nassau*, putting her searchlights out of action and killing many of the crews. The *Nassau* attempted to ram, but the *Spitfire* escaped by putting her helm hard over, and the two ships ran into one another, port bow to port bow. The *Spitfire*'s bridge and funnels received the full blast of the *Nassau*'s 11 in. guns. The side plating was torn off her forecastle, and the bridge, searchlight platform, mast, foremost funnel, boats and davits were completely demolished. The Germans thought they had sunk her, but she managed to get clear, and eventually proceeded to the Tyne at reduced speed with 20ft of German plating as a memento of her exciting encounter. The *Garland* also endeavoured to return to the *Tipperary*'s assistance but was driven off to the eastward, rejoining the remainder of the flotilla shortly before midnight.

86. When the enemy first opened fire, the *Broke*, followed by the *Sparrowhawk*, altered course outwards to fire her starboard after tube, and then resumed course. A few minutes later searchlights were directed on her by a large ship on the starboard beam. After waiting a short pause for the after tube to be fired, the *Broke* put her helm hard-a-starboard, but just then a shell hit the lower bridge, killing everyone on it and jamming the helm. She therefore continued to circle and rammed the *Sparrowhawk* just before the bridge, cutting right into her. Whilst the two ships were locked together, the *Contest* added to the confusion by ramming the *Sparrowhawk* and cutting off five feet of her stern. The *Broke*, who had suffered very heavy casualties from the enemy's gun-fire, succeeded in extricating herself from the wreckage, and steaming North at slow speed eventually proceeded to the Tyne. The *Sparrowhawk* drifted to the north-eastward and was abandoned and sunk about 9 am, after the *Marksman* had attempted to tow her. The remainder of the flotilla, consisting of the *Achates*, *Ambuscade*, *Ardent*, *Fortune*, *Porpoise* and *Unity*, appears to have altered course to the eastward on the enemy opening fire, and after proceeding about three miles in that direction resumed a Southerly course. The *Unity* and *Contest*,

---

[9] She eventually sank at 1.45 am.

[10] The *Rostock* was torpedoed, but she cannot be definitely allotted to the *Spitfire*, as several torpedoes were fired at this time.

however, lost touch with the flotilla, the former joining the 9th and 10th, and the latter, with a damaged stem, steering to the north-eastward, took no further part in the battle. On the British side this phase of the action resulted in the disablement of the *Tipperary*, *Sparrowhawk*, *Broke* and *Spitfire*, and the eventual loss of the first two. On the German side the *Rostock* and *Elbing*, which were abreast of the van of the 1st Squadron on the engaged side, turned away from the torpedoes fired by the 4th Flotilla, and in order to avoid masking the fire of the battleships endeavoured to pass through the line. During this manœuvre the *Rostock* was torpedoed by the 4th Flotilla and the *Elbing* was rammed by the *Posen*. Both vessels were eventually abandoned and sunk by the Germans, the former at 3.45 am and the latter at 2 am.

87. The flotilla as an organised force now consisted of only the *Achates*, *Ambuscade*, *Ardent*, *Fortune*, *Porpoise* and *Garland*.[11] Their Easterly course and subsequent alteration to the South were again leading them rapidly towards the High Sea Fleet, and about midnight enemy ships were sighted on the starboard side. These at once opened fire, sinking the *Fortune* and hitting the *Porpoise* in the after boiler room. The latter, screened by steam and the smoke of the sinking *Fortune*, was able to make her escape slowly to the northward. The *Ambuscade* after firing a torpedo was chased off to the eastward with the *Achates*, the former joining up with the *Castor* and the latter returning to Rosyth. The *Garland* made off to the north-eastward after firing a torpedo. The *Ardent*, on the other hand, proceeded to repeat the manœuvre which had just brought about the loss of the *Fortune*. After retiring to the eastward she resumed a Southerly course, and converging on the enemy's South-Easterly course, suddenly ran right into them again. She at once fired a torpedo, but as it left the tube the two leading ships opened a devastating fire and quickly reduced her to a wreck. After firing for about five minutes they ceased fire and switched off searchlights. The next squadron opened fire at point blank range, the survivors took to the water and the *Ardent* sank with colours flying.

The result of this phase of the action was the destruction of the *Fortune* and *Ardent* and the disablement of the *Porpoise*. Torpedo hits were claimed by the *Garland* and *Ambuscade*, but the German ships were undamaged.

Those vessels of the flotilla that remained capable of action were now scattered and dispersed and took no further effective part in the operations. The 4th Flotilla had ceased to exist as an organised force.

The results of the two encounters between the 4th Flotilla and High Sea Fleet are summarised below:

---

[11] The *Garland* rejoined just before midnight.

Approximate Time	Vessel	Damage and Subsequent Proceedings	Torpedoes Fired
11.30	Tipperary	Disabled by gun-fire. Sunk at 1.45 am.	2
11.35	Spitfire	In collision with Nassau.	2 (possibly hit Rostock)
11.30	Garland	Fired torpedo; lost flotilla, but rejoined before midnight.	1
11.30	Contest	Fired torpedo; rammed Sparrowhawk, lost flotilla and took no further part in the action.	1
11.30	Unity	Lost flotilla and joined 9th and 10th Flotilla.	–
11.35	Broke	Damaged, and heavy casualties from gun-fire; returned to Tyne.	1 (possibly Rostock)
11.35	Sparrowhawk	Completely disabled by collision with Broke and Contest. Sunk by gun-fire next day owing to difficulty of towing.	1 (possibly Rostock)
11.30	Achates, Ambuscade, Ardent, Fortune, and Porpoise	Altered course to eastward. Ambuscade fired two torpedoes.	2
11.30	Elbing (German)	Rammed and disabled by Posen; sunk by enemy at 2 am.	–
11.30	Rostock (German)	Torpedoed and disabled. Sunk by enemy at 3.45 am.	–
Midnight	Fortune	Sunk by gun-fire.	–
Midnight	Porpoise	Disabled by gun-fire. Escaped to northward.	–
Midnight	Achates	Retired to eastward.	–
Midnight	Ambuscade	Fired one torpedo; retired to eastward.	1
Midnight	Garland	Fired one torpedo; retired to north-eastward.	1
0.20	Ardent	Sunk by gun-fire.	1

88. The 4th Flotilla's heavy losses on the night of the 31st must be attributed to a defective system of command and tactics, rather than to any particular efficiency on the part of the enemy. The sea was smooth and the enemy ships

were in sight at a comparatively close range[12] for some time before they opened fire. In short, the conditions were ideal for torpedo attack. Although everything depended on getting in the first blow, the flotilla continued a steady course and speed without change of range or deflection. That under these conditions the enemy only succeeded in finally disabling one destroyer by gunfire does not indicate any very high gunnery standard. The hesitation of the flotilla in attacking which placed the initiative completely in the enemy's hands arose partly from doubt as to the movements of the enemy and disposition of their own forces,[13] whilst the failure of the rear and centre to carry out any organised attack after fire was first opened must be put down to an over-centralised system of flotilla command which broke down with the disablement of *Tipperary*.

The necessity of separating the command of the flotilla or half flotilla from the executive command of an individual boat had never been recognised in the British service. The result of expecting one man without a staff to manoeuvre an individual destroyer during the terrible stress and strain of a night action and at the same time to exercise general tactical control over a number of boats can be seen on the night of the 31st. The system of command fell to pieces with the first blast of the enemy's guns, for no organised attempt was thereafter made either to attack or avoid the enemy. The majority of the boats were merely guided by the sub-conscious idea of resuming their original course after getting clear of the enemy, a procedure that could only lead to a repetition of the first encounter. Tactical co-operation with the Battle Fleet was also lacking, for not a single signal was made either during or after the fighting reporting the position and course of the enemy to the Commander-in-Chief.

---

[12] The range was certainly under 2,000 yards.

[13] The Commander-in-Chief knew the enemy's course by 10.45 pm, but it was not passed on to any squadrons or flotillas. *Official Despatches*, 309, *Achates* (r): 'I respectfully submit that in future the maximum amount of information may be given to destroyers as to the disposition of our own forces'. Fawcett and Hooper, *Fighting at Jutland*, 323, Navigating Officer of *Broke*: 'Our chief anxiety was that we were unaware of the relative positions of any of our ships or squadrons except the Battle Fleet, and also we did not know the position of the enemy'. *Spitfire* (Fawcett and Hooper, *Fighting at Jutland*, 337): 'We had absolutely no idea of where the enemy were, and only a very vague idea of the position of our own ships'. *Sparrowhawk* (Fawcett and Hooper, *Fighting at Jutland*, 347): 'We sighted three ships on our starboard beam steering approximately the same course as ourselves, but steaming a little faster, and we reported these ships to Captain (D), informing him that at least one of these ships was a three-funnelled light cruiser. He replied that he thought them to be our 1st Light Cruiser Squadron'. (The 1st Light Cruiser Squadron was with the battle cruisers about 18 miles from the 4th Flotilla.) *Marksman* (Fawcett and Hooper, *Fighting at Jutland*, 368): 'As we had little or no information as to the relative position of ourselves to the other ships and squadrons of the Fleet . . .' *Faulknor* (Fawcett and Hooper, *Fighting at Jutland*, 388): 'We were not certain of the whereabouts or disposition of most of the Battle Fleet, and as for that of the other British destroyer flotillas' [*sic*].

13th Flotilla (Diagram 52)

89. On the Commander-in-Chief ordering the destroyers to take station for the night, the 12th and 13th, 9th and 10th (the Harwich detachment) Flotillas took up a position astern of the eastern flank of the Battle Fleet. At 9.35 pm the 12th Flotilla[14] was in station, two cables astern of the *Agincourt*. At 9.45 pm it reduced speed and by 10.45 pm[15] was five miles astern of the 5th Division. Up till 11.30 pm, the 9th and 10th Flotillas[16] were on the starboard beam of the 12th, and the 13th Flotilla[17] was on the starboard beam of the 9th and 10th. When the enemy engaged the 4th Flotilla at 11.30 pm many shots fell amongst the 9th, 10th and 13th Flotillas,[18] which were in the line of fire. The *Champion*, leading the 13th, thereupon altered course to the eastward,[19] and increased to high speed without signal – a manoeuvre which completely disorganised her own flotilla, of which only the *Moresby* and *Obdurate* managed to maintain touch. The remainder followed astern of the 9th and 10th Flotillas in a long straggling line without their senior officer being aware of this addition to his forces. The 12th Flotilla was also forced off its course to the north-eastward and had to reduce speed in order to let the *Champion* pass ahead.

British destroyers were between the *Champion* and the enemy, but the orthodox method of attack is from ahead, and there was nothing to prevent her increasing speed and maintaining a Southerly direction so as to get into a favourable position. After proceeding about six miles to the eastward, the *Champion* altered course to the South and the *Marksman* and *Maenad*, which

---

[14] Consisting of *Faulknor* (Captain D), *Obedient, Mindful, Marvel, Onslaught, Maenad, Narwhal, Nessus, Noble, Marksman, Opal, Nonsuch, Menace, Munster* and *Mary Rose*.

[15] *Faulknor* (r); *Official Despatches*, 332.

[16] Consisting of *Lydiard, Liberty, Landrail, Laurel, Moorsom* and *Morris*. The *Termagant* and *Turbulent* were temporarily attached to the 13th Flotilla and the *Moorsom* was ordered to return to her base at 9.57 pm.

[17] Consisting of *Champion* (Captain D), *Obdurate, Moresby, Nerissa, Termagant, Nicator, Narborough, Pelican, Petard* and *Turbulent*.

[18] *Nerissa* (r): 'Many salvos fell between *Nerissa* and *Moresby*' (*Official Despatches*, 235). *Liberty* (r): '11.30. Fire was opened on the flotilla by about four heavy ships which appeared to be 4,000 yards on our port beam' (*Official Despatches*, 259). *Champion* (r): 'About 11.30 heavy firing was opened on our starboard beam, apparently at some of our destroyers between the 13th Flotilla and the enemy' (*Official Despatches*, 224).

[19] *Lydiard* (r): '*Champion* suddenly increased to high speed and disappeared to starboard' (*Official Despatches*, 255). *Landrail* reports: '11.30. Fire was opened to starboard of us . . . during it *Champion* went on at high speed and disappeared without a signal' (*Official Despatches*, 258). *Champion* states 'about 11.30 heavy firing was reported on our starboard beam. I hauled out to the eastward as I was unable to attack with any of our flotilla, our own forces being between me and the enemy. Destroyers of the 13th Flotilla with the exception of *Obdurate* and *Moresby* lost touch with me during the night' (*Official Despatches*, 225).

had become separated from the 12th Flotilla, took station astern about 2.30 am. In retiring to the eastward and afterwards steering a Southerly course, the *Champion* repeated the mistake of the 4th Flotilla, but when she sighted the enemy, consisting of four ships of the *Deutschland* class, it was getting light, and they could be seen about two miles away bearing West. The Germans apparently did not see the British in the half light and did not open fire. The *Champion* again altered course to the eastward[20] at 2.34 am, but the *Moresby* considering some action imperative, hoisted 'Compass West' to point out the enemy, hauled out to port and attacked on her own initiative, firing one torpedo. This apparently sank the German torpedo boat V.4, but not having seen the *Moresby*, the enemy put her loss down to a mine. No report was made to the Commander-in-Chief.

About 2.45 the *Champion* altered course to the northward to close the Commander-in-Chief in accordance with the latter's signal made at 2.20 am. At about 3.30 am four enemy torpedo boats were sighted steering South at about 3,000 yards range. They attacked with torpedoes and the *Champion* appears to have replied with one round from her 6 in. guns,[21] but she made no attempt to follow them and they quickly disappeared in the mist. They were probably G.37, G.38 and G.40, and V.45, returning with 1,250 men from the *Lützow*, and it is unfortunate that a light cruiser and four destroyers should have allowed them to escape without pursuit. Scheer states that these four torpedo boats engaged British cruisers and destroyers on two occasions, and that during the last action G.40 was hit in the engine room and had to be taken in tow. The failure to follow up the enemy is therefore all the more regrettable.

On the way North survivors of the *Ardent* and *Fortune* were picked up. The *Champion*, *Moresby*, *Obdurate* and *Maenad* then returned to their base, whilst the *Marksman*, after sinking the *Sparrowhawk*, joined the 1st Battle Squadron. The proceedings of the remainder of the 13th Flotilla will be considered in conjunction with the 9th and 10th.

9th and 10th Flotilla (Diagram 52)

90. When the *Champion* crossed the bows of the 9th and 10th Flotilla, the *Lydiard* (the Senior Officer of the 9th and 10th Flotilla) altered course to the south-eastward, followed by the *Unity* from the 4th Flotilla and the seven boats of the 13th Flotilla which had just lost touch with the *Champion*. The shots directed at the 4th Flotilla continued to fall spasmodically in the direction of

---

[20] The *Champion* makes no mention of sighting the enemy battleships in her report, but the alteration of course corresponds with the time of the *Moresby*'s report.

[21] Some of the destroyers accompanying the *Champion* also appear to have opened fire.

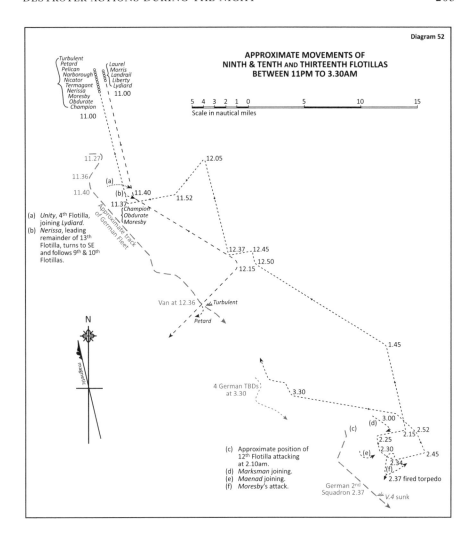

Diagram 52

APPROXIMATE MOVEMENTS OF NINTH & TENTH AND THIRTEENTH FLOTILLAS BETWEEN 11PM TO 3.30AM

Scale in nautical miles

(a) *Unity*, 4th Flotilla, joining *Lydiard*.
(b) *Nerissa*, leading remainder of 13th Flotilla, turns to SE and follows 9th & 10th Flotillas.

(c) Approximate position of 12th Flotilla attacking at 2.10am.
(d) *Marksman* joining.
(e) *Maenad* joining.
(f) *Moresby*'s attack.

the 9th and 10th, and the object in view was to work round to the other side of the enemy ships.[22] At about midnight, course was altered to SW, which took the majority of the flotilla across the head of the enemy's line about 0.25 am, but the last four boats passed very close. The *Narborough* and *Pelican* sighted enemy ships on the starboard quarter at short range, whilst the *Petard* had to alter course to avoid being rammed by the leading ship. The enemy switched on searchlights and opened fire on the last two boats – the *Petard* and *Turbulent*. The former received several hits and the latter was sunk with all hands, either by ramming or gun-fire.[23]

---

[22] *Lydiard*'s (r); *Official Despatches*, 255.
[23] *Editor's note*: *Turbulent* was not rammed; Campbell (*Jutland*, 396) says that she was one of several British destroyers 'sunk by 5.9in shells from the *Westfalen* and other battleships'.

At 1.30 course was altered to the westward to close the *Castor*. At 5.35 am the 9th and 10th Flotilla, which was short of fuel, proceeded to its base, and the stragglers of the 13th Flotilla were ordered to close the battle cruisers.

The action taken by the 9th and 10th Flotillas at 11.30 pm was similar to that of the 4th and *Champion*'s detachment – a retirement to the eastward followed by a Southerly course. Although there seems to have been no idea of attacking, the flotilla found itself in an excellent position to do so. The line of 13 destroyers was right across the van of the whole enemy Battle Fleet, but it was a long straggling inarticulated line, lacking cohesion and offensive power. It was left to the enemy to attack, and the *Turbulent* was sunk in the same manner as the *Tipperary*, *Fortune* and *Ardent*. There was also the same doubt as to the identity of the enemy ships,[24] and the same neglect to report the position of the enemy to the Commander-in-Chief.

12th Flotilla (Diagram 53)

91. At 11.45 pm the *Faulknor*, leading the 12th Flotilla, was pressed off her course to the southward by the *Champion*, *Obdurate* and *Moresby*. She altered course to the eastward and later to the north-eastward, reducing speed to allow the *Champion* to pass ahead. As the flotilla was turning to SE, two enemy cruisers suddenly appeared on the starboard side close to the rear of the line. The *Menace* had to put her helm hard over to avoid collision, and the *Nonsuch*[25] turned to the eastward and increased to full speed. The cruisers were probably the *Pillau* and *Frankfurt* of the 2nd Scouting Group, which apparently took a more Northerly course than the remainder of the fleet after the action with the 4th Flotilla. As a result of this encounter the *Nonsuch* lost touch with the flotilla. She fell in with the *Acasta* about 8 am and towed her to Aberdeen.

At 0.20 am the flotilla resumed its Southerly course. At about 1.45 am the *Faulknor* and *Obedient* sighted strange ships on the starboard bow steering SE. They proved to be the 2nd Squadron of the High Sea Fleet. The *Faulknor*, who was leading with the 1st and 2nd Divisions, disposed on the starboard and port quarter respectively, at once altered parallel to the enemy, increased speed to 25 knots, and ordered the 1st Division[26] to attack. But the enemy had sighted the destroyers, and turning away was temporarily lost to view. Thereupon the

---

[24] *Pelican* (r), 'at 0.40 . . . observed two ships which were at first taken to be our light cruisers' (*Official Despatches*, 234). *Narborough* (r), 'at 0.30 am . . . This vessel was thought to be one of our light cruisers or an armoured cruiser of the *Warrior* class, one of which had been on our starboard quarter during the first watch' (*Official Despatches*, 230).

[25] *Nonsuch* (l). 'Two German cruisers passed astern and opened fire; attempted to fire torpedo. Increased to 33 knots'.

[26] *Obedient*, *Marvel*, *Mindful* and *Onslaught*.

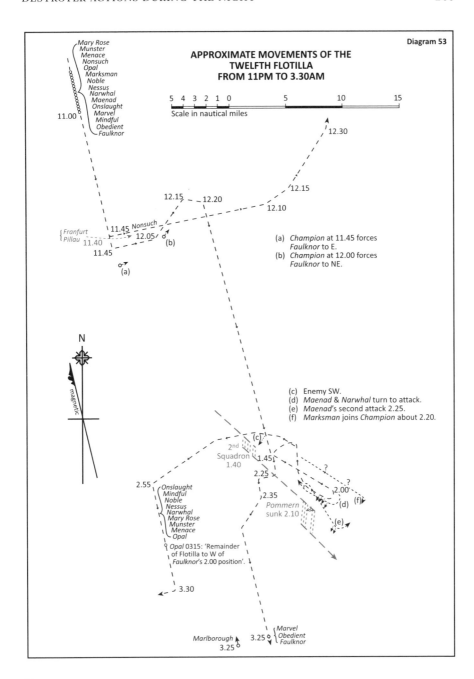

Note:

The content of *Opal*'s 0315 signal was missing from the original and has been inserted.

Faulknor recalled the 1st Division and ordered it to take station astern. The whole flotilla then proceeded at 25 knots in a South-Easterly direction to get into a favourable position for attacking. In the meanwhile the *Faulknor* found time to report the position and course of the enemy to the Commander-in-Chief,[27] and at about 2.00 she turned some 16 points to starboard, followed by the *Obedient*, *Marvel* and *Onslaught*. The *Mindful*, which originally had been astern of the *Obedient*, only having two boilers available, was left some distance behind. The *Maenad*, who had expected the attack to be made to starboard, held on to the south-eastward to admit of her tubes being trained to port, and turned about five minutes after the *Faulknor*, followed by the *Narwhal*. The *Faulknor* and the three destroyers following her, sighted the enemy immediately after their turn was completed, and all fired torpedoes. The *Mindful*, which was apparently still steering in a South-Easterly direction, appears to have sighted the enemy on her starboard bow whilst the *Faulknor* was delivering her attack, and to have made straight for the German line, but being masked by the destroyers astern of the *Faulknor* she had to turn away to avoid being rammed. The *Faulknor* and *Obedient* each fired two torpedoes, and the *Onslaught* and *Marvel* four each. One of them hit the *Pommern*, the third ship in the enemy's line, which blew up with a terrific explosion[28] at 2.10 am. The destroyers came under a heavy fire, the *Onslaught*'s bridge and chart house were totally wrecked, the Captain mortally wounded and the 1st Lieutenant killed.

92. The *Maenad* and *Narwhal* appear to have delivered their attack about ten minutes after the *Faulknor*, the former firing one torpedo and the latter two. The *Maenad* then turned approximately 16 points to starboard and delivered a second attack by herself, firing two torpedoes. None of these took effect.[29] The *Maenad* then ran down to the south-eastward and joined up with the *Marksman* and *Champion* about 2.30 am.

Nothing definite can be said as to the movements of the *Nessus*, *Noble*, *Opal*, *Menace*, *Munster* and *Mary Rose* after the *Faulknor* turned to the north-westward, for no reports from these vessels can be traced. They may or may not

---

[27] 0152, 'Enemy's Battle Fleet steering SE, approximate bearing SW. My position 10 miles astern of 1st Battle Squadron'. *Faulknor* reports that this signal was made twice on power but was not answered.

Editor's note: Possibly because of heavy W/T traffic, with ships on both sides tending to signal at full power (Howland, 'Naval Radio').

[28] '... and directly ahead of us saw a huge pillar of fire shoot up to the sky. It looks to us like the trail of a gigantic rocket ... The ship must have been blown literally to atoms, for a few minutes later not the slightest trace of her could be seen'. Von Hase (I.D. 1220), 39.

[29] *Maenad* states that the range was between 4,000 and 5,000 yards. But the enemy probably turned away, and the 4 in. guns are reported as hitting with 6,000 yards on the sights. Individual torpedo attacks cannot be expected to succeed at such long ranges.

have followed the *Maenad* and *Narwhal*, but they did not fire any torpedoes,[30] and it may therefore be assumed that they took no part in the attack. The proceedings of the *Marksman* are also obscure. After the *Faulknor*, etc., had delivered their attack, cruisers were seen approaching from the rear of the enemy's battle line. They opened a heavy fire and drove the *Faulknor*'s detachment off to the north-eastward.[31] As soon as they were clear *Faulknor* altered course to the SW and gradually to the South with the intention of keeping in touch. A cruiser was sighed about 2.25 am, but after that the enemy was not seen again.[32]

The *Faulknor* proceeded to join the Battle Fleet, taking station on the quarter of the 5th Division at 3.40 am. In the meanwhile, at 3.20 am, the *Opal* had reported the remainder of the flotilla 15 miles to the westward of the *Faulknor*'s 2 am position, and at 3.46 am the *Faulknor* ordered them to conform to her movements.

The command of the 12th Flotilla compares very favourably with that of the 4th, 9th, 10th and 13th Flotillas on the night of the 31st. The initiative was not left to the enemy; an attack was organised, and an attempt was made to get into a suitable position before delivering it. It is also noticeable that the flotilla leader endeavoured to communicate the position and course of the enemy to the Commander-in-Chief. The attack was, however, only a partial one; only six destroyers participated, and only 16 torpedoes were fired out of a possible 60.

Generally speaking, the British flotillas do not appear to have taken full advantage of their opportunities on the night of the 31st. Their system of command and organisation proved inadequate to meet the conditions of modern battle, and they were also seriously handicapped by lack of information as to the disposition and movements of their own and enemy forces.

Night had fallen on the flotillas taking up a position astern of the fleet. Break of day found them scattered and dispersed and the German Fleet passing Horns Riff.

93.[33] Such was the Battle of Jutland, whose reverberations were felt in every

---

[30] Analysis of Torpedo Firing in the Battle of Jutland, 1918, C.B. 1384.
Editor's note: A copy of this document can be found in TNA: ADM 186/586.

[31] The *Faulknor* reports that the cruisers which drove her off to the north-eastward 'altered back towards their own fleet and continued to attack the destroyers astern of us'. It is possible that these cruisers drove the remainder of the flotilla out of range and prevented them attacking.

[32] When last seen the enemy battle line was steering SSW, and this was signalled to the Commander-in-Chief by the *Faulknor* at 2.12 am. It was made twice on power but was not answered.

[33] *Editor's note*: Beatty probably agreed with these concluding paragraphs – they are highlighted in the margin in his copy.

corner of the globe, and which by virtue of the strength of the forces confronting one another and the magnitude of the issues involved must rank as one of the great naval battles of the world.

To the Germans it was a day very different from that of their vainglorious toasts,[34] and they were successful only in avoiding a disastrous defeat. To the British it was a day of trial, when the thought and work of two generations were brought to the bar of reality and put to the test. The bed-rock qualities of the Navy stood unshaken, but the system of tactics and fleet command did not stand the strain.

It has been said that a great victory would have given us no more than we had. This is a lame commentary on the battle. It is not only a repudiation of the teachings of Nelson and Mahan, but it involves an entire misconception of the subsequent workings of the submarine campaign, and reduces contemporary British strategy to the level of a farce. It is better to look facts in the face. The battle of Jutland can only be regarded as the beginning of a great battle which was never driven home. By studying its history we may redeem our shortcomings and discover another and sounder conception of tactics and command.

---

[34] *Editor's note*: The reference here is the British belief that, before the war, German naval officers often drank toasts to 'Der Tag' – the great future day when Germany would defeat Britain at sea. This idea was vigourously denied by one German naval officer, who assured the British naval attaché, 'on his honour, that such a toast was absolute unknown [*sic*], and moreover was contrary to the rules of the Service' (Seligmann, *Naval Intelligence from Germany*, 222).

APPENDIX A:
PRELIMINARY DISTRIBUTION OF BRITISH SHIPS, WITH NAMES OF COMMANDING OFFICERS[1]

On Tuesday, May 30, 1916, the sea-going ships of the Grand Fleet were distributed between the three northern bases as follows:

AT SCAPA FLOW

Iron Duke, Captain Frederic C. Dreyer, C.B. (Fleet Flagship), flying the flag of Admiral Sir John Jellicoe, G.C.B., K.C.V.O., Commander-in-Chief. Vice-Admiral Sir Charles Madden, K.C.B., C.V.O., Chief-of-Staff: Commodore Lionel Halsey, C.M.G., Captain-of-the-Fleet

Attached to Fleet Flagship:

Destroyer
Oak, Lieutenant-Commander Douglas Faviell, M.V.O.

Flotilla Leader
Abdiel, Commander Berwick Curtis (Fitted as minelayer)

Light Cruiser
Active, Captain Percy Withers

Seaplane Carrier
Campania (was unable to raise steam in time to sail with the Fleet, left Scapa at 1.30 am, but was ordered back with defects at 4.30 am, 31st)

Kite Balloon Ship
Menelaus (did not sail)

1st BATTLE SQUADRON

Marlborough, Captain George P. Ross, flying the flag of Vice-Admiral Sir Cecil Burney, K.C.B., K.C.M.G., Second in Command of the Grand Fleet. Captain E. Percy F. G. Grant, Chief-of-Staff

Revenge, Captain Edward B. Kiddle

Hercules, Captain Lewis Clinton-Baker

Agincourt, Captain Henry M. Doughty

Colossus, Captain Alfred D. P. R. Pound, flying the flag of Rear-Admiral Ernest F. A. Gaunt, C.M.G.

Collingwood, Captain James C. Ley

Neptune, Captain Vivian H. G. Bernard

---

[1] Reproduced from Harper's Report, p. 5.

St. Vincent, Captain William W. Fisher, M.V.O.

Attached to 1st Battle Squadron:
Light Cruiser
Bellona, Captain Arthur B. S. Dutton
(*Royal Sovereign*, which had commissioned on April 18, 1916, and arrived at Scapa Flow on May 25, did not proceed to sea with the Fleet)

4th BATTLE SQUADRON
Benbow, Captain Henry W. Parker, flying the flag of Vice-Admiral Sir Doveton Sturdee, Bart., K.C.B., C.V.O., C.M.G.
Bellerophon, Captain Edward F. Bruen
Temeraire, Captain Edwin V. Underhill
Vanguard, Captain James D. Dick
Royal Oak, Captain Crawford Maclachlan
Superb, Captain Edmond Hyde-Parker, flying the flag of Rear-Admiral Alexander L. Duff, C.B.
Canada, Captain William C. M. Nicholson

Attached to 4th Battle Squadron:
Light Cruiser
Blanche, Captain John M. Casement
(*Emperor of India*, Second Flagship of this Squadron, was at this time refitting at Invergordon; the flag was flown temporarily in *Superb*)

3rd BATTLE CRUISER SQUADRON
Invincible, Captain Arthur L. Cay, flying the flag of Rear-Admiral The Hon. Horace L. A. Hood, C.B., M.V.O., D.S.O.
Indomitable, Captain Francis W. Kennedy
Inflexible, Captain Edward H. F. Heaton-Ellis, M.V.O.

To this Squadron were temporarily attached:
Light Cruisers
Chester, Captain Robert N. Lawson, belonging to 3rd Light Cruiser Squadron
Canterbury, Captain Percy M. R. Royds

2nd CRUISER SQUADRON
(Organised that day out of the ships of the old 2nd and 7th Cruiser Squadrons)
Minotaur, Captain Arthur C. S. H. D'Aeth, flying the flag of Rear-Admiral Herbert L. Heath, M.V.O.
Hampshire, Captain Herbert J. Savill
Cochrane, Captain Eustace La T. Leatham
Shannon, Captain John S. Dumaresq, M.V.O.
(*Achilles* was away refitting, and *Donegal* on detached service.)

4th LIGHT CRUISER SQUADRON
Calliope, Commodore Charles E. Le Mesurier
Constance, Captain Cyril S. Townsend
Comus, Captain Alan G. Hotham

Caroline, Captain H. Ralph Crooke
Royalist, Captain The Hon. Herbert Meade, D.S.O.

4th FLOTILLA
Flotilla Leaders
Tipperary, Captain Charles J. Wintour (Captain D IV)
Broke, Commander Walter L. Allen

Destroyers
Achates, Commander Reginald B. C. Hutchinson, D.S.O.
Porpoise, Commander Hugh D. Colville
Spitfire, Lieutenant-Commander Clarence W. E. Trelawney
Unity, Lieutenant-Commander Arthur M. Lecky
Garland, Lieutenant-Commander Reginald S. Goff
Ambuscade, Lieutenant-Commander Gordon A. Coles
Ardent, Lieutenant-Commander Arthur Marsden
Fortune, Lieutenant-Commander Frank G. Terry
Sparrowhawk, Lieutenant-Commander Sydney Hopkins
Contest, Lieutenant-Commander Ernald G. H. Master
Shark, Commander Loftus W. Jones
Acasta, Lieutenant-Commander John O. Barron
Christopher, Lieutenant-Commander Fairfax M. Kerr
Owl, Commander Robert G. Hamond
Hardy, Commander Richard A. A. Plowden
Midge, Lieutenant-Commander James R. C. Cavendish
Ophelia, Commander Lewis G. E. Crabbe (temporarily attached)
(*Cockatrice* and *Paragon* of this Flotilla were away refitting, and *Victor* remained in
   harbour.)

PART OF 11th FLOTILLA
Light Cruiser
Castor, Commodore James R. P. Hawksley, M.V.O. (Commodore F, Captain D XI)

Destroyers
Marne, Lieutenant-Commander George B. Hartford
Manners, Lieutenant-Commander Gerald C. Harrison
Michael, Lieutenant-Commander Claude L. Bate
Mons, Lieutenant-Commander Robert Makin

12th FLOTILLA
Flotilla Leaders
Faulknor, Captain Anselan J. B. Stirling (Captain D XII)
Marksman, Commander Norton A. Sulivan
Obedient, Commander George W. McO. Campbell

Destroyers
Maenad, Commander John P. Champion
Opal, Commander Charles G. C. Sumner

Mary Rose, Lieutenant-Commander Edwin A. Homan
Marvel, Lieutenant-Commander Reginald W. Grubb
Menace, Lieutenant-Commander Charles A. Poignand
Nessus, Lieutenant-Commander Eric Q. Carter
Narwhal, Lieutenant-Commander Henry V. Hudson
Mindful, Lieutenant-Commander John J. C. Ridley
Onslaught, Lieutenant-Commander Arthur G. Onslow, D.S.C.
Munster, Lieutenant-Commander Spencer F. Russell
Nonsuch, Lieutenant-Commander Herbert I. N. Lyon
Noble, Lieutenant-Commander Henry P. Boxer
Mischief, Lieutenant-Commander The Hon. Cyril A. Ward, M.V.O.
(*Napier* and *Mameluke* of this Flotilla were away refitting; they returned to Scapa in time to screen the Battle Fleet into the base on its return.)

AT INVERGORDON
2nd BATTLE SQUADRON
King George V, Captain Frederick L. Field, flying the flag of Vice-Admiral Sir Martyn Jerram, K.C.B.
Ajax, Captain George H. Baird
Centurion, Captain Michael Culme-Seymour, M.V.O.
Erin, Captain The Hon. Victor A. Stanley, M.V.O., A.D.C.
Orion, Captain Oliver Backhouse, C.B., flying the flag of Rear-Admiral Arthur C. Leveson, C.B.
Monarch, Captain George H. Borret
Conqueror, Captain Hugh H. D. Tothill
Thunderer, Captain James A. Fergusson
Attached to 2nd Battle Squadron:
Light Cruiser
Boadicea, Captain Louis C. S. Woollcombe, M.V.O.

1st CRUISER SQUADRON
Defence, Captain Stanley V. Ellis, flying the flag of Rear-Admiral Sir Robert Arbuthnot, Bart., M.V.O.
Warrior, Captain Vincent B. Molteno
Duke of Edinburgh, Captain Henry Blackett
Black Prince, Captain Thomas P. Bonham

PART OF 11th FLOTILLA
Flotilla Leader
Kempenfelt, Commander Harold E. Sulivan

Destroyers
Ossory, Commander Harold V. Dundas
Mystic, Commander Claud F. Allsup
Morning Star, Lieutenant-Commander Hugh U. Fletcher
Magic, Lieutenant-Commander Gerald C. Wynter

Mounsey, Lieutenant-Commander Ralph V. Eyre

Mandate, Lieutenant-Commander Edward McC. W. Lawrie

Minion, Lieutenant-Commander Henry C. Rawlings

Martial, Lieutenant-Commander Julian Harrison

Milbrook, Lieutenant Charles G. Naylor

Moon, Commander (acting) William D. Irvin (on patrol; joined up with her flotilla about 2 pm, May 31)

(*Marmion* and *Musketeer* of this Flotilla were away refitting.)

AT ROSYTH

Lion, Captain Alfred E. M. Chatfield, C.V.O. (Battle Cruiser Fleet Flagship), flying the flag of Vice-Admiral Sir David Beatty, K.C.B., M.V.O., D.S.O. Captain Rudolph W. Bentinck, Chief-of-Staff

5th BATTLE SQUADRON

Barham, Captain Arthur W. Craig. Flying the flag of Rear-Admiral Hugh Evan-Thomas, M.V.O.

Valiant, Captain Maurice Woollcombe

Warspite, Captain Edward M. Phillpotts

Malaya, Captain The Hon. Algernon D. E. H. Boyle, C.B., M.V.O.

(*Queen Elizabeth* of this Squadron was under refit.)

1st BATTLE CRUISER SQUADRON

Princess Royal, Captain Walter H. Cowan, M.V.O., D.S.O., flying the flag of Rear-Admiral Osmond de B. Brock, C.B.

Queen Mary, Captain Cecil I. Prowse

Tiger, Captain Henry B. Pelly, M.V.O.

2nd BATTLE CRUISER SQUADRON

New Zealand, Captain John F. E. Green, flying the flag of Rear-Admiral William C. Pakenham, C.B., M.V.O.

Indefatigable, Captain Charles F. Sowerby

(*Australia*, Flagship of this Squadron, was absent refitting at Devonport; the flag was flown temporarily in *New Zealand*.)

1st LIGHT CRUISER SQUADRON

Galatea, Commodore Edwyn S. Alexander-Sinclair, M.V.O.

Phaeton, Captain John E. Cameron, M.V.O.

Inconstant, Captain Bertram S. Thesiger, C.M.G.

Cordelia, Captain Tufton P. H. Beamish

2nd LIGHT CRUISER SQUADRON

Southampton, Commodore William E. Goodenough, M.V.O., A.D.C.

Birmingham, Captain Arthur A. M. Duff

Nottingham, Captain Charles B. Miller

Dublin, Captain Albert C. Scott

3rd LIGHT CRUISER SQUADRON

Falmouth, Captain John D. Edwards, flying the flag of Rear-Admiral Trevylyan D. W.
   Napier, M.V.O.
Yarmouth, Captain Thomas D. Pratt
Birkenhead, Captain Edward Reeves
Gloucester, Captain William F. Blunt, D.S.O.

PART OF 1st FLOTILLA
Light Cruiser
Fearless, Captain Charles D. Roper (Captain D I)

Destroyers
Acheron, Commander Charles G. Ramsey
Ariel, Lieutenant-Commander Arthur G. Tippet
Attack, Lieutenant-Commander Charles H. N. James
Hydra, Lieutenant Francis G. Glossop
Badger, Commander Charles A. Fremantle
Goshawk, Commander Dashwood F. Moir
Defender, Lieutenant-Commander Lawrence R. Palmer
Lizard, Lieutenant-Commander Edward Brooke
Lapwing, Lieutenant-Commander Alexander H. Gye
(*Botha*, *Archer*, *Jackal* and *Tigress* of this Flotilla were away refitting, and *Phoenix*
remained in harbour.)

13th DESTROYER FLOTILLA
Light Cruiser
Champion, Captain James U. Farie (Captain D XIII)

Destroyers
Nestor, Commander The Hon. Edward B. S. Bingham
Nomad, Lieutenant-Commander Paul Whitfield
Narborough, Lieutenant-Commander Geoffrey Corlett
Obdurate, Lieutenant-Commander Cecil H. H. Sams
Petard, Lieutenant-Commander Evelyn C. O. Thomson
Pelican, Lieutenant-Commander Kenneth A. Beattie
Nerissa, Lieutenant-Commander Montague G. B. Legge
Onslow, Lieutenant-Commander John C. Tovey
Moresby, Lieutenant-Commander Roger V. Alison
Nicator, Lieutenant Jack E. A. Mocatta
(*Negro*, *Nereus*, *Paladin*, *Penn* and *Pigeon* of this Flotilla were away refitting and
Nepean remained in harbour)

PART OF 9th FLOTILLA
Lydiard, Commander Malcolm L. Goldsmith
Liberty, Lieutenant-Commander Phillip W. S. King
Landrail, Lieutenant-Commander Francis E. H. G. Hobart
Laurel, Lieutenant Henry D. C. Stanistreet

PART OF 10th FLOTILLA

Moorsom, Commander John C. Hodgson
Morris, Lieutenant-Commander Edward S. Graham
Turbulent, Lieutenant-Commander Dudley Stuart
Termagant, Lieutenant-Commander Cuthbert P. Blake

Seaplane Carrier

Engadine, Lieutenant-Commander Charles G. Robinson

APPENDIX B:
ORGANISATIONS OF THE BRITISH FLEET[1]

BATTLE FLEET

	Organisation No. 5		Organisation No. 2	
2nd Battle Squadron	King George V, Ajax, Centurion, Erin	1st Division	King George V, Ajax, Centurion, Erin	1st Division (2nd Battle Squadron)
	Orion, Monarch, Conqueror, Thunderer	2nd Division	Orion, Monarch, Conqueror, Thunderer	
4th Battle Squadron	Iron Duke, Royal Oak, Superb, Canada	3rd Division	Iron Duke, Royal Oak, Superb, Canada	2nd Division (Iron Duke and 4th Battle Squadron)
	Benbow, Bellerophon, Temeraire, Vanguard	4th Division	Benbow, Bellerophon, Temeraire, Vanguard	
1st Battle Squadron	Colossus, Collingwood, Neptune, St. Vincent	5th Division	Marlborough, Revenge, Hercules, Agincourt	3rd Division (1st Battle Squadron)
	Marlborough, Revenge, Hercules, Agincourt	6th Division	Colossus, Collingwood, Neptune, St. Vincent	

[1] Reproduced from Harper's Report, p. 106.

Attached Cruisers: {
Boadicea
Blanche
Bellona
Active
}

Attached {
Oak
Abdiel
}

5th BATTLE SQUADRON

Barham	*Warspite*
Valiant	*Malaya*

BATTLE CRUISERS
Lion

1st Battle Cruiser Squadron	2nd Battle Cruiser Squadron	3rd Battle Cruiser Squadron
Princess Royal	*New Zealand*	*Invincible*
Queen Mary	*Indefatigable*	*Inflexible*
Tiger		*Indomitable*

LIGHT CRUISERS

1st Light Cruiser Squadron	2nd Light Cruiser Squadron	3rd Light Cruiser Squadron
Galatea	*Southampton*	*Falmouth*
Phaeton	*Birmingham*	*Yarmouth*
Inconstant	*Nottingham*	*Birkenhead*
Cordelia	*Dublin*	*Gloucester*
		Chester

CRUISER SQUADRONS

1st Cruiser Squadron	2nd Cruiser Squadron
Defence	*Minotaur*
Warrior	*Hampshire*
Duke of Edinburgh	*Cochrane*
Black Prince	*Shannon*

LIGHT CRUISER SQUADRON

4th Light Cruiser Squadron.

Calliope	*Caroline*
Constance	*Royalist*
Comus	

LIGHT CRUISER - *Canterbury*

DESTROYER FLOTILLAS.

12 Flotilla	11th Flotilla	4th Flotilla
Faulknor	*Castor*	*Tipperary*
Marksman	*Kempenfelt*	*Broke*
Obedient	*Ossory*	*Achates*
Maenad	*Mystic*	*Porpoise*

Opal	*Moon*	*Spitfire*
Mary Rose	*Morning Star*	*Unity*
Marvel	*Magic*	*Garland*
Menace	*Mounsey*	*Ambuscade*
Nessus	*Mandate*	*Ardent*
Narwhal	*Marne*	*Fortune*
Mindful	*Minion*	*Sparrowhawk*
Onslaught	*Manners*	*Contest*
Munster	*Michael*	*Shark*
Nonsuch	*Mons*	*Acasta*
Noble	*Martial*	*Ophelia*
Mischief	*Milbrook*	*Christopher*
		Owl
		Hardy
		Midge

1st Flotilla	13th Flotilla	9th and 10th Flotillas
Fearless	*Champion*	*Lydiard*
Acheron	*Nestor*	*Liberty*
Ariel	*Nomad*	*Landrail*
Attack	*Narborough*	*Laurel*
Hydro	*Obdurate*	*Moorsom*
Badger	*Petard*	*Morris*
Goshawk	*Pelican*	*Turbulent*
Defender	*Nerissa*	*Termagant*
Lizard	*Onslow*	
Lapwing	*Moresby*	
	Nicator	

SEAPLANE CARRIER
Engadine

ORGANISATION OF THE GERMAN FLEET
BATTLESHIPS

3rd Squadron

König	
Grosser Kürfurst	5th Division
Kronprinz	
Markgraf	
Kaiser	
Kaiserin	6th Division
Prinzregent Luitpold	

1st Squadron	Friedrich der Grösse (Fleet Flagship) Ostfriesland Thüringen Helgoland Oldenburg	1st Division
	Posen Rheinland Nassau Westfalen	2nd Division
2nd Squadron	Deutschland Hessen Pommern	3rd Division
	Hannover Schlesien Schleswig-Holstein	4th Division

CRUISERS

1st Scouting Group (Battle Cruisers).	2nd Scouting Group (Light Cruisers).	4th Scouting Group (Light Cruisers).
Lützow	*Frankfurt*	*Stettin*
Derfflinger	*Wiesbaden*	*München*
Seydlitz	*Pillau*	*Hamburg*
Moltke	*Elbing*	*Frauenlob*
Von der Tann		*Stuttgart*

DESTROYER FLOTILLAS

Rostock (light cruiser), 1st Leader of Torpedo Boats.	*Regensburg* (light cruiser), 2nd Leader of Torpedo Boats.
First half of 1st Flotilla	2nd Flotilla
3rd Flotilla	6th Flotilla
5th Flotilla	9th Flotilla
7th Flotilla	

Note: Each Flotilla consisted of 11 destroyers, and was divided up into two Half-Flotillas, the 1st Flotilla consisting of the 1st and 2nd Half-Flotillas, the 2nd Flotilla consisting of the 3rd and 4th Half-Flotillas, and so on.

APPENDIX C:

BRITISH CASUALTIES[1]

SHIP	OFFICERS Killed.	Wounded	Prisoners of War	MEN Killed.	Wounded	Prisoners of War
Marlborough	-	-	-	2	-	-
Colossus	-	-	-	-	5	-
Barham	4	1	-	22	36	-
Valiant	-	-	-	-	1	-
Warspite	1	3	-	13(2)	13(1)	-
Malaya	2	-	-	61(4)	33	-
Lion	6	1	-	93(2)	43	-
Princess Royal	-	1	-	22(2)	77	-
Queen Mary (sunk)	57	2	1	1,209	5	1
Tiger	2	-	-	22	37	-
Indefatigable (sunk)	57	-	-	960(5)	-	2
Invincible (sunk)	61	-	-	965(5)	-	-
Southampton	-	1	-	35(1)	40	-
Dublin	1	-	-	2	24	-
Chester	2	3	-	33	39	-
Defence (sunk)	54	-	-	849(4)	-	-
Warrior (sunk)[2]	1	2	-	70	25	-
Black Prince (sunk)	37	-	-	820(5)	-	-
Calliope	-	2	-	10	7	-
Defender	-	-	-	1	2	-
Tipperary (sunk)	11	-	-	174	2	8
Broke	1	3	-	46	33	-
Porpoise	-	-	-	2	2	-
Spitfire	-	3	-	6	16	-
Ardent (sunk)	4	1	-	74	1	-
Fortune (sunk)	4	-	-	63	1	-
Sparrowhawk (sunk)	-	-	-	6	-	-
Shark (sunk)	7	-	-	79	2	-
Acasta	1	-	-	5	1	-
Moorsom	-	-	-	-	1	-
Turbulent (sunk)	5	-	-	85	-	13
Castor	-	1	-	13	22	-
Nessus	2	-	-	5	7	-
Onslaught	3	-	-	2	2	-
Nestor (sunk)	2	-	5	4	-	75

[1] Reproduced from Harper's Report, 117–18.

[2] Casualties sustained prior to loss of ship.

Nomad (sunk)	1	–	4	7	–	68
Petard	2	1	–	7	5	–
Onslow	–	–	–	2	3	–
Total:	328	25	10	5,769	485	167

Numbers in brackets indicate the number of civilians included.

GERMAN CASUALTIES

	OFFICERS		MEN	
Ship	Killed	Wounded	Killed	Wounded
Ostfriesland	–	–	1	10
Oldenburg	4	3	4	11
Rheinland	–	1	10	19
Nassau	2	2	10	13
Westfalen	–	1	2	7
Pommern (sunk)	71	–	769	–
Schlesien	–	1	1	–
Schleswig-Holstein	–	–	3	8
König	1	1	44	26
Grosser Kurfürst	3	1	12	10
Markgraf	–	1	11	12
Kaiser	–	–	–	1
Seydlitz	5	4	93	46
Moltke	–	–	17	22
Derfflinger	1	2	153	24
Von der Tann	1	3	11	32
Lützow (sunk)	5	5	106	49
Pillau	–	–	4	23
Frankfurt	1	1	2	20
Wiesbaden (sunk)	27	–	543	–
Elbing (sunk)	–	1	4	9
Rostock (sunk)	1	–	13	6
Stettin	–	1	9	26
München	1	4	7	15
Hamburg	1	4	13	21
Frauenlob (sunk)	17	–	325	–
S.32	–	–	3	1
G.40	–	–	1	1
B.98	–	1	2	10
V.48 (sunk)	6	–	84	–
V.4 (sunk)	1	–	17	4
VI Flotilla	–	3	3	13
IX Flotilla	12	–	108	15
Total	160	40	2,385	454

APPENDIX D:

DAMAGE SUSTAINED BY BRITISH SHIPS[1]

Lion

Received about 12 hits from large projectiles.

1.   Struck fore end of sick bay skylight, then upper deck plating and inboard side of 4 in. armour, where it exploded.

2 and 3.   After end of forecastle, exploded on striking upper deck, and causing many casualties amongst 4 in. gun's crews.

4.   Just above forecastle deck (starboard) and caused cordite fire near port side after 4 in. guns.

5.   Pierced mainmast.

6.   Struck 'Q' turret, when trained on port beam. Front roof plate forced off and entire turret's crew killed, due to cordite fire in working chamber, hoist and waiting tray. Magazine was flooded.

7.   12-in. shell (probably a ricochet) pierced blast screen, and dropped between blast screen and middle funnel without exploding.

8.   Pierced fore end of blast screen (port) and struck middle funnel casing. Exploded and caused a lot of local damage.

9.   Entered ship's side, struck upper deck, and was deflected up, passing through forecastle deck. This shot caused a severe fire in cabins on entry.

10 and 11.   Struck side armour close together, midway between main and upper decks. Armour damaged, but not pierced.

12.   Struck sheet cable holder and passed through forecastle deck and side plating.

Repairs were completed on July 19, 1916.

Princess Royal

Received about 6 hits from large projectiles.

1.   Struck 'X' turret armour, killing four men and putting turret out of action, through armour being driven in.

2.   Struck just above joint of 6 in. and 9 in. side armour (starboard). Passed through and burst port side.

3.   Struck 2 ft. below main deck (port), and pierced 9 in. armour, burst inside, causing many small fires.

4.   Entered Admiral's pantry and exploded on striking upper deck, causing fire, and many casualties from gassing and burns.

5.   Struck starboard strutt [sic] of foremast about 20 ft. above forecastle nearly half severing it, passed through funnel and more than half severed the port strutt [sic]. The mast was unaffected and director firing continued.

6.   Struck edge of muzzle of right gun of 'Q' turret, and apparently exploded in the air.

Repairs were completed on July 15, 1916.

---

[1]   Reproduced from Harper's Report.

Tiger

Received about 10 hits from large projectiles.

1. On after plate of side armour (port) near water line. Plate slightly displaced and wing compartment flooded.
2. On port side of 'X' turret close to deck. Armour broken, but gun mounting unaffected.
3. Struck 9 in. belt port side. Plate pushed in about 3 in.
4. Through 6 in. armour just below upper deck (port). Shell burst inside and caused local damage.
5. Between forecastle and upper decks (port). Struck and cracked 'A' turret armour.
6. Entered between forecastle and upper decks (port). Burst inside and caused local damage.
7. Struck starboard cable holder, shattering it, passed through forecastle deck and exploded.
8. Struck forecastle deck (port) and burst inside.
9. Through shelter deck, hit forecastle deck, but did not penetrate.
10. Struck roof of 'Q' turret, knocked off centre sighting hood. Turret not put out of action.

Repairs were completed on July 2, 1916.

Barham

Received about 6 hits from large projectiles.

1. Through upper deck (starboard) and exploded between upper and main decks.
2. Through upper deck (starboard) and exploded between upper and main decks. One fragment entered lower conning tower.
3. Through superstructure (starboard) and exploded on forecastle deck.
4. Through forecastle deck, exploding inside.
5. Through side plating between upper and main decks (starboard), exploding inside and causing fire.
6. Struck armour belt port side. Armour not damaged but driven in ¾ in.

Repairs were completed on July 4, 1916.

Malaya

Received 7 hits from large projectiles.

1. On lower tier of armour. Armour pushed in slightly.
2. On upper tier of armour. Splash off face of plate.
3 and 4. Close together, inner and outer bottoms torn away just below armour shelf.
5. Through forecastle deck and burst causing cordite fire in starboard battery, 102 casualties. No. 3 casemate gun had to be replaced.
6. On lower boom stanchion, damage to superstructure.
7. Middle roof plates of 'X' turret. No material damage inside turret.

Repairs were completed on June 24, 1916.

Warspite

Received 13 hits from large projectiles.

1. On unarmoured side (starboard) between main and middle decks. Burst inside.
2. On unarmoured side (port) between main and middle decks. Burst in Captain's quarters.
3. Through 6 in. armour, 3 ft. above middle deck. Burst inside.
4. Through upper deck. Burst inside.
5. Through 6 in. armour between main and upper decks. Burst inside.
6. On main armour, breaking off top corner of armoured plate. Burst inside.
7. Through 6 in. armour and exploded inside.
8. Through upper deck, causing small fire.
9. Through after funnel, struck armour gratings and deflected up and burst starboard side.
10. Struck upper deck, exploded on impact, caused small cordite fire.
11. Through after funnel, deflected up by armour gratings and passed through shelter deck.
12. Struck deck edge of fore shelter and burst inside, causing fire.
13. Struck after side of after communication tube, half severed it and turned it through 60°, then burst.

Repairs were completed on July 20, 1916.

Marlborough

1. Torpedo. Struck about 18 ft. below water line and 3 ft. before fore end of boiler room.

Repairs were completed on August 2, 1916.

Southampton

Received 18 hits from 5.9 in. and below.

1. Struck upper deck, making small hole.
2. Struck immediately below upper deck and burst in cabin.
3. Passed through deadlight and struck ammunition hoist.
4. Cracked 1½ in. protective plating along seam.
5. Struck ship's side, pierced 1½ in. protective plating and burst inside.
6. Struck ship's side and apparently exploded on impact.
7. Pierced starboard side of forecastle, did not burst.
8. Burst inside.
9. Struck forecastle deck and burst, putting both starboard and port guns out of action, set fire to cordite charges. The flame passed down adjacent ammunition hoist but no further.
10. Struck forecastle, and burst on impact.
11. Pierced 1¾ in. protective plating. Small damage.
12. Struck mast 9 ft. above forecastle and caused fire on mast.
13. Slight damage.

14.   On protective plating, causing indentations and one small hole.
15.   ”   ”   ”
16.   ”   ”   ”
17.   ”   ”   ”
18.   ”   ”   ”
Repairs were completed on June 20, 1916.

Dublin

Received 8 hits.
1.   After end of forecastle, did considerable damage.
2.   After davit of 30 ft. cutter, local damage.
3.   Shell pierced protective and side plating in No. 4 bunker, but did no further damage.
4.   Through top corner of chart house.
5.   Pierced ship's side above protective plating, burst on mess deck.
6.   Pierced ship's side above upper deck and burst on deck.
7.   Indented protective and side plating.
8.   Pierced ship's side forward, apparently did not burst.
Repairs were completed on June 17, 1916.

Chester

Received about 17 hits.
1.   On protective plating (starboard), which had to be renewed.
2.   On protective plating (port). Plate renewed.
3.   On protective plating (port). Plate renewed.
4.   Port side upper edge of side armour.
5.   Port bow.
Most of the others burst on upper deck, causing much damage and many casualties.
S. 1 gun damaged by splinter and condemned.
P. 1 gun. Direct hit on gun.
S. 2 gun. Breech mechanism damaged by splinter.
S. 4 gun. Shield struck and bent.
Repairs were completed on July 25, 1916.

Broke

Received about 9 hits and damaged by collision.
Repairs were completed on August 31, 1916.

Contest

Collision, damage to bow.
Repairs were completed on June 19, 1916.

Spitfire

Received about 2 hits, bow damaged by collision.
Repairs were completed on July 31, 1916.

Acasta

> Received about 2 hits, probably 5.9 in.
> Repairs were completed on August 2, 1916.

Onslow

> Received about 5 hits, three 5.9 in. and 2 4.1 in.
> Repairs were completed on August 8, 1916.

Porpoise

> Received about 2 hits, air chamber of spare torpedo burst.
> Repairs were completed on June 23, 1916.

Defender

> 1 hit from a 12 in. shell.
> Repairs were completed on June 23, 1916.

Onslaught

> About 1 hit, fore end of ship.
> Repairs were completed on June 23, 1916.

Petard

> About 3 hits.
> Repairs were completed on June 27, 1916.

Moorsom

> About 1 hit.
> Repairs were completed on June 17, 1916.

DAMAGE SUSTAINED BY GERMAN SHIPS[2]

Lützow

> Received about 40 hits – finally unable to steam and was sunk by a German
>   torpedo.
>   *Lion* and *Princess Royal*, 3.48 to 4.30
>   *Lion* and *Princess Royal*, about 6 pm (badly hit)

Seydlitz

> Received about 24 hits from large projectiles and 1 torpedo – 3 smaller hits.
> Apparently all turrets were hit except foremost one.
> No. 4 turret received 2 hits and all the crew were killed.
> Several 5.9 in. guns were put out of action.
> Was in great danger of sinking.
>   *Tiger*, 4.26 and 4.50 – 5.10
>   *Hercules*, 7.12
>   *Royal Oak*, 7.16

---

[2] The identification of the ships by whom the damage was inflicted is probably fairly correct, but there is insufficient data to guarantee its accuracy.

Revenge
Acasta, 1 torpedo 6.12
Ready for sea on September 16, 1916.

Derfflinger

Received about 20 hits from large projectiles and 9 smaller hits.
Two after turrets hit and put out of action and crews killed.
Several 5.9 in. guns put out of action.
Princess Royal, 3.40 – 4.30 and again 8.21 – 8.30
Valiant, 4.50 – 5.10
Agincourt, perhaps 6.24
Benbow, Colossus, Revenge, Royal Oak, 7.12 – 7.21
Ready for sea on November 3, 1916.

Moltke

Received about 4 hits from large projectiles and several smaller hits.
New Zealand, Indomitable, 8.26 – 8.42
5th Battle Squadron, 4.10 – 4.30
Ready for sea, August 7, 1916.

Von der Tann

Received about 4 hits from large projectiles.
Fore turret put out of action. After turret hit, not much damage.
Barham, 3.40 – 4.30
Tiger, Revenge, 7.10 – 7.20
Repairs took about six weeks.

König

Received about 10 hits from large projectiles.
Fore part flooded and a heavy list to port.
Iron Duke, 6.25 – 6.40
Marlborough, 7.10 – 7.20
Ready for sea, August 3, 1916.

Grosser Kurfurst

Received about 8 hits from large projectiles.
Marlborough
Orion
Ready for sea on July 18, 1916.

Markgraf

Received about 5 hits from large projectiles and possibly a torpedo.
Barham, Agincourt, 7.06

Kaiser

Received about 2 hits from heavy projectiles.
Ready for sea on June 14, 1916.

Ostfriesland
Hit a mine on her way home.
Ready for sea on July 29, 1916.

Helgoland
Received 1 hit from heavy projectile.
There is also a report that she struck a mine.
Ready for sea on June 19, 1916.

Oldenburg
Received 1 hit, 4 in. high explosive at night.
Ready for sea on June 19, 1916.

Rheinland
2 medium calibre hits.

Nassau
2 small calibre hits. High explosive or shrapnel.
Also damaged by ramming British destroyer.

Westfalen
1 medium calibre hit.

Schlesien
Received 1 hit from large calibre projectile.
Battle cruisers, 8.21 - 8.30

Schleswig-Holstein
Received 1 hit from large calibre projectile.
Battle cruisers, 8.21 - 8.30

Pommern
Received 1 hit from large calibre projectile.
Battle cruisers, 8.21 - 8.30
Torpedoed and sunk by 12th Flotilla, 2.10 am, June 1.

Pillau
Received 1 hit from large calibre projectile.
Funnels and superstructure damaged.

Frankfurt
Received 1 large hit and 3 medium.

Stettin
2 medium calibre hits.

München
5 medium calibre hits.

Hamburg
4 medium calibre hits.

S.32

    3 small calibre hits.

G.40

    1 medium calibre hit.

B.98

    1 small calibre hit.

S.52

    Received unknown number of hits.

S.36

    Received unknown number of hits.

APPENDIX E:

LIST OF SHIPS SUNK

British	Enemy
BATTLESHIPS	
–	*Pommern*
BATTLE CRUISERS	
Queen Mary	*Lützow*
Indefatigable	–
Invincible	–
ARMOURED CRUISERS	
Defence	–
Warrior	–
Black Prince	–
LIGHT CRUISERS	
–	*Wiesbaden*
–	*Elbing*
–	*Rostock*
–	*Frauenlob*
DESTROYERS	
Tipperary	*V.*48
Ardent	*V.*4
Fortune	*V.*27
Sparrowhawk	*S.*35
Shark	*V.*29
Nestor	–
Nomad	–
Turbulent	–

APPENDIX F:
SUMMARY OF REPORTS OF ENEMY RECEIVED IN *IRON DUKE*[1]

RECEIVED BETWEEN 2.20 pm AND 3.35 pm.

REPORTS OF ENEMY LIGHT CRUISERS[2]

1. Received 2.18 pm from *Galatea*. At 1420 in 56° 48' N, 5° 21' E, 2 cruisers ESE.
2. Received 2.30 pm from *Galatea*. At 1430, in 56° 30' N, 5° 19' E, 1 cruiser, East, steering SSE.
3. Received 2.34 pm from *Galatea*. Enemy ships reported are 2 destroyers.
4. Received 2.35 pm from *Galatea*. At 1430, in 56° 50' N, 5° 19' E, smoke ENE.
5. Received 2.51 pm from *Galatea*. At 1445, in 56° 52' N, 5° 33' E, smoke, 7 vessels, turned North.
6. Received 3.05 pm from *Falmouth*. At 1500, in 56° 59' N, 5° 31' E, 3 cruisers, East course North.
7. Received 3.08 pm from *Galatea*. At 1507, in 56° 59' N, 5° 27½' E, course NNW. Enemy altered course NW.
8. Received 3.21 pm, from *Lion*. At 1515, in 56° 48' N, 5° 17 E, course NE. (received as N 40 E by Commander-in-Chief) 23 knots.
9. Received 3.24 pm, from *Nottingham*. At 1522, in 56° 46' N, 5° 14' E, smoke ENE. 5 columns.
10. Received 3.27 pm, from *Galatea*. At 1515 (position omitted) smoke ESE steering WNW.
11. Received 3.35 pm, from Admiralty. At 2.31 pm in 56° 57' N, 6° 9' E, enemy light cruiser.

RECEIVED BETWEEN 3.40 pm and 4 pm

REPORTS OF ENEMY BATTLE CRUISERS

12. Received 3.40 pm, from *Lion*. At 1535 in 56° 53' N, 5° 28' E, enemy battle cruisers, five in number, North-East.
13. Received 3.41 pm, from *Galatea*. At 1535 in 57° 04' N, 5° 10' E, light cruisers altered course to South.
14. Received 3.44 pm, from *Falmouth*. At 1538 in 57° 10' N, 5° 14' E, enemy E by S. Course SE. 21-25 knots.
15. Received 3.45 pm, from *Lion*. At 1545 in 56° 53' N, 5° 33' E, Course of enemy S 55 E.
16. Received 3.55 pm, from *Lion*. At 1550 in 56° 53' N, 5° 31' E, engaging enemy.

---

[1] The substance of the reports is given, but not necessarily the actual signals.

[2] The times of receipt are from *Official Despatches*, Appendix II, except that of the Admiralty report, which is from *Iron Duke's* wireless entry log.

17. Received 3.59 pm, from *Galatea*. At 1555 in 57° 03' N, 5° 27 E, own course ESE, 28 knots, enemy bearing E.S.E, Course ESE.

RECEIVED BETWEEN 4.30 and 5 pm

REPORTS OF ENEMY BATTLE FLEET

18. Received 4.30 pm, from *Southampton*. At 1630 in 56° 38' N, 6° 07' E, one cruiser SE, course NE, Commander-in-Chief asks at 4.41 to check repeat. Repeated at 5 pm in original form.
19. Received 4.38 pm, from *Champion*. At 1630 in 56° 51' N, 5° 46' E, Enemy's Battle Fleet, centre SE. Course ENE.
20. Received at 4.38 pm, from *Southampton*. At 1638 in 56° 34' N, 6° 20' E. Enemy Battle Fleet, approximately SE. Course North.
21. Received about 5.05 pm[3] *Lion* at 1645 in 56° 36' N, 6° 04' E, 26-30 battleships bearing SSE steering SE.
22. Received 5 pm[4] from *Southampton*. At 1646 in 56° 29' N, 6° 14' E. Enemy Battle Fleet, centre East, course North.
23. Received 5 pm, Admiralty at 1609 in 56° 27' N, 6° 18' E. Enemy Battle Fleet, course NW, 15 knots.
24. Received 5 pm from *Southampton*. At 1700 in 56° 33' N, 6'° 00' E. Enemy Battle Fleet, East 10 to 11 miles, course North.

RECEIVED BETWEEN 5.35 pm and 6.14 pm

CONTACT SIGNALS (Diagrams 18 and 19)

25. *Falmouth* to *Black Prince* (SL). Received about 5.36 pm. Battle cruisers engaged to SSW. 1735.
     This is the first signal of contact, but was not received in *Iron Duke*. The *Falmouth* was about 5 miles North of *Lion*. The *Black Prince* was approximately 13 miles SSW from *Iron Duke*, but she was only 4½ miles from *Duke of Edinburgh*, and the latter was 5½ miles from *Marlborough*. It was therefore possible to establish visual connection between the *Iron Duke* and *Lion*.
26. *Southampton* to Commander-in-Chief. Received 5.48 (W/T). Enemy's Battle Fleet has altered course NNW. My position Lat. 56° 46' N, 5° 40' E. 1740. [*Official Despatches*, 456 gives 5.40. This is too early. *Iron Duke* did not receive it until 5.48. *Iron Duke* (s[1]), 5.48; *Benbow* (s), 5.52; *Southampton* (w/e), 5.44; *New Zealand* (s), 5.47. *Falmouth* (s), 5.43. *Southampton*'s signalled position was 5 miles South of her actual position. The signal gives no bearing of enemy, which greatly reduces its value.]
27. *Black Prince* to Commander-in-Chief and *Minotaur* W/T. Received 5.42. Battle cruisers bearing South, 5 miles. My position Lat. 56° 59' N, Long. 5° 24' E. 1740.

---

[3] *Iron Duke* (s[1]) 5.05 *Minotaur* (s) 5.10. *Marlborough* (s) 5.08.

[4] *Iron Duke* (w/e) 5.19. *Marlborough* (w) 5.15. *Official Despatches* says 5 pm.

[*Black Prince's* signalled position was about S 27 W, 17 miles from Commander-in-Chief by *Iron Duke's* reckoning. This would place battle cruisers SSW 21½ miles from *Iron Duke*. *Black Prince* was actually about 7 miles 60° from her signalled position. *Official Despatches*, 456 has 'Enemy Battle Cruisers', but *Iron Duke* (s¹), also *Marlborough* (s) has 'Battle Cruisers', and Commander-in-Chief assumed them rightly to be Beatty's squadron (Jellicoe, *Grand Fleet*, 344).]

28. *Defence* to *Minotaur* (W/T and SL). Received 5.46. Ships in action bearing SSW, steering NE. My position 57° 07' N, 5° 38' E. ° 1745.

[*Iron Duke* (s¹), 5.46; *Benbow* (s), 5.49; *Marlborough* (w), 5.49. The *Defence* was actually 2½ miles 74° from above position. This signal would make ships in action S by W by Commander-in-Chief's reckoning, about 45° on starboard bow. This was the boom and flash of Beatty's guns, but Commander-in-Chief thought they might be the enemy's battle cruisers (Jellicoe, *Grand Fleet*, 344).]

29. *Falmouth* to SO Cruisers (SL). Received 5.48. Two heavy enemy ships bearing SSE, steering NE. My position 57° 07' N, Long. 5° 45' E. 1745.

[Not in *Iron Duke* (s¹), *Marlborough* (s), 5.50. The heavy enemy ships may possibly have been the *König* and *Grosser Kurfürst*, then about 14 miles S 7 E from the *Falmouth*, or, more probably, the 1st S.G., then bearing 10 miles S 30 E. If this signal was received in the *Iron Duke* it would place the enemy sharp on the *Iron Duke's* starboard bow about 20 miles. The *Falmouth's* actual position was 5¾ miles 220° from position signalled.]

30. *Southampton* to Commander-in-Chief and SO, BCF. Received 5.52 (W/T). Enemy Battle Fleet has altered course to North. Enemy battle cruisers bear SW from enemy Battle Fleet. My position 56° 50' N, 5° 44' E. 1750.

[This makes the *Southampton* about 24 miles S 2 W from *Iron Duke's* reckoning and would have been a valuable report if it had given the bearing of the enemy. The bearing of the battle cruisers from Battle Fleet was evidently intended to be NE. The report placed the enemy roughly 26 miles, 15° from *Iron Duke's* starboard bow. *Southampton* was actually 7 miles 323° from signalled position.]

31. Admiralty [to] Commander-in-Chief. Received 5.53. Enemy main force at 4.30 pm in 56° 31' N, 6° 5' E, steering North, 15 knots. 1745.

[This signal would place the enemy at 5.50 pm, S 15 E, 26 miles from *Iron Duke's* reckoning, approximately 2 points on the starboard bow. This is only 4 miles 270° from the actual position of the head of the German line in 56° 31' N, 6° 15' E at 4.30 pm. The initial westerly error compensates for the German north-westerly course at 5 pm, and gives a very good estimate of German position, though the course and speed did not hold good.]

32. *Marlborough* to Commander-in-Chief. Received 6 pm (SL).[5] Our battle cruisers bearing SSW steering East 3 to 4 miles, *Lion* leading ship. 1800.

   Note: Lion had been in sight from *Marlborough* since 5.45 pm.

33. *Southampton* to Commander-in-Chief and SO, BCF. Received 6.03 (W/T).[6]

---

[5] *Iron Duke* (s¹), 5.55; *Marlborough* (s), 6.00.

[6] *Iron Duke* (s¹), 6.03; *Benbow* (s), 6.07; *New Zealand* (w), 6.07; *Marlborough* (s), 6.06; *Falmouth* (s), 6.07.

Urgent. Have lost sight of enemy's Battle Fleet. Am engaging enemy battle cruisers. Position 56° 57' N, 5° 43' E. Course NNE, 26 knots. 1800.

[This was the *Southampton*'s last wireless message before deployment. The positions in 1750 and 1800 are 7 miles apart, giving her a speed of 42 miles. *Southampton*'s actual position is 4½ miles 298° from above position.]

34. *Lion*. Received 6.06. *Lion* to Commander-in-Chief (SL). Enemy's battle cruisers bearing SE. 1806.

[The *Lion* was about S 18 W 2½ miles from *Iron Duke*. This would place enemy battle cruisers about SSE of *Iron Duke* 7 miles, on the port bow of the fleet (going South at the time). The Commander-in-Chief thereupon turned to a SE course (Jellicoe, *Grand Fleet*, 347).]

35. *Marlborough* to Commander-in-Chief. Received 6.07 (SL) 5th Battle Squadron bearing SW. 1805.

[This places 5th Battle Squadron approximately 8 miles on starboard beam of *Iron Duke*.]

36. *Barham* to Commander-in-Chief (Flags). Received 6.12. Enemy in sight SSE. 1810.

[*Iron Duke* (s¹), 6.12; Jellicoe, *Grand Fleet*, 347, 6.15. This would place the enemy at 6.12 about 5 miles, 40° on *Marlborough's* bow on the Commander-in-Chief's basis of a five-mile visibility. Lord Jellicoe's diagram I in *Grand Fleet* shows the German van 7 miles, 31° on *Marlborough's* bow, in approximately its correct position.]

37. *Lion* to Commander-in-Chief. Received 6.14 (SL). Sighted enemy's Battle Fleet SSW. 1814.

[*Iron Duke* (s¹), 6.14; Jellicoe, *Grand Fleet*, 347, 6.14. This makes enemy about 5 miles 34° on *Marlborough's* bow.]

38. *Southampton*. Received 6.24. Enemy Battle Fleet bears 10 to 11 miles SSE. Course NE. My position Lat. 56° 58' N, Long. 5° 51' E. 1820.

Iron Duke (s¹), 6.18; *Marlborough* (w), 6.21; *Benbow* (s), 6.22; *New Zealand* (w), 6.22; *Falmouth* (s), 6.23. This position received after deployment gives the *Southampton* an easterly course from 1800; it may, however, have been meant for the position of the enemy, in which case it was approximately correct, for the *König* was in 56° 58½' N, 5° 55' E. course NE at 6.20, two miles to eastward of the above position of the *Southampton*.

APPENDIX G:

GERMAN SIGNALS

The following list contains the more important German signals bearing on the Battle of Jutland as decoded and registered at the Admiralty between May 30 and June 1, 1916. They are extracted from Room 40 records, Volumes 896 and 897. The five figured number is the serial number as given in the Records. The first time represents the German time group converted to Greenwich Mean Time, the second the time received in Room 40 from the intercepting Station, and the third is the time the decoded messages was passed to the Operations Division.

1.

No. 20272.
From Flag.
To Ostfriesland.   May 30, 9.44 am/9.52/11.30.
    For A.S. Fleet.
Be assembled in the outer Roads by 9 pm at the latest.
                                      (*Sgd*.) Commander-in-Chief.

2.

No. 20274.
From Bruges.
To All Ships.   May 30, ——/10.04 am/11.50.
Reckon on the proceeding out of our forces on May 31 and June 1.
    Note: There was some doubt as to whether the word 'our forces' meant enemy (*i.e.*, British) forces or our (i.e., German) forces. It was translated 'our forces' but its meaning was afterwards discovered to be 'enemy (i.e., British) forces'; see Birch and Clarke.

3.

No. 20280.
From Flag.
To Ostfriesland.   May 30, 11.31 am/12.36/2.40 pm
    For 1st Mine S. Divn.
U.R. (an Aux. M.S.D.).
A.C., 2nd Battle Squadron.
    U.F. (1st M.S. Division) is to go this afternoon with gear from square 55° 1' - 7° 25' E to square 54° 33' - 7° 25' E, from F and E to Place 8; on Wednesday commencing at dawn seek enemy submarines West of Heligoland and Amrum Bank; one half-flotilla is to search to-night Place 8 to Place 1.
                                       (*Sgd*.) A.C., 1st Cr. Sq.

4.

No. 20293.
From Flag.
To Ostfriesland.   May 30, 3.36 pm/4.40/5.08.
    For High Sea Fleet.
    On May 31, most secret (/) 2490.
    (*Note.*-Remainder of signal not intercepted.)

                                            (*Sgd.*) Commander-in-Chief

---

5.

No. 20306.
From ——.
To ——.   May 30, 4.45 pm/5.19/7.30.
    For War Lightship E of Jade.
    Out lights to be shown for proceeding out – from 2 am to 4.30 am.
                            (*Sgd.*) Fortress Commandant Wilhelmshaven.

6.

No. 20310.
From Flag.
To Ostfriesland.   May 30, 6.41 pm/6.43/8.10.
    For High Sea Fleet.
    Flag to take over wireless in Deutsche Bucht at 11 pm.
                                        (*Sgd.*) Commander-in-Chief.
    (*Note.*- The preliminary to any important operation.)

7.

No. 20318.
From Heligoland.
To Flag.   May 30, 9.15 pm/10.39/12.30 am.
    For U.R. (An Auxiliary M.S.D.)
    A.C., 1st C.S.
    U.F. (1st M.S.D.)
    U.N. (Auxiliary M.S.D. of Wilhelmshaven).
    On Wednesday at dawn search with gear ways D and F return journey without gear
via Places 7 and 8, after ascertaining the facts in accordance with 1837 (our No. 20304)
(search) ways A, B, C with gear.
                    (*Sgd.*) E. H. (Chief of a Flotilla of North Sea Outpost Boats).

8.

No. 20332.
From Fleet Flagship.
To Arcona.   ——/May 31, 7.52 am/8.28.
(Preamble) From 5th of 4th Half-Flotilla, U.66.
    For Commander-in-Chief.
Eight large warships, course —— (group unintelligible) in Area 3 (57° 36' N, 0° 15' W).
                                            (*Sgd.*) ——

9.

No. 20373.
From Flag of A.C., 1st SG.
To U.A. (C.-in-C.)   May 31, 3.46 pm/4.05/5.40.
    For U.A.

Six enemy battle cruisers and light forces in square (?) 56° 51', 5° 19', steering SE. 1st Scouting Group steering SSE at 18 knots. Am engaged with six battle cruisers. Own main force report position.

                                              (*Sgd.*) A.C., 1st Scouting Group.

10.

No. 20377.
From Flag.
To Rostock.   May 31, 4.21 pm/5.50/5.56.
    For O.C., 1st Torpedo Division.
    Torpedo boats of our own main force assemble on the leading ship.

                                              (*Sgd.*) Commander-in-Chief.

11.

No. 20383.
From Flag.
To Ostfriesland.   May 30, 5.41 pm/7/May 31, 6.40 pm.
    For High Sea Fleet.

The head of the 3rd Battle Squadron will pass (warlightship) at 5.30 am. 2nd Battle Squadron will take part in the undertaking (and will) join up with the 1st Battle Squadron. Direction of the W/T in the German Bight will be carried out by Wilhelmshaven 3rd Entrance, which will have the W/T call (of the Commander-in-Chief, High Sea Fleet).

                                              (*Sgd.*) Commander-in-Chief.

Note from Room 40: Made last night in a new cypher, only now decyphered.

12.

No. 20388.
From Neumünster, NIC.
To Flag of C.-in-C.   May 31, 10.18 am/12.08/7.20 pm.
    For Commander-in-Chief.
    Weather report Firth of Forth, —— Wind West —— hazy, barometer 767.
    Reports of this type are generally only observed when the Fleet is at sea.
                                            (*Sgd.*) Neumünster, NIC.

(*Note*: Delay due to new key.)

13.

No. 20391.
From Rostock.
To N.M.   May 31, 5.59 pm/7.27/7.40.
    For High Sea Fleet.

1st Scouting Group to move off in *echelon* as observation is impossible against the sun.

                                                (*Sgd.*) A.C., 1st C.S.

14.

No. 20394.

From ——.

To ——.   May 31, ——/6.08 pm/8.05.

The Route from Squares 54° 3' - 5° 15'; 53° 33' - 5° 45' – Area 7 – is free of mines, and also from Horns Riff East of Amrum Bank.

Count on meeting our own Outpost Forces on May 31 and June 1.

(*Sgd.*) ——

15.

No. 20398.

From Frankfürt.

To Flag.   May 31, 7.22 pm/7.43/9.07.

For Commander-in-Chief.

The *Lützow* is being fired on from the NE by strong enemy forces.

(*Sgd.*) A.C., 2nd Scouting Group.

16.

No. 20399.

From Flag.

To Derfflinger.   May 31, 8.12 pm/8.17/9.31.

For O.C.'s 1st and 2nd Torpedo Division.

All torpedo boats to be sent to the night attack, under the command of the O.C., 1st Torpedo Division.

(*Sgd.*) Commander-in-Chief.

17.

No. 20400.

From Hamburg.

To Arcona.   May 31, 7.50 pm/9.50/9.40.

For 3rd Submarine Half-Flotilla.

2nd of 2nd Submarine Half-Flotilla.

3rd of 4th Submarine Half-Flotilla.

All submarines ready for service and U.67 at once advance to the North. Report position at 6 am.

(*Sgd.*) O.C. Submarines.

18.

No. 20401.

From Stettin.

To ——.   May 31, 8.21 pm/8.23/9.45.

There are four small enemy cruisers in square 56° 45' - 5° 40'.

(*Sgd.*) A.C., 4th Scouting Group.

19.

No. 20402.
From (missed).
To (missed). May 31, 8.31 pm/8.31/10.
    For O.C., 2nd Torpedo Division.
    The allotted flotillas are to attack independently.
        (*Sgd.*) O.C., 1st Torpedo Division.

20.

No. 20404.
From ? Regensburg.
To Flag. May 31, 8.36 pm/8.31/10.02 (*sic*).
    For Commander-in-Chief.
O.C., 1st Torpedo Division.
From square 56° 55', 5° 30', the 2nd TBD Flotilla to advance on the Sector ENE - ESE, the 12th TBD Half-Flotilla on the sector ESE - SE. *Note.*-The flotillas had been launched to the attack before signal 2212 (our 20399) was made.
        (*Sgd.*) O.C., 2nd Torpedo Division.

21.

No. 20406.
From (missed).
To (missed). May 31,——/9 pm/10.25.
    For 2nd and 6th TBD Flotillas.
    At 11 pm the rear ship of our own main force was in square 56° 33' - 5° 30' lower part – on a southerly course.
        (*Sgd.*) O.C., 2nd Torpedo Division.

22.

No. 20407.
From Rostock.
To Flag of Commander-in-Chief. May 31, 8.56 pm/10.20/10.40.
    For 5th Flotilla (TBD).
        7th Flotilla (TBD).
    The 7th TBD Flotilla is to advance from 56° 35' - 5° 30' E, sector SE to S by E, 5th Flotilla sector S by E to SSW.
        (*Sgd.*) O.C., 1st Torpedo Division.

23.

No. 20408.
From Hannover.
To Flag. May 31, 9.27 pm/9.33/9.45.
    Enemy in sight ahead. Four ships in 56° 27' - 5° 30'.
        (*Sgd.*) 2nd A.C., 2nd B.S.

24.

No. 20409.
From Rostock.
To Flag.   May 31, 9.39 pm/9.44/10.50.
    For 18th TBD Half-Flotilla.
    With reference to 1127 (20408). Attack the enemy.
                                          (*Sgd.*) O.C., 1st Torpedo Division.

25.

No. 20410.
From Flag of Commander-in-Chief.
To H.S. Fleet.   May 31, 9.14 pm/10.39/10.55.
    For H.S. Fleet.
    Our own main body is to proceed in [*sic*] maintain course SSE ¼ E, speed 16 knots.
                                                  (*Sgd.*) Commander-in-Chief.

26.

No. 20411.
From Flag of Commander-in-Chief.
To H.S. Fleet.   May 31, 9.29 pm/10.39/10.55.
    For H. S. Fleet.
    2nd Battle Squadron behind 3rd Battle Squadron. All large cruisers in the rear. 2nd
Scouting Group ahead. 4th Scouting Group to starboard.
                                                  (*Sgd.*) Commander-in-Chief.

27.

No. 20413.
From Flag.
To H.S. Fleet.   May 31, 9.46 pm/9.54/11.10.
    For H.S. Fleet.
    Own main body course SSE ¾ E.
                                                  (*Sgd.*) Commander-in-Chief.

28.

No. 20414.
From Flag.
To Heligoland NIC.   May 31, 9.06 pm/9.52/11.10.
    For Airship Detachment.
    Early air reconnaissance at Horns Riff is urgently requested.
                                                  (*Sgd.*) Commander-in-Chief.

29.

No. 20415.
From 3rd Boat of 3rd TBD Half-Flotilla.
To Rostock.   May 31, 9.50 pm/9.50/11.05.
    In 56° 45' - 5° 55' E.
    Five small enemy cruisers many destroyers turning to starboard. I am steering NW.
                                                  (*Sgd.*) 2nd TBD Flotilla.

30.

No. 20421.
From Neumünster, NIC.
To Flag.   May 31, 9.30 pm/10.40/12.10.

For Commander-in-Chief.

Destroyers have taken up position five sea miles astern of the enemy main Fleet.

(*Sgd.*) Neumünster, NIC.

(As this message comes from Neumünster it is probably an English intercept).

31.

No. 20422.
From Flag.
To Rostock.   May 31, 10.32 pm/10.43/11.15.

For H.S. Fleet.

Main Fleet steering SE by S.

(*Sgd.*) Commander-in-Chief.

32.

No. 20423.
From Rostock.
To Flag of C.-in-C.   May 31, 10.32 pm/10.43/12.15 am.

For All TBD Flotillas.

Be assembled by 4 am at Horns Riff or course round Skaw.

(*Sgd.*) O.C., 1st Torpedo Division.

33.

No. 20426.
From Arcona.
To Flag.   May 31, 10.07 pm/10.56/12.35 am.

For O.C., Submarines, High Sea Fleet.

U.19, U.22, U.64 are leaving the Ems for the North at high speed.

(*Sgd.*) 3rd Submarine Half-Flotilla.

34.

No. 20427.
From Flag.
To   König.   May 31, 9.50 pm/11.06/12.30 am.

For Flag.

Lützow at 11.30 pm with four destroyers in 56° 33' – 5° 55', course SSW. Speed 13 knots.

(*Sgd.*) 4th of 1st TBD Half-Flotilla

35.

No. 20428.
From Rostock.
To 1st of 3rd TBD Half-Flotilla.   May 31, 11.06 pm/11.25/12.50 am.

For H.S. Fleet.

Own main body at 1 am, 56° 15' – 5° 42' E. Course SE ¾ E.

(*Sgd.*) Commander-in-Chief

36.

No. 20429.
From Rostock.
To ——.   May 31, 10.50 pm/11.23/12.50 am.
   For H.S. Fleet.
Enemy destroyers in 56° 3′ N., 5° 55′ E. Course S. Full speed.

(*Sgd.*) 7th TBD Flotilla

37.

No. 20430.
From Flag.
To H.S. Fleet.   May 31, 11.30 pm/11.43/1 am.
   For H.S. Fleet.
Or our main forces are to resume course SE by South.

(*Sgd.*) Commander-in-Chief.

38.

No. 20433.
From Flag.
To Ostfriesland.   May 31, 11.36 pm/11.37/1.05 am.
   For Ostfriesland.
The course ordered is SE ¾ S.

(*Sgd.*) Commander-in-Chief.

39.

No. 20438.
From Heligoland, NIC.
To Arcona.   May 31, 7.50 pm/11.57/1.30 am.
   3rd Submarine Half-Flotilla.
   3rd of 4th Submarine Half-Flotilla (U.67).
   Heligoland NIC.
   For 2nd of 2nd Submarine Half-Flotilla (U.51).
Submarines ready for service and U.67 at once to advance North. At 6 am report position.

(*Sgd.*) O.C., Submarines.

40.

No. 20439.
From 1st Boat of 3rd TBD Half-Flotilla.
To Flag.   May 31, 11.52 pm/12.30/1.35 am.
   For O.C., 1st TB Division.
      O.C., 2nd TB Division.
      Commander-in-Chief.
   Am going round the Skaw.

(*Sgd.*) 2nd TBD Flotilla.

41.

No. 20440.
From 3rd of 1st TBD Half-Flotilla.
To Flag.   June 1, 0.17 am./1.44/2.00.
   For A.C., 1st C.S.
   Position of *Lützow* at 2 am, 56° 26' N., 5° 41' E. Course S. Speed 7 knots.
                                        (*Sgd.*) 3rd of 1st TBD Half-Flotilla.

42.

No. 20442.
From 4th Boat of 17th TBD Half-Flotilla.
To Flag.   June 1, ——/0.32 am/2.05.
   For O.C., 2nd Torpedo Division.
           Commander-in-Chief.
           H.S. Fleet.
   In square 56° 21' – 5° 53' E, enemy destroyers in sight, course 29°.
                                        (*Sgd.*) G.42 or 52.

43.

No. 20444.
From Flag of Commander-in-Chief.
To Rostock.   June 1, 0.43 am/0.48/2.20.
   For Lützow.
   Own main body's position at 2.30 am, 55° 57', 6° 15 E.
                                        (*Sgd.*) Commander-in-Chief.

44.

No. 20448.
From ? Regensburg.
To Flag.   June 1, 1.59 am/1.50/3.15.
   For High Sea Fleet.
       All TBD Flotillas.
   All TBD Flotillas are to assemble at the head of the 3rd Battle Squadron.
                                        (*Sgd.*) O.C., 2nd TBD Division.

45.

No. 20456.
From Flag.
To H.S. Fleet.   June 1, 2.30 am/2.35/4.00.*
   For Fleet.
   Main Fleet in 55° 33' – 6° 50'. Course SE by S. Speed 16 knots.
                                        (*Sgd.*) Commander-in-Chief.

*(*Note*: As this signal was sent to Commander-in-Chief at 3.29 am this must be 4 am
summer time.)

46.

No. 20462.
From Flag of Commander-in-Chief.
To Moltke.   June 1, 3.24 am/3.44/5.05.
    For A.C., 1st C.S.
    1st Scouting Group to proceed in.

                                                        (*Sgd.*) Commander-in-Chief.

47.

No. 20464.
From Flag.
To H.S. Fleet.   June 1st, 3.38 am/3.51/5.10.
    For Fleet.
        2nd SG astern.
        4th SG ahead.
    O.C., 1st T.D. distribute TBD's for submarine protection.
    2nd BS proceed in.

                                                        (*Sgd.*) Commander-in-Chief.

48.

No. 20465.
    From Flag.
    To H.S. Fleet.   June 1, 3.54 am/4.8/4.15.
        For Fleet.
    Course S. Proceed in East of Amrum Bank.

                                                        (*Sgd.*) Commander-in-Chief.

EDITOR'S AFTERWORD

False ideas have thus obtained credence because the historian has not thrown his investigating net wide enough. What we want is a picture of the conflicting elements which an admiral had before him; let us see him in the middle of his distractions; point out to us the information, or the lack of information, on which he had to act. So far as possible, put us in his position and make us think what we ourselves should have done. This will give us a true idea of war – war as it really is, with the drawn curtain hiding the enemy's movements. Criticism of what a commander did should, if it is to be of any value to a student, be based on the information that commander had at the time, and not on information placed subsequently at our disposal.[1]

It is not difficult to separate the good from the bad in the *Naval Staff Appreciation*. In part because it was written so soon after the war, without the advantage of access to German records, there are a number of minor errors of fact (which ship scored hit 'x', etc.). These have been discussed in the Editor's Notes in each chapter, but are not particularly important. There are, however, significant flaws in the volume, most especially the very obvious bias against Jellicoe and the Battle Fleet proper, which call into question the merit of the Dewars' evaluation. Nevertheless, many of their conclusions are valid, and well in keeping with modern analysis. Their critiques fall into several categories, as discussed below.

'Jellicoe Bad / Beatty Good'

Put as charitably as possible, there are a number of places in the *NSA* where the authors show obvious partiality for the BCF and Beatty, typified by their

---

[1] Richmond, 'Naval History from the Naval Officer's Point of View', 46–7.

constant reference to 'the Commander-in-Chief', rarely referring to Admiral Jellicoe by name. While there is no evidence that Beatty had any input into the writing of the *Appreciation*, it is certain that Kenneth Dewar was no fan of Jellicoe; Dewar tells of a meeting with the admiral in May 1917, during which the latter said '. . . that I had a reputation for independent opinions and it was evident from his tone that he did not count this unto me for righteousness'.[2]

There was clearly no love lost between the two men, and Dewar was allied with, and perhaps assisted, the officers who worked towards Jellicoe's ousting as First Sea Lord in 1917.[3] And while Dewar had a poor opinion of Jellicoe, he had a high regard for Beatty, considering him 'a clear-sighted man of unconscious courage'.[4] During the war, Dewar was at least partially plugged-in with the officers of the BCF, exchanging letters with two of Beatty's staff officers, William Chalmers and Reginald Plunkett (later Reginald Ernle-Erle-Drax), who served as Beatty's War Staff Officer from 1913 to January 1917.[5] It is therefore easy to see where Kenneth Dewar's affiliations lay when he began work on the *Naval Staff Appreciation*, and his brother Alfred fully shared his high regard for Beatty.[6]

Unfortunately, the Dewars were unable to lay their prejudices aside when they came to write about Jutland. It is interesting that noted historian Arthur Marder, who corresponded with Kenneth Dewar after the Second World War, would describe him as 'among the most perceptive thinkers in the Navy of his generation', but was also forced to admit that he 'always seemed to have a chip on his shoulder'.[7] Despite the undoubted merits of his writing, he had difficulty seeing beyond his own particular viewpoint.[8] One of his contemporaries wrote of him that '. . . he was, without any doubt, a clear and original thinker. He also had the defects of these qualities, amongst others a contemptuous attitude towards anything with which he disagreed, a certain exudation of omniscience in argument, and a growing intolerance'.[9]

Even his longtime correspondent, Reginald Drax, would later describe Dewar as 'a disappointed, angry man and much inclined to be hyper-critical'.[10]

---

[2] Dewar, *Navy from Within*, 213.

[3] Davison, 'Striking a Balance between Dissent and Discipline', 48–9.

[4] Dewar, *Navy From Within*, 244.

[5] Correspondence in NMM: DEW 2/Part 1; Wilson, *Biographical Dictionary of the Twentieth Century Royal Navy*, 1:1116

[6] As is clear from his review of Corbett's treatment of Jutland; see [Alfred Dewar], 'Naval Operations of War, Vol. III, the Battle of Jutland'.

[7] Marder, *From the Dardanelles to Oran*, 59.

[8] Marder, *FDSF*, 4:135 n.

[9] Goldrick, 'The Founders', 9.

[10] Letter from Admiral Drax to Arthur Marder, 18 August 1959, CAC: DRAX 6/18.

Certainly this comes through clearly in the *Naval Staff Appreciation*, where positive comments on Jellicoe's handling of the Grand Fleet are few and very far between. However, what was much worse, and quite unacceptable, were the accusations that a timid Admiral Jellicoe was strictly on the defensive (Chapter II, Section 20), and that 'it is impossible to resist the conclusion that the Commander-in-Chief had abandoned any idea of renewing the action' the day after the battle (Chapter XI, Section 81). Moreover the Dewars flirted with a very serious charge when they wrote:

> . . . it is difficult to trace any definite purpose in the British movements during the night [after the day action]. No instructions were issued as to the Commander-in-Chief's intentions, no organised attempt was made to obtain information of the enemy's movements, and when definite intelligence from the Admiralty supplied absolute confirmation of the enemy's course, nothing was done to intercept him.
>
> This is the darkest part of the battle. The question of deployment and the question of turning away from torpedo attack are points which belong to the sphere of tactics, but the question of pursuing the enemy was a very different one. It was an irredeemable charge[11] which was not done (Chapter XI, Section 81).

This comes perilously close to accusing Jellicoe of the charge that got Admiral Byng shot in 1757 – that 'he did not do his utmost to take or destroy every ship which it shall be his duty to engage. . . '.[12] It amounts almost to an accusation of cowardice.

The concepts of honour and duty were integral to naval officers during the Great War era – even if perhaps foreign qualities in some early 21st-century circles. Impugning the intentions – for example, by suggesting that the Commander-in-Chief decided to 'deploy away from the enemy' (Chapter X, Section 62) – and reputation of a leader as beloved and respected as Jellicoe[13] was certainly going too far, and more importantly, patently untrue. If nothing else, throughout the entire war the Grand Fleet was possessed by the burning desire to come to grips with the High Seas Fleet, and that temper could not

---

[11] Here the word is used in the sense of a obligatory duty.

[12] Creswell, *British Admirals of the Eighteenth Century*, 94.

[13] See, for example, Marder, *FDSF*, 3:45, 3:336–7. An interesting case is gunnery officer Commander Cecil B Prickett, who served in *New Zealand*, *Princess Royal* and *Lion* during the war, and was originally in the Beatty camp. However, after he became acquainted with Earl Jellicoe when he was Governor-General of New Zealand, he came away converted to the pro-Jellicoe side (editor's phone conversation and email with Prickett's grandson, March 2004).

have been maintained throughout four tedious years had the Fleet's senior leadership not been imbued with the same spirit. Indeed, Marder was convinced that Jellicoe possessed the offensive spirit.[14]

Had the Dewars been equally critical of David Beatty, the *Naval Staff Appreciation* would have much more value. Unfortunately, they glossed over or ignored Beatty's lapses and were very quick to praise him. There are numerous examples of this scattered through the text – the omission of the BCF steaming in a circle at 7.05 pm (even though that movement is subtly hinted at in Diagram 34[15]) is one such,[16] but a more serious one is their take on the separation of the 5th BS from the main body of the BCF at the very start of the action, and the consistent breakdown in signalling between the two forces. They note the ten mile separation between *Barham* and *Lion* that occurred when the former didn't follow *Lion*'s 2.32 pm turn to the SSE (Chapter III, Section 34), but there is no discussion as to the reasons behind the delay. One suspects that they were hesitant to criticise the signalling arrangements in Beatty's flagship (although there is a school of thought that suggests Evan-Thomas ought to have followed the turn on his own initiative[17]). Another breakdown in signals procedure led to the delay in the 5th BS reversing course after the German battle fleet had been sighted, and again, the Dewars avoid all discussion of this in Chapter V.[18]

A more glaring omission is the lack of criticism of Beatty for not keeping Jellicoe properly informed both of his own movements, and more importantly, the position of the enemy. The authors of the *NSA* do point out the need for visual links between the detached forces (Chapter VII, Section 48) and suggest that the obvious value of the comparatively new technology of wireless telegraphy had led officers to forget the importance of keeping a chain of ships in visual contact so as to correct the inevitable mistakes in position that would occur. However, that very same section notes that Evan-Thomas' 5th BS should have reported losing sight of the German battle fleet at roughly 5.30 pm, but is silent with regard to the BCF's same lack of attention to what was, after all,

---

[14] Marder, *FDSF*, 3:230.

[15] It is not mentioned in the *Admiralty Narrative*, either, though the same diagram is reproduced.

[16] Interestingly, in his autobiography Kenneth Dewar records the exact opposite of the facts: he has Beatty remembering his battle cruisers turning a complete circle, and Harper charting two separate half-circles, the 'evidence' supporting the latter! Dewar, *Navy From Within*, 267.

[17] Gordon (*Rules of the Game*, Chapter 6), analyses this delay in much detail – including the important point that Evan-Thomas had not received a copy of the Battle Cruiser Fleet's Orders.

[18] Once again, this is a topic which Gordon discusses in detail (*Rules of the Game*, Chapter 8).

a fundamental battle cruiser task. The Dewars also make no mention of Jellicoe's plaintive 'Where is Enemy's BF?' signal at 6.01 pm.

Admiration for Beatty is at its height in Chapter X. Phrases like 'Admiral Beatty, however, appreciated the significance of the new formation' (Section 64); 'at 7.20, as at 6.15, the BCF indicated the course to take' (Section 68); and 'Admiral Beatty had turned at once to the sound of the guns' (Section 71), will not have gone unnoticed, and were hardly suitable for an objective analysis of the battle.

A more balanced view of the two most senior British officers leads to the conclusion that both Jellicoe and Beatty were competent officers, who made both good and bad decisions during the battle. Although as Commander-in-Chief, the final blame for the unsatisfactory outcome ultimately rests on Jellicoe's shoulders, the reality is that an examination of the performance of the two is not a zero-sum game.

Command and Staff

Clearly, Jellicoe did not possess the qualities the Dewar brothers sought in an ideal commander-in-chief. These qualities were set forth in a pre-war series of articles by Kenneth Dewar, which prefigure many of the criticisms that would appear in the *Appreciation*, even using some of the same examples and phrases.[19] They were an attempt to address an issue raised at the very outset of the *Naval Staff Appreciation*: 'an adequate system of staff work and command' (Introduction, Section 7). Command, staff work and battle tactics were inextricably linked in the Dewars' thought.

In his articles, Kenneth Dewar argued that in a military leader the power of decision was the prime requirement, since 'rapidity and consistency' in carrying out a mediocre plan would obtain better results than delay and changes in pursuit of an ideal plan.[20] The commander should therefore possess 'great personal bravery, power of decision, fearlessness of responsibility and untiring energy'[21] – qualities the Dewars' undoubtedly saw in Beatty, but not in Jellicoe.

But modern battle would move too fast for the commander to manage it personally. As Kenneth Dewar wrote,

The increased speed and certainty of movement of ships, the terribly demoralizing [*sic*] effect of shell and torpedo fire, and the multiplication of weapons and types of ships will demand a higher standard of direction than that

[19] [Kenneth Dewar], 'Executive Command and Staff in Naval Warfare'.
[20] [Kenneth Dewar], 'Executive Command and Staff in Naval Warfare', part 1, 62.
[21] [Kenneth Dewar], 'Executive Command and Staff in Naval Warfare', part 1, 61–2.

which sufficed in the sailing ship period. The various phases will develop much more quickly, and the rapidity of action and counter-action will necessitate a higher degree of initiative and co-operation.[22]

To meet these challenges, a commander needed an effective staff:

> The staff has mainly to work with abstract things, to forecast and foretell the nature and conditions of war, and to evolve doctrines and plans of, [*sic*] strategy, tactics, command, training, etc.; such work must be based on historical analysis, an intelligent forecast of future possibilities and a careful balancing of various material and immaterial forces. It demands the service of critical and constructive minds and the power of reasoned thought and imagination. Its members must be trained to deal with basic principles and to express it's [*sic*] group ideas and thoughts in intelligible language.[23]

There was nothing original in this; it was directly based on the role of the Prussian general staff, as developed by Field Marshal Helmuth Graf von Moltke during the nineteenth century. Although a 'War Staff' had been established within the Admiralty in January 1912,[24] it did not fulfil the range of functions outlined by Dewar in the passage just quoted; it had not had sufficient time before the war, and its organisation was too imperfect. Most importantly, it could not provide the prerequisite for tactical success: a naval service that was based on the principles of 'centralised direction, decentralised command, a common doctrine and an aggressive offensive'.[25] The commander would provide the method of attack, but it would be executed by subordinates acting in a cooperative fashion acting on their own initiative. Dewar recognised that initiative was a 'two-edged weapon', and that it could lead to chaos on the battlefield unless all officers '. . . speak a common language and act in accordance with common principles, so that they may act in the same direction though not necessarily in the same way of carrying out the wishes of the supreme command'.[26]

The Navy lacked these common principles because it lacked a strong staff system, and the result was a too heavy reliance on centralised command, which could only further inhibit initiative. It was in essence a vicious circle that could

---

[22] [Kenneth Dewar], 'Executive Command and Staff in Naval Warfare', part 3, 1.

[23] [Kenneth Dewar], 'Executive Command and Staff in Naval Warfare', part 1, 73.

[24] For the background of the War Staff in this period, see Hamilton, *Making of the Modern Admiralty*, 213–71, and Black, *British Naval Staff*, 53–169.

[25] [Kenneth Dewar], 'Executive Command and Staff in Naval Warfare', part 2, 246.

[26] [Kenneth Dewar], 'Executive Command and Staff in Naval Warfare', part 3, 11.

only be broken by instituting a staff that could bring together doctrine and training so that in battle officers would act in unison in spite of rapidly changing circumstances and unexpected situations.

These themes run through the *Naval Staff Appreciation*, and form the core of many of the criticisms to be found in its pages. Keeping these views in mind, we can turn at other aspects of the *NSA*.

The Grand Fleet Battle Orders[27]

The *Naval Staff Appreciation* was intended primarily as a tactical analysis of Jutland, and it is here that the Dewars level their most damaging criticisms of Jellicoe. His Grand Fleet Battle Orders, as the embodiment of the admiral's tactical intentions, are subjected to an extended and highly unfavourable critique (Chapter II). The details of the tactical ideas will be dealt with in the next section; the question addressed here is the nature and purpose of the GFBOs themselves.

Some additional context may be of value. As the Dewars note, 'When war broke out there was no comprehensive or authoritative tactical doctrine, and conflicting views were held on fundamental questions of principle' (Chapter II, Section 9). The lack of a comprehensive doctrine was not due to negligence on the part of the Admiralty; it was the result of a considered policy. There was a widespread view at the time that British tactical thought in the sailing era had been stymied by an Admiralty-imposed doctrine of the single line of battle as embodied in the so-called 'Permanent Fighting Instructions'; the upshot of this was that throughout the late nineteenth and early twentieth centuries the Admiralty avoided anything that could be construed as an 'official' system of tactics.[28] Thus we find the Admiralty writing to the commander-in-chief of the Mediterranean Fleet in 1903 that

> their Lordships wish you distinctly to understand that they do not contemplate issuing any definite instructions on the subject of fighting formations or battle tactics. They feel that to the several Flag Officers in command of Fleets it must be left to decide how best to fight those fleets under the circumstances of every case.[29]

---

[27] *Note by Stephen McLaughlin*: The following sections were largely incomplete at the time of Bill Schleihauf's death, so what follows is mostly my work. Although I believe Bill's thinking and mine were developing along similar lines, this cannot be proven; therefore the views expressed here should be attributed to me.

[28] See, for example, Laughton, 'Article IX – Naval Warfare'. For a convincing alternate view regarding both the 'Permanent' Fighting Instructions and the line of battle, see Creswell, *British Admirals in the Eighteenth Century*.

[29] Admiralty to Admiral Sir Compton Edward Domvile, 26 October 1903; TNA: ADM 144/17, courtesy of Simon Harley.

Not that officers were left without any guidance at all; as Prince Louis of Battenberg, the director of Naval Intelligence, noted in 1904,

> Detailed reports, with plans of all the principal tactical exercises carried out are issued to the Fleet, with a short précis of the principal features of each exercise . . . there is ample material therein for officers who take the trouble to study them to form their own conclusions. If a textbook were issued, it would mean that they were saved the trouble of study by having their conclusions drawn for them, which would be getting near the system of 'Fighting Instructions' which brought Matthews and Byng to grief.[30]

The Admiralty did not depart substantially from this policy in the last years before the war. In late 1913 Battenberg, now First Sea Lord, while agreeing with a proposal that the Naval War Staff compile a book on tactics, insisted that it should not be called a 'Text Book' or 'Manual':

> What is wanted is a compilation of all that has been tried up to date both in the fleet and on the tactical board, accompanied by critical analysis . . . It is quite understood that flag officers shall be given a free hand as to how they will fight their commands but we ought to give them every assistance in forming their opinions . . . [31]

Although the policy that flag officers were free to devise their own tactics is clearly still in force, Battenberg accepted the idea of the Naval Staff providing some form of tactical guidance, and on the eve of the war, the Admiralty was considering the 'formation of a new "Training Division" of the Admiralty War Staff, for the co-ordination of tactical ideas and methods'; but this process was interrupted by the outbreak of war.[32]

---

[30] Marder, *Anatomy of British Sea Power*, 423–4 n.18. The reference is to Thomas Mathews (note spelling), who commanded the British fleet at the indecisive Battle of Toulon in 1744.

[31] 'The Naval War Staff, 1911-1914' (TNA: ADM 1/8377/120). Battenberg's comments are included in the fold-out side-by-side comparison of opinions at the end of this file. These comments probably date from latter part of 1913, as they pertain to the 'Report of the Committee Appointed to Consider the Organisation and Training of the Royal Naval War College . . .', which took evidence in May and June of that year (Admiralty Library, Portsmouth, P 771).

[32] 'Agenda for War Conference'; TNA: ADM 137/1939, 12. The conference was to be held on 24–25 July 1914, but was cancelled due to the European crisis. The 'Training Division' eventually materialised as the Training and Staff Duties Division of the Naval Staff in December 1917; see Admiralty, Naval Staff, Training and Staff Duties Division, *Naval Staff of the Admiralty*, 91–2 (Admiralty Library).

Thus when Jellicoe assumed command of the Grand Fleet on 4 August 1914 there was no navy-wide tactical system in place; his predecessor, Admiral Sir George Callaghan, had issued instructions in the form of memoranda (see Annexe V), but even taken together these did not amount to a complete tactical system; had the fleet gone into battle under Callaghan, much would have depended upon the degree of mutual understanding between him and his subordinates, as developed in discussion, conferences and exercises. This goes far to explain Jellicoe's reluctance to supplant Callaghan at the outset of the war[33] – if the Germans had offered immediate battle, this mutual understanding between the new commander-in-chief and his subordinates would have been lacking.

To rectify this situation, Jellicoe began a programme of intensive fleet exercises; in parallel with these, he began issuing tactical instructions by signal. On 18 August 1914 these were compiled into a three-page memorandum, the first of what would become the Grand Fleet Battle Orders (GFBOs). These were followed by revisions, additions, and addenda, until by December 1915 the GFBOs amounted to about seventy-five pages.[34]

But while the GFBOs filled the gap that the Dewars had identified in British tactical thought – the lack of a 'comprehensive or authoritative tactical doctrine' (Chapter II, Section 9) – they also believed that Jellicoe had created a 'centralised system of command' (Chapter II, Section 12) that gave 'no opportunity for the initiative of subordinates' (Chapter II, Section 23). This meant that Jellicoe's tactics were dependent upon signals from the commander-in-chief; but according to the Dewars 'Signals alone have . . . always failed to obtain a high degree of co-operation' (Chapter II, Section 22 n.57). While admitting that the 'direction of the battle should be centred in the Commander-in-Chief', the Dewars argued that

> instead of trusting to signals to meet emergencies as they arise, or to cut-and-dried plans for meeting emergencies which may not arise . . . [the commander] should rely on the trained judgment and spontaneous action of subordinates to carry out his ideas (Chapter II, Section 23).

---

[33] *Jellicoe Papers*, 1:9, 41–2. This reluctance has sometimes been attributed to Jellicoe wishing to avoid the responsibility of commanding the Grand Fleet, but his concerns over the possible consequences of the sudden removal of Callaghan seem genuine.

[34] After the war, photostatic copies of the GFBOs were gathered into three volumes; see TNA: ADM 116/1341 (before Jutland), ADM 116/1342 (after Jutland), and ADM 116/1343 (in force at Jutland). Excerpts can be found in *Jellicoe Papers*, 1:52–63, 243–53. See also Annexe II in this book for a selection of material from the orders in force at Jutland.

There is a good deal of truth to the Dewars' condemnation, but like so much else in the *Naval Staff Appreciation*, it is overstated and lacks context. If the GFBOs were overly-specific in many places, they also gave subordinates the rationale for many of Jellicoe's tactical precepts – in many places they are more like tactical lectures, explaining why it was important for the battle fleet to manoeuvre in a certain way, or how cruisers should carry out their scouting role, or the best methods for destroyers to attack the enemy's battle line if the opportunity presented itself. In short, the GFBOs were Jellicoe's method of creating and promulgating doctrine.

But while Jellicoe's underlying tactical principles are embedded in these 'lectures', as the Dewars noted, 'The principles of tactics tend to be lost sight of in long detailed instructions' (Chapter II, Section 11). There can be no disputing the fact that the GFBOs were a somewhat jumbled mass of material, with fundamental principles scattered amid orders for specific signals, manoeuvres and formations. Beatty, who assumed command of the Grand Fleet in November 1916, began an overhaul of the orders with his first GFBOs (March 1917), adding a two-page preface that summarised his most important tactical concepts.[35] In the January 1918 edition these were labelled 'General Principles', and the old GFBOs were divided into separate 'Grand Fleet Battle Instructions' (GFBIs) and 'Grand Fleet Manoeuvring Orders' (GFMOs). But while his GFBIs and GFMOs were better organised than Jellicoe's GFBOs, they were also longer and adhered to many of the same principles.[36] Marder provides a fair summary: 'Under both Jellicoe and Beatty . . . the G.F.B.O.s remained excessively wordy, endeavouring as they did to cover all possibilities'.[37]

In the end, we must remember, when criticising Jellicoe's GFBOs, the conditions he faced. It was not the ideal situation the Dewars described when they wrote:

> If tactical principles, standing orders for manœuvring, etc., were embodied in a suitable manual, and continually revised in the light of current experience, an

---

[35] Harper believed that the March 1917 GFBOs were primarily the work of Jellicoe and his staff, and Beatty simply issued them; see Harper to Frewen, 23 December 1944; reproduced in *Beatty Papers*, 2:478–9.

[36] In addition to the set in ADM 116/1342, there are excerpts from Beatty's January 1918 GFBIs in *Beatty Papers*, 1:456–506. There is also a complete set of the January 1918 GFBIs and GFMOs in the US National Archives, presumably issued to the American 6th Battle Squadron when it was attached to the Grand Fleet; NARA: RG 45, Box 225, 'IY – Grand Fleet Battle Instructions & Orders', Folder 5.

[37] Marder, *FDSF*, 3:277.

Admiral on taking command should only have to prepare a short memorandum explaining his particular methods of attack (Chapter II, Section 10).

In fact, there was no 'suitable manual', so in his GFBOs Jellicoe had to combine tactical principles, manoeuvring orders and description of 'his particular methods of attack'. With ships continually joining the fleet, new divisions and flotillas being formed, and officers arriving from other commands, Jellicoe had to promulgate his doctrine in a single accessible form; if in compiling the GFBOs he erred by providing for too many specifics, we would be wise to bear in mind the words of Captain Wayne Hughes, who noted that 'if one must err it is better to do so on the side of too much rather than too little doctrine'.[38]

Jellicoe's Tactics

If one looks past the Dewar brothers' carping criticisms, Chapter II of the *Naval Staff Appreciation* provides an accurate summary of the main features of Jellicoe's tactics: his favoured formation was the single line of battle, with all the dreadnoughts keeping together, and the ideal situation was action on parallel courses. The fleet would deploy at long range, and would gradually close with the enemy as British fire grew in effectiveness (the September 1914 GFBOs envisaged ranges between 12,000 and 9,000 yards, increased to between 15,000 and 10,000 yards by the time of Jutland).[39] The Grand Fleet's numerical superiority would be used to concentrate fire on the leading German battleships, while the battle cruisers and the fast battleships of the 5th BS would attack the flanks (van and rear) of the enemy's line. The fleet's cruisers, light

---

[38] Hughes, *Fleet Tactics*, 30. A final point: Historically, Royal Navy usage defined 'orders' as commands that must be obeyed, whereas 'instructions' were general guidelines. As a result, because they were labelled 'orders', Jellicoe's GFBOs have sometimes been interpreted as mandatory commands. But Jellicoe does not appear to have accepted (or even been aware of) this distinction – and the same could probably be said of most of his admirals and captains. As a result the Grand Fleet Battle Orders combine both 'instructions' and 'orders'. See [Richmond], 'Orders and Instructions' for a discussion of the general point.

[39] Professor Jon T Sumida argues that Jellicoe did not intend to fight at long range, but at medium ranges – which he defines as 7,000–10,000 yards – delivering a massive 'pulse' of fire for 5–8 minutes before ordering a simultaneous turn-away to avoid torpedoes fired by the German battle line. Sumida calls this hypothesis the 'new technical-tactical synthesis', arguing that the GFBOs were a stopgap, and that as soon as Jellicoe had accumulated the ships and fire-control gear necessary, he intended to introduce his new scheme. Having read a substantial number of pre-war and wartime tactical documents, I find this hypothesis unconvincing, and therefore have taken no account of it in what follows. Readers wishing to explore Sumida's ideas should see the following articles: Sumida, 'A Matter of Timing' and 'Expectation, Adaptation, and Resignation'. For opposing arguments, see Brooks, 'Preparing for Armageddon' and McLaughlin, 'Battle Lines and Fast Wings'.

cruisers and destroyers would prevent their German counterparts from interfering with the work of the battleships.

The Dewars take issue with most of these tactical concepts. The fundamental disagreement is with the single line of battle as a fighting formation. They note that

> In the sailing ship period, the rigid formula of the long line always failed to bring about decisive results, and it was finally discredited after numerous failures and endless courts-martial (Chapter II, Section 16).

The problem with the line as they saw it was that it made it almost impossible to achieve any form of concentration on the enemy:

> the whole art of tactics consists in massing superior forces against part of the opposing fleet, and battles are not won by applying equal pressure all along the line. In every case there is one part of the line the defeat of which will bring about the collapse of the whole (Chapter II, Section 17).

In the eyes of the Dewars and others of like mind, the single line could not concentrate on a part of the enemy's fleet, and therefore its revival in the early years of the twentieth century was a fundamental error based on a profound ignorance of the lessons of the past. In seeking an alternative, they looked for their inspiration to Nelson's crushing victory at Trafalgar (21 October 1805). Instead of manoeuvring to form line of battle against the Franco-Spanish fleet, Nelson approached headlong in two divisions, slicing the enemy line into three separate pieces that could be individually overwhelmed. The Dewars believed that, like Nelson's fleet at Trafalgar, a large modern fleet should be divided into independently manoeuvring units that would act in accordance with general instructions issued by the commanding admiral; any attempt at centralised control by a single admiral would inevitably break down in the smoke and confusion of battle.

This method of attack came to be known as 'divisional tactics', and there was certainly much to be said in their favour, but the Dewars, in their zeal to promote them, overlooked several factors that should have moderated their criticisms of Jellicoe's tactics as applied at Jutland. For example, they ignored the fact that there was a difference in basic competence between the French and Spanish navies faced by Nelson and the German navy faced by Jellicoe. Nelson knew his captains and crews were superior in seamanship and gunnery to his enemies, and the implications of this were recognised by the historian Sir Julian Corbett – who was definitely not an advocate for the line of battle – when he noted of Nelson's approach at Trafalgar that 'against an enemy of equal spirit each ship must have been crushed as she came into action'.[40] Unlike Nelson, in the High Seas Fleet Jellicoe faced a competent enemy, a fact he recognised all too clearly: 'The German Fleet has shown itself to be highly efficient and their gunnery in any action in which they have not been hopelessly inferior has been markedly excellent.'[41] Jellicoe believed – correctly – that he was dealing with an opponent with whom it would have been unwise to take the sort of tactical liberties that Nelson had.

Another fundamental difference between Nelson's day and Jellicoe's concerned the ability of ships in line to concentrate their fire. The Dewars wrote:

> The word concentration is used here in its tactical and not in its gunnery sense. At the time of Jutland the technique of modern gun concentration was comparatively undeveloped, but tactical concentration is as old as fighting at sea (Chapter II, Section 17 n.34).

This statement is to some degree nonsensical, since the entire purpose of *tactical* concentration in the sailing era was to bring a preponderance of *gunfire* against a single enemy vessel or group of vessels – that is, to achieve gunnery concentration. Given short-ranged guns with limited arcs of fire, concentration could be achieved only by bringing two or more ships against one enemy vessel. Matters were entirely different with dreadnoughts, thanks to long-ranged guns that could be concentrated on a single enemy simply by having several ships aim their turrets at the same target. Certainly there were fire-control issues to be sorted out, but before Jutland it was believed that these had been solved:

> When concentration is possible, *pairs* will give the best results, as mutual interference to observation of fire is then practically negligible; three or four ships can, however, concentrate effectively on one if the conditions are sufficiently good to admit of spotting and so keeping the range.[42]

Although this view proved optimistic, there seemed to be good reason for Jellicoe and other advocates of the single line to believe that massing gunfire

---

[40] Corbett, *Fighting Instructions*, 300. For Corbett's view that the line of battle was a 'fetish', see p 284.

[41] Jellicoe to Admiralty, 19 November 1914; *Jellicoe Papers*, 1:97.

[42] GFBOs, XV – 'Distribution of Gunfire' (December 1915), TNA: ADM 116/1343; emphasis in the original. See also Home Fleets General Order No. 15, 'Distribution of Gunfire' (8 December 1913), 2–3, for several methods of concentrating fire; TNA: ADM 137/260.

could achieve decisive results without the need for the 'tactical concentration' by manoeuvre.

The differing views on the nature of concentration are directly connected to the role of the fast battleships of the 5th BS and of the battle cruisers in a fleet action. Jellicoe's instructions to the 5th BS are a good example of the Dewars' contention that the GFBOs attempted to lay down cut-and-dried rules for too many possible situations – what to do if the fleet deploys towards or away from Heligoland, if the enemy battle cruisers are at the head or tail of his line, if the British battle cruisers are present or absent – nevertheless, the basic concept is clear: the fast battleships will use their speed to 'attack the enemy van [or rear] ships from a commanding position'.[43] In other words, they would concentrate their fire on the head or tail of the German fleet; Jellicoe envisaged them operating as much as five or six miles ahead of the line of battle. The battle cruisers would play a similar role, if they were not too busy coping with their opposite numbers.[44]

To the Dewars, however, there was no advantage in this employment of fast ships:

> the 5th Battle Squadron and Battle Cruiser Force were detached from [the line of battle], and at first sight this might seem to imply an intention for this fast and powerful force to co-operate with the Battle Fleet in an overwhelming attack on part of the High Sea Fleet. But this was apparently not the intention of the Orders, for these vessels were merely directed to engage the opposing battle cruisers and prolong the line of deployment . . . (Chapter II, Section 17).

The difference between Jellicoe's intentions and the Dewars' interpretation is stark: to Jellicoe, the fast squadrons would be used to attack the enemy 'from a commanding position' and so help to achieve an overwhelming concentration of fire; but to the Dewars, since these units would merely 'prolong the line of deployment', they could not assist in achieving a meaningful 'tactical' concentration.

These disagreements outlined above could be put down to differences of opinion over details; but the *Naval Staff Appreciation* also levels a more damning charge at Jellicoe:

---

[43] GFBOs, V – 'Orders for 5th Battle Squadron'; TNA: ADM 116/1343.

[44] GFBOs, XXIV – 'Duties of Battle-Cruisers, Cruisers, and Light-Cruisers in a Fleet Action', sec. b, Battle Cruisers; TNA: ADM 116/1343.

The theory of the defensive is . . . so consistently implied in the Grand Fleet Orders,[45] that a determination to run no risks must be regarded as part of its Commander-in-Chief's considered policy (Chapter II, Section 20).

Certainly defensive precautions form a major theme of the GFBOs, especially regarding underwater weapons; the dangers of mines and torpedoes clearly weighed heavily on Jellicoe's mind. In his 30 October 1914 letter to the Admiralty (reproduced in Annexe I), he had noted:

It is quite within the bounds of possibility that half our battlefleet might be disabled by under-water attack before the guns opened fire at all, if a false move is made, and I feel that I must constantly bear in mind the great probability of such attack and be prepared tactically to prevent its success.

Jellicoe's concerns fell into three general areas; submarine traps, the use of mines by the High Seas Fleet, and torpedo attacks by the enemy's destroyers. By limiting discussion of these issues to the GFBOs, the Dewars give the impression that these concerns were the products of Jellicoe's own cautious imagination. In point of fact many of the Royal Navy's senior officers shared these concerns. For example, as early as August 1912 his predecessor, Admiral Sir George Callaghan, had noted: 'We believe that it is the intention of certain foreign powers to use both destroyers and submarines in combination with the battle fleet in action . . .'[46] Even the aggressive Admiral Beatty turned away from an imaginary periscope during the Dogger Bank action (24 January 1915). Nor was the fear of submarines purely speculative; they had already caused grievous losses, and as Jellicoe wrote:

The submarine menace both before action, during passage south, and during action is going to be our great trouble. All our tactical games show how difficult they are to deal with in action, and how very easy their chances of hitting a line after deployment . . . [47]

---

[45] Here the Dewars have made a terminological error: the 'Grand Fleet Orders' were entirely separate from the Grand Fleet *Battle* Orders; the former cover a wide variety of topics, including orders for exercises, gunnery practices, movements of individual ships, procedural matters, etc. Specimens can be found in TNA: ADM 137/2020 and ADM 137/4051.

[46] Callaghan to Admiralty, 3 August 1912, quoted in Brooks, 'Grand Battle-Fleet Tactics', 195.

[47] Jellicoe to Beatty, 23 June 1915; *Jellicoe Papers*, 1:168–9.

Thus, while the Dewars dismiss the possibility of submarines being used in a fleet action (Chapter II, Section 24), attributing Jellicoe's concerns to cautiousness, this was in fact a more general concern among the RN's senior officers, and had been tested in tactical games. The assumptions underlying this concern may have been incorrect, but no one could know this until the issue was tried in actual combat.

The same can be said of the other elements of the 'theory of the defensive' that the Dewars detected in the GFBOs. This can clearly be seen regarding the tactical use of mines. As early as 1906 the naval attaché in Germany noted this possibility,[48] and in 1911 the German naval journal *Mitteilungen aus dem Gebiete des Seewesens* published an article that discussed the use of mines during a fleet action.[49] It is therefore hardly surprising that the GFBOs warned:

> When engaging the enemy's battlefleet it must be borne in mind that all German destroyers carry mines, and that it is therefore highly dangerous to cross a locality that has been occupied by those vessels.[50]

But it is important to stress that this concern was also not unique to Jellicoe; admirals usually considered more aggressive than Jellicoe were equally worried about the mine threat. Admiral Sir Frederick Doveton Sturdee, whose views on tactics were otherwise very different to those of Jellicoe, noted in the tactical instructions he issued before the Battle of the Falkland Islands (8 December 1914), that 'The danger from mines dropped by the retiring enemy Cruisers must be guarded against. Ships should avoid crossing any track passed over by the enemy . . .'[51] Beatty showed a similar concern about the possibility that the German destroyers were manoeuvring to drop mines in his path during the battle of Dogger Bank (24 January 1915).[52] This was simply another of the ideas prevalent in the Royal Navy prior to Jutland.

Jellicoe's views on the role of his destroyers also reflected widespread views; before the war there had been extensive discussion of whether their primary duty was to attack the enemy's battle fleet with their torpedoes, or to defend

---

[48] Heath's report, 16 November 1906; Seligmann (ed.), *Naval Intelligence from Germany*, 196.

[49] See the translation in 'Mining Warfare – A Sketch of Possibilities'; NARA: RG 38, Folder P-11-b.

[50] Grand Fleet Battle Orders, 18 August 1914; TNA: ADM 116/1341.

[51] Sturdee's memorandum, 25 November 1914; CAC: SDEE/2/6 part 13, Folder labelled 'Fighting Instructions'.

[52] Goldrick, *The King's Ships were at Sea*, 265–6.

their own fleet against torpedo attacks by the enemy's destroyers.[53] In his 1912 'War Orders' Jellicoe came down firmly on the offensive side of the debate: 'The purpose of . . . the Destroyers . . . is to attack the enemy's Battle Line'.[54] But by the time the first GFBOs were issued on 18 August 1914, a defensive turn of mind is evident, and the destroyers' tasks are evenly split between attacking the enemy's battle fleet and guarding their own against German torpedo attacks.[55] By the end of August, the balance had tipped decisively toward defence: 'It is impressed on all destroyer officers that their primary duty is to stop the German destroyers by engaging them in close action.'[56]

The reason for this evolution from offensive to defensive use of destroyers was Jellicoe's firm belief that 'we shall probably be largely outnumbered in torpedo craft'.[57] In October 1915 he 'assumed that the Germans will have at least eight flotillas, viz., eighty-eight boats' – a number that would overwhelm his cruiser screen.[58] The only way to stop a German torpedo onslaught on this scale, in Jellicoe's view, was to use his destroyers defensively.

These fears regarding torpedoes and mines turned out to be exaggerated – but this fact came to light *as a result* of Jutland; given the predicted effectiveness of these weapons, widely canvassed by their enthusiasts before the war, caution was probably wise until the event proved otherwise. Put another way, the Dewar brothers build their case for a super-cautious Jellicoe by ignoring the fact that his concerns were shared by many senior officers, even ones regarded as more aggressive.

If Jellicoe's tactics erred on the side of caution, the divisional tactics the Dewar brothers so ardently advocated would have been out-and-out reckless in the visibility conditions prevailing at Jutland. Separated divisions operating beyond the range of mutual support exposed a stronger fleet to the danger of piecemeal defeat, as the GFBOs expressly pointed out.[59] Poor visibility would make the isolation of an independently-manoeuvring formation all the more likely, and it was for this reason that Admiral May, in his pre-war tactical

---

[53] For a complete discussion of this topic, see Brooks, 'Grand Battle-Fleet Tactics: From the Edwardian Age to Jutland'.

[54] 'The Use of Torpedo Craft and Light Cruisers', 'My War Orders and Dispositions . . . . Prepared when in 2nd Division, Home Fleet', reproduced in *Jellicoe Papers*, 1:25.

[55] GFBOs, 'Destroyer Flotillas', 18 August 1914; TNA: ADM 116/1341. Reproduced in *Jellicoe Papers*, 1:57–8.

[56] GFBOs IV, 'General Remarks', GFBOs, Addendum No. 2, 31 August 1914; TNA: ADM 116/1341; reproduced in *Jellicoe Papers*, 1:60.

[57] GFBOs, Destroyer Addendum, 1 October 1915; TNA: ADM 116/1643.

[58] GFBOs, Destroyer Addendum, para. 24, 1 October 1915; TNA: ADM 116/143.

[59] GFBOs, V, 'Orders for 5th Battle Squadron', para. 4; VII, 'Battle Tactics', para. 3; VIII, 'Conduct of a Fleet in Action', para. 8.

exercises, discussed only 'Divisional Attack in *Clear* Weather' [emphasis added].[60] Visibility at Jutland was not at all clear, and even the German Official History noted:

> In view of the low visibility then ruling and the lateness of the hour, co-operation between squadrons acting independently would have been so uncertain that the danger of the enemy overwhelming a part of the British Fleet with the whole of his force could not be overlooked.[61]

Indeed, Admiral Sturdee – a proponent of divisional tactics – noted in his report that 'There was considerable difficulty in distinguishing friend from foe owing to these large fleets meeting in varying visibility'.[62]

A final comment about divisional tactics before moving on: despite the fact that the *Appreciation* praises the German system of command for its decentralisation, divisional tactics seem to have played no role in the High Seas Fleet's tactical thinking; as the German official history noted,

> . . . the German plan of battle differed in no way from the British, namely, that the squadrons should, on encountering the enemy, deploy from a wide preparatory formation into a line of battle from which all guns could be brought to bear simultaneously, with the enemy being abaft the beam, if possible.[63]

In fact, despite the Dewar brothers' insistence on the evident superiority of divisional tactics, it would seem that none of the world's navies adopted them before or during the First World War, with the exception of the Russian navy.[64] Their arguments for decentralised tactics were valid, but by insisting that they should have been employed at Jutland, where conditions were so clearly unsuited to them, the Dewars actually undermined their case.

The Performance of British Officers

While the courage, seamanship and technical skills of the Royal Navy's officers at Jutland are unquestioned, there remains the fact that many failed to show initiative in the stress of combat. The *Appreciation* points out a number of instances of this, especially during the night after the battle; perhaps the most

---

[60] May, *Notes on Tactical Exercises. Home Fleet. 1909-1911*, 237–410; Admiralty Library.

[61] Tarrant, *Jutland*, 147, quoting Groos, *Der Krieg in der Nordsee*, 5:306–8.

[62] 'Vice-Admirals' Reports, 4th Battle Squadron'; *Official Despatches*, 123. See also the report of *Superb*, where it is noted that the 'Chief difficulty throughout action was making certain between friend and foe'; *Official Despatches*, 367.

[63] Marder, *FDSF*, 3:119–20 n. 33, quoting Groos, *Der Krieg in der Nordsee*, 5:300–1 n.

[64] Hone, 'United States: The US Navy', 273–5; McLaughlin, 'Russia: Rossiikii imperatorskii

egregious examples concerned sightings of the German battle cruiser *Seydlitz*. Badly damaged and proceeding independently, at about 10.30 pm she ran into *Thunderer* (2nd Battle Squadron, 2nd Division), challenged her with *German* recognition signals (red and green lights), and yet *Thunderer* did nothing before the wounded German ship slipped back into the darkness.[65] Next, at about 12:30 am, *Seydlitz* bounced off the 1st Battle Squadron (which had fallen behind the fleet because of flagship *Marlborough*'s reduced speed due to torpedo damage); challenged by *Revenge*, she gave the wrong reply, but the British ship still did not open fire.[66] A single salvo probably would have finished off *Seydlitz*, but she was allowed to go on her way unmolested.

There is, however, a mitigating factor: the Russo-Japanese War had demonstrated that it was unwise for a battle fleet to reveal its location to prowling torpedo craft, and this consideration seems to have been uppermost in the mind of *Thunderer*'s captain, who stated that he did not open fire because 'it was considered inadvisable to show up [the] battle fleet'.[67] Similarly, *Agincourt*, the second ship astern of *Revenge*, also saw the *Seydlitz* but her captain decided against challenging her as he did not want to 'give our Division's position away'.[68] Clearly they considered it vital to keep the fleet's position concealed lest enemy flotilla craft locate and attack it.

Less explicable is the fact that none of these ships reported what they had seen to Jellicoe; moreover, the *Malaya* and *Valiant* of the 5th Battle Squadron saw German battleships at about 11:30 pm, and also failed to make any report to the Commander-in-Chief.[69] Nor did any of the destroyers report their run-ins with German heavy ships, except for Captain A J B Sterling, commanding the 12th Destroyer Flotilla in *Faulknor*; unfortunately not one of his three reports was received by Jellicoe.[70] Destroyer W/T sets were relatively weak, and *Faulknor*'s reports may simply have been lost in the clutter of radio noise, or the Germans may have been jamming.

The destroyers were involved in short, sharp actions that gave little opportunity for them to make reports until afterwards; most of them probably

---

flot', 232; Evans and Peattie, *Kaigun*, 144–6. Among the American supporters of divisional tactics was Dudley Knox; see his article '"Column" as a Battle Formation', which calls them 'group tactics'.

[65] *Official Despatches*, 114.

[66] *Official Despatches*, 68, 86.

[67] *Official Despatches*, 114.

[68] *Official Despatches*, 93.

[69] *Official Despatches*, 211, 219–20.

[70] *Official Despatches*, 478; Marder, *FDSF*, 3:166.

assumed that their leaders would handle any communications necessary. But none of the leaders did so. The most likely explanation is that they didn't realise that what they had seen was important; as the Dewars note,

> Admiral Jellicoe states that it [i.e., the stationing of the destroyers five miles astern of the battle fleet] was intended to provide the Battle Fleet with a screen against torpedo attack, and also to give them a chance of attacking the enemy's heavy ships should they also be proceeding to the southward. But this was not communicated to the destroyers, and not a word was told them of the formation and disposition of their own fleet nor of the position and probable course of the enemy (Chapter XI, Section 76).

This was certainly a serious lapse on the part of Jellicoe and his staff. The destroyers, not having been briefed on the location of their own fleet, often hesitated before taking action when unknown ships loomed out of the darkness. Moreover, since they had not been informed of Jellicoe's intentions – keeping the enemy fleet to the westward by barring its path – they did not realise that the appearance of the German capital ships astern of the battle fleet and heading eastwards was an important piece of information. So they did not report it.

The above points are not meant as excuses for inactivity; at best, they are partial, not complete, explanations. Individual failures can always be pardoned, but the fact that so many officers at Jutland did not take action when presented with opportunities to strike at the enemy leaves one with the uncomfortable impression that, with some notable exceptions, something was fundamentally wrong with the Royal Navy's officer corps. Certainly Jellicoe himself had doubts about the quality of his senior officers; in 1915 he noted that his 'Vice-Admirals are always a little shaky'; he also worried that the strain was too much for the more elderly admirals.[71] Ten days before Jutland, Jellicoe wrote to the first sea lord to discuss possible commanders for the 1st Battle Squadron, and his evaluation of the candidates makes for depressing reading. Charles Madden, Jellicoe's Chief of Staff, was the best of the bunch, but he was more useful where was. Of the rest, only Vice-Admiral Sir Stanley Colville stood out, and even so Jellicoe noted that he was 'not . . . brilliant but he is sound, has had more experience than anyone else and is physically fit'.[72] Hardly a ringing endorsement of the man who would lead the entire British battle line!

---

[71] Letter to Admiral Sir Henry Jackson, First Sea Lord, 16 June 1916 (*Jellicoe Papers*, 1:167).
[72] Letter to Admiral Sir Henry Jackson, 21 May 1916 (*Jellicoe Papers*, 1:241).

Among the explanations for the apparent dearth of talent in the Royal Navy's senior ranks is the possibility that some peacetime practices in officer postings were given too much weight in wartime, that seniority counted for too much in spite of the urgent demands of war. Perhaps there was also insufficient ruthlessness in weeding out substandard men. There are hints of these factors being at work, but without an in-depth study of the Royal Navy's officer corps in this era, it is impossible to be certain if these causes were operating, and, if so, to what degree.

In recent times historians have ascribed the failings noted at Jutland to more fundamental causes; Stephen Roskill, for example, contends that

> . . . the whole system of training junior officers in the *Britannia* and later at Osborne and Dartmouth Colleges was based on unquestioning discipline and absolute subordination to authority. More gold braid, we were taught, necessarily meant more wisdom; and any signs of originality were frowned on if not actively suppressed. This state of affairs lasted into my own time at the naval colleges (1917–20), and indeed until World War II.[73]

Andrew Gordon, while agreeing with these observations, digs deeper for their roots, arguing that a Victorian passion for order and control fostered the hierarchical system described by Roskill.[74] These are very large issues – too large to discuss usefully here. For the Dewars, however, the inadequacies of British officers were due to more immediate causes. In his pre-war articles Kenneth Dewar had noted that

> . . . when everything is regulated from above, initiative and enthusiasm amongst subordinates are quickly killed, and . . . if such qualities are not developed amongst juniors, they will be wanting in the senior ranks.
>
> . . .
>
> . . . an army or navy's system of command and the character of its officers react on each other, and . . . a centralized [*sic*] and formal system destroys initiative and enthusiasm.[75]

---

[73] Roskill, *Admiral of the Fleet Earl Beatty*, 186; see also 21–2, where Roskill says that the training of naval cadets 'stifled any tendency to show originality'.

[74] Gordon, *Rules of the Game*, *passim*; see also Gordon, '1914-18: The Proof of the Pudding' for a condensed version of this thesis.

[75] [Kenneth Dewar], 'Executive Command and Staff in Naval Warfare', part 1, 65 and part 3, 3.

These views are reflected in the *Appreciation*, where there are frequent references to the evils of centralisation (e.g., Chapter IX, Section 57; Chapter XII, Section 88). Despite a tendency to attribute all failings to this cause, there is probably much truth to this claim.

Finally, there was the problem of the unknowns of naval warfare in the early twentieth century. Although he was greatly influenced by the *Naval Staff Appreciation*, Churchill's broader intellect recognised something the Dewars failed to grasp:

> . . .nothing like this particular event [i.e., Jutland] had ever happened before, and nothing like it was ever to happen again. The 'Nelson touch' arose from years of fighting between the strongest ships of the time. Nelson's genius enabled him to measure truly the consequences of any decision. But that genius worked upon precise practical data. He had seen the same sort of thing happen on a less great scale many times over before the Battle of Trafalgar. Nelson did not have to worry about underwater damage. He felt he knew what would happen in a fleet action. Jellicoe did not know. Nobody knew.[76]

How effective was long-range gunfire? How many hits would it take to disable a dreadnought? Could enemy destroyers be stopped before they launched shoals of torpedoes? No one knew the answer to these questions. As a result there was perhaps a lack of confidence – not the boastful confidence of pre-war days, but the quiet confidence that comes from knowing, as Nelson and his captains knew, what to expect of their ships, their men, their weapons – and of their enemies.

For Jellicoe in particular, those unknowns were magnified by a simple fact: the Grand Fleet was the final safeguard of the British Empire and the Allied cause. If it vanished in some great cataclysm, not only the periphery, but the British Isles themselves would be vulnerable to invasion and defeat. Aware of the great responsibility that rested upon his shoulders, confronted by the untested potential of underwater weapons, and possessing a calculating mind that emphasised dangers over opportunities, Sir John Jellicoe erred on the side of caution at Jutland. He was certainly no Nelson; but then again, perhaps even Nelson would have been daunted by the responsibilities and unknowns that loomed in the mists of Jutland.

Lessons Learnt

The central tactical concept advocated so forcefully in the *Naval Staff Appreciation of Jutland* – the need for decentralisation – had become generally

---

[76] Churchill, *World Crisis*, vol. 3, pt. 1, pp. 131–2.

accepted in the Royal Navy by the 1930s,[77] but it would be going too far to claim that this demonstrated the influence of the *Appreciation* itself. Few officers had access to it after its recall in 1922, and fewer still after most copies were destroyed in 1930. It would be more correct to trace the acceptance of this idea more directly to Jutland; as Stephen Roskill wrote, '. . . it is no exaggeration to say that in the early 1920s the Royal Navy was obsessed by the lessons learnt from the indecisive clash with the High Seas Fleet in May 1916'.[78]

The need for more decentralisation was one of those lessons. If, as Roskill maintains, the 1920s was a 'period of tactical sterility',[79] the 1930s saw a blossoming of tactical innovations, many of which had their roots in the dissatisfaction with the results of Jutland. Night fighting by destroyers and capital ships was honed to a fine edge, and methods for close-range fighting – now considered by many officers as best suited to the British navy's strengths – were investigated. Much of this tactical ferment was fuelled by concerns over the fact that both the United States and Japan were outspending the Royal Navy when it came to capital ship modernisation, leading to a desire to compensate for ageing equipment by better tactics.[80] In many ways the centrepiece of these tactical innovations was decentralisation; as the U.S. naval attaché reported in November 1938, during a conversation with a British captain who had been on the staff of the Tactical School, the latter

. . . stated with emphasis that the present School of British Tactics considers tactical decentralization as almost a fetish. This he ascribes to the lessons of the war . . . He is in general agreement with this fundamental idea, but believes it is now being carried somewhat too far as regards the battle line.[81]

Although decentralisation is not necessarily the same thing as the Dewar brothers' brand of divisional tactics, there can be no doubt that several prominent British commanders of the Second World War did employ such tactics – Commodore Henry Harwood used them at the battle of the River Plate

---

[77] The published sources for tactics between the world wars are far from complete; most useful is Moretz, *Royal Navy and the Capital Ship in the Interwar Period*, Chapter 7; Roskill, *Naval Policy between the Wars*, 1:531–7, provides some material, based for the most part on reminiscences and correspondence; and Sumida, '"The Best Laid Plans"' offers some interesting insights.

[78] Roskill, *Naval Policy Between the Wars*, 1:533.

[79] Roskill, *Naval Policy Between the Wars*, 1:534.

[80] Sumida, '"The Best Laid Plans"', 687–8.

[81] U.S. naval attaché, London, 'British Naval Tactics', 29 November 1938; NARA: RG 38, P-11-b, folder 'Tactical Policy, and Tactics, British Navy'.

(13 December 1939),[82] Admiral Sir John Tovey granted *Rodney*'s captain freedom to manoeuvre independently 'provided he conformed generally to the Admiral's movements' during the final action with the *Bismarck*[83] (a proviso that Captain Dalrymple-Hamilton interpreted very broadly, with Tovey's approval) and Admirals Cunningham and Fraser were proponents of decentralised tactics.[84]

If Jutland eventually fostered a trend toward decentralisation, it also provided another element that made it worthwhile: battle experience. The twin bogeyman of the torpedo and mine were cut down to proper size and the exaggerated fears of their dangers no longer dominated tactical thought as they had in 1914–18. Without the confidence gained from the experience of actual battle, it is unlikely that British naval officers would have handled their ships as boldly as they did in the second war, no matter how much decentralisation had been encouraged in peacetime. It is almost impossible to imagine an admiral of the First World War taking a battleship up a narrow fjord infested with destroyers and U-boats; but that is exactly what Admiral Sir William Whitworth did with *Warspite* on 13 April 1940.[85] The battle of the Barents Sea (31 December 1942) offers another example of a group of ships handled boldly in the face of superior forces. The attack by 26th Destroyer Flotilla on the Japanese heavy cruiser *Haguro* (16 May 1945) was a classic example of an aggressive flotilla action at night. Other examples could be found – as could counter-examples. The point can certainly be argued, but the impression remains that on the whole in the Second World War the Royal Navy was led by bolder senior officers than it had been in the first war.

For all the flaws of the *Naval Staff Appreciation*, its core principle – the need to foster tactical decentralisation and the initiative of subordinates – was a key asset in the greater and more desperate fight the Navy would face in the Second World War. Although many of the first war's lessons were lost or misunderstood, the doctrine of decentralisation ensured that the Royal Navy would have the resilience to cope with the challenges when the new war came.

* * *

The lessons of Jutland were taken to heart by the RN. Those lost are commemorated in stone and the occasional ceremony, but their real memorial lies within the Royal Navy's 21st-century doctrine:

[82] Roskill, *Naval Policy Between the Wars*, 2:533 n.4.
[83] Grenfell, *The Bismarck Episode*, 178. Tovey had commanded the destroyer *Onslow* at Jutland.
[84] Sumida, "'The Best Laid Plans'", 695–6.
[85] Roskill, *HMS Warspite*, 202–8.

Modern communications present commanders with two interconnected challenges. The first is the risk of superior levels of command 'micro-managing' operations at lower levels. The second is too heavy a reliance on communications, which has the effect of undermining the longer-term ability of subordinates to take the initiative . . . [Commanders must] avoid over immersion in matters of detail that are the job of their staff, and delegate as much as possible to subordinates. They issue clear and concise orders and leave their staff to work out the details.[86]

---

[86] *British Defence Doctrine*, 2001, Chapter Seven: 'The Philosophy of Command', 7-1 and 7-4.

Annexe I:
Jellicoe's Letter to the Admiralty, 30 October 1914

This is the well-known letter from Admiral Jellicoe to the Admiralty, referred to several times in Chapter II of the Naval Staff Appreciation, *outlining his intended tactics should he encounter the German Fleet – paragraphs 10 and 11 are often quoted. Arthur Marder has pointed out that it was written just before the court martial of Admiral Troubridge for the escape of* Goeben *to Turkey. This letter has been transcribed from* The Jellicoe Papers, *edited by A. Temple Patterson, 1:75–9. The 1st and 3rd Destroyer Flotillas referred to were part of the Harwich Force, under Commodore Reginald Tyrwhitt.*

Iron Duke
30th October, 1914.
The experience gained of German methods since the commencement of the war makes it possible and very desirable to consider the manner in which these methods are likely to be made use of tactically in a fleet action.

2. The Germans have shown that they rely to a very great extent on submarines, mines, and torpedoes, and there can be no doubt whatever that they will endeavour to make the fullest use of these weapons in a fleet action, especially since they possess an actual superiority over us in these particular directions.

3. It, therefore, becomes necessary to consider our own tactical methods in relation to these forms of attack.

4. In the first place, it is evident that the Germans cannot rely with certainty upon having their full complement of submarines and minelayers present in a fleet action, unless the battle is fought in waters selected by them and in the Southern area of the North Sea. Aircraft, also, could only be brought into action in this locality.

5. My object will therefore be to fight the fleet action in the Northern portion of the North Sea, which position is incidentally nearer our own bases, giving our wounded ships a chance of reaching them, whilst it ensures the final destruction or capture of enemy wounded vessels, and greatly handicaps a night destroyer attack before or after a fleet action. The Northern area is also favourable to a concentration of our cruisers and torpedo craft with the battlefleet; such concentration on the part of the enemy being always possible, since he will choose a time for coming out when all his ships are coaled and ready in all respects to fight.

6. Owing to the necessity that exists for keeping our cruisers at sea, it is probable that many will be short of coal when the opportunity for a fleet action arises, and they might be unable to move far to the Southward for this reason.

7. The presence of a large force of cruisers is most necessary, for observation and for screening the battlefleet, so that the latter may be manoeuvred into any desired position behind the cruiser screen. This is a strong additional reason for fighting in the Northern area.

8. Secondly, it is necessary to consider what may be termed the tactics of the actual

battlefield. The German submarines, if worked as expected with the battlefleet, can be used in one of two ways:

(a) With the cruisers, or possibly with destroyers.

(b) With the battlefleet.

In the first case the submarines would probably be led by the cruisers to a position favourable for attacking our battlefleet as it advanced to deploy, and in the second case they might be kept in a position in rear, or to the flank, of the enemy's battlefleet, which would move in the direction required to draw our own Fleet into contact with the submarines.

9. The first move at (a) should be defeated by our own cruisers, provided we have a sufficient number present, as they should be able to force the enemy's cruisers to action at a speed which would interfere with submarine tactics.

The cruisers must, however, have destroyers in company to assist in dealing with the submarines, and should be well in advance of the battlefleet; hence the necessity for numbers.

10. The second move at (b) can be countered by judicious handling of our battlefleet, but may, and probably will, involve a refusal to comply with the enemy's tactics by moving in the invited direction. If, for instance, the enemy battlefleet were to turn away from an advancing Fleet, I should assume that the intention was to lead us over mines and submarines, and should decline to be so drawn.

11. I desire particularly to draw the attention of Their Lordships to this point, since it may be deemed a refusal of battle, and, indeed, might possibly result in failure to bring the enemy to action as soon as is expected and hoped.

12. Such a result would be absolutely repugnant to the feelings of all British Naval Officers and men, but with new and untried methods of warfare new tactics must be devised to meet them.

I feel that such tactics, if not understood, may bring odium upon me, but so long as I have the confidence of their Lordships I intend to pursue what is, in my considered opinion, the proper course to defeat and annihilate the enemy's battlefleet, without regard to uninstructed opinion or criticism.

13. The situation is a difficult one. It is quite within the bounds of possibility that half our battlefleet might be disabled by under-water attack before the guns opened fire at all, if a false move is made, and I feel that I must constantly bear in mind the great probability of such attack and be prepared tactically to prevent its success.

14. The safeguard against submarines will consist in moving the battlefleet at very high speed to a flank before deployment takes place or the gun action commences.

This will take us off the ground on which the enemy desires to fight, but it may, of course, result in his refusal to follow me.

If the battlefleets remain within sight of one another, though not near the original area, the limited submerged radius of action and speed of the submarines will prevent the submarines from following without coming to the surface, and I should feel that after an interval of high speed manoeuvring I could safely close.

15. The object of this letter is to place my views before their Lordships, and to direct their attention to the alterations in pre-conceived ideas of battle tactics which are forced

upon us by the anticipated appearance in a fleet action of submarines and minelayers.

16. There can be no doubt that the fullest use will also be made by the enemy of surface torpedo craft.

This point has been referred to in previous letters to their Lordships, and, so long as the whole of the First Fleet Flotillas are with the Fleet, the hostile destroyers will be successfully countered and engaged.

The necessity for attaching some destroyers to Cruiser Squadrons, alluded to in paragraph 9, emphasizes the necessity for the junction of the 1st and 3rd Flotillas with the Fleet before a fleet action takes place.

17. It will, however, be very desirable that all available ships and torpedo craft should be ordered to the position of the fleet action as soon as it is known to be imminent, as the presence of even Third Fleet vessels after the action or towards its conclusion may prove of great assistance in rendering the victory shattering and complete.

The Channel Fleet should be accompanied by as many destroyers, drawn from the Dover or Coast patrols, as can be spared.

I trust that their Lordships will give the necessary orders on the receipt of information from me of an impending fleet action.

18. In the event of a fleet action being imminent, or, indeed, as soon as the High Sea Fleet is known to be moving Northward, it is most desirable that a considerable number of our oversea submarines should proceed towards the Fleet, getting first onto the line between the Germans and Heligoland in order to intercept them when returning. The German Fleet would probably arrange its movements so as to pass Heligoland at dusk when coming out and at dawn when returning, in order to minimise submarine risk. The opportunity for submarine attack in the Heligoland Bight would not therefore be very great, and from 4 to 6 submarines would be the greatest number that could be usefully employed there. The remainder, accompanied by one or two light cruisers, taken, if necessary, from the Dover patrol, should work up towards the position of the fleet, the light cruisers keeping in wireless touch with me.

The Admiralty's response:
Admiralty,
7th November 1914.

I have laid before My Lords Commissioners of the Admiralty your letter of the 30th ultimo., and I am commanded by them to inform you that they approve your views, as stated therein, and desire to assure you of their full confidence in your contemplated conduct of the Fleet in action.

2. My Lords will, as desired, give orders for all available Ships and Torpedo Craft to proceed to the position of the Fleet Action on learning from you that it is imminent.

Annexe II:
Excerpts of the Grand Fleet Battle Orders in Force at Jutland

The following sections have been extracted in their entirety from the GFBOs (dated December 1915) that were in force in the Grand Fleet at Jutland. Italics are as in the original.

V. ORDERS FOR 5TH BATTLE SQUADRON.

(b) Battle Stations

5. When practicable, on or shortly before deployment, the Commander-in-Chief will order the 5th Battle Squadron to take station either at the van, forming part of the fleet, or as a fast division some 4 to 5 miles ahead of it, or at the rear.

6. If the two fleets deploy towards Heligoland and both our own and the enemy's battle cruisers are present, the 5th Battle Squadron will take station at 'L' (see page 41 [*this refers to the deployment diagram; see Diagram 28*]) in the van.

7. If the two fleets deploy away from Heligoland and the Battle Cruiser Fleet is at the van the 5th Battle Squadron will state station at 'M' (see page 41) in the rear, in which case the duty of the Rear-Admiral is to engage the rear of the enemy and to render a turning away movement on his part an operation which places him in a disadvantageous position.

8. If the fleets deploy in opposite directions, the Rear-Admiral commanding 5th Battle Squadron is to be at the opposite end of the line to our Battle Cruisers.

9. Whatever the direction of deployment, in the absence of our own and the enemy's battle cruisers, the Rear-Admiral will endeavour to place the 5th Battle Squadron at the van of our line to attack the enemy van ships from a commanding position and to cover and support the cruisers and light-cruisers stationed at the van. It may be desirable that the 5th Battle Squadron should draw ahead of our van and towards the engaged bow to force in the enemy cruisers and to deny to them a favourable position from which to attack our fleet; such action will also ensure a favourable position for our cruisers, light-cruisers, and destroyers from which the enemy line may be successfully attacked with torpedo and gunfire.

10. If the enemy battle-cruisers are at the van of their fleet and ours are absent, it will become the primary duty of the 5th Battle Squadron to attack them; the squadron should be sufficiently far ahead not to crowd or hamper the cruisers, light-cruisers and destroyers in the van; a position six miles two points from right ahead on the engaged side will be suitable in weather of good visibility. Should a turn of sixteen points bring the 5th Battle Squadron to the rear of our line, it is to attack the enemy's rear if opportunity offers, being careful to avoid his torpedo fire. When attacking the rear, the ships should be in open order so as to reduce the risk of injury from torpedo fire.

11. The Rear-Admiral must be most careful to avoid having his ships between the two battle fleets when fire is opened, or in such a position that the smoke of his ships hampers the fire of our battlefleet. This caution is particularly necessary if the 5th Battle Squadron is proceeding towards our van.

12. Should the 5th Battle Squadron and the enemy's battle-cruisers both be at the van of their respective fleets and the enemy battle-cruisers then turn to take station in rear of their battlefleet, it is probable that this will be the prelude to a turn of 16 points by the whole enemy fleet. The 5th Battle Squadron is to follow the enemy's battle-cruisers' motions and passing <u>about 1 mile on</u> the disengaged side of our own Battlefleet is to take station in rear, turning at once should the signal '02' or '21' be hoisted.

13. The 5th Battle Squadron is to form part of our battle line for purposes of Distribution of gunfire unless ordered by signal to the contrary.

VI. DEPLOYMENT

The Battlefleet will be deployed by the Oblique pendant, by Equal Speed manoeuvring signal, by Equal Speed pendant, or by Forming and Disposing signal, according to the bearing of the enemy's centre relative to the course of the Fleet and the time available.

(a) Forming the Line of Battle by Oblique Pendant

2. When 'Line of Battle' is formed by Oblique pendant, officers commanding columns are to order the course and speed of their ships so as to develop the most effective gun power of the *Fleet as a whole* in the shortest possible time.

When line of battle is formed, the distance between the leading ship of one division and the rear ship of the preceding division is to be one cable more than the distance apart of ships in column.

Whilst forming the line, the commander of the van column is to increase speed up to within one knot of the maximum speed available, the increase being greatest when the angle between the original and new courses is small, but a speed of eighteen knots is not ordinarily to be exceeded.

Great care must be observed by leading ships of columns, not to turn too far during deployment, or it may be necessary to turn back again and kink the line, especially if the rear ship of the column next ahead turns outside her proper position in the line, or is astern of her station.

It is preferable that leading ships of divisions should turn short of the correct deployment course, the only ill effect of which is to slightly delay the final turn into line.

During deployment Commanding Officers of divisions should watch the ships of their divisions which are astern of them; a wavy line with inefficient gunfire often implies faulty leading.

The Commander-in-Chief in the centre will haul down the signal for the speed of the Fleet as a whole as soon as the deployment is developed.

(b) Use of Syren when Deploying

3. It may be necessary to commence deployment at once without waiting for flag or searchlight signals to be answered. In this case, the Commander-in-Chief will at once turn as necessary, sounding one or two short blasts on the syren to indicate whether he is turning to starboard or to port; commanders of columns are then to turn in the same direction. Such syren signals are to be made at short intervals until repeated by

commanders of adjacent columns, and close watch is to be kept for the puffs of steam as the sound of the syren cannot always be heard.

Signals to indicate the method of deployment, and the course to be steered will be made as usual to enable commanders of columns to deploy correctly, but the first action is to be taken on hearing the Commander-in-Chief's sound signal, and without waiting for the flag signals to be hauled down.

It is possible that the first turn may be a feint; the commanders of columns should therefore not turn too far until they are satisfied by the Commander-in-Chief's signals that he is deploying into line of battle.

(c) Instructions for Deploying in Low Visibility

4. In low visibility, if the enemy is sighted near the beam bearing and time does not admit of redisposing the guides, line of battle will usually be formed on the wing column nearest the enemy.

If the enemy be sighted at close quarters by the commander of a wing column, he must decide immediately as to the course to be steered and the manner of bringing his column into action, at the same time signalling his course and speed and using the syren as described above; adjacent columns must at once deploy or turn together to support. In some cases it may be desirable for the wing column to continue on approximately the same course, other columns forming astern.

VII. BATTLE TACTICS

The Commander-in-Chief controls the whole Battlefleet *before* deployment and on deployment except in the case of low visibility mentioned in *paragraph 4, Section VI*.

He cannot be certain, *after* deployment, of being able to control the movements of three battle squadrons when steaming fast and making much funnel smoke; with the noise and smoke of battle added the practicability of exercising general control will be still further reduced.

2. It therefore becomes necessary to decentralise command to the fullest extent possible, and the Vice-Admirals commanding squadrons have discretionary power to manoeuvre their squadrons independently whilst conforming generally to the movements of the Commander-in-Chief and complying with his known intentions. As the Commander-in-Chief is in the centre he will ordinarily control the movements of the 4th Battle Squadron should separate action by that squadron become necessary, but as the fleet is manoeuvred by divisions in the 5th organisation after deployment, the Vice-Admiral, 4th Battle Squadron, will control the movements of his division, conforming generally to the movements of the division led by the Commander-in-Chief unless any contrary directions are given. Similarly the Rear-Admirals, 1st and 2nd Battle Squadrons, control the movements of their divisions unless they receive directions from the Commander-in-Chief or the Vice-Admirals of their squadrons.

3. In all cases the ruling principal is that the *'Dreadnought'* fleet as a whole keeps together, attempted attacks by a division or squadron on a portion of the enemy line being avoided as liable to lead to the isolation of the ships which attempt the movement, and, so long as the fleets are engaged on approximately similar courses, the squadrons should form one line of battle.

4. The Fleet is to be guided generally by the movements of the division led by the Commander-in-Chief, which should be considered the rallying point.

The movements of the Commander-in-Chief must therefore be very carefully watched and his wishes if possible anticipated. Signals may either be indistinguishable or they may take too long to get through a large fleet. This does not mean that they will not be made, but the movement signalled may be commenced before the executive is given. It is hoped that difficulties in signalling will be largely overcome by the use of wireless telegraphy.

5. Assuming good visibility and favourable weather, and non-deployment earlier on the part of the enemy, I shall probably deploy or move to a flank with 'A' arcs bearing at a range of about 18,000 to 20,000 yards so as to be in a favourable position for opening fire in good time, whilst, if the enemy delays his deployment, our fleet will be able to concentrate its whole force on the leading ships of his columns.

6. I attach the greatest importance to making full use of the fire of our heavier guns in the early stages at long range. Close action is to the German advantage if they intend to use large numbers of auxiliary craft to strengthen their attack on our fleet; assuming this to be their intention, if our long range fire is effective, there is a good chance of the German fleet being thrown into partial confusion before his attack can be developed with consequent loss of initiative and interference with their preconceived plan. German ideas before the war undoubtedly favoured a short range action in which their secondary armament and torpedo craft were to play an important part.

7. The officer leading the line of battle is to be guided by the instructions in *Section VIII* for adjusting course and speed to the best advantage of the whole line; it is improbable that any signalled directions will be made to him. In weather of good visibility, the range should be between 15,000 and 10,000 yards; the latter being reached as the enemy's fire is overcome; in the early stages of action I do not desire to close the range much inside 14,000 yards.

The torpedo menace must always be borne in mind. Assuming the fleets on parallel courses with their vans approximately abeam of one another; although at normal ranges our van is comparatively safe from torpedo attack from the enemy's battle line, the centre and rear are vulnerable should the lines close within the running range of the torpedo. It is quite possible the enemy may now possess torpedoes of 15,000 yards running range or more.

Until the enemy is beaten by gunfire it is not my intention to risk attack from his torpedoes, although it is always possible that if we were inferior in strength on meeting it might become necessary to close sufficiently to attack by torpedoes. Such a move would, however, be ordered by me, and generally speaking it is to be understood that my intention is to keep outside torpedo range of the enemy's battle line. As indicated above, with the two vans approximately abeam and the fleets on parallel courses, our van could afford to be at a shorter range than our rear, and it is quite conceivable that the action might develop on such lines, our van squadron gradually closing with a view to obtaining decisive results with gunfire and for the purposes of firing their torpedoes, but not being followed to that close range by our centre or rear.

A further factor affecting the distance of our various squadrons or divisions from the enemy is the maximum range at which their guns are capable of engaging. This must necessarily be taken into account.

8. Exercises at sea and exercises on the Tactical Board shew that one of the most difficult movements to counter on the part of the enemy is a 'turn away' of his line of battle, either in succession or otherwise. The effect of such a turn (which may be made for the purpose of drawing our fleet over mines or submarines) is obviously to place us in a position of decided disadvantage as regards attack by torpedoes fired either from ships or destroyers. If the turn is not followed the enemy runs out of gun range. If it is followed we have to accept a disadvantageous position for a length of time dependent on our excess of speed over the enemy's battle line. This excess may be expected to be 1½ to 2 knots, due to the presence of the German 2nd Squadron.

9. It may be expected that I shall not follow a decided turn of this nature shortly after deployment as I should anticipate that it is made for the purpose of taking us over submarines. The Flag Officer leading the line of battle should exercise great judgment therefore, in 'leading in' to keep the range or close to it.

10. It is undesirable to create too marked a 'bend' in the line, by the whole line altering course in succession, as the mobility of the fleet is somewhat hampered thereby; a turn by squadrons or divisions is preferable and is the method intended to be used unless the alteration of course is small. If the Flag Officer commanding a squadron alters course without making a signal the whole of his squadron should follow in his wake; if he desires to turn his squadron by divisions, or even sub-division, he will do so by signal; or he may make a signal to his own division only, in which case the other division should act similarly if the conditions render it desirable. At the rear where the Rear-Admiral is leading the squadron it might be desirable for the Vice-Admiral to order the movements of the two divisions of his squadron.

11. The 'Dreadnought' fleet will concern itself with the 1st, 2nd and 3rd German Battle Squadrons. It is anticipated that our 3rd Battle Squadron will be available to deal with the 4th and 5th German Battle Squadrons; in any case it is doubtful whether these ships could take part in action with our 'Dreadnought' fleet owing to their inferior speed.

Annexe III:
Cover Letter for Admiral Jellicoe's Despatch

Transcribed from Cmd 1068, Battle of Jutland Official Despatches, *1–4. The accompanying Narrative has not been reproduced.*

No. 1396/H.F. 0022.
'Iron Duke',
18th June 1916.
Sir,

Be pleased to inform the Lords Commissioners of the Admiralty that in accordance with the instructions contained in their Lordship's telegram No. 434 of 30th May, Code time 1740, the Grand Fleet proceeded to sea on 30th May 1916.

2. The instructions given to those portions of the fleet that were not in company with my flag at Scapa Flow were as follows:

To Vice-Admiral Sir Thomas Jerram, with Second Battle Squadron at Invergordon:

'Leave as soon as ready. Pass through Lat. 58° 15' N, Long. 2° 0' E, meet me 2 pm to-morrow 31st, Lat. 57° 45' N, Long. 4° 15' E. Several enemy submarines known to be in North Sea.

Acknowledge.

1930 (Code time).'

To Vice-Admiral Sir David Beatty, Commanding the Battle-cruiser fleet at Rosyth, with the Fifth Battle Squadron, Rear-Admiral Hugh Evan-Thomas in company:-

'Urgent, Priority.

Admiralty telegram 1740.

Available vessels, Battle-cruiser Fleet, Fifth Battle Squadron and TBDs including Harwich TBDs proceed to approximate position Lat. 56° 40' N, Long. 5° 0' E. Desirable to economise TBD's fuel. Presume you will be there about 2 pm tomorrow 31st. I shall be in about Lat. 57° 45' N, Long. 4° 15' E by 2 pm unless delayed by fog.

Third Battle Cruiser Squadron, 'Chester' and 'Canterbury' will leave with me. I will send them on to your rendezvous.

If no news by 2 pm stand towards me to get in visual touch.

I will steer for Horn Reef from position Lat. 57° 45' N, Long. 4° 15' E.

Repeat back rendezvous.

1937 (Code time).'

3. I felt no anxiety in regard to the advanced position of the force under Sir David Beatty, supported as it was by four ships of the Fifth Battle Squadron as this force was far superior in gun power to the First Scouting Group and the speed of the slowest ships was such as to enable it to keep out of range of superior enemy forces.

4. The operation, however, showed that the ships of the Third Squadron of the High Sea Fleet possess an unexpected turn of speed for at any rate a short period. The 'Queen Elizabeth' class are nominally 25-knot vessels. The official Quarterly Return of British

and Foreign War Vessels gives the 'König' and 'Kaiser' classes a designed speed of 20.5 knots. I have always expected that they might reach 22 knots for a short distance, but the fact that the Fifth Battle Squadron was unable to increase its distance from the German ships when steaming at their utmost speed comes as an unpleasant surprise and will have considerable effect on the conduct of future operations. It is quite evident that all German ships possess a speed much in excess of that for which they are nominally designed.

5. When Sir David Beatty sighted the enemy battle-cruisers he adopted the correct and only possible course in engaging and endeavouring to keep between the enemy and his base. Whether the First Scouting Group was supported or not, his duty would be to engage and keep touch with the enemy vessels of similar class to his own, so long as he was not in manifestly inferior force. In this case he had a great superiority, and there could be no question as to his action.

6. The disturbing feature of the battle-cruiser action is the fact that five German battle-cruisers engaging six British vessels of this class, supported after the first twenty minutes, although at great range, by the fire of four battleships of the 'Queen Elizabeth' class, were yet able to sink the 'Queen Mary' and 'Indefatigable'. It is true that the enemy suffered very heavily later, and that one vessel, the 'Lützow', was undoubtedly destroyed, but even so the result cannot be other than unpalatable.

The facts which contributed to the British losses were, *first*, the indifferent armour protection of our battle-cruisers, particularly as regards turret armour and deck plating, and, *second*, the disadvantage under which our vessels laboured in regard to the light. Of this there can be no question.

But it is also undoubted that the gunnery of the German battle-cruisers in the early stages was of a very high standard. They appeared to get on to their target and establish hitting within two or three minutes of opening fire in almost every case, and this at very long ranges of 18,000 yards. The German vessels appear to use some such system of fire as the Petravic method[1] as the guns do not go off exactly together, and it unquestionably gives excellent results. The 'spread' for both direction and elevation is very small and the rapidity of fire very great.

7. Once we commence hitting, the German gunnery falls off, but – as shown by the rapidity with which the 'Invincible' was sunk at a later stage – their ships are still able to fire with great accuracy even when they have received severe punishment.

8. The fact that the gunnery of the German battlefleet when engaged with our battlefleet did not show the same accuracy must not, I think, be taken as showing that the standard is not so high as with their battle-cruisers, as I am inclined to the opinion that we then had some advantage in the way of light, although it was very bad for both sides.

9. The German organisation at night is very good. Their system of recognition signals is excellent. Ours is practically nil. Their searchlights are superior to ours and

---

[1] *Editor's note*: The Petravic 'method' was a gyroscopically-stabilised sight, at the gun itself, designed by the Austro-Hungarian inventor Julius von Petravic. Better than nothing, it would not be as effective as the British 'Henderson Gear' mounted on the director sight that entered British service post-Jutland. Petravic obtained US patent 1,032,022 in July 1912.

they use them with great effect. Finally, their method of firing at night gives excellent results. I am reluctantly compelled to the opinion that under night conditions we have a good deal to learn from them.

10. The German tactics during the action were those which have always been anticipated, and for which provision has been made so far as is possible in my Battle Orders. The 'turn away' of the enemy under cover of torpedo boat destroyer attacks is a move most difficult to counter, but which has been closely investigated on the Tactical Board. Vice-Admiral Sir Doveton Sturdee has rendered me much assistance in the study of this particular movement and in devising a counter to it. There is no real counter. Nothing but ample time and superior speed can be an answer, and this means that unless the meeting of the fleets takes place fairly early in the day it is most difficult, if not impossible, to fight the action to a finish. In this particular case, thanks to the fact that the enemy did not, as far as can be seen, expect to find our whole fleet present, there was not time for him to lay a prepared mine area, and not much time to place his submarines, although many submarines were present.[2] It is unlikely that in future operations we shall be so favoured in this respect, and the element of time will therefore be still more important. I foreshadowed in my letter of Oct. 30th, 1914, No. 339/HF/0034,[3] in which their Lordships expressed concurrence, A.L. of November 7th, 1914, M.03177/14, the possibility of it being actually necessary purposely to delay bringing the fleet to close action for some time on account of the possibilities which the mine and submarine give for preparing a trap on a large scale, and it should be understood that this possibility still exists, and will be increased as the enemy gets stronger in submarines.

11. It was unnecessary for me to give any special orders to the flag officers during the action. Events followed the course that was expected. All squadrons and flotillas took up their stations as directed in the Battle Orders with most commendable accuracy under very difficult circumstances. The torpedo attacks launched by the enemy were countered in the manner previously intended, and practised, during exercises, and the fleet was manœuvred to close again after these attacks by the method which had been adopted for this purpose. The handling of the large fleet was immensely facilitated by the close co-operation and support afforded me by the flag officers.

12. One of the features of the action was the large number of torpedoes that crossed our line without taking effect on any ship except the 'Marlborough'. Sir Cecil Burney estimates that at least twenty-one torpedoes were seen to cross the line of his squadron. All were avoided by skilful handling, except that single one, and it is notable that the 'Marlborough' herself evaded seven. Similarly the Fifth Battle Squadron, in rear of the First Battle Squadron, avoided a considerable number and other squadrons had similar experiences.

It is of supreme importance to keep from the knowledge of the enemy the fact that ships were able to avoid torpedoes by seeing the track, as it would not be beyond the ingenuity of the Germans to devise a means of preventing any track being left.

13. The experience and results of the action, particularly the knowledge we now

---

[2] *Editor's note*: In fact, neither British nor German submarines were present.

[3] *Editor's note*: Reproduced in Annexe I.

have of the speed of the enemy's Third Squadron, must exercise considerable influence on our future dispositions and tactics. It will, for instance, not be advisable in future to place our Fifth Battle Squadron in a position removed from support. I have these questions under consideration and will submit my conclusions to their Lordships.

14. A narrative of the action is enclosed.[4]

I am, Sir,

Your obedient Servant,

J. R. JELLICOE,

Admiral.

The Secretary of the Admiralty.

Annexe IV:
Enemy Sighting Reports, 8 pm Through Midnight, 31 May

Extracted from Official Despatches, *467–76.*

Time of Despatch	From	To	Message
8.09	SO 3rd LCS	SO BCF	Ships bearing N by W.
8.14	Commodore F	SO 2nd BS	Enemy's Destroyers bearing NW (passed to C-in-C 8.26 pm).
8.15	*Princess Royal*	SO BCF	I think *Princess Royal* must have run over a Submarine. Ship is not making water. There was a very heavy bump.
8.15	Commodore F	SO 4th LCS and *Kempenfelt*	12 enemy Destroyers NW.
8.25	*Canada*	C-in-C	Have received on D wave 14 groups, apparently German. Call signs RZ RZ RZ.
8.28	*Falmouth*	C-in-C and SO BCF	Urgent. Am engaging Enemy's Cruisers. My position Lat. 56° 47' N, Long. 5° 46' E.

[4] *Editor's note*: Not reproduced.

8.33	*Inconstant*	SO BCF and C-in-C	Submarine, Lat. 56° 56' N, Long. 6° 06' E.
8.38	C-in-C	*Comus*	Who are you firing at? Reply: Enemy's BF bearing West.
8.46	C-in-C	SO BCF	Indicate the bearing of the Enemy (logged by SO BCF as having been received from *Galatea*. Vide 2100 SO BCF to *Galatea*)
8.46	*Falmouth*	C-in-C, SO BCF	Battle Cruisers unknown. Bearing of Enemy N. Course of Enemy WSW. Position of reporting ship Lat. 56° 42' N, Long. 5° 37' E.
8.50	SO 2nd LCS	C-in-C	Enemy's Destroyers are attacking West. (Not logged as having been received in *Iron Duke*).
8.51	*Black Prince*	C-in-C	Urgent. Submarine on port hand, Lat. 56° 55' N, Long. 6° 11' E.
8.57	*Southampton*	C-in-C	Urgent. Am engaging Enemy Destroyers. Enemy ships bearing W from me, number unknown. My position Lat. 56° 38' N, Long. 6° 09' E.
8.59	*Lion*	C-in-C	Urgent. Enemy Battle Cruisers and pre-Dreadnought Battleships bear from me N 34° W, distant 10 to 11 miles, steering SW. My position Lat. 56° 40' N, Long. 5° 50' E, course SW, 17 knots.
9.00	*Caroline*	SO 2nd BS	Three ships bearing N.W. 8,000 yards. May be attacking with torpedoes. Apparently old battleships. (Not logged in *KGV* signal log).
9.05	SO BCF	Galatea	Your 2046. N by W. (Time of Origin: 9.00. Received in *Iron Duke* 9.04 pm)
9.05	SO 1st BS	C-in-C	Urgent. Enemy Destroyers are attacking Light Cruisers from Westward.

9.06	SO 2nd BS	*Caroline*	Negative. Those ships are our Battle Cruisers (this is the response to *Caroline*'s 9.00 signal)
9.06	*Caroline*	SO 2nd BS	Those are evidently Enemy ships. (Also made by Commodore F at 9.15 pm)
9.06	SO 2nd BS	*Caroline*	If you are quite sure attack.
9.10	*Southampton*	C-in-C	Enemy reported in my 2055 has been driven to the NW. My position Lat. 56° 31' N, Long. 6° 09' E.
9.27	*Marksman*	Captain D12	Permission to attack Enemy bearing South.
9.38	SO BCF	C-in-C	My position now Lat. 56° 35' N, Long. 5° 41' E, course SW, speed 17 knots. Enemy's bearing N by W, steering WSW (Received in *Iron Duke* 9.41 pm).
9.55	Admiralty	C-in-C	Three Destroyer flotillas have been ordered to attack you during the night.
9.58	*Garland*	Captain D4	German Destroyers steering SE.
9.58	Admiralty	C-in-C	At 9 pm rear ship of Enemy BF in Lat. 56° 33' N, Long. 5° 30' E, on southerly course. (Received in *Iron Duke* at 10.23 pm).
10.00	*Contest*	Captain D4	German Destroyers steering SE.
10.03	*Garland*	Captain D4	German Submarines astern
10.25	Captain D4	C-in-C	Submarine five miles North of Dragonfly (?) at 10 pm.
10.27	*Contest*	Captain D4	*Contest* fired one round at three German Destroyers astern steering SE.
10.30	*Canada*	C-in-C	*Contest* to Captain D. Urgent. German TBD steering NE.

10.30	*Garland*	Commodore F	*Garland* fired at Enemy's Destroyers astern.
10.40	*Boadicea*	*Thunderer*	Enemy's ships on starboard beam.
10.41	Admiralty	C-in-C	At 10.41 pm the Admiralty informed the Commander-in-Chief that they enemy was believed to be returning to its base as its course was SSE ¾ E and speed 16 knots. (*This is a paraphrase of the actual signal sent*)
10.43	*Fortune*	Captain D4	*Fortune* fired one round at 9.55 pm in direction torpedo came from.
10.46	C-in-C	Commodore F	Urgent. Are you engaging Enemy's Destroyers? Reply: No. (Reply via *Kempenfelt*.)
10.48	*Contest*	Captain D4	Destroyers off starboard quarter steering E.
10.50	Commodore F	C-in-C via *Kempenfelt*	My position, course and speed South 17 knots, have been engaged by Enemy Cruisers. (This signal crossed 2243 from C-in-C)
10.55	*Porpoise*	Captain D4	German Destroyer astern steering East.
11.30	*Birmingham*	C-in-C, SO BCF	Urgent. Priority. Battle Cruisers, unknown number, probably hostile, in sight, NE course S. My position Lat. 56° 26' N, Long. 5° 42' E.
11.38	SO 2nd LCS via *Nottingham*	C-in-C, SO BCF	Urgent. Have engaged Enemy's Cruisers 10.15 pm, bearing WSW. (Received in *Iron Duke* 11.38 pm)
11.47	*Ambuscade*	Captain D4	Have fired two torpedoes and heard one explosion. (Via *Indomitable* to SO BCF)

Annexe V:
Pre-war Tactical Instructions, 1913–1914

The Admiralty-issued Instructions, and two memoranda from Admiral Sir George Callaghan, Commander-in Chief Home Fleet, are reproduced here (italics, etc., as in the original). The first document, 'Instructions for the Conduct of a Fleet in Action', were the only thing that could be considered a tactical publication approved by the Admiralty; traditionally included in the Signal Book, they are a rather generic set of instructions, some of them dating back to the early eighteenth century. In March 1913 Callaghan had submitted a draft update of these, but the Admiralty War Staff criticised his submission as being 'much too detailed to be issued as general instructions from the Admiralty', and most of the Callaghan's suggestions were rejected. As a result, the instructions as issued (too late to appear in the Signal Book, they were distributed separately) reverted for the most part to their earlier form. Callaghan therefore issued two memoranda that laid out his tactical instructions in more detail. (See NMM, Thursfield Papers, THU 107, 'Development of Tactics in the Grand Fleet', 2 February 1922, for more details.)

(Secret)   October, 1913.
M./0426/13/A.

INSTRUCTIONS FOR THE CONDUCT OF A FLEET IN ACTION.

I.

In carrying out the intentions of the Admiral, Commanders of Squadrons, divisions or sub-divisions should be given a wide discretion as to the conduct of the ships under their immediate orders.

II.

Mutual Support.

Commanders of squadrons, divisions, sub-divisions, or any columns detached from the main body of the fleet, and ordered to attack the enemy, independently, should be careful not to expose their commands to the fire of a superior force by closing him prematurely, and should endeavour to bring their ships into action at a time and in a manner which will enable all portions of the fleet to give the most effective support to one another.

   The above does not imply that all portions of the fleet necessarily come into action at the same time, but if it is the intention of the Admiral that this should be so every effort should be made to bring it about, as its importance may be very great.

III.

General Instructions.

(1) **Guide.**

   The leading ship of a column will always become the guide of the column without signal; if the leading ship is so damaged as to be obliged to quit the line, her next astern automatically becomes guide (*see* Article X).

(2) **Manœuvring and Gunfire.**

Commanders of squadrons, divisions or sub-divisions and Captains of ships should exercise discretion as to manœuvring their squadrons, divisions or sub-divisions or ships to develop the maximum fire on the enemy and to avoid interfering with the fire of, or firing into, other columns or ships. It is of greater importance to manœuvre squadrons, divisions, sub-divisions, or ships so that alterations of course are small, and sudden and large changes of range or bearing are avoided, than to follow strictly in the wake of the guide of the column.

(3) **Rear Ships.**

When the line of battle has been formed, the rear ships, if out of range, are to be brought into action, as soon as possible under the senior officer of their divisions (or sub-division) without further orders, by increasing speed and forming them on a line of bearing, if necessary.

IV.

Ships to Reform without Signal if necessary.

If, during an engagement, a column should be thrown into disorder, the line is to be reformed as expeditiously as possible, ships taking station in the sequence in which they find themselves, without waiting for the signal to do so.

V.

Signal to Open Fire.

Although the signal "open fire" may have been made, it should not be obeyed by ships which are out of effective range of the enemy, or by those which, from their position, are liable by their fire to damage friendly ships. Firing over another ship during battle is not justifiable, owing to the possibility of guns being pointed on the wrong target, but fire may be continued over torpedo craft which are proceeding to attack the enemy.

VI.

Ships not to Separate.

No ships are to quit the line (or any position in which they have been specially stationed for a definite purpose) to pursue the enemy's ship or ships which may be disabled or are attempting to escape, until ordered to do so by the Admiral or the commander of their squadron or division, or by the commander of their column if detached.

VII.

Disabled Ships to Maintain Station as long as Practicable.

Though a ship be partially disabled and hard pressed by the enemy in action, the Captain is to use his utmost endeavour to maintain the position of the ship in the line, but if, in consequence of a loss of speed or control, temporarily or otherwise, he is unable to do so, he should haul out of line, when possible, on the disengaged side, at the same time making a signal to show he is doing so. The ship is to take station in the rear of the line and resume action as quickly as possible.

VIII.

Disablement of the Admiral or the Commander of a Squadron or Division.

If the Admiral or the Commander of a squadron or division be disabled or killed during an action the Officer next in seniority in the fleet, squadron or division is to be informed at once, and is to assume command of the fleet, squadron or division.

If any flag officer be disabled or killed, his flag is to be kept flying until the battle is ended, or the enemy be no longer in sight.

IX.

Flagship Disabled.

If the flagship of the Admiral be disabled in action, he will take such steps as he may consider desirable to enable him to continue to exercise his command.

If the flagship of any other flag officer be disabled in action, he is not to call a ship out of the line during the action in order to embark in her, but, if a subsequent opportunity offers he may transfer his flag to another vessel (not already carrying a flag), one of his own command for preference.

X.

Sudden Appearance of the Enemy at Night or in a Fog.

Should the fleet fall in suddenly with the enemy, it may happen that part of the fleet may come into action without the Admiral being able to make signals for the order of the attack; the officer in command of that portion of the fleet will then act according to his own discretion and as the circumstances of the case may require.

Notes:-

(i)   The term "Admiral" signifies the senior officer present, whether he be the Commander-in-Chief or not.

(ii)   The word "signal" means any form of communication available, whether made by visual, wireless telegraphy or other method.

The instructions for the conduct of a fleet in action contained in the "Signal Manual" (pp. 74-77) and in the "Flotilla Signal Book" (pp. 250-252) are hereby cancelled.

Admiralty, *October, 1913.*

Source: OU 6183, *Naval Tactical Notes, Volume I, 1929*; TNA: ADM 186/80).

<u>**CONFIDENTIAL.**</u>

'*Neptune*' at Portsmouth,

5th December, 1913.

H.F. 0235.

Memorandum.

Remarks on the conduct of a fleet in action, based on the experience gained in the manœuvres and exercises of the home fleets during the year 1913.

One of the most important points to which attention has been drawn by the exercises carried out during the year is the need for officers in command of squadrons, flotillas and in certain cases of individual ships, to be prepared to act on their own initiative.

It is possible, up to the time when the enemy is reported, for an Admiral to station and control generally a fleet consisting of vessels of all descriptions; it is then possible for him to control the movements of all ships within W/T range, except those which are actually in contact with the enemy, and to direct their movements, with a view to concentration of the main forces and to keeping touch with the enemy fleet, etc. As, however, the distance between the opposing fleets lessens, a time arrives when the conduct of the main body (the battle-fleet and the vessels in company with it) must become the Admiral's chief concern, and he can no longer pay the same attention to his detached and advanced ships, which must consequently be handled by their Senior Officers (or Captains if acting singly) without waiting for the Admiral's orders.

As the fleets approach one another the above applies in a still greater degree until, ultimately, the Admiral's whole attention must be given to the battle-fleet; and the vessels in company with it – be they cruisers, light-cruisers, or destroyers – should expect neither signals nor instructions as to what is required of them. This principle must be carried a step further when the battle-fleets reach the range at which fire is opened generally, for then it may no longer be possible for one officer to retain close control of a large battle-fleet, and column commanders must be given considerable freedom to act as circumstances may require.

The above remarks trace, in a general way, the sequence of control which we must be prepared for; they do not imply, however, that the Admiral will not continue to exercise control so long as it is possible for him to do so. It follows that Officers commanding squadrons and flotillas in the first place, and all officers in command in the second place, must at all times be ready to act, if circumstances require it, on their own initiative and judgement in assisting the Admiral to defeat the enemy. Once the battle-fleets are engaged, vessels outside the line of battle must not rely on receiving orders; none should remain inactive if they are able to make effective use of their force.

2. The aim of the battle-fleet is the destruction of the enemy's battle-fleet by gunfire aided by torpedo fire when opportunities offer.

To enable this to be done with the greatest certainty and in the shortest time, it is of primary importance that the whole attention of ships in the line should be given to their opposite numbers, and that they should be free of anxiety as to the attack of other vessels not in the line, whether these be battle-cruisers, cruisers, light cruisers, or torpedo craft, each and all of which possess the power to inflict great damage if the opportunity is given to them. The duty of thus guarding our battle-fleet clearly belongs to vessels of generally similar type to those of the enemy which require to be dealt with, but it does not therefore become a purely defensive one; they require to attack a well as defend, and to attack in preference, because by so doing, their force is applied to more positive advantage, and the initiative is taken from the enemy.

3. It remains to consider, briefly, what are the principal functions, *in a fleet action*, of the different types of vessels which may be present with the battle-fleet.

Battle-Cruisers. The primary function must be that of engaging the battle-cruisers of the enemy. There are many reasons for this, the most important being that, owing to their great power and speed, battle-cruisers, if not in the line of battle, can force all inferior vessels to give way, and, consequently, if the enemy's battle-cruisers are not "held," their power to inflict damage on ships of weaker types is unchecked, and they are able to assume positions from which they can concentrate on, or enfilade, the line of battle, cover the attack of light-cruisers and torpedo craft, etc.

If the enemy has no battle-cruisers with his fleet, the function of our battle-cruisers may be an equally definite one; they may be employed as a fast division of the battle-fleet, or comparative freedom of action may be given to the Admiral commanding to attack the enemy in the manner (indicated above) he may judge best.

Cruisers. The primary function of cruisers in a fleet action must be that of engaging the cruisers of the enemy, observing that, in the absence of battle-cruisers, vessels of the more powerful cruiser type may be able, if not themselves engaged, to act in the same manner as the battle-cruisers.

Cruisers are also required to guard the battle-fleet from attack by light-cruisers and torpedo craft, their positions being governed by this object as well as that of inflicting damage on the enemy.

Light-Cruisers. The functions of these vessels are numerous and include:

The protection of their own battle-fleet from the attack of the enemy's light-cruisers and torpedo craft.

The attack of the enemy's light-cruisers.

The attack of the enemy's torpedo craft.

(*NOTE.* These functions are not stated in the order of their importance, which necessarily must be governed by the circumstances existing at the time.)

As regards the protection of their own battle-fleet, light-cruisers can, to a certain extent, act with their gunfire as the anti-torpedo boat armament of the battle-fleet, although, if large numbers of enemy torpedo craft are attacking together, it will probably be necessary for the light-cruisers to engage them at point blank range, or even to endeavour to run them down.

The best initial positions for the light-cruisers must depend to a proportional extent on the numbers present, and on the positions of the cruisers; if the numbers are few, a position ahead or slightly on the inner bow of their own battle-fleet is suitable; it is desirable that other cruisers or light-cruisers should be stationed astern or on the inner quarter to protect the rear, though this will usually be of less importance than the protection of the van and centre from the attacks from ahead. In these positions they are well placed for acting (on an interior radius) against the enemy's light cruisers and torpedo craft with their gunfire, or against his battle-fleet with torpedo fire, or for supporting the attack of our flotillas.

If the numbers are greater, light-cruisers may also be well employed with the battle-cruisers or acting independently against the enemy's ships and torpedo craft.

Destroyer Flotillas. The functions of the destroyers in a fleet action are:

(1st)   To attack the enemy's ships with torpedoes.

(2nd)   To attack the enemy's torpedo craft.

(*NOTE.* The relative importance of these two functions may sometimes be reversed, but the chances of exercising the second are considered to be more uncertain, and reliance cannot be placed on our torpedo craft being able to engage those of the enemy before the reach positions from whence they can fire their torpedoes at our battle-fleet.)

Destroyers will usually be best stationed from one to two miles ahead or astern of the column to which they are attached, these positions being assumed after line of battle is formed. Prior to forming line of battle, i.e., during the approach, the flotillas should be astern or on the quarter of the wing column, or stationed on a compass bearing, so as not to impede the heavy ships when they deploy.

4. In the preceding paragraphs the functions of vessels of different types in a fleet action have been stated separately, but co-operation is at all times important and opportunities for this are certain to occur.

5. Premature attack by vessels of any type is to be avoided; in weather of normal visibility the battle-fleet is the hinge on which the action turns, and therefore, until the battle-fleet is engaged, vessels of small power should not expose themselves to destruction by greatly superior forces unless there is need for or advantage in their doing so.

6. It must be borne in mind that preconceived ideas on action may be upset by unlooked-for tactics by the enemy; it is for this reason, as much as for any other, that officers must be trained to at on their own initiative, when it is clear that by doing so they can make the best use of the power of the ships they command, and materially assist in the enemy's defeat.

(Sgd.) G.A. CALLAGHAN,
Admiral,
Commander-in-Chief.

The Flag Officers, Commodores, and Captains
    Of the First and Second Fleets, and the
    Captains (D) of the First Fleet.
Copies to Vice-Admirals, Second and Third Fleets for
    issue on mobilisation to the Flag Officers and
    Captains of the 6th and 7th Cruiser Squadrons and
    7th Battle Squadron.
Copy to Admiralty, Commander-in-Chief, Mediterranean,
    China, East Indies, and Cape, and Admiral of
    Patrols.

Source: Naval Historical Branch, Backhouse Papers, Box 1, Folder T94608.

SECRET.   Copy No. 199.
'*Neptune*', at Portsmouth,
14th March 1914.
H.F. 03.
MEMORANDUM.

CONDUCT OF A FLEET IN ACTION.
COMMANDER-IN-CHIEF'S INSTRUCTIONS.
(*Supplementary to the Instructions issued by the Admiralty (M 0426 13/A of October 1913), and to be kept with them*).

A. REMARKS ON ACTION TACTICS.

Size of the fleet must influence tactics. It must be recognised that the tactics of a fleet composed of three or more squadrons of battleships, in addition to battle-cruisers, cruisers, etc., opposed to a fleet of similar strength, are necessarily different from those of a fleet of one or two squadrons opposed to another or correspondingly similar numbers.

Whilst, in both cases, concentration of force is necessary in order (*a*) to establish superiority of fire on the enemy's columns, and (*b*) to give the enemy no chance of employing tactics which will enable him to isolate a portion of our fleet, it is probable that control of a small fleet can be retained in the hands of one officer for a considerably longer time than would be the case with a large fleet. As the size of the fleet increases, the greater will be the need to decentralise the control to the column commanders.

2. *Control of the Fleet*. Assuming good visibility, I intend to exercise control over the whole fleet during the approach, disposing it as may be best for subsequent deployment, and ordering the deployment when the time arrives. After the Fleet has deployed and fire is generally opened, I shall continue to control that portion of the fleet (van, centre or rear) in which I am, but the control of other portions or of squadrons detached must be delegated to their commanders, subject to the general instructions given below or to others which I issue.

I shall endeavour to complete the deployment of the fleet in sufficient time, in order that superiority of fire may be established from the commencement of the action; late deployment may lead to ships being under fire when they cannot return it effectively.

My object will be, *if possible*, to attack the enemy's van, but I shall not delay deployment on this account.

In low visibility, it is more difficult to forecast the tactics to be employed since much will depend on the general conditions at the time and the information received as to the order and strength of the enemy's fleet.

The above statement of my intentions is issued for the guidance of Flag Officers and Captains, but it is not to be taken as restricting my freedom to act otherwise should the circumstances require it.

3. *Range*. The following considerations must be taken into account:

(a) Early hits are of paramount importance on account of their moral effect, as well as by reason of actual damage inflicted.

(b) No definite result will be obtained if the range is too great for effective gunnery, but, provided that the range we select is not too great for our control of fire, closer ranges are undesirable in the early stages because they (i) expose the fleet to torpedo fire from the enemy's ships, and (ii) are more suited to the tactics of the enemy's torpedo craft which may be sent to attack our columns.

For ships of the all-big-gun type, in fine clear weather, deliberate fire may well be opened at about 15,000 yards; 8,000 to 10,000 yards should suffice for *effective* range at which superiority of fire may be established; ranges below 8,000 yards are to be expected towards the later stages of action in order to press home advantage and obtain decisive results.

In weather of limited visibility, the range of action must necessarily be smaller, and may, in practice, be expected to settle itself.

In rough weather, the ranges given above will be less according to the state of the sea.

For battleships of the '*King Edward VII*' and earlier type, the limits of effective range in fine weather may be considered as 7,000 to 9,000 yards, but as the power of these ships chiefly lies in their main armament guns, when in the same column as ships of the all-big-gun type, the range should be governed by the requirements of the latter.

B. GENERAL INSTRUCTIONS.

4. The following general principles should be adhered to in action, unless the circumstances are such as to require otherwise.

(1) *Formation*. The battle formation of a column will be line ahead, at close order.

Circumstances may sometimes require a column of ships to be formed on a line of bearing, or to be turned out of line ahead by Blue pendant, but it should be borne in mind that, in line ahead, station keeping is easier and the line is less liable to be thrown into disorder; moreover, in any formation other than line ahead, course cannot safely be altered without signal, while signal communication in action is likely to be slow and uncertain, and may become impossible.

(2) *Leading ships*. The leading ship of a column engaged with an enemy's column on approximately similar course should endeavour, in the absence of other instructions, and whilst the two columns maintain their courses, to keep the enemy's leading ship slightly abaft her beam; *i.e.*, if the bearing is drawing aft, she may alter course gradually towards the enemy so as to maintain a suitable range and keep her whole broadside bearing, *while drawing forward of the enemy's beam if able to do so*; similarly, if the bearing is drawing forward, she may alter course gradually away from the enemy, or increase her speed.

If the enemy's leading ship turns away, it will probably be necessary to turn towards her to keep within effective range.

If the two fleets are on approximately opposite courses, the leading ship should, when abreast the enemy's centre, and in the absence of other instructions, alter course gradually inwards in such a manner as to obtain a relative position suitable for effective gunfire, without leading the column so close as to endanger the leading ships from the concentrated fire of the enemy's rear or from torpedo fire.*

The above remarks are written for the guidance of the leading ships of columns; they do not and cannot apply literally in all cases, as, for example, in the case of a wing division attacking the van or rear of an enemy's column which is already engaged; nor are they intended to limit the exercise of discretion by officers leading the line, as it is impracticable to provide for special cases.

NOTE – A rough rule for the leading ship is to keep the relative bearing of the enemy's rear ship constant from the time when the first alteration inwards is made; at short ranges the first alteration inwards should be made later.

(3) *Weather*. The conditions as regards wind, sea, and light (including direction of sun), may be such as to render it of great importance to secure or to maintain the most favourable position for effective gunnery, or to avoid being placed at a serious disadvantage; under these circumstances, some departure from the instructions given above in (*2*) may be advisable according to the conditions existing.

The leeward position, with the wind on the bow on the engaged side, is usually the better, but the force of the wind and state of the sea may also influence the matter; in very strong winds less importance attaches to the lee-gauge, and in a rough sea the windward position may have decided advantages.

In fine or moderate weather, the main consideration is that of being in a position where gun and funnel smoke from our own ships do not interfere with gunlaying and observation of fire, either of the firing ship or others ahead and astern of her; in bad weather, smoke interference is less probable, but interference by spray over the gunsights must be taken into account.

(4). *Attack on the rear.* If the circumstances require it, the commander of the rear division or rear sub-division should form his ships on a line of bearing to maintain their most effective gunfire or to meet an attack on the rear, but this line of bearing should seldom be continued for more than four points from right astern. If, however, an attack on the rear cannot be met effectively in this manner, or should the ships attacking the rear cross to the opposite side of the line, he should take such other action as he considers expedient.

(5). *Caution to be observed if engaging a fast division.* The enemy may endeavour through the tactics of a fast division to draw off a portion of our fleet from the action between the main bodies, so that after accomplishing its object the fast division may, by its superior speed, rejoin its own fleet, leaving the ships engaged with it astern. When opposed to ships of much superior speed, caution is therefore necessary to avoid ruses of this nature.

(6). *Torpedo fire.* When in line ahead, alterations of course of not more than a point may be made by ships to enable torpedoes to be fired, speed being increased to keep the ship abreast of her station in the line and to allow her to resume it without hampering her next astern.

(Caution is necessary to avoid risk or damage to consorts when firing torpedoes, more especially those fired from a stern tube or fitted with angle gyroscope).

(7). *Speed.* Subject to maintaining a good position, the speed of a column in the line of battle should be less than the maximum, in order to facilitate station keeping, reduce smoke, and leave something in hand for emergency.

At medium speeds gunlaying is easier, whether by director or otherwise, owing to the effect of helm on course and heel being less than at high speeds.

(8). *Repeating Ships.* With a large fleet repeating ships are necessary for the rapid conveyance of signals in the opening stages of action; it is doubtful, however, whether they will be of any utility after effective range is reached, and, if they are not, their Commanding Officers are to use their discretion as to the manner in which they join in the action.

The duty of a repeating ship attached to a squadron is not only to repeat all signals made by the Senior Officer of the squadron, but also to make every endeavour to see that such signals are seen and understood. Consequently, repeating ships are to consider themselves free to leave their station for the purpose of getting signals through, so long as they remain within effective visual signalling distance of the flagship to which they are attached.

It is probable that one or two repeating ships will be detailed for special attendance on the Admiral to enable him to signal up to the last moment. If two ships are thus detailed, it is to be clearly understood that one is to remain close to the Admiral, whilst the other takes whatever steps are necessary to pass his signals through in the shortest possible time.

C. PREPARATIONS TO BE MADE.

5. On the signal being made to prepare to engage, or for 'immediate action', or whenever the enemy's ships are fallen in with, every Captain is, without waiting for further orders, to raise steam for full speed and to prepare his ship for battle with the utmost dispatch.

D. SHIPS REJOINING THE FLEET SHORTLY BEFORE OR AFTER ACTION HAS COMMENCED.

6. An action between large fleets is likely to be brought about through the medium of cruisers, of which some, at least, will be required to keep touch with the enemy until the battle fleets are within sight of one another, and it is to be expected that vessels (cruisers) thus employed will not be present at the commencement of an action.

Captains of single ships closing the fleet shortly before, or after the commencement of an action, should, if possible, rejoin their squadrons, but, if this is impracticable, or another course is clearly advisable, they are to use their discretion as to the position to assume, and are to act on their own initiative in the manner they judge to be most advantageous.

When two or more vessels of similar class, which have become detached from their squadrons, are able to join one another, they should usually do so, the senior officer taking the junior under his orders.

E. ABSENCE OF SPECIAL DIRECTIONS.

7. Whenever junior flag officers or captains find themselves without special directions during an action, either from inability to make out or receive the Admiral's signals or from unforeseen circumstances rendering previous orders inapplicable, they are to act as their judgment shall dictate in making every effort to damage the enemy. If under these circumstances, vessels are detached from the main body owing to temporary disablement or other causes, they should usually attach themselves to some formed body of friendly ships rather than attempt individual action.

F. SHIPS WATCHING THE ENEMY TO SIGNAL HIS MOVEMENTS.

8. If any enemy's or strange ship or ships be sighted, the vessels appointed to watch their motions are to use every possible endeavour to keep them in sight so as to give the Admiral, by signal, all information as to the enemy's class, numbers, order, course, and speed; if there is danger of the ships keeping touch being driven off by superior force, the Admiral should be informed at once.

Vessels ordered to keep in touch with the enemy for the purpose of giving information to the Admiral are not to expose themselves to disablement, and consequent failure to perform their appointed duties, unless the circumstances require it and their orders cannot otherwise be carried out.

NOTES – (i) The term 'the Admiral' signifies the senior officer present, whether he be the Commander-in-Chief, or not.

(ii)   The word 'signal' means any form of communication, whether made by visual, W/T, or other method.

(Sgd.) G.A. CALLAGHAN,
Admiral,
Commander-in-Chief.

The Flag Officers and Officers commanding
H.M. ships of the Home Fleets, the Cap-
tain (T) and Captains (D) of the First Fleet.
(Copy to Admiral of Patrols).

Source: Naval Historical Branch, Backhouse Papers, Box 1, Folder T94621.

Annexe VI:
Surviving Copies of the *Naval Staff Appreciation of Jutland*: A Bibliographical Note
By Stephen McLaughlin

The *Naval Staff Appreciation of Jutland* was printed in February 1922 by H M Stationery Office Press, Harrow, for the Admiralty; in size, the book was royal octavo (defined as 10in x 6.25in [254mm x 159mm]; the actual size, after trimming, as in this case was 9.72in x 6.10in [247mm x 155mm]), and it was bound in cardboard covers, each copy having a copy number stamped on the front cover. The binding was glued to a cloth strip.

One hundred copies of the *NSA* were printed. The number and date are confirmed by the printer's note at the foot of the table of contents page.[1] The number of copies is further confirmed by a note in the Beatty Papers at the National Maritime Museum.[2] Nevertheless, there has been considerable confusion over the years regarding the number printed, even amongst people deeply involved in the controversy. For example, J E T Harper wrote: 'At first, 12 numbered copies were issued to Board of Admiralty etc'.[3] A typed note pasted into Jellicoe's copy claims that only seven copies were printed. More recently, Arthur J Marder said that 'About 300 copies' were originally printed, but gives no basis for this number.[4] However, Roskill correctly states that 'about 100 copies' were printed.[5]

As part of the research for this book, I made an effort to track down all the surviving copies of the *Naval Staff Appreciation of Jutland*; citations in various books identified four extant copies, and during a trip to England in January 2015 I was able to see all four of them.[6] There may yet be other survivors, but I have not been able to trace them. The four known copies are:

- National Maritime Museum, Greenwich, London: Beatty Papers, BTY/22/9. Copy No. 1.[7] This was the copy from which the microfilm, now at UC Irvine, was made (see below).
- British Library, London: Keyes Papers, Add. MS. 82490. Copy No. 2 (vol. CXVIII of the Keyes Papers; also given as MSS 7/3).

---

[1] I am grateful to Matthew Seligmann for explaining the significance of this notation to me.

[2] NMM: BTY/9/5.

[3] Harper to Oswald Frewen, 23 December 1944; ROSK 3/11, reproduced in *Beatty Papers*, 2:478–9.

[4] Marder, *FDSF*, 3:ix; Rasor, *Battle of Jutland*, 129, repeats this figure.

[5] Roskill, *Admiral of the Fleet Earl Beatty*, 333.

[6] A 1938 note in the Chatfield Papers (NMM: CHT/8/2) states that only three copies were known to be extant at that time. Since four copies definitely exist, one of them must have been overlooked by the author of this note.

[7] Bill Schleihauf apparently thought this was copy 16, but I checked the cover and spine; although both are faded and, in the case of the spine, wrinkled and cracked, I saw no sign of a '6' after the '1'. So this would appear to be copy No. 1.

- Churchill Archives Centre, Churchill College, Cambridge: Roskill MSS, ROSK 3/13. Copy No. 4. This copy once belonged to Frank Spickernell, Beatty's secretary.
- British Library, London: Jellicoe Papers, Add. MS. 49042. Copy No. 7.

Some brief notes describing the peculiarities of each of these copies can be found at the end of this section.

In addition to these original copies, a microfilm version also exists:

- University of California, Irvine, Langston Library: Microfilm M 000147. This microfilm copy was made for Arthur J Marder. Although the copy number is not visible, the university's catalog notes that it was photographed from the Beatty Manuscripts, i.e., copy no. 1 (NMM, BTY/22/9). This is confirmed by a comparison of the marginal notes. The microfilm also includes several memoranda relating to the *NSA*.

Online access:

- The British Library has digitized the Jellicoe Papers, including Add. MS. 49042: http:www.bl.uk/manuscripts/Viewer.aspx?ref=add_ms_49042_fs001r.
- A PDF, based on a print-out of the microfilm at UC Irvine, is available, but the quality is marginal: http:analysis.williamdoneil.com/Hist/Jutland_Staff_Appreciation—txt_undr.pdf.

Some information survives on the copies issued to other individuals:

- Copy No. 5, issued to K G B Dewar; this copy is not amongst the Dewar Papers at the National Maritime Museum; it was presumably turned in when ordered in 1922 and later destroyed.
- Copy No. 9, issued to Sir Julian Corbett; in 1938 this copy was apparently in the Admiralty's secretariat, and it was noted that it could 'be retained by the First Sea Lord [Chatfield] if desired'.[8] It does not appear to be in the Chatfield Papers at the National Maritime Museum.
- Copy number unknown: issued to Admiral Sir Herbert Richmond; apparently not in the Richmond Papers at the NMM.
- Copy number unknown: issued to Admiral J E T Harper, but not listed as amongst the Harper Papers at the British Library.[9]
- Copy number unknown: given or loaned to Winston Churchill in 1924, when he was writing his *World Crisis*.[10]

---

[8] Note dated 8 March 1938; NMM: CHT/8/2.

[9] Bill Schleihauf's original manuscript indicated that he saw this copy, but I think he may have seen the copy in the Keyes Papers, and perhaps got his notes confused.

[10] Prior, *Churchill's 'World Crisis' as History*, 198, 207, 308 n.47, 309 n.79.

Other copies presumably were issued to the members of the Board of Admiralty and other officers for review, but no further information regarding them has come to light.

Some additional materials relevant to the *Naval Staff Appreciation of Jutland* are available. Most significant are the original typescript drafts of the *NSA* in the papers of Alfred C Dewar, now held at the library of the National Museum of the Royal Navy in Portsmouth (MSS 265, Box No. 2: Jutland). There is some correspondence related to the publication of the *NSA* and the origins of the *Admiralty Narrative* in the papers of Kenneth Dewar at the National Maritime Museum (NMM: DEW/4), but the material here is not extensive. Finally, in the Marder Papers at UC Irvine there is a memorandum by Lt. John Pollen, defending the diagrams of the *NSA* against Jellicoe's criticisms; although undated, internal evidence indicates it was written about 1923 (Marder Papers, Box 27, Folder 1).

Notes on the Individual Copies

Copy No. 1: On flyleaf: '1st Sea Lord's Copy', with Beatty's signature below. Marginal notations throughout, but the majority of these are simple pencil marks emphasising portions of the text. A few of these have been noted at the appropriate points in this book. Some notes seem to be associated with the composing of the *Admiralty Narrative*, indicating chapters to be omitted from the latter.

Copy No. 2: Numerous pencil marks in the margins, usually in the form of vertical lines emphasising passages or entire sections; very few actual notes. Inserted into an envelope pasted on the flyleaf, labelled (in pencil) 'Memorandum in Staff Appreciation of Jutland' are two documents: a joint memorandum from Keyes and Chatfield to Beatty recommending that the *NSA* not be issued (dated 14 August 1922),[11] and a note from the Secretary of the Admiralty, dated 6 April 1932, asking Keyes to return his copy of the *NSA*. Obviously, he did not comply.[12]

Copy No. 4: Pencilled note at top of flyleaf: 'Sec to 1 S L'. Inked note at top of flyleaf: 'From Geoffrey Blake to S.W. Roskill August 1960'. Inked note pasted on lower part of flyleaf:

This is one of ___[?] only 2 or 3 copies of the original Naval Staff Appreciation of Jutland which survived Madden's order of 1928 that [?] they [?] be destroyed. Written by A.C. & K.G.B. Dewar it is critical of Jellicoe. It seems to have been the foundation for Churchill's account in the World Crisis. This copy was _____[?] by Sir Frank Spickernell (Beatty's Sec) & was obtained from him by Admiral Blake.

SR [presumably 'Stephen Roskill']

13/1/56

---

[11] Reproduced in *Beatty Papers*, 2:455–6.

[12] Letters between Beatty and Keyes expressing their intention not to return their copies can be found in *Keyes Papers*, 2:299.

There are numerous light pencil marks, usually in the form of brackets surrounding parts of the text, throughout the copy. Included in the same folder as the *NSA* are two letters from Vice-Admiral Sir Geoffrey Blake to Stephen Roskill, describing how he came to acquire the manuscript from Spickernell's widow.

Copy No. 7: This copy has been rebound; on the spine a note indicates that it was 'Presented by the Jellicoe Trustees' to the British Museum; it was received by the museum in April 1957. There are numerous written marginal notes throughout the text; most if not all of these were apparently written by Jellicoe's long-time friend Frederic Dreyer (so identified by John Brooks based on the handwriting). Dreyer seems to have had free run of the Jellicoe papers before they were deposited at the British Museum (perhaps as one of the trustees of the papers). A handwritten note on the inside cover states that:

> This very discreditable book was never issued as a Secret or Confidential book – but only <u>seven copies</u> were completed, of which this is one.
>
> It was written by two brothers – ~~Commander~~ newly promoted Captain K.G. Dewar R.N. and retired Lieutenant A.C. Dewar R.N. neither of whom was distinguished as a Naval Officer.
>
> The few copies completed (six) are known to have been shown to various people as '<u>The Naval Staff Appreciation of Jutland</u>' – which it certainly was not.
>
> <u>In that disguise</u> it did a great deal of harm. It was not stated <u>that the Board of Admiralty had refused to approve</u> it.
>
> In place of this book the Admiralty <u>in 1924</u> issued <u>The Narrative</u> which though not so outrageous and misleading as this book is <u>a mean drab [?] book</u>, which, 'inter alia' omits to mention <u>the crucial fact</u> that the Admiralty at 10.10 pm GMT on night of Jutland battle had de-cyphered <u>an urgent signal</u> made by Vice Admiral Scheer the German Commander in Chief calling for Zeppelin reconnaissance over the Horn Reefs. This Admiralty failed to tell this to Jellicoe.

There is also a typed note pasted in on the original flyleaf:

> Copy numbered '7', of a book entitled '<u>Naval Staff Appreciation of Jutland</u>' (with appendices and diagrams).
>
> This book was never issued as a C.B. (Confidential Book) but its get up gave the erroneous impression that it was. It was written by two inexperienced Officers, neither of whom was present at the Battle of Jutland. It is a stupid book suggesting that the Grand Fleet should have carried out <u>divided</u> tactics in the Jutland misty atmosphere.
>
> <u>In 'The Tactical Manual' issued in 1922 by the Naval Staff</u> single line was advocated and practical adherence to Jellicoe's 1916 Grand Fleet Orders.
>
> The two books mentioned above and issued in close succession thus advocated opposed principles.

Not surprisingly, most of the marginal notations indicate Dreyer's disapproval of the text, and the word 'Rubbish!' appears frequently.

BIBLIOGRAPHY

Official Publications(in chronological order)

Cmd. 1068. *Battle of Jutland, 30th May to 1st June 1916. Official Despatches with Appendices* (London: HMSO, 1920; reprinted by the Naval & Military Press Ltd. in 2006, with the original charts reduced to single-page size).

The Official Record of the Battle of Jutland, 31st May to 1st June, 1916. Usually referred to as the 'Harper Record'; although readied for publication, in September 1920 the Board of Admiralty decided against its issue; it was eventually published in 1927 (see Cmd. 2870, below).

CB0938, *Naval Staff Appreciation of Jutland.* Written by the Dewar brothers between November 1920 and January 1922, it was too controversial for release and all but a handful of copies were destroyed. This is what is being reprinted here. For details on the surviving copies, see Annexe VII.

Corbett, Sir Julian, *Naval Operations*, Volume III (London: Longmans, Green and Co., 1923). Published 'By Direction of the Historical Section of the Committee of Imperial Defence', the Admiralty was not happy with Corbett's interpretation and insisted on a disclaimer being included, indicating that 'Their Lordships find that some of the principles advocated . . . especially the tendency to minimise the importance of seeking battle and of forcing it to a conclusion, are directly in conflict with their views'. Corbett was barred from making any reference to the work of Room 40. Reissued in 1940 with additional material (see below).

Narrative of the Battle of Jutland (London: HMSO, 1924). A heavily-censored version of the *Naval Staff Appreciation*, with several chapters omitted and most of the more critical judgments deleted. Admiral Jellicoe nevertheless submitted a number of objections, which were made into an appendix, with the Admiralty's responses included as footnotes to Jellicoe's text.

Cmd. 2870. Harper, Captain J E T, *Reproduction of the Record of the Battle of Jutland Prepared by Captain J.E.T. Harper, M.V.O., R.N. and Other Officers by the Direction of the Admiralty in 1919-1920* (London: HMSO, 1927). Basically the 'Harper Record' of 1920, without the diagrams (copy courtesy of John Tennier).

Corbett, Sir Julian, *Naval Operations*, Volume III (London: Longmans, Green and Co., 1940). This second edition, revised by the secretary of the Historical Section of the Committee of Imperial Defence, Lt.-Colonel E Y Daniel (who had steered the original edition to press after Corbett's death), included material on Room 40's decryption work, as well as other updates; unfortunately, many copies were destroyed by enemy action before they could be sold. Happily, a facsimile has been reprinted: London: The Imperial War Museum, and Nashville Tennessee: The Battery Press, 1995.

Primary Sources

Birch, Frank and Clarke, William F. (Hans Joachim Koerver, ed.), *Room 40: German Naval Warfare 1914-1918*, 2 volumes. Berlin?: Hans Joachim Koerver, 2009. A transcription of 'A Contribution to the History of German Naval Warfare 1914–1918' (TNA: HW 7/1 – HW 7/4), with an introduction by Koerver.

Exercise Jutland Tribute - Hydrographic Survey Results – report of the 1991 diving expedition, courtesy of Warrant Officer Robert Myers.

Joint Doctrine & Concepts Centre, JWP-0-01 *British Defence Doctrine* (Second Edition), October 2001.

Sighting Device for use On Ships, Julius von Petravic, US Patent 1,032,022.

The Navy List for August 1914. The CD-Rom version available from 'Archive Britain' was used (www.archivebritain.com).

Admiralty Library, Portsmouth:

C.B. 3013/B.R. 1875. Naval Staff, Training and Staff Duties Division, *The Naval Staff of the Admiralty. Its Work and Development* (Admiralty, September 1929).

Eb 012. May, Admiral Sir William, *Notes on Tactical Exercises. Home Fleet. 1909-1911* (Admiralty, 19 September 1911).

P 771. 'Report of the Committee Appointed to Consider the Organisation and Training of the Royal Naval War College, and its Relations to the Naval War Staff' (London: HMSO, 1913).

British Library, London:

Jellicoe Papers, Add. MSS. 49012. 'My War Orders and Dispositions . . . Prepared when in 2nd Division, Home Fleet'.

Jellicoe Papers, Add. MS. 49042. *Naval Staff Appreciation of Jutland*, copy No. 7.

Keyes Papers, Add. MS. 82490. *Naval Staff Appreciation of Jutland*, copy No. 2.

Caird Library, National Maritime Museum, Greenwich:

Beatty Papers, BTY/9/5. Correspondence.

Beatty Papers, BTY/22/9. *Naval Staff Appreciation of Jutland*, copy No. 1.

Chatfield Papers, CHT/8/2. Note dated 8 March 1938.

[Kenneth] Dewar Papers, DEW2/Part 1, DEW/3, DEW/4. Various correspondence and papers related to the *Naval Staff Appreciation of Jutland*.

Thursfield Papers, THU/107. Captain H G Thursfield, 'Development of Tactics in the Grand Fleet', Royal Naval Staff College, Greenwich, Session 1921-22, Lecture No. I, delivered 2 February 1922.

Churchill Archives Centre, Churchill College, Cambridge:

Daniel Papers, DANL 2. Diary of Admiral Sir Charles Saumarez Daniel, 1915-1916.

Drax Papers, DRAX 1/61. DRAX 6/18. Correspondence.

Roskill Papers, ROSK 3/11. Harper to Oswald Frewen, 23 December 1944.

Roskill Papers, ROSK 3/13. *Naval Staff Appreciation of Jutland*, copy No. 4.

Sturdee Papers, SDEE/2/6 part 13. Folder labelled 'Fighting Instructions', memorandum dated 25 November 1914.

The National Archives (formerly the Public Record Office), Kew:

ADM 1/7506. 'Combined Manoeuvres Mediterranean and Channel Fleets, 1901'. Report of Admiral Sir A K Wilson, 4 October 1901.

ADM 1/8377/120. 'The Naval War Staff, 1911-1914'.

ADM 1/8682/124. 'HMS *Campania*: movements prior to the Battle of Jutland'.

ADM 1/8697/64. 'Publication of Jutland material. Amendments to proofs submitted by Mr Winston Churchill'.

ADM 116/1341. Grand Fleet Battle Orders, vol. I (before Jutland).

ADM 116/1342. Grand Fleet Battle Orders, vol. II (after Jutland).

ADM 116/1343. Grand Fleet Battle Orders, vol. III (in force at Jutland). A more accessible version is the transcription produced by Brad Golding, P.O. Box 440 Mitcham Victoria 3132, Australia.

ADM 137/260. Home Fleets General Orders No. 15, 'Distribution of Gunfire', 8 December 1913.

ADM 137/293. Grand Fleet Gunnery and Torpedo Orders.

ADM 137/302. Reports of ships at Jutland; many of these were published in Cmd 1068, *Battle of Jutland*, but some technical material considered confidential (e.g., concerning gunnery) was not included in the published versions.

ADM 137/1939. Proposed Flag Officers' Conference at Spithead, Agenda for War Conference.

ADM 137/2020. Grand Fleet Orders, 'Exercises carried out on 13-14 June', 8 July 1915.

ADM 137/2135. Battle Cruiser Force Signal Orders (1 August, 1918) [an extract showing destroyer fuel endurance may be found online at www.gwpda.org/naval/wrndd001.htm].

ADM 137/4051. Grand Fleet Orders.

ADM 144/17. Admiralty to Admiral Sir Compton Edward Domvile, 26 October 1903.

ADM 186/80. Admiralty, Tactical Division, Naval Staff, OU 6183, 'Naval Tactical Notes, Volume I', May 1929.

ADM 186/586. Admiralty, Gunnery Branch, CB 1384, 'Analysis of Torpedo Firing in the Battle of Jutland,' January 1918.

HW 3/2: Birch, Frank, 'An Admiralty Telegram', 10 August 1924.

HW 7/1 through HW 7/4. Birch, Frank and Clarke, William F, 'A Contribution to the History of German Naval Warfare 1914-1918', 1920.

National Archives and Record Administration, Washington, D.C. (Downtown branch):

RG 38, Folder P-11-b. 'Mining Warfare – A Sketch of Possibilities', (translation of an article from *Mitteilungen aus dem Gebiete des Seewesens*, 1911).

RG 38, Folder P-11-b. 'Tactical Policy, and Tactics, British Navy'. Report from U.S. naval attaché, London, 'British Naval Tactics', 29 November 1938.

RG 45, Box 225, 'IY – Grand Fleet Battle Instructions & Orders', Folder 5. Grand Fleet Battle Instructions and Grand Fleet Manoeuvring Orders, January 1918.

National Museum of the Royal Navy's Library, Portsmouth:

Alfred C Dewar Papers, MSS 265, Box No. 2: Jutland. Papers related to the *Naval Staff Appreciation of Jutland* and the *Narrative of the Battle of Jutland* (the 'Admiralty Narrative').

Naval Historical Branch, Portsmouth:

Backhouse Papers, Box 1, Folder T94608: Remarks on the Conduct of a Fleet in Action, Based on the Experience Gained in the Manœuvres and Exercises of the Home Fleets during the Year 1913, 5 December 1913.
Backhouse Papers, Box 1, Folder T94621: Conduct of a Fleet in Action: Commander-in-Chief's Instructions, 14 March 1914.

University of California, Irvine, Langston Library:

Marder Papers, Box 1. Correspondence.
Marder Papers, Box 27, Folder 1. Memorandum by Lt. John Pollen, ca. 1923.
Microfilm M 000147. *Naval Staff Appreciation of Jutland*, taken from Beatty's copy in the National Maritime Museum.

Secondary Sources

Note that articles were published anonymously in the *Naval Review*, as a means of fostering debate without fear of retribution. Authors of articles published from the journal's inception up to 1930 are identified by James Goldrick in 'Author List for *The Naval Review*, 1913–1930', published as Appendix C in Goldrick and Hattendorf (eds), *Mahan is Not Enough*, pp. 341–405. The names of authors identified through this list are included in [square brackets].

Anon., *German Warships of World War I: The Royal Navy's Official Guide to the Capital Ships, Cruisers, Destroyers, Submarines and Small Craft, 1914-1918* (Annapolis: Naval Institute Press, 1992).
Bacon, Reginald H, *The Life of John Rushworth Earl Jellicoe* (London: Cassell and Company, 1936).
————————, 'Mr. Churchill and Jutland', in George Sydenham *et al.*, *The World Crisis by Winston Churchill: A Criticism* (1928; reprint edition, Port Washington, NY: Kennikat Press, 1970).
Beatty, David, *The Beatty Papers: Selections from the Private and Official Correspondence of Admiral of the Fleet Earl Beatty*, ed B McL Ranft, vol I, *1902-1918*; vol II, *1916-1927* (London: Navy Records Society, 1989–1993).
Beesly, Patrick, *Room 40: British Naval Intelligence 1914-18* (London: Hamish Hamilton, 1982).
Bennett, Geoffrey, *The Battle of Jutland* (London: B. T. Batsford Limited, 1964).
————————, 'The Harper Papers', *The Quarterly Review* (London: John Murray), January 1965, pp 16–25.
Black, Nicholas, *The British Naval Staff in the First World War* (Woodbridge, Suffolk: The Boydell Press, 2009).

Brooks, John, *Dreadnought Gunnery and the Battle of Jutland: The Question of Fire Control* (London: Routledge, 2005).

_____, 'Grand Battle-Fleet Tactics: From the Edwardian Age to Jutland', in Robert J Blyth, Andrew Lambert and Jan Rüger (eds), *The Dreadnought and the Edwardian Age* (Farnham, Surrey: Ashgate Publishing Limited, 2011), pp 183–212.

_____, 'Preparing for Armageddon: Gunnery Practices and Exercises in the Grand Fleet Prior to Jutland', *Journal of Strategic Studies*, vol. 38, no. 7 (December 2015), pp 1006–23.

Brown, David K, 'Torpedoes at Jutland', *Warship World*, vol 5, no 2 (Spring 1995), pp 24–6.

Campbell, John, *Jutland: An Analysis of the Fighting* (London: Conway Maritime Press, and Annapolis, MD: Naval Institute Press, 1986).

Chatfield, Alfred Ernle Montecute, *The Navy and Defence* (London: William Heinemann, Ltd, 1942).

Churchill, Winston S, *The World Crisis, 1916-1918*, vol 3, part 1 (London: Thornton Butterworth Limited, 1927).

Corbett, Julian, *Fighting Instructions, 1530-1816* (London: Navy Records Society, 1905; reprint edition, New York: Burt Franklin, 1967).

_____, *Maritime Operations in the Russo-Japanese War, 1904-1905* (Annapolis: Naval Institute Press, 1994).

_____, *Some Principles of Maritime Strategy* (Longmans, Green & Co., 1911; reprint edition, London: Naval & Military Press, 2003).

Creswell, John, *British Admirals of the Eighteenth Century: Tactics in Battle* (London: George Allen & Unwin Ltd., 1972).

Davison, Robert L, '"Auxillium ab Alto" - The Royal Navy Executive Branch and the Experience of War', *The Northern Mariner/Le marin du nord*, vol XV, no 3 (July 2005), pp 87–105.

_____, *The Challenges of Command: The Royal Navy's Executive Branch Officers, 1880-1919* (Farnham, Surrey: Ashgate Publishing Limited, 2011).

_____, 'Striking a Balance between Dissent and Discipline: Admiral Sir Reginald Drax', *The Northern Mariner/Le marin du nord*, vol. XIII, no. 2 (April 2003), pp 43–57.

[Dewar, Alfred C], 'Naval Operations of War, Vol. III, the Battle of Jutland', *Naval Review*, vol XII, no 2 (May 1924), pp 286–300.

Dewar, Kenneth G B, 'Battle of Jutland', *Naval Review*, part 1: vol XLVII, no 4 (October 1959), pp 400–16; part 2: vol XLVIII, no 1 (January 1960), pp 25–47; part 3: vol. XLVIII, no. 2 (April 1960), pp. 146–58.

_____, 'The Executive Command and Staff in Naval Warfare', *Naval Review*; part 1: vol I, no 1 (February 1913), pp 59–76; part 2: vol I, no 3 (August 1913), pp 229–51; part 3: vol II, no 1 (February 1914), pp 1–11.

_____, *The Navy From Within* (London: Victor Gollancz, 1939).

Dreyer, Frederic C, *The Sea Heritage: A Study of Maritime Warfare* (London: Museum Press, 1955).

Ejstrud, Bo, 'A Near Miss: Heavy Gun Efficiency at Jutland', *Warship International*, vol XLI, no 2 (2004), pp 159–71.

Evans, David C and Peattie, Mark R, *Kaigun: Strategy, Tactics, and Technology in the Imperial Japanese Navy, 1887-1941* (Annapolis: Naval Institute Press, 1997).

Fawcett, H W, and Hooper, G W W (eds), *The Fighting at Jutland: The Personal Experiences of Sixty Officers and Men of the British Fleet* (privately printed, 1921; reprint edition, Rochester: Chatham Publishing, 2001).

Friedman, Norman, *Naval Firepower: Battleship Guns and Gunnery in the Dreadnought Era* (Barnsley: Seaforth Publishing, 2008).

_____, *Naval Weapons of World War One: Guns, Torpedoes, Mines and ASW Weapons of All Nations* (Barnsley: Seaforth Publishing, 2011).

Gibson, Langhorne and Harper, J E T, *The Riddle of Jutland: An Authentic History* (New York: Coward-McCann, 1934).

Goldrick, James, 'The Founders', in Peter Hore (ed), *Dreadnought to Daring: 100 Years of Comment, Controversy ad Debate in The Naval Review* (Barnsley: Seaforth Publishing, 2012), pp 1–17.

_____, *The King's Ships were at Sea: The War in the North Sea, August 1914-February 1915* (Annapolis: Naval Institute Press, 1984).

_____, and Hattendorf, John B. (eds.), *Mahan is Not Enough: The Proceedings of a Conference on the Works of Sir Julian Corbett and Admiral Sir Herbert Richmond* (Newport, Rhode Island: Naval War College Press, 1993).

Gordon, Andrew, '1914-18: The Proof of the Pudding', in Geoffrey Till (ed), *The Development of British Naval Thinking: Essays in Memory of Bryan Ranft* (Abingdon: Routledge, 2006), pp 89–102.

_____, *The Rules of the Game: Jutland and British Naval Command* (London: John Murray, 1996).

Grant, Robert M, *U-Boat Intelligence 1914-1918* (Hamden Connecticut: Archon Books, 1969).

Grenfell, Russell, *The Bismarck Episode* (1948; reprint edition, London: Faber and Faber Limited, 1968).

Gröner, Erich, *German Warships 1815–1945*, vol 1, *Major Surface Vessels* (Annapolis: Naval Institute Press, 1990).

Halpern, Paul G, *A Naval History of World War I* (Annapolis: Naval Institute Press, 1994).

Hamilton, C I, *The Making of the Modern Admiralty: British Naval Policy-Making, 1805-1927* (Cambridge: Cambridge University Press, 2011).

[Hammick, A R], 'Dardanelles Notes', *Naval Review*, vol IV (1916), pp 198–269.

Harland, John, *Seamanship in the Age of Sail* (Annapolis: Naval Institute Press, 1984).

Hase, Georg von, *Kiel and Jutland* (London: Skeffington & Son, n.d.).

Herwig, Holger H, *'Luxury' Fleet - the Imperial German Navy 1888-1918* (London: George Allen & Unwin, 1980).

Hezlet, Arthur, *Electronics and Sea Power* (New York: Stein and Day, 1975).

Hines, Jason, 'Sins of Omission and Commission: A Reassessment of the Role of Intelligence in the Battle of Jutland', *Journal of Military History*, vol 72, no 4 (October 2008), pp 1117–53.

Hone, Trent, 'United States: The U.S. Navy' in: Vincent P O'Hara, W David Dickson and Richard Worth (eds), *To Crown the Waves: The Great Navies of the First World War* (Annapolis: Naval Institute Press, 2013), pp 257–307.

Howland, Vernon W, 'Naval Radio: Introduction and Development 1900-1920', *Warship International*, vol XXXVII, no 2 (2000), pp 119–51.

Hughes, Wayne P, *Fleet Tactics and Coastal Combat* (2nd ed., Annapolis: Naval Institute Press, 2000).

Hunt, Barry D, *Sailor-Scholar: Admiral Sir Herbert Richmond, 1871-1946* (Waterloo, Ontario: Wilfred Laurier University Press, 1982).

Irving, John, *The Smoke Screen of Jutland* (London: William Kimber and Co. Limited, 1966).

James, William, *Admiral Sir William Fisher* (London: Macmillan & Co., 1943).

Jellicoe, John Rushworth, *The Grand Fleet 1914-1916: Its Creation, Development and Work* (London: Cassell and Company, 1919).

_____, *The Jellicoe Papers: Selections from the Private and Official Correspondence of Admiral of the Fleet Earl Jellicoe of Scapa*, ed A Temple Patterson, vol I, *1893-1916*; vol II, *1916-1935* (London: Navy Records Society, 1966–8).

Keyes, Roger, *The Keyes Papers: Selections from the Private and Official Correspondence of Admiral of the Fleet Baron Keyes of Zeebrugge*, vol II, *1919-1938*, ed Paul G Halpern (London: Navy Records Society, 1980).

Knox, Dudley W, '"Column" as a Battle Formation', *United States Naval Institute Proceedings*, vol 39, no 3 (September 1913), pp 949–58.

Lambert, Andrew, 'The Development of Education in the Royal Navy: 1854-1914', in Geoffrey Till (ed), *The Development of British Naval Thinking: Essays in Memory of Bryan Ranft* (Abingdon: Routledge, 2006), pp 34–59.

Lambert, Nicholas, '"Our Bloody Ships" or "Our Bloody System"? Jutland and the Loss of the Battlecruisers, 1916', *The Journal of Military History*, vol 62, no 1 (January 1998), pp 29–55.

Laughton, John Knox, 'Article IX – Naval Warfare', *The Edinburgh Review or Critical Journal*, vol CLXII, no 331 (July 1885), pp 234–64.

Layman, R D, *Naval Aviation in the First World War* (Annapolis: Naval Institute Press, 1996).

Lyle, Colin, 'Jutland, or a Second "Glorious First of June"?', *The Mariner's Mirror*, vol 82, no 2 (May 1996), pp 190–9.

Macintyre, Donald, *Jutland* (New York: W. W. Norton & Co., 1958).

Mahan, Alfred Thayer, *The Influence of Sea Power upon History, 1660-1783* (4th ed., Boston: Little, Brown, 1893).

March, Edgar J, *British Destroyers 1892-1953* (London: Seeley Service & Co., 1966).

Marder, Arthur J, *The Anatomy of British Sea Power: A History of British Naval Policy in the Pre-Dreadnought Era, 1880-1905* (reprint; New York: Octagon Books, 1976).

_____, *From the Dardanelles to Oran: Studies of the Royal Navy in War and Peace 1915-1940* (London: Oxford University Press, 1974).

_____, *From the Dreadnought to Scapa Flow: The Royal Navy in the Fisher Era, 1904-1919* (5 volumes) (Oxford: Oxford University Press, vol I, *1904-1914: The Road to War* (1961); vol II, *The War Years: to the Eve of Jutland* (1965); vol III, *Jutland and After: May 1916-December 1916* (second edition, 1978); vol IV, *1917: Year of Crisis* (1969); vol V, *1918-1919: Victory and Aftermath* (1970).

McBride, Keith Donald, untitled letter in *The Mariner's Mirror*, vol 83, no 1 (February 1997), pp 97–8.

McLaughlin, Stephen, 'Battle Lines and Fast Wings: Battlefleet Tactics in the Royal Navy, 1900-1914', *Journal of Strategic Studies*, vol 38, no 7 (December 2015), pp 985–1005.

_____, 'Equal Speed Charlie London: Jellicoe's Deployment at Jutland', in John Jordan (ed.), *Warship 2010* (London: Conway, 2010), pp 122–39.

McLaughlin, Stephen, 'Russia: Rossiiskii imperatorskii flot', in Vincent P O'Hara, W David Dickson and Richard Worth (eds), *To Crown the Waves: The Great Navies of the First World War* (Annapolis: Naval Institute Press, 2013), pp 213–56.

Mead, Hilary P, 'Jutland Signals', *The Mariner's Mirror*, vol 43, no 3 (1957), pp 232–3.

Moretz, Joseph, *The Royal Navy and the Capital Ship in the Interwar Period: An Operational Perspective* (London: Frank Cass, 2002).

Mountbatten, Louis, 'The Battle of Jutland: An Appreciation Given at the Annual Jutland Dinner in H. M. S. *Warrior* on 25 May 1978', *The Mariner's Mirror*, vol 66, no 2 (May 1980), pp 99–111.

Patterson, A Temple, *Jellicoe* (London: Macmillan, 1969).

Prior, Robin, *Churchill's 'World Crisis' as History* (Beckenham, Kent: Croom Helm Ltd., 1983).

Rasor, Eugene L, *The Battle of Jutland: A Bibliography* (Westport, Connecticut: Greenwood Press, 1992).

Raven, Alan and Roberts, John, *British Battleships of World War Two* (Annapolis: Naval Institute Press, 1976).

[Richmond, Herbert W], 'A Fighting Instruction', *Naval Review*, vol III, no 2 (May 1915), pp 185–95.

_____, 'Naval History from the Naval Officer's Point of View', in *Naval and Military Essays: Being Papers Read in the Naval and Military Section at the International Congress of Historical Studies 1913* (Cambridge: University Press, 1914), pp 39–54.

_____, 'Orders and Instructions', *Naval Review*, vol I, no 3 (August 1913), pp 280–95.

_____, *Portrait of an Admiral: The Life and Papers of Sir Herbert Richmond*, ed. Arthur J Marder (Cambridge, Massachusetts: Harvard University Press, 1952).

Roskill, Stephen, *Admiral of the Fleet Earl Beatty: The Last Naval Hero. An Intimate Biography* (London: Collins, 1980).

_____, *HMS Warspite: The Story of a Famous Ship* (Annapolis: Naval
    Institute Press, 1997).

_____, *Naval Policy Between the Wars*, vol 1: *The Period of Anglo-American
    Antagonism 1919-1929*; vol. 2: *The Period of Reluctant Rearmament 1930-1939*
    (London: Collins, 1968–1976).

Scheer, Reinhard, *Germany's High Sea Fleet in the World War* (London: Cassell and
    Company, 1920). Recently reprinted, with an introduction by Markus Faulkner
    and Andrew Lambert (Barnsley: Frontline Books, 2014).

Schleihauf, William, 'A Concentrated Effort: Royal Navy Gunnery Exercises at the
    End of the Great War', *Warship International*, vol XXXV, no 2 (1998), pp 117–39.

_____, 'What Happened to the *Campania*?', *The Mariner's Mirror*, vol
    90, no 4 (November 2004), pp 464–6.

Seligmann, Matthew (ed.), *Naval Intelligence from Germany: The Reports of the
    British Naval Attachés in Berlin, 1906-1914* (Aldershot, Hants: Ashgate Publishing
    Limited for the Navy Records Society, 2007).

Sumida, Jon Tetsuro, '"The Best Laid Plans": The Development of British Battle-
    Fleet Tactics, 1919-1942', *The International History Review*, vol XIV, no 4
    (November 1992), pp 681–700

_____, 'Expectation, Adaptation, and resignation: British Battle Fleet
    Tactical Planning, August 1914-April 1916', *Naval War College Review*, vol 60, no
    3 (Summer 2007), pp 101–22.

_____, 'A Matter of Timing: The Royal Navy and the Tactics of
    Decisive Battle, 1912-1916', *The Journal of Military History*, vol 67, no 1 (January
    2003), pp 85–136.

Tarrant, V E, *Jutland: The German Perspective* (Annapolis: Naval Institute Press,
    1995).

True, Arnold E, 'The Effects of Meteorological Conditions on Tactical Operations at
    Jutland', *United States Naval Institute Proceedings*, vol 66, no 1 (whole no 443;
    January 1940), pp. 9–17.

Wegener, Wolfgang, *The Naval Strategy of the World War* (E S Mittler & Son, 1929;
    English edition translated by Holger H Herwig: Annapolis: Naval Institute Press,
    1989).

Willis, Sam, *The Glorious First of June: Fleet Battle in the Reign of Terror* (London:
    Querus, 2011).

Wilson, Alastair, *A Biographical Dictionary of the Twentieth Century Royal Navy*, vol
    1: *Admirals of the Fleet and Admirals* (Barnsley: Seaforth Publishing, 2013).

Yates, Keith, *Flawed Victory* (Annapolis: Naval Institute Press, 2000).

INDEX

The *NSA*'s numerous references to a very large number of ships and formations make a comprehensive index practically impossible. Only the most important persons, ships, events and topics are therefore included here. Entries for individual ships refer to major events – attacks made, damage sustained, sinking, etc. German ships are indicated by the abbreviation 'Ger'; all other ships are British. Sub-entries prefaced by '*At Jutland*' are in chronological rather than alphabetical order.

Abbreviations:

Formations: BCF = Battle Cruiser Fleet; BCS = Battle Cruiser Squadron; BF = Battle Fleet; BS = Battle Squadron; CS = [Armoured] Cruiser Squadron; HSF = High Seas Fleet (Ger); LCS = Light Cruiser Squadron; SG = Scouting Group (Ger).

Ships: B = Battleship; OB = pre-dreadnought battleship; BCr = Battle Cruiser; Cr = Armoured Cruiser; LCr = Light Cruiser; D = Destroyer.

Ranks: Adm = Admiral; VA = Vice-Admiral; RA = Rear-Admiral; Cmdre = Commodore; Capt = Captain; Cmdr = Commander; Lt-Cmdr = Lieutenant-Commander; SO = Senior Officer (of any rank).

Numbered Formations, British

1st Battle Squadron (*Marlborough*) 41; composition 209; *At Jutland*: second engagement 146, 147, 148n.44, 149, 150n.51; falls behind fleet during night 184; joined by destroyers 202; encounters *Seydlitz* 261

2nd Battle Squadron (*King George V*) 41; composition 212; *At Jutland*: second engagement, 146, 153; fails to follow BCF 156–7, 163; misidentifies German ships 164, 192; and 4LCS 166; encounters *Seydlitz* 261

3rd Battle Squadron (pre-dreadnoughts): in GFBOs 20, 275; not sent to join Jellicoe 43, 44

4th Battle Squadron (*Benbow*) 41; composition 210; *At Jutland*: second engagement 146, 147, 149

5th Battle Squadron (*Barham*) xxxiv, 41, 42, 47, 150, 189n.77, 246; composition 213; in GFBOs 20, 22, 25, 32, 124n.21; speed of 78–9; *At Jutland*: delay in coming into action 53–4, 57–8; Run to the South 62–3, 68; delayed turning away from HSF 73–4, 76–8, 79; Run to the North 77–80, 81, 85, 92–3; fails to report position of HSF 100–1; deployment 110, 116, 118, 122–4, 130, 134–5; after deployment 138, 144, 145, 150n.51, 165; night 171, 178, 179, 180, 184, 185, 188; hits scored on enemy 189n.77

1st Battle Cruiser Squadron (*Princess Royal*) 41; composition 213. *See also* Battle Cruiser Fleet/Force

2nd Battle Cruiser Squadron (*New Zealand*) 41; composition 213; approach 47, 55, 56, 69; hits scored on enemy 189n.77. *See also* Battle Cruiser Fleet/Force

3rd Battle Cruiser Squadron (*Invincible*) 41, 45, 89, 136, 145; composition 210; *At Jutland*: sent to support BCF 84; in action 92–6, 98; mistaken by Germans for Battle Fleet, 97, 145; takes station ahead of BCF 119–21; *Invincible* sunk 130–2; takes station astern of BCF 142; German flotillas attack 150n.51; hits scored on enemy 189n.77

1st Cruiser Squadron (*Defence*) 41, 98, 212

2nd Cruiser Squadron (*Minotaur*) 41, 45, 94, 167, 170n.9, 177–8, 210

1st Light Cruiser Squadron (*Galatea*) 41; composition 213; *At Jutland*: approach 55, 59; Run to the North 76; deployment, 97n.29; second engagement 126; sweep to west 155; night 167, 200n.13

2nd Light Cruiser Squadron (*Southampton*) 41; composition 213; *At Jutland*: approach 55, 59; sights HSF 72n.9; Run to the North 76; deployment 124, 126; drives off German destroyers 165; night 167, 180, 192

3rd Light Cruiser Squadron (*Falmouth*) 41; composition 214; *At Jutland*: approach 55, 59; Run to the North 76; joined by *Canterbury* 94; deployment 110, 124, 126; second engagement 151, 155; engages 4SG 157, 161; night 167, 187

4th Light Cruiser Squadron (*Calliope*) 41; composition 210–11; *At Jutland*: deployment 110, 126; second

engagement 136, 141, 147, 148, 149, 152, 153, 146, 165–6; at dusk 161, 162, 164; night 167, 170n.7

1st Destroyer Flotilla (part; *Fearless*) 41, 126, 127, 128, 168, 214

4th Destroyer Flotilla (*Tipperary*) 41, 96n.26, 126, 141, 168, 182–3; composition 211; in night actions 196–8, 201, 202, 204

9th Destroyer Flotilla (part; *Lydiard*) 41, 55, 59, 61, 65, 127, 129, 141, 168, 183; composition 214; in night actions, 201, 202–4

10th Destroyer Flotilla (part; *Moorsom*) 41, 124, 127, 168, 183; composition 215; in night actions, 201, 202–4

11th Destroyer Flotilla (part; *Castor*) 41, 126, 127, 147, 149, 152, 156, 168, composition 212–13; in night actions 177, 179, 194, 196

12th Destroyer Flotilla (*Faulknor*) 41, 110, 126, 128, 141, 168; composition 211–12; in night actions 185, 201, 202, 204–7

13th Destroyer Flotilla (*Champion*) 41, 55, 59, 63, 65, 75, 76, 96n.26, 127, 129, 141, 168, 183; composition 214; in night actions, 202–2

Numbered Formations, German
1st [Battle] Squadron (*Ostfriesland*) 72; *At Jutland*: first engagement 118, 130, 132; second engagement 139, 142, 155; at dusk 162; in night actions 170, 171, 179, 183, 198

2nd [Battle] Squadron (*Deutschland*) 50, 72; *At Jutland*: second engagement 139, 156, 157; engages BCF at dusk 160–1; night 170, 171, 175n.31, 179; attacked by British destroyers 185, 202, 204

3rd [Battle] Squadron (*König*) 72; *At Jutland*: sighted by 1SG 73; first engagement 118, 129n.42, 130n.48, 132; second engagement 142, 150, 155; at dusk 162; night 170, 171, 179

1st Scouting Group (*Lützow*) 42; *At Jutland*: approach 51, 55–6, 58, 72; Run to the South 68, 76; Run to the North 92, 96; deployment 108, 121n.12; engages 3BCS 130n.47, 145; second engagement 136, 139–40, 156; engages BCF at dusk 160–1; night 170, 179

2nd Scouting Group (*Frankfurt*): 50; *At Jutland*: approach 51, 53–5, 73, 76; encounters *Chester*, 3BCS 89, 92–4; encounters 1CS 97–8; deployment 121n.12, 145; at dusk 161; in night actions 179, 180n.43, 182–3, 194, 196, 204

4th Scouting Group (*Stettin*) 72; *At Jutland*: at dusk 156, 157, 159, 161; in night actions 170, 179, 180

1st Destroyer Flotilla (first half) 72, 133, 145n.35, 148

2nd Destroyer Flotilla 66, 155, 156, 165n.116, 179n.42

3rd Destroyer Flotilla 72, 96n.23, 128n.35, 133, 145, 148, 150n.51, 154n.61

5th Destroyer Flotilla 72, 149, 150n.51, 155n.67

6th Destroyer Flotilla 96, 146, 150n.51, 179n.42; 11th Half Flotilla 51, 72, 147n.43; 12th Half Flotilla 51, 93n.10, 94, 95n.18, 110, 120, 150n.51, 155, 156, 158

7th Destroyer Flotilla 72, 182, 196n.5; 13th Half Flotilla 164

9th Destroyer Flotilla 56, 66, 94, 95n.18, 96, 110, 120–1, 146, 150n.51, 179n.42; 17th Half Flotilla 66n.29, 147n.43, 149n.50; 18th Half Flotilla 149n.49

A

Abdiel (Minelayer) 180

Acasta (D) 94, 96–7, 98, 144n.29, 204, 225

Achates (D) 197, 198, 199, 200n.13

Admiralty: *At Jutland*: orders GF to sea 40; informs C-in-C HSF still in Jade 50, 56–7; recalls Harwich Force 88; signals position of HSF to C-in-C 181, 184, 187, 192; fails to pass information to C-n-C 190

Admiralty Narrative. See *Narrative of the Battle of Jutland*.

Agincourt (B) 147, 148, 166, 184, 201, 261

Airship Detachment, airships (Zeppelins) 39, 40, 50–1, 175n.32, 187, 238, 297

Ambuscade (D) 197, 198, 199

Arbuthnot, RA Sir Robert (SO 1CS in *Defence*) 98–9

Ardent (D) 183, 198, 199, 202, 204, 228

B

B.98 (Ger D) 228

Baltic Sea 10–11, 14, 50n.52

Barham (B): *At Jutland*: approach 53; delay in following BCF 57; Run to the South 63, 73–4; delay in turning north 76–7, 79; reports to C-in-C 104, 108; deployment 122–3, 135; hits scored 166; damage to 77, 81, 100, 222

battle (general): importance of 10, 14–16

Battle Cruiser Fleet/Force (BCF; *Lion*) xvii, xix, xx; *At Jutland*: approach 50, 53–6, 68–9; signalling problems 57–8, 74n.18, 246; Run to the South 59–65, 71–2; Run to the North 75–81; renews engagement with 1SG 92; makes complete circle xxi, 142n.17, 246; action with 1SG, (Ger) 2BS at dusk 159–61; night 178, 185, 187–8; hits scored on enemy 189n.77

Battle Fleet xx, 45, 70, 243, 262; *At Jutland* approach to BCF 82–4, 88, 89, 92; deployment 95, 98, 100, 104, 106, 107, 110, 112, 118, 126, 130; first engagement 128, 129; second engagement 136, 140–4, 148–9, 150–3, 155; at dusk 158, 161–3; night 167, 170, 172, 177–8, 181–4, 185, 187–8; hits scored on enemy 189n.77

Battle Fleet (Ger): *At Jutland*: Hipper seeks to close with 55; attacked by British destroyers 67; sighted by BCF 70, 72–4, 246; Run to the North 75, 77; reported to C-in-C 85, 86; Hipper retires on 92, 97; attempts to assist *Wiesbaden* 98; engages 1CS 99; approach to British battle Fleet 100, 102n.49, 104, 106, 107–8, 112; first engagement 129; second engagement 140, 144–5, 149, 152; at dusk 158, 162; night 170, 181, 184, 185, 187n.73, 204, 206n.27; returns to harbour 189

Battle of Jutland, 30th May to 1st June 1916. Official Despatches with Appendices ('Official Despatches') xx, xxxi, 6n.15, 57

Beatty, VA Sir David (SO BCF) xx, 41; and 'Harper Record' xxi–xxii; and *NSA* xxiii–xxiv, xxvii; praised by *NSA* 246–7; recommends Kenneth Dewar to Churchill xxvi–xxvii; revises GFBOs 252; *At Jutland*: approach 53, 56, 57–8; Run to the South 65, 68–9; Run to the North 70–1, 74, 76, 81, 84, 92; deployment 107–8, 112; first engagement 120; second engagement 142, 155, 159; night 178, 187–8

Birmingham (LCr) 180, 183, 188

Black Prince (Cr) 83, 99, 100; sunk 183, 228

Broke (D) 183, 196–8, 199, 200n.13, 224

C

Callaghan, Admiral Sir George: and pre-war tactics 18–9, 26, 251, 257, 283–93

Campania (Seaplane carrier) 45n.31

Caroline (LCr) 164–5, 167n.1, 177

Casualties: British 219–20; German 220

Castor (D) 194, 196, 198, 204

Champion (LCr) 185, 187, 201–2, 204, 206

Chatfield, Capt Alfred Ernle Montacute (*Lion*) xxiii, xxiv, 142n.17, 295, 296

Chester (LCr): 93–4, 224

Churchill, Winston 57, 264, 295, 296; his *World Crisis* and *NSA* xxvi–xxvii, 57, 61n.9, 114n.17, 116

Committee of Imperial Defence (CID) xxi–xxii, xxiii

Contest (D) 197–8, 199, 224

Corbett, Sir Julian Stafford 116, 295; and *Naval Operations* (Official History) xii, xxiii, xxv n.33, xxvi, xxx; and *NSA* xxiii–xxvi, xxx; on Nelson's tactics 254–5

D

damage: to British ships 221–5; to German ships 166, 225–8

Defence (Cr): *At Jutland*: crosses bow of BCF 119; engages 2SG and *Wiesbaden* 97–8; sunk 99–100, 122, 135, 171, 172, 228

Defender (D) 225

deployment at Jutland 107–16; on centre column 112–13; on port wing 108, 110; on starboard wing 106, 110; completed 129; movements of cruisers, destroyers during 126–7. *See also* Grand Fleet Battle Orders; Tactics

Derfflinger (Ger BCr): *At Jutland*: approach 56; Run to the South 60n, 62–3, 66, 68; sights HSF 73; Run to the North 78, 79, 92; sinks *Invincible*

130–2; second engagement 139–40, 142–3; night 179; damage to 62, 143, 159–60, 166, 171, 226

destroyer attacks 149; British 65–8, 76; German 94–5, 120–1, 133–4, 145–8, 157–8

Dewar, Capt Alfred Charles xxii–xxiii, 5n.13, 295; publishes review of Corbett's Jutland volume xxvi; opinion of Beatty 244

Dewar, VA Kenneth Gilbert Balmain xxiii, xxix; assists Churchill xxvii; opinions of Beatty and Jellicoe 244; *Royal Oak* court martial xxiii; views on staff and command 247–9; views on tactics 254–5, 263–4

Dogger Bank, Battle of (24 January 1915) xx, 42n.22, 58, 143n.22, 257, 258

Dreyer, Capt Frederic (*Iron Duke*) 115, 297

Dublin (LCr) 180, 188, 224

E

Elbing (Ger LCr) 51, 56, 183, 198, 199, 228

Engadine (Seaplane carrier) 54–5, 58

Evan-Thomas, RA Hugh (SO 5BS) 73, 84–5; and delay in following BCF 57–8, 246; and delay in turning north 74n.18; and deployment 122, 134

F

Falmouth (LCr): *At Jutland*: approach 54; Run to the North 76; sighted by *Black Prince* 83, 100; engages *Wiesbaden* 126; first engagement 128, 141; actions at dusk 159, 161, 164–5, 170

Faulknor (D) 200n.13, 204, 206, 207

Flanders U-boat Flotilla (Ger) 39, 40

Fortune (D): sunk, 183, 198, 199, 204, 228; survivors rescued 202

Frankfurt (Ger LCr) 204, 227

Frauenlob (Ger LCr): sunk 180, 228

Friedrich der Grosse (Ger B) 7, 56, 86, 99, 118, 142

G

G.40 (Ger D) 202, 228

Galatea (LCr) 46–7; *At Jutland*: sights enemy ships 47, 50, 51, 69, 82, 84; draws enemy ships to NW 53–4, 59; Run to the North 76; speed reduced 126; night 168

Garland (D) 182, 196–8, 199

Gordon, Andrew xxxi, 263

Grand Fleet xvii; compared with High Seas Fleet 117–18; organisations 215–17; during the night 167–8, 171; rendezvous with BCF 41–2

Grand Fleet Battle Orders (GFBOs) 19–37, 249–60; centralisation 21, 30–3; concentration 24; concentration of fire 253–4; cruisers 22–3, 253–4; defensive conception of 28–9, 256–9; deployment 108, 272–3; deployment diagram 22, 124, 128, 141, 150, 177–8; destroyers 23, 26–8, 253–4, 258–9; fighting ranges 20, 253, 274; general principles 273–5; purpose of 249–53; reference positions 170; role of 5BS, BCF 20, 22, 25, 32, 124, 253, 256, 271–2; sighting reports 106; single line 253; torpedoes, mines and submarines 19, 20–1, 257–8, 274–5

Grosser Kurfürst (Ger B) 166, 171, 226

H

Hamburg (Ger LCr) 227

Harper, VA John Ernest Troyte xx–xxii, xxiii, xxvii, 4, 8, 252n.35, 294, 295

'Harper Record' xxi–xxii, xxiii, xxv, xxvi, 6, 8

Harvey, Major Francis J W RMLI 61

Harwich Force xxxv, 24, 35, 40, 43–5, 88, 187, 268, 276

Hase, Cmdr Georg von (gunnery officer,

Derfflinger) 67, 73, 79, 80, 98, 99, 131, 144–5

Helgoland (Ger B) 166, 227

Heligoland Bight: Battle of (28 August 1914) xx, 43; German control of 11–12; German swept channels ('ways') through 75, 173, 175; minefields in 12–13, 173

High Seas Fleet: compared with Grand Fleet 117–8; organisation 217–18; decentralisation of command in 179n.42; importance of 10–14; night actions 170, 171, 196; supports U-boats 12–13; returns to harbour 189

Hipper, VA Franz (SO Ger 1SG): At *Jutland*: sights BCF 55; impressed by 5BS gunnery 63n.15; launches destroyer attack 66; takes station ahead of HSF 68, 72–3; Run to the North 79, 89, 92; mistakes 3BCS for main British fleet 97; engages 3BCS 130; abandons *Lützow* 139; unable to board *Seydlitz* or *Moltke* 144

Hood, RA the Hon. Sir Horace (SO 3BCS in *Invincible*) 84, 92, 93, 95, 120, 130

Hughes, Capt Wayne (USN) 253

I

Indefatigable (BCr): sunk 62, 71n.6, 171, 172, 228

Indomitable (BCr) 95, 121n.12, 187

Intelligence Division 78–9, 87, 175, 190–1, 191n.86, 191n.87, 250. *See also* Room 40

Invincible (BCr): position of wreck surveyed xxi, 8, 132n.56; At *Jutland*: sent to support BCF 84, 92; engages 2SG 94–5, 97; sunk 121, 130–2, 171, 172, 228

Iron Duke (B): signal logs 2n.1, 3–5; At *Jutland*: positions 46, 82; and *Lion*, difference in reckoning between 84,

88–91, 104; sights *Lion* 102; deployment 112; first engagement 129, 138n.48; second engagement 144, 147, 149, 152, 153, 156, 166, 172; at dusk 162; night 170, 178, 185

J

Jellicoe, Adm Sir John (C-in-C, Grand Fleet): and 'Admiralty Narrative' xxvi; and 'Harper Record' xxi–xxii; and night after battle 173–5, 178, 182, 185–8, 200, 262, 191–2; concerns regarding underwater weapons 257–9, 264; deployment decision 107–16; evaluation of his admirals 262; evaluation of HSF 255; Jutland despatch cover letter 276–9; letter of 30 Oct. 1914 23–4, 30, 257, 268–70; *NSA* alleges caution of 245, 256–8; offensive spirit of 245–6; sighting reports received by 82–6, 229–32; tactics of 253–9; turns away from torpedo attack 147; turns towards enemy 154; unaware of ship losses 172

Jerram, VA Sir Thomas (SO 2BS) 192

Jones, Lt-Cmdr Loftus (*Shark*) 95–6

Jutland Controversy xii, xvii–xxix, 294

K

Kaiser (Ger B) 166, 171, 226

Keyes, Adm Sir Roger xxiii n.23, xxiv, xxv n.31, 296

König (Ger B): speed of 78–9, 117n2; At *Jutland*: sighted by Hipper 72; engages 5BS 77–8; engages *Defence* 99n.39; first engagement 118, 130, 132; second engagement 139, 142; damage to 129n.40, 166, 171, 189, 226

L

Lion (BCr) 41, 47; At *Jutland*: approach 53–6, 57, 58; Run to the South 59–61, 63, 68, 69; Run to the North 72–6, 79, 92, 95; and *Iron Duke*, difference in reckoning between 84, 88–91; in contact with battle fleet 102, 104, 108; deployment 112; second engagement 136, 152, 155; makes complete circle xxi, 142n.17; engages 1SG (Ger) at dusk 2BS 156, 159, 161, 162; night 170, 178, 192; requests recognition signals from *Princess Royal* 178n.41; damage to 60, 61, 75–6, 81, 119, 171, 221

Long, Walter (1st Sea Lord) xxi

Lützow (Ger BCr): *At Jutland*: approach 55, 56, 184, 189; Run to the South 60–1, 66–8; Run to the North 92, 97, 99; second engagement 155, 159; night 171, 179, 184; sunk 189, 228; survivors 187, 188, 202; damage to 139, 166, 171, 225

Lydiard (D) 127, 202

M

Maenad (D) 185, 187, 201–2, 206

Magic (D) 194

Malaya (B): *At Jutland*: engages HSF 77–8; deployment 116, 134; night 261; damage to 78, 81, 100–1, 171, 222

Marder, Arthur Jacob xviii, xxvii–xxviii, xxx–xxxi, 114, 116, 244, 246

Markgraf (Ger B) 129n.42, 166, 171, 226

Marksman (D) 185, 187, 197, 200n.13, 201–2, 206, 207

Marlborough (B): *At Jutland*: deployment 102, 106, 108, 110, 118, 122, 135; torpedoed 128, 137–8; second engagement 141, 142, 146–8, 166; speed reduced 171–2, 261; astern of station 178, 179; ordered back to base 184, 187; damage to 223

Marne (D) 194

Marvel (D) 206

May, Admiral of the Fleet Sir William: and pre-war tactics 18n.2, 19, 26, 29, 259–60

Menace (D) 204

Mindful (D) 206

Moltke (Ger BCr) 15; *At Jutland*: approach 56; Run to the South 63n.16; Hipper attempts to board 144; night 179; damage to 68n.43, 171, 226

Moorsom (D) 65, 66, 225

Moresby (D) 28n.47, 76, 185, 187, 201, 202, 204

München (Ger LCr) 227

N

Narborough (D) 65, 203, 204n.24

Narrative of the Battle of Jutland ('Admiralty Narrative') xviii, xxv–xxvi, 170n.8, 191–2, 246n.15, 296

Narwhal (D) 206–7

Nassau (Ger B) 183, 196n.7, 197, 199, 227

Naval Operations ('Official History') xxii, xxiii, xxvi, xxx, 57

Naval Staff Appreciation of Jutland: influence of xxv–xxix; on GFBOs 251–2, 256; recalled and suppressed xxiv–xxv; surviving copies of 294–7; views on Jellicoe and Beatty 243–6; writing of xxii–xxv

navigation xxxii–xxxiii, 3

Nelson, VA Horatio, First Viscount xix, 17, 208; command method 31–2; tactics of 24n.34, 254–5; Trafalgar 254, 264

Nestor (D) 65–7, 96n.26, 128; sunk 67, 228

Neumünster (Ger wireless intercept station) 51, 182, 184n.62, 190, 235, 239

night actions 167–207; battleships fail to report 261; defective system of command 199–200, 207; destroyers fail to make reports 204, 261–2; *Faulknor*'s reports 206–7, 261; Jellicoe fails to inform destroyers of intentions 194–5; sighting reports 279–82

Nomad (D) 65–7, 128, 155n.67; sunk 67, 228

Nonsuch (D) 204

O

Obdurate (D) 65, 185, 187, 201, 202, 204

Obedient (D) 204, 206

officers, lack of initiative of 17, 18n.3, 128–9, 260–4

Official Despatches. See *Battle of Jutland, 30th May to 1st June 1916. Official Despatches with Appendices*

Oldenburg (Ger B) 227

Onslaught (D) 206, 225

Onslow (D) 28n.47, 76, 97–9, 118n.8, 225

Opal (D) 207

Ostfriesland (Ger B) 5, 183, 189, 227

P

Pelican (D) 65, 203, 204n.24

Petard (D) 64–7, 68n.37, 128, 144n.29, 203, 225

Pillau (Ger LCr) 51, 94, 183, 204, 227

Plunkett(-Ernle-Erle-Drax), Cmdr Reginald 244

Pollen, Lt-Cmdr John F H xxiii, xxv, xxv n.33, 4, 7, 296

Pommern (Ger OB) 161; sunk 185, 206, 227, 228

Porpoise (D) 182, 196–8, 199, 225

Posen (Ger B) 161n.96, 183, 198, 199

Princess Royal (BCr) 58; *At Jutland*: Run to the South 60–3, 68; signals to C-in-C 74n.20, 75; Run to the North 92; deployment 97; first engagement 134; night 171; *Lion* requests recognition signals from 178n.41; damage to 62, 81n.46, 161, 221

Q

Queen Mary (BCr): *At Jutland*: Run to the South 60n, 61n.7, 68n.43; sunk 63–4, 71n.6, 117n.1, 171, 172, 228

R

Regensburg (Ger LCr) 51; *At Jutland*: approach 56; Run to the South 66–7, 72; engages *Shark* 95–6; night 179n.42, 188

Reproduction of the Record of the Battle of Jutland. See 'Harper Record'.

Revenge (B) 148, 166, 184, 261

Rheinland (Ger B) 227

Room 40 (also 'Special Intelligence') xxxv, 28, 189–91; role in strategy 15–16; signals deciphered by 233–42; source for *NSA* 4–5; tracks German fleet movements 40, 42n.22, 43, 44, 50n.50, 56–7, 87, 175; tracks U-boat movements 21n.19, 191

Roskill, Capt Stephen W xxviii, 57–8, 116, 263, 265, 294, 296

Rostock (Ger LCr) 72; first engagement 133n.60; in night actions 179n.42, 182, 183, 197n.10, 199; sinks 198, 228

Royalist (LCr) 164–5, 167n.1, 177

Rutland, Flight-Lt F J 58

S

S.32 (Ger D) 96n.23, 128n.35, 133, 148, 228

S.35 (Ger D) sunk 149n.49, 166, 228

S.36 (Ger D) 149n.50, 228

S.52 (Ger D) 149n.50, 228

Scheer, Admiral Reinhard (C-in-C, Ger High Sea Fleet): 38, 50, 39; *At Jutland*: receives U-boat reports of British movements 51; and first turn-away 132; mistakes position of British main fleet 94, 132, 145; turns back toward British 139–40; and second turn-away 7, 144–5, 150; orders course for Horns Reef 155; possible routes home of 173–6; orders destroyers to attack during night 178–9

Schlesien (Ger OB) 161, 227

Schleswig-Holstein (Ger OB) 161, 227

Seydlitz (Ger BCr): At *Jutland*: approach 56; Run to the South 61n.7, 66; torpedoed 68n.37, 96, 97, 128; Run to the North 92; second engagement 139, 142, 143n; engaged by BCF at dusk 159, 161n.96; night 179, 189, 261; damage to 68n.43, 144, 166, 171, 225

Shark (D) 28n.47, 92, 94–7, 110, 128, 228

signals, signalling: deciphered German 233–42; excessive British 150–1; logs 3–5; methods of xxxiii–xxxiv; sighting reports 229–32, 279–82

Southampton (LCr): At *Jutland*: approach 55; Run to the South 59; sights German battle fleet 70; sighting reports of 73, 85–6, 100, 102, 104, 110n.11, 116, 136–7, 170, 193; deployment 126, 136; at dusk 165; night action 180, 181; damage to 223–4

Sparrowhawk (D) 183, 196n, 197–9, 200n.13, 202, 228

Spitfire (D) 183, 197–9, 200n.13, 224

Special Intelligence. *See* Room 40.

Staff: At *Jutland*: 9, 18, 19, 30, 180, 188, 200; qualities necessary in 247–9

Sterling, Capt A J B (SO 12 Flotilla, in *Faulknor*) 261

Stettin (Ger LCr) 227

Sturdee, VA Sir Frederick Charles Doveton (SO 4BS, in *Benbow*) 130n.52, 146, 258, 260

submarines (British) 189

Sumida, Jon T 253n.39

T

tactical units xxxiv–xxxv

tactics: Admiralty and 249–50; at Trafalgar 254–5; centralised 254; concentration 10, 24, 254–6, 288; concentration of fire 255; decentralised 29, 248, 265–6; deployment (general) 22, 83n.8, 102–4; divisional 134n.62, 138, 142, 254, 259–60; Fighting Instructions 249; German 260; post-war 265–6; pre-war 17–19, 283–93; single line 19–20, 24, 29, 254; *See also* deployment at Jutland, Grand Fleet Battle Orders.

Thunderer (B) 261

Thuringen (Ger B) 183

Tiger (BCr): At *Jutland*: approach 57; Run to the South 60–1, 64, 65, 66n, 69; Run to the North 76, 92; first engagement 134; engagement at dusk 159; damage to 60, 81, 222

Tipperary (D): in night actions 183, 196–8, 200; sunk 199, 204, 228

Trafalgar, Battle of (21 October 1805) 254–5

Turbulent (D) 47; At *Jutland*: torpedo attack on 1SG 66, 68n.37, 128n.38; in night actions 183; sunk 203, 204, 228

Tyrwhitt, Cmdre Reginald (SO Harwich Force) 43–4, 88

U

U-boats: and commerce warfare 11–12; prize regulations imposed on 38; reported sightings of, at Jutland 21n.19, 140–1, 165n.117; stationed off British bases 39n.7, 45–7, 51

Unity (D) 182, 196, 197–8, 199, 202

V

V.4 (Ger D): sunk 185, 202, 228

V.27 (Ger D): sunk 66, 228

V.29 (Ger D): sunk 66, 228

V.48 (Ger D): sunk 96n.23, 228

Valiant (B): At *Jutland*: Run to the

North 76, 78, 81; fails to report
   position of HSF 101; reports position
   of HSF 104; at 'Windy Corner' 122,
   135; second engagement 166; fails to
   report during the night 261
visibility: and divisional tactics 259–60;
   At Jutland: for airships 51; for
   Engadine's aircraft 54; during
   approach 55; during the Run to the
   South 69; during the Run to the
   North 73, 76, 100–1; for 3BCS 94; for
   Battle Fleet 98n.32; deployment and
   104, 107, 108, 111, 115, 118n.9, 134;
   during first engagement 129, 130; and
   sinking of *Invincible* 131; during
   second engagement 143, 145, 150,
   154n.63; at dusk 167n.1
Von der Tann (Ger BCr): *At Jutland*:
   approach 56; sinks *Indefatigable* 62;
   damages *Warrior* 99n.40; night 179;
   damage to 63n.15, 68n.43, 166, 171,
   226

W

Warrior (Cr): *At Jutland*: engages 2SG
   97, 98; crosses bows of BCF 119;

seriously damaged 99, 122–3, 135,
   171, 172; sinks 228
Warspite (B): *At Jutland*: Run to the
   South 73; sights HSF 74; Run to the
   North 77; helm jams 99, 122–4;
   damage to 78, 81, 171, 223
Westfalen (Ger B) 139, 156, 170, 179,
   203n.23, 227
Wemyss, Admiral Sir Rosslyn xx, xxi
Wiesbaden (Ger LCr): *At Jutland*:
   approach 51; engaged by 3BCS 94;
   engaged by 1CS, *Onslow* 98–9;
   engaged by Battle Fleet 118, 126, 129;
   torpedoes *Marlborough* 138; attempts
   to rescue crew of 140, 150n.51;
   damage to 94, 97, 166; sunk 171, 228
Wilson, Admiral of the Fleet Sir Arthur
   29n.50, 30, 43, 44, 86, 87, 114
'Windy Corner' 126

Y

Yarmouth (LCr) 47, 141

Z

Zeppelins. *See* Airships, Airship
   Detachment